Sereno E. Todd, Making of America Project

The Young Farmer's Manual

detailing the manipulations of the farm in a plain and intelligible manner. With

practical directions for laying out a farm and erecting buildings, fences, and farm

gates.

Sereno E. Todd, Making of America Project

The Young Farmer's Manual
detailing the manipulations of the farm in a plain and intelligible manner. With practical directions for laying out a farm and erecting buildings, fences, and farm gates.

ISBN/EAN: 9783337362423

Printed in Europe, USA, Canada, Australia, Japan

Cover: Foto ©Andreas Hilbeck / pixelio.de

More available books at **www.hansebooks.com**

THE

YOUNG FARMER'S MANUAL:

DETAILING THE

MANIPULATIONS OF THE FARM IN A PLAIN AND INTELLIGIBLE MANNER.

WITH PRACTICAL DIRECTIONS FOR

LAYING OUT A FARM, AND ERECTING BUILDINGS, FENCES, AND FARM GATES.

EMBRACING ALSO

THE YOUNG FARMER'S WORKSHOP:

GIVING

FULL DIRECTIONS FOR THE SELECTION OF GOOD FARM AND SHOP TOOLS, THEIR USE AND
MANUFACTURE, WITH NUMEROUS ORIGINAL ILLUSTRATIONS OF FENCES, GATES,
TOOLS, ETC., AND FOR PERFORMING NEARLY EVERY BRANCH OF
FARMING OPERATIONS.

BY S. EDWARDS TODD.

NEW YORK:
C. M. SAXTON, BARKER & COMPANY.
No. 25 PARK ROW.
1860.

EDWARD O. JENKINS,
Printer and Stereotyper,
No. 26 FRANKFORT STREET.

PREFACE.

"A useful book may live from age to age,
And those unborn may read its printed page."—J. W. BARBER.

THE chief object of this little volume is, to instruct the *young* farmer how to perform the various operations of the farm in a skillful, economical, and workmanlike manner. From my early boyhood I have been engaged in the cultivation of the soil, and I have always experienced a very great disadvantage and inconvenience in not having a *text-book* to assist me in putting tools and agricultural implements in proper order, and in *handling* them with skill and dexterity. Knowing well what difficulties and embarrassments a young farmer is sure to meet with, and understanding what instructions he will be most likely to need, it has been my aim to *supply* that knowledge which has for so long a time been called for by the *young* farmers of America. I have not written for farmers of mature age and long experience, to whom the contents of most of these paragraphs *may* appear too *common-place*, but for the *sons* of farmers, and those who are leaving the merchants' counters and the mechanics' shops to engage *practically* in that honest, honorable, and noble calling—the cultivation of the soil.

I have come directly from the *farmer's workshop*, from the

(3)

stercorary, from the *ditch*, and from *following the plow*, with tow-frock, and overalls, and India-rubber boots on, all bespattered with mud, with callous hands and stiff fingers, to show *young* farmers *how to work*.

Most writers on agricultural subjects have appeared to take it for granted, that every one already understands the *practical* operations in the various branches of business connected with the farm (see "Introduction"); therefore we have no elementary works in our agricultural libraries, and when young men commence *practically* in any branch of farming operations, they are at a great loss how to perform, in a workmanlike manner, many of the most common operations of the farm without an experienced foreman.

It has been my aim to lay down most reliable directions in all my details; and the young farmer can carry this volume into his workshop or into the field, and learn from its pages how to perform every job in a workmanlike, easy, and most expeditious manner.

I have endeavored to make use of simple and intelligible language, which none can fail to understand; and have numbered the paragraphs, so that when reference is made to a subject the reader may be able to turn at once to the paragraph, which will *explain more particularly* what he may desire to know.

My manner of writing it has been to pen my own ideas, and then on any subject which might not seem very clear, to confer with such experienced and skillful farmers as Hon. David Crocker and Deacon Isaac Bower, who are known to be thorough-going farmers and producers of neat cattle, and to whose inspection I submitted my MS. for criticism.

In regard to *tools*, and especially *edged* tools, I have conferred

with many of our best mechanics, and I have not, as yet, been
able to detect anything in this work which does not coincide with
the most approved views and practices for manufacturing and
for putting tools in order.

The figures of tools and implements have been drawn *with my
own pencil*, and I have penned nothing which has not been well
tested, and have introduced no tools, or implements, which can
be considered of doubtful utility. The reader will find about
every tool which is represented in the following pages—and
scores of others also—in my possession, which are in prime order.

The chapter on *fencing* and *fence tools*, a portion of which has
been *re-written*, was published in the volume of Trans. of the
N. Y. State Agricultural Society for 1858; and it is a source of
great chagrin to me that I did not have the *proof-sheets* in time
to correct the numerous typographical errors, and to place some
of the cuts *right side up*, and others in *their appropriate places*.
Some of them were placed on the *side*, and some *topsy turvy*,
while several of them, instead of being inserted where they were
described, under their appropriate heads, were placed in another
part of the chapter, where they were simply alluded to. *I grin
and bear it* as well as any one *ought to*. Some of the cuts were
not *engraved* like the original drawings, and have since been *re-
engraved*.

Reference is frequently made to subjects in another volume,
which will follow this in a succession of paragraphs and illustrations, which will relate more particularly to the cultivation of the
soil and raising crops.

There are *ten* ways of performing most of the operations of
the farm; there is a *right* way, and a *wrong* way; an *easy* way,
and a *hard* or very laborious way; a *skillful*, and an *awkward*

way; a *neat,* and a *slovenly* way; and an *economical,* and a very *expensive* way. As a general rule, *tyros,* and, many times, "*old uns,*" too, are very liable to perform every job and handle every tool in one of these sinister ways.

Now, one laudable object in this treatise is, to furnish plain directions, which, with the exercise of a little skill and common sense, will turn our awkward, unskillful farmer-boys into skillful, neat, and economical farmers.

A copious index will be found at the end of the volume, by which the reader will be able to turn without any difficulty to any subject, or cut of tool or implement. The first column of figures refers to the paragraphs in which whatever is referred to may be found; and the second column refers to the page of the book. Reference is frequently made to paragraphs, in different parts of this book, where the subject under consideration is more fully explained, which should be looked out when reading.

Stimulated by an ardent desire to give an efficient and skillful direction to the energies of the *young* American farmer, and elevate him to that high and noble standing which the Creator designed for him, I send forth this volume, hoping that my labors of love will be appreciated, not only by my contemporaries, but by thousands yet unborn, when I am sleeping in the dust.   S. E. T.

LAKE RIDGE, TOMPKINS CO., N. Y., 1860.

INTRODUCTION.

"The sounds of active industry
I love—I love them all :
The banging of the hammer, the whirring of the plane,
The crashing of the busy saw, the creaking of the crane."—ANON.

THE age has passed in which the hard-fisted cultivator of the
soil was looked upon as an illiterate plebeian, and the last beams
of its twilight are dancing about *us*. Our worthy grandfathers
taught their sons that, if they were able to read, intelligibly, the
Bible and the " Babes in the Woods," which usually constituted
their library, and could write a legible hand, and keep their debit
and credit so that no one could *cheat* them, they would have all
the education that would ever be of any practical advantage to
them in agricultural pursuits. Our fathers allowed us to *exceed*
the boundaries which restrained them, and permitted us to look
into geography, natural philosophy, and chemistry, as applied to
agriculture ; and, after long importunity, allowed us to lay aside
those old *Bull Plows*, with wooden mold-boards, and those clumsy,
awkward, heavy, ill-shapen tools, for those which had been manufactured of better materials,·and of forms more in accordance
with the most approved mechanical and philosophical principles.
Our forefathers were taught, and they inculcated the same pre-
cept, that if a boy or man happened to be so unaccountably
stupid that he would not be likely to make a successful doctor, or
lawyer, or merchant, or mechanic, he must be a *farmer ;* but *we*

have manfully *broken off* this tyrannical yoke of "old fogy" con-
ventionalism, and teach our sons that we need the most *active,
promising, intelligent,* and *skillful* men and boys, for farmers; and
if a boy happens to be deficient in the attic story, he must *learn
a trade,* and be a mechanic.   Our forefathers brought up their
sons to feel that farmers belonged to an inferior *caste ;* and many
of our fathers and fastidious mothers taught their children, that
manual labor was *dishonorable* and *degrading,* and that, in order
to be respected in the world, they must have a situation *behind
the merchant's counter,* or study theology, or jurisprudence.   But
we, at the present day, teach those under our care, that there is
a no more honorable, nor respectable, nor honest livelihood, than
that of cultivating the soil, and its kindred arts and sciences.
And we teach them also, that, in order to be a *thorough-going,
energetic,* and *successful* farmer, a man must be *educated ;* that he
must have a good smattering of agricultural chemistry, natural
philosophy, geology, mineralogy, botany, and a good peep into
vegetable physiology, and arithmetic and geometry, &c.; and
must have a good understanding, also, of the manufacture of
agricultural implements, according to the most convenient and
approved form and weight; and must know how to handle them
with skill and dexterity.   Therefore,

A FARMER MUST BE A MAN OF THOUGHT AND INVESTIGATION.

No man can reasonably expect to succeed in the thorough
cultivation of the soil, and raise good crops on his farm from year
to year, as long as he lives, and not impoverish it, but leave it in
as good, or even a better state of fertility at the end of his days,
unless he is *a man of thought,* accustomed to devise the best and
most practicable arrangements and systems of management, not
only for *producing,* but for *consuming* the productions of the farm.
(See How TO MAKE A GOOD FARM BETTER, in next vol.)   He
must not always be "whistling along for want of thought," but
he must think *beforehand*—not a year afterwards—what he can
do *practically* to bring all his practices and farming operations to
a greater degree of perfection for the year to come, than they were

the past season. He must make note of his *failures* in every operation, and endeavor to have everything performed in the most seasonable time, and in the most economical and farmer-like manner. And-

A FARMER MUST BE A LABORING MAN.

On the other side of the great water, the *landlord*, the *farmer*, and the *laborer*, exist in three distinct personages ; but in America, for the most part, these three are united in *one*. The most successful cultivators of the soil in America, whose opinions on agricultural subjects and whose practices are eagerly sought, and widely disseminated and adopted, are most generally men who are not ashamed nor mortified to be seen in a ditch, with a tow frock on, or holding the plow, or swinging 'the cradle. Reason and experience teach us that manual labor is by no means incompatible with the growth and vigor of our intellects. Philosophy and long experience have furnished us with the most indubitable demonstration that *active, energetic, manual* employment, imparts *vigor* to the corporeal system, and that vigor of the body invigorates the brain. Our systems are so constituted, that while our *hands* are engaged in manual operations, the head and the heart may be led on to knowledge. It injures no one to labor with his hands; and, although we were doomed to toil by the Creator, (Gen. 3: 19,) it is one of the greatest temporal blessings, in disguise, which mortals are permitted to enjoy. If a farmer's business should be so extensive that all his time is consumed in *planning* and in *superintending*, or if he is able to glide along through the world *passively*, still he ought to have a good understanding of manual operations, so as to be able to instruct those in his employ how to handle their tools with skill and efficiency. No man ever shortened his days by energetic, manual labor, *alone ;* but *bad habits* have sent thousands to an untimely grave, whose demise was *attributed* to " *hard work.*" Intellectual culture and manual labor must go hand in hand. The time is fast hastening on, when the hands of hard-fisted industry will sway the destiny of the world.

A FARMER SHOULD BE A GOOD MECHANIC,

theoretically, if he is not *practically.* There are so many branches
of mechanical operations connected with farming, such as making
farm gates, and fences, harrows, field-rollers, and tools of every
description, and repairing old ones, and putting edge tools
in order, and such like, that he who must necessarily depend
entirely on some one else to perform every little job, cannot
expect to succeed in farming operations like him who will accustom himself to handle mechanical tools with dexterity.   More
than one-half of our country mechanics, who work at their trade
for a livelihood, are *incompetent* to perform a difficult job, in a
neat and workmanlike manner, without a *foreman.*   For this
reason, if for no other, a farmer should be a good mechanic, in
order to give proper directions *how* a piece of work should be
performed, or whether or not it is *perfect* or *faulty* after it is
finished.

A FARMER SHOULD BE A MACHINIST.

Now that so many new machines are being manufactured and
introduced for performing the labors of the farm, a farmer needs
the skill and discernment of an ingenious machinist, in order to
understand whether a machine has been manufactured according
to the most approved mechanical principles or not, and to detect
at a glance any imperfection in its construction (see FITTING UP
MACHINERY, in the next vol.); and in case a machine fails in consequence of little imperfections in its manufacture, to be able to
repair it *himself,* or to direct another to do it, in a workmanlike
manner.

A FARMER SHOULD BE A GOOD ENGINEER.

Agriculture now is ranked among the *arts* and *sciences* of the
first order.   Indeed, the cultivation of the soil has been not improperly styled the "mother of arts."   Perhaps in no other single
art and science can there be found such a variety of simple and
complex, cheap and expensive, tools and implements, as in agriculture.   Consequently, in order to be able to work, or manage,

or handle with skill and efficiency, such a variety of implements and tools, a man needs an eye like a serpent, an ear like a roe, the perception of an elephant, and the skill and acumen of a honey-bee. He needs to have a good knowledge *of the strength of materials*—which lies at the very foundation of successful engineering—that he may be able to determine, without hesitancy, whether the various parts of a tool are of the correct proportion, (see next vol.,) or ·whether one part of a machine is made four times lighter, or heavier, as the case may be, than is required, or is necessary. It is important for him to know whether, in erecting buildings, the stress on the different parts is so great, or so small, as to need a timber one foot square, or six inches square. He should have a perception so acute when running any kind of machinery as to determine, in an instant, by the *sound* and *clatter*, whether the motion is too high or too low, or uniform, or variable, or when anything is not in complete running order. He should be able to tell whether he is hauling with his team a number of hundred pounds of redundant material in a given machine ; and whether his team moves, or the parts of machinery run, at the most effective velocity or not. (See VELOCITY OF SAWS.) A farmer should understand well the *principles of draught*, (see next vol.,) that he may not break his tools unnecessarily, nor use up the energies of his team to no good purpose. These are but a very few of the qualifications which ought to be prominent characteristics of every successful cultivator of the soil ; and besides these, it is of primary importance that a farmer should understand, well,

THE PROPER APPROPRIATION OF THE FORCES OF THE FARM.

" The prudent foreman now, with timely care,
 Forecasts his labors ; gives to each his share.
 No force is misapplied : he keeps in view
 The faithful, trusty, and the *idle*, too,
 With plans well formed for every future day,
 His forces execute without delay."—EDWARDS.

Why does one farmer often accomplish as much, or even more

labor with two workmen, than his neighbor does with *four* laborers of equal strength? Why do the operations on one farm move on most effectively in every respect, without any hurry, or bluster, or fretting, or worrying of teams, while on the next farm all is hurry and excitement, and but little work done? The answers to these interrogations may all be expressed in few words, which cannot be gainsayed: *A want of wise plans, and an improper appropriation of the forces of the farm.*

Every farmer, in order to be successful, must have well-digested plans for performing every operation connected with his business. He can never hope to be successful who goes to work at random. A successful farmer will be a *thinking* man; and all his plans will be so harmonious, that little, if any, of his available force will be improperly appropriated, under any circumstances. He will never send two laborers to perform a little job which one can do in about the same period of time. It cannot be denied that multitudes of pretty good farmers are most stupendously deficient on this point; and it is no uncommon occurrence to see them employ two, three, and even *four* laborers to do what one hand could perform very advantageously. There are very many operations on the farm which one hand cannot do to any good advantage; but when one man can perform a given piece of work alone by working four times as long as it would require four men to do it, as a general rule, in practice, it will be found to be most economical, on the score of expense, to employ but *one* hand at such a job. It cannot be expected that uninterested laborers will care but little how many of them are sent by their employer to perform a given job; therefore the skillful and successful farmer, whether he is a tyro or not, should always *think* a moment, whether more than one hand is really needed, and whether one will not perform a certain job about as quickly as *two* will do it.

The practice of some farmers always is, if there is a job or two of labor at a distant part of the farm which one hand could do in an hour or so most advantageously, to send three or four to do it, thinking that if one man can do it in two hours, two men will be able to do it in one hour; and four men can do it in half an hour.

Did such reasoning hold good, there would be a loss of time by sending four hands. Suppose, for instance, the work is so far distant as to occupy ten minutes in going to it and ten minutes in returning. Now one laborer will go and do the job in two hours and twenty minutes, or in one hundred and forty minutes, when he will be ready for another job. But if *four* men are employed, each one consumes twenty minutes in going to and returning from the job, which will consume one hundred and ten minutes, providing they perform the job in thirty minutes. With good faithful laborers, those who will work faithfully when alone, there is almost always *a loss of time*, in proportion to the number employed. There will be some waiting, one for another, which cannot conveniently be avoided. And more than all, when a lot of men work together, it often seems at first sight that they are driving the job with great rapidity, when, if the labor performed were divided up into plots, so that each could see exactly how much he had accomplished, they would all be ashamed that they had done so little. But it is much the wisest policy, many times, to have a lot of hands work together, because some men do not like to work alone, and they *cannot* work alone ; and if set to work alone, they *cannot work*, and they *will not try*. This is a weakness not uncommon to many pretty active men. They need the little stimulus of example; and many times, men who are good for nothing when alone will accomplish a large day's work if they can have only the company of another individual, whether he is an associate laborer or not. On this point the tyro must exercise all possible acumen; and if it is his misfortune to have in his employ a laborer not unlike the one just alluded to, he should have every plan wisely laid *beforehand*, so that when his workmen have finished one job, he will be ready to give orders, with promptness, who shall go to this piece of work, and who shall do that. There will be time enough consumed in going to and returning from labor on a large farm, when the plans are ever so well laid ; but unless some *forethought* is exercised little will be accomplished.

It is no uncommon occurrence on some farms to see two men

sent to get one team, and go half a mile or more to get a load of rails, or wood, or stone, or such like. We will grant that they may work advantageously in loading and unloading; but if it consumes twenty minutes in going to, and twenty more in returning from their work, there is a loss of forty minutes with one laborer, which might have probably been appropriated to some good purpose. Now let forty minutes be taken from every two hours during the entire day, and one third of his time will amount to nothing. Allowing fifteen or twenty minutes for one man to put on a load of rails, or of wood, if two were able to do it in half that time, there would be a waste of time. In hauling dirt, gravel, peat, muck, or manure, two men, and many times *three*, are sent with *one team* and one cart, or wagon, to haul such substances the distance of one fourth of a mile, or even more. Suppose, after loading, it requires only five minutes to drive to the place for unloading, and five minutes to return. If two laborers are employed, and both go to unload, there will be a loss of time of one man, of ten minutes each load; amounting to more than two hours *lost time* during the working hours of one day.

In mowing grass with scythes, or cradling grain, one man usually, especially if he will work alone, will cut more than half as much as two; and as the number of hands are increased in one company at such work, the less labor will be performed in proportion to the number of workmen employed. Why? Because even when they are all faithful as possible, there will of necessity be a vast amount of waiting one for another. Suppose, for instance, there are five mowers, or cradlers. It will usually be seen that one who *sets in* first will work one or two minutes before there will be an opportunity for the last one to commence. Now, they will all work fifteen or twenty rods, and perhaps not half that distance, when there will be another halt until all come up even, when the scythes must be whet. Then there is a delay of one for the other all day; and it many times will amount to . more than the working hours of one man in one day. And, besides, the labor performed will be most astonishingly less, in proportion to the number of hands employed, than if one or two laborers only worked together. And, furthermore, when a lot of hands are mowing, or cradling together, each one is prompted, by the recital of some nonsensical story or startling adventure, to relate something similar, in order to disclose his own indomitable perseverance, or prowess, or magnanimity : and if there be half a score, all must wait to hear it. The true remedy is, to set a few hands at work in one field, and a few in another field,—when there will usually be a little ambition on the part of faithful workmen to perform quite as much, or a little more, and a little better, than the other party.

It is no uncommon thing to see two men sent to the woods to split rails, stakes, or the like, with but one beetle, and as many wedges and glats, as one man only needs. Two laborers can work together very advantageously in splitting such materials only when each one has all the tools which one man requires. But when two men have but one beetle, and a corresponding number of wedges, if they are ever so faithful, there must necessarily be a loss of time,—unless one hand confines himself closely to splitting, while the other chops off the cuts, and peals and piles whatever the other splits. But pealing, piling up, and cutting the cuts, are usually much less than half the labor required, to make rails and stakes. The true and economical way, when two men are employed to split rails together, is, to furnish each one with a beetle, an axe, and as many wedges as he needs. And then let both work together, when opening the cuts, each one having a good handspike, especially when the cuts are large ; and when a cut is separated, let each one take one half to split into rails; and they will not be in each other's way; and all their time and labor will be most economically appropriated. (See SPLITTING RAILS, par. 63.)

In digging post-holes, two men are very frequently seen at work with but one set of tools. Under such circumstances, it is almost impossible for two laborers to dig in a day twice as many holes as one man alone will dig. When each one must of necessity wait a few minutes when he wants to use a tool, for the other to finish using it, for the time there will be a loss of time; and in a few days, those lost, idle moments, when a laborer is receiving seventy-five cents or more per day, will soon amount to enough to purchase a set of tools.

During the season of haying and harvesting in particular, the tyro should see to it that every plan is most wisely and economically laid, in disposing of the manual forces of the farm. Whether he leads the van in active labor, or only superintends, he should, as occasion requires, think what disposition he may make of his ‿orces, in order to accomplish the greatest amount of labor in a given time. If, for example, it will be necessary to spread, or turn, or air a lot of hay, in some distant field, which one man will be able to do in half an hour or so, let one only go and do it. Let one hand only get a team, instead of sending *two*. When there are more than two hands in loading, let two pitch while one loads: because one man can load for two pitchers just as well as for one. When the distance is half a mile or more from the barn to the field, and it is convenient to have two teams to haul with, three hands will accomplish more at hauling hay and grain, by putting on two loads in the field and driving them to the place of unloading, and unloading both wagons, than they will to use only *one* wagon and one team : because there will be less time not appropriated to useful labor when there are *two* teams, than when but *one* is used. In hauling anything any considerable distance, in order to appropriate the working hours to the most economical purpose, each man should have a team, so that all his time may be consumed, if not in *active* labor, in something which consumes time, such as simply driving a team with a load.

In hauling heavy logs or timber, where two or more hands are absolutely necessary in loading, in order to lose no time of workmen, each one should have a team; and then two, three, or more, as may be necessary, should load one team, and then another; and then each man drive a team to the place of unloading, when no time need be consumed to no purpose.

I have been led to pen these thoughts in consequence of having seen so much injudicious and uneconomical appropriation of the manual forces of the farm ; and by those, too, who were always grumbling, and complaining that their work was *always behind ;* and that they were not able to get laborers to perform as much in a day for themselves, as when they were in the employ of some of their neighbors. I might expatiate upon the subject to four times its present length, with seeming propriety ; but enough has been said to induce the tyro *to think* and plan for himself, and to appropriate his forces according to the circumstances of the occasion.

It may be urged that hard-working laborers need *rest ;* and that it seems rather like a disposition to *overreach* the limits of fairness and propriety. It is granted that they need rest ; but there is no danger that they will not avail themselves of all the time, necessary or not, to reinvigorate their partially exhausted faculties. They will seldom consider any number of hours spent in idleness, in the *light of rest ;* nor will they seldom feel willing to make any greater exertion, when they are in active labor, if half their time is consumed in idleness, than they do when they work during all the working hours of one or of many days. There are always rainy days, and portions of days, during the year, when laborers cannot labor at all advantageously ; but they must receive the same wages that they do when they are earning, in a day, twice the sum which they receive per day. But, when the weather is fair, it is but just and right that all the forces should be brought into operation, in the most economical and effective manner. The tyro should plan work for his hands on the preceding day, so that each one, as soon as he rises in the morning, can start immediately to his business, without hanging around a half-hour or more, before he knows what to go about. Let one man go and feed the teams ; and another do this, and another do that job, until breakfast time, and in this way a long catalogue of little jobs will be performed, during the season, which otherwise would have gone undone. Another consideration of vast importance is,

THE COÖPERATION OF THE WIFE.

" Good husband without it is needful there be :
*Good housewife within is as needful as he.''—*TUSSER.

However judiciously and economically the plans for the operations of the farm may be laid, if a man and his wife do not *harmonize*, most completely, in prosecuting their labors, he had better
at once dispose of his farm, and lay by the avails of it for decrep-
itude and old age, and work out by day's work. The *housewife*
and her operations are *the great regulator* of the operations of the
farm. There is too much truth in the old maxim, for fiction, that
" if a man would succeed well in his livelihood, he must ask his wife."
A very great fault among many farmers is, they do not consult
their wives in relation to matters with reference to which it is
highly proper they should have a word or two to say. We com-
miserate the man who bears the reproach of a *hen-pecked husband ;*
and, when we see a wife ruling, and engineering in-doors and out
of doors, we think that if she had a husband *far superior to her-
self*, she would be a woman of sterling worth. It cannot be
denied that wives have often made, to their husbands, some most
capital suggestions, in reference to the operations of the farm;
and it must be acknowledged, that many women are far more
capable of planning judiciously, and carrying on more economically the operations of the farm, than their husbands. But if a
wife superintends and executes, in the best manner, the *in-door*
operations, nothing more should be required of her. I know that
very many men consider it a little beneath them to consult their
wives with reference to any of their plans; and they will never
suffer their wives to know, if they can prevent it, any thing about
their income or expenditures, or their debit or credit. But it is
a matter of doubt whether there ever was an instance in which a
man habitually consulted his wife, when, as a consequence, it
proved detrimental, or a disparagement to him in any respect.
There can be no impropriety in the practice of some men, of
allowing the housewife to know exactly all about the income and

expenditures, the debit and credit of the farm; and if these wise ones, who congratulate themselves that they have a most perfect knowledge of the best manner of performing the operations of the farm, would confer a little more with their wives, their wisdom would be greatly increased.

> " A man may spare and yet be bare,
> If his wife be *naught*—if his wife be *naught* !
> But a man may *spend*, and have cash to *lend*,
> If his wife be *aught*—if his wife be *aught* !"

THE

YOUNG FARMER'S MANUAL.

CHAPTER I.

SELECTING THE MOST SUITABLE LOCATION FOR THE BUILDINGS
OF A FARM.

"Be this our home—that ever hallowed spot,
To plant a palace or a lowly cot."

1. THE first and very important consideration with a young
farmer, as soon as he comes into possession of a farm, is, to have
all his buildings situated in the most convenient location, with
reference to each other and to the different fields of the farm.
If a farm is broken up by gullies and deep ravines, if convenience
of access to fields on both sides of them is any object, the young
farmer should endeavor to have his buildings located at the most
desirable point. If a farm is rather undulating, or nearly level,
and its boundaries at nearly right angles, it is not attended with
much difficulty to select a site for the farm buildings which shall
prove most convenient in every respect. It is always most
desirable to have every field as convenient of access from the
barn as possible. This is desirable, not only for the sake of
convenience, but for the sake of economy in the expenses of
travelling, with or without loads, to and from the fields. Some
people will select only a high spot of ground for locating farm
buildings, and never even think of consulting convenience of

(27)

access to the distant parts of a farm. Americans almost universally will erect their buildings along the highway, even when such
a location would place them entirely on one side of their farm.
When the boundaries of a farm are in the shape of a wedge,
which is not unfrequently the case, and the barn is located on the
small end, it makes a vast amount of unnecessary travel and
labor in hauling the produce of distant fields to the barn, and in
returning the manure to them. Streams of water and springs
often influence the young farmer in choosing the most desirable
and convenient location for buildings; but streams of water can
be so easily turned from their natural course, and the water of
springs can be brought in pipe or tube at so small an expense,
and up hill, too, that these considerations should have but little
weight in selecting the location for the buildings of a farm.
When the farm is composed of only forty or fifty acres, and is
located in a square compass, if the buildings are all located on
one side of it the inconvenience is not so great as it is when the
buildings are all on one side of a large farm. Convenience would
dictate that the buildings should be located as near the middle of
the farm as is practicable.

2. It is true that there are many advantages in having the
buildings of the farm located on the borders of the highway;
but it is a very rare instance in which the disadvantages attending the performance of the labors of the farm—if the farm is a
large one—would not have a preponderating influence if they
were fairly and impartially compared. There are some farmers
who have torn away from the very common custom of building
along the highway, and have located their buildings in the centre
of the farm, and the result is, the most distant fields are situated
nearer the barn, and much less time is spent in going to and from
them. Should the centre of a farm be an undesirable location,
on account of low, wet ground, it would be far better to locate a
little at one side of the centre, than to be placed entirely at one
side of the farm.

3. If I were to commence on a new farm of only fifty, or of
two hundred acres, on which there were no streams or springs

of water, I would dig a large, deep well in the centre of the farm, and erect a wind wheel for pumping the water; and here I would locate the buildings, and would lay out a lane each way from the centre of the farm, north, south, east, and west, so that cattle could go to and come from any field to the water without crossing another field. The land appropriated to lanes would produce pasture, and therefore would not be useless. If it were only "*the fashion*" to have the buildings of a farm located near the centre of it, the inconveniences arising from having the buildings located entirely at one side of it would seem almost intolerable. It will require no more land for the sites of buildings, and for pleasure grounds and yards, in the centre of a farm, than would be occupied near the borders of the highway.

4. For the arrangement and disposition of buildings, and for plans of dwelling-houses, and plans of out-buildings—as a chapter of proper length on that subject would swell this Treatise far beyond its prescribed limits—young farmers who are interested in this subject, will find all that the most fastidious can desire on this subject, in works devoted to that subject.

PLOTTING THE FARM AND LAYING OUT THE FIELDS.

5. Every farmer should draw a Plan of his farm on a large sheet of drawing-paper, which may be inclosed in a wooden frame, or it may be delineated on a large board, neatly planed. Let the Deed of a farm be taken to a good surveyor, who has the proper instruments, and he will be able to delineate the shape of any farm, with the different distances of a proper proportion to each other, with the outside lines running at the same angle in the plan that they do on the farm. The larger the plan is, the better it will be. The next step will be, to lay out the farm into fields of the most convenient shape and size. If the farm is a large one, the fields may be proportionately large; but if the farm is small, and the proprietor designs to keep a limited number of cattle, or animals of any kind, the fields must be small. It should always be the aim, in dividing a farm into fields, by fences, to have the boundaries of each field run about at right

angles. But when a farm is cut up with highways, railroads, and deep gullies, which do not run parallel with the outside boundaries, the young farmer must exercise a little judgment and skill in giving them a shape that will be most convenient of access from the barn. If the buildings are so located that the fields must necessarily be all on one side of a lane, leading to the barn, it would be more convenient to have the fields eighty or one hundred rods long, and of a narrow width, and let them extend from the farther boundary of the farm to the lane, than to have the fields square and be obliged to cross one or two fields in order to reach a distant field. Sometimes it seems desirable to make the fields of an irregular shape, in order to allow animals in each field to have access to water. But it is not always advisable to give a field an irregular shape for the sake of a stream of water, when it can be brought to that field for a small expense. It is always desirable to have the fields of a uniform size, especially when one adopts, in raising crops, a rotation system.

6. The first settlers of our country were accustomed to locate their buildings almost anywhere; and to clear and cultivate the best and dryest land first; and to fence around those parts of the farm which were too wet to plow, and to keep them for pasture only. The result was, that the fields of many farms were as irregular in shape as a shapeless rock. When the location is such that such places can be drained, the fences should be made in the desired places, and all wet places and corners made dry by ditching. Having decided upon the form and size of each field, let marks be delineated in the plan to represent the fences. Let each field be designated in the plan by some name, or title, or by some tree, or rock, or pool, or they may be designated as the fields A, B, C, &c. This plan, or map, should be placed where every one connected with the farm could see it often, and understand the location of every field, and woods, and yard, and building, from the map. Now, if there are little streams running across the farm, let them be represented by dotted lines, running at about the same angle in the map that they do on the farm. When under-drains are made in any field, dotted lines should be

made on the map to represent them. The distances should be accurately measured in the field,—how many rods from a given corner a certain ditch crosses the boundary of such a field, and how many rods it runs in a given direction, and how many rods from a certain corner it crosses the fence towards the outlet. Should there be branches in a main ditch, let the distance from a given side of the field be accurately measured, in rods or feet, and noted down with the dotted lines on the map. All this will not require as much time, if everything is performed systematically, as I have consumed in penning these few thoughts. If the ditches are filled with tile, stone, or wood, in any form, let it be noted on the map, and also the *time* when the ditches were made.

7. The advantage to be derived from knowing exactly, to one foot or less, where an under-drain is located, may often be of more or less pecuniary profit, in case a certain ditch should fail to discharge the surplus water where it is located, in consequence of some little obstruction, which could be readily found if the exact location of the drain were known. (See DRAINING, 395.)

8. If a young farmer should happen to settle on a farm where all the necessary buildings are erected and the fields laid out, he may frequently obviate many very great inconveniences, by altering the shape of his fields, and by removing the out-buildings to a more desirable and convenient location.

GENERAL REMARKS AND SUGGESTIONS IN REFERENCE TO ERECTING FARM BUILDINGS.

9. Every man who has a lot of farm buildings to erect, needs all the forethought and experience of him who has had the supervision of erecting the necessary buildings of a large farm, in order that he may be able to plan everything judiciously, and see that every part of a job is executed economically and substantially. Erecting buildings is a piece of labor which is not to be performed every year of a man's life; and it is almost always quite impracticable to undo, and perform correctly, a job in building that has been done amiss. Not one in fifty knows how to take advantage of common circumstances in erecting his build-

2

ings; and but few know really what materials are actually necessary, or know how to obtain them in the most economical and expeditious manner. A few practical suggestions on this subject may be of almost incalculable advantage to the young farmer.

10. When a man of little experience is about to commence building, he should make a most vigorous effort to ascertain what kind of buildings—how large or how small, whether of wood, brick, or stone—he really needs. It may save him several hundreds of dollars, to first procure the excellent periodicals published on this subject; as in them he will find an almost unlimited variety of ground plans and elevations of buildings. In order to build most economically, the stone and sand should all be hauled in the winter, when the labors of the farm are not on hand; and boards and plank should be well-seasoned, not less than one year, before they are worked up. In the meantime, the beginner should confer with those who have had experience in planning buildings; and endeavor to have every plan arranged in the most complete and economical manner. Always, if possible, commence building *in the spring;* because the weather is usually more favorable, and the days are longer, and workmen will perform full one quarter or one third more, than they will be able to do in the short, unfavorable, and cold days of autumn. We will commence with

THE DWELLING-HOUSE.

11. Every dwelling-house needs a good cellar beneath it. And in order to have it cool in summer, and dry and warm in winter, the foundation walls should be built not less than twenty inches above the level of the ground, after the ground has been levelled off, in order to furnish sufficient space for the cellar windows. The surface of the ground should always *descend* a little from the house in order to carry off the surface water. Before the cellar walls are laid, a good drain should be cut not less than six inches *deeper* than the bottom of the cellar, and a little trench dug entirely around the bottom of the cellar leading into the main ditch. Now, let water be poured into the trench to ascer-

tain whether it will flow out freely into the main ditch. If water will run out of the trench into the main ditch, lay pipe or sole tile, having not less than an inch and a half calibre, in this trench entirely around the cellar, and cover them with hard dirt, well tramped down on the tile. These tile will carry off all water that would find its way into the cellar. Let tile be laid in the main drain. Two inch tile is sufficiently large. Never trust to a drain filled with stone about a cellar, or beneath any building; because they will be filled with some obstruction in a few years. Let the main drain extend into the cellar a foot or two. Let the bottom of the cellar be a few inches highest in the centre. If it is convenient, let a lead pipe extend from the bottom of the rain-water cistern through the foundation of the cellar, having a faucet or plug in the end, so that when the cistern needs to be emptied, or the cellar-bottom needs cleaning, water may be let out of the cistern on the cellar bottom, and allowed to escape through a hole in a flat stone into the drain. All the surplus water of the cistern, during heavy rains, should pass off through the tile for the purpose of keeping the passage clear. Never build a dry wall around a cellar under any building; because you will wish a thousand times in less than five years, that the stone had been laid up in good mortar. (Read paragraph 187, to learn the best manner of laying stone walls.) Remember that roots and fruit will freeze much sooner in a damp cellar than they will in a dry one. Make calculations to have sufficient space in the cellar to allow a tall man to walk erect in it, and carry a basket of potatoes on his shoulder. If a building is large and heavy, the foundation stone should be sunk six inches below the bottom of the cellar; and the stone walls should in no case be less than twenty inches in thickness. Thirty inches thick would be far better.

12. In hauling the stone for the cellar wall, the young farmer should endeavor to select those first which have a good face side, and reject all ill-shapen ones; and when unloading them, let them be well spread out, with the face side up, and corner-stones

by themselves, so that a stone-mason will be able to select readily such as he needs, first or last.

13. In localities where building-stone is very scarce, and the subsoil is very compact and hard, the cellar walls may be built with a small amount of stone, after the manner of building in this region. Excavate the ground of the size of the cellar, about one foot deep, and build the foundation wall two feet high, making calculations to grade up on the outside nearly one foot high. Let the wall above the ground be carried up with square timber to the desired height. There should be a narrow space between the timbers, as frost will not pass timbers of the same thickness, when there is a space between them, as soon as it will one solid stick: and so with stone foundations. If a wall is built of two courses of stone, the frost will be excluded from the cellar much longer than it will if the stones extend entirely across the wall.

Now, let the cellar be dug about three and a half feet below the *bottom* of the walls, leaving a square shoulder of earth, not less than two feet wide, entirely around the cellar; and let this shoulder of earth be well plastered with water-lime mortar, both on the side and on the top. This shoulder will be found a very convenient shelf to place barrels on in the winter. I know of cellars that have been built in this manner fifteen years, and are now as good as when they were first built. But the frost must be kept out of such cellars, or it will injure such plastering, and make it peel off. The middle of such cellars should be the highest, and a gutter made around the outside to carry off the water. My own cellar is built in this manner; and although it has been built ten years, and has been injured by the frost only a little in two places, still I regret that the walls were not built from the bottom of the cellar with good stone. These considerations with reference to the foundation wall, are equally applicable to the foundation of a barn or other out-buildings. Every building should have a good stone wall under it, laid up in *lime mortar*.

14. In building the superstructure, as a general rule, timber is made use of which is nearly twice as large as is necessary. It is better to have the frame timber too large than too small. Sills, one foot square, lying on a good stone wall, are more than twice as large as is necessary. And, besides, such large timber is very liable to be affected with the "dry rot." Sills, six by eight, or ten inches square, are sufficiently large for any building that is erected on a wall, whether dwelling-house or barn.* For small building, sills that are six inches square are infinitely better than if they were four times as large. When a tree is a large one, of which it is desirable to make a sill or other timber, let it be slit at the saw-mill of the desired size. A tree will often turn out four good sticks of timber when sawed, besides some boards or plank; whereas, if it was scored and hewed only one stick could be obtained. Where the plates of a building are supported by studs between the posts, if they are five by eight inches square, they will be sufficiently strong for the roof of any ordinary building. As most kinds of timber, with the heart of the tree in the middle of the stick, is liable to check and crack open, often to its great injury, if a tree is slit through the middle for a couple of plates, they will not check. If there is a large seam in the middle of the tree, a plank or two may be sawed out of the middle, and the plates cut out of the soundest wood.

15. *The Roofs* of buildings are often made too flat for profit. A flat roof, whatever the materials are of which it is made, is far more liable to leak than a steep roof, and it will leak much sooner than if it were steeper; and the same roof will be serviceable full ten years longer if built with a half pitch, than it will if built with a quarter pitch.† A roof looks far better, and is more

* A large church was recently taken down in this town, the sills of which were of the best of white oak, one foot square, and although the outside was as sound and tough as good spoke timber, about one-third of the middle of the sills was nothing but a mass of "dry rot." The rationale is, that the sills could not season only in part, because they were so large.

† When a building is sixteen feet wide, and the ridge of the roof is four feet higher than the top of the plates, the roof is said to have a *quarter*, or *one-fourth pitch*. When the ridge of the roof is eight feet higher than the top of the plates, and the building sixteen feet wide, it is said to have a *half-pitch*.

durable, when it has about *one-third pitch*, than if it is built flatter. When a roof, covered with wooden shingles, has *one-half pitch*, the shingles may be completely worn out before that roof will leak. And another consideration of great importance is, in countries like this, where snow falls deep, the roofs of buildings should have not less than one-third pitch, because the steeper the roof is, the less liable a body of snow is to lodge on it; and a body of snow that would thrust the plates apart, or injure the roof, if it had but a fourth pitch, would not remain on a steep roof. When heated air from any of the rooms below the roof melts the snow on the roof in cold weather, the water thus formed will run down to the eaves, and freeze before it falls into the eaves-troughs; and if there is much snow on the roof, and the roof has less than one-third pitch, ice will continue to form at the eaves, until it becomes so thick that the water will flow back under the shingles, and fall down on the walls in the upper rooms. This is of very common occurrence in this region, and many costly walls in elegant dwellings have been seriously damaged in this way.

16. The remedy is, steeper roofs, with the eaves projecting beyond the sides of the building, not less than two feet, measuring horizontally. If the roof projects two feet or more, and is rather steep, there will not be as much water and ice; and should it freeze at the eaves, there will not be enough on the roof to cause the water to flow back under the shingles above the plates.

17. The beginner should be careful to see that when a house or any other building is framed, some means is devised to prevent the middle of the building from spreading. Jobbers are not particular on this point, and many times the plates at the middle of the building will be thrust apart several inches, to the great injury of the building. Sometimes a scantling bolted from near the foot of one rafter to the other, called a *collar*, on each of the rafters, will be sufficient. In large buildings, if the roof is not supported by purline plates and posts, the foot of the rafters should be secured by means of a *truss*, or a *tie* and *king-post* and *struts*. Sometimes this may be most effectually prevented, as in a hay

barn, where a beam would be very much in the way, by fitting a brace, without mortises, and bolting one end of it to the middle post just below the plate, and the other end to the upper side of the beam which supports the floor. Braces in such places, when put in with tenon and mortise, almost always give way, and it is not safe to rely upon them.

18. When a roof is covered with wooden shingles, a little care should be exercised in having the shingles *three courses thick*. The distance which one course of shingles is laid above the other, is called *laying to the weather*. If shingles are laid six inches to the weather, and the greater part of them are a little *less* than eighteen inches in length, the shingles will not be of three thickness over the entire roof; but there will be many places at the butts of each course, where the top end of the under course does not extend far enough up the roof to receive the water as it falls from the butts of the outside course. A new roof often will leak because the shingles are laid more than one-third of their length to the weather; whereas, the courses should be laid a little less than one-third the length of the shortest shingles.

OUT-BUILDINGS.

19. Many farmers seem to prefer a lot of small detached barns to one large one. But those who have ever had a cluster of small barns, and afterwards came in possession of one larger one, greatly prefer a large one to a lot of small ones. On the score of economy, one large barn that will contain as much as three or four small ones, will cost nearly one half less to erect it; and a number of small ones are never as convenient as one large one. The young farmer, as a general rule, need have no apprehensions that he will erect a barn larger than is necessary, for the complaint almost always is a want of barn room. Barn room usually is all occupied; and in most instances it pays a good interest; but so much redundant house room as is too frequently met with, is a decided disadvantage to a farmer. A few years ago barns were built with posts only twelve and fourteen feet in length; because it was so laborious and expensive pitching hay or grain

to the top of them. But now that we have very efficient horse elevators, out-buildings should be made much higher than they formerly were. It costs but a trifle more to frame a post twenty-four feet long than it costs to frame one fourteen feet long ; and it requires no more rafters, and roof boards, and shingles, to cover a high building than a low one. The posts of a large barn may just as well be, and ought to be, twenty-four feet long, as to be shorter. If such posts are eight inches square no one need have any fears that they would ever prove too small; providing every one is well braced. Every additional brace gives additional stiffness to a building ; and the young farmer should insist on having the foot of every post braced, where they will not be in the way, with as long braces as there is room for receiving; and *each end should be well pinned.* One brace at the foot of a post, is more effectual in rendering a high building stiff, than two braces at the top of it. The braces in a barn frame may face with the inside of the posts ; and then they can cross the girts ; and braces as long as can be received between the posts can be used without interfering with the girts or studs.

20. Jobbers will usually mutter and grumble when requested to put in long braces on the *inside* of posts ; and will deny the importance of having long braces, and of having the ends of them well pinned. But these ideas have not been penned without knowing from experience how a building should be braced, in order to render it as stiff as possible with a given quality and form of materials. It is by no means the largest timbers that can be worked into a building, which impart the greatest strength and stiffness to the frame ; but it is the *manner in which the framing is performed.* Every tenon, where it is possible, should pass *entirely through a sill or post;* and be well pinned with very tough pins. The girts—or girders—should never be placed more than four feet apart. If they are much farther apart, the outside boards, which are nailed to them, will not be as firm as they should be. The main beams should be not less than fourteen feet from the floor ; so as to allow sufficient room for a load of hay or grain to pass under them. If such beams are eight by

ten inches square, and supported at proper distances with middle posts, they will be large enough for any barn. The beginner should, at the commencement of a job, give the foreman directions to let the ends of every beam *into the posts* not less than half an inch, so that the superincumbent pressure will not all rest on the tenons.

21. The sleepers or joists of the principal floor should be stiff enough to sustain any team and load without bending ; and they never should be placed more than three feet apart from centre to centre, even when two inch plank is used for the floor. Two inch basswood plank, thoroughly seasoned, with the edges plowed with a half-inch plow, a half-inch deep, and a tongue neatly fitted, like Fig. 1, will make as neat a barn floor as any

FIG. 1.

MANNER OF UNITING BARN-FLOOR PLANK.

one can desire. Fig. 2 represents the best manner of uniting the

FIG. 2.

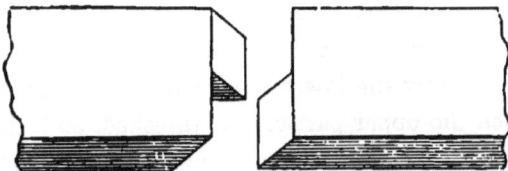

MANNER OF MAKING END JOINTS TO FLOORING.

ends of plank or floor boards. In the absence of good plank, a double floor of inch boards will subserve a good purpose. In this case, a good coating of tar, or lime and tar, should be laid between them for the purpose of excluding wire-worms and all other insects, and for rendering the floor tight and firm.

22. When there are a number of different kinds of timber in the frame, such as soft and hard wood, the proprietor should see that the workmen have three or four different sizes of nails in their boxes. Every good joiner knows that it is not always practicable to drive ten or twelvepenny nails into seasoned, hard

2*

wood.   In nailing on siding or inch boards, if the timber is hard wood, nails of a smaller size should be used.   Let a workman attempt to nail on a half-inch board with tenpenny nails driven into a stud of sugar maple, thoroughly seasoned; and after the nail has entered about one inch it will bend or break; and the siding will most assuredly be split.   Let sixpenny nails be used for nailing into hard wood, and eights and tens—according to the thickness of the boards—when the studs, posts, or girders are of soft wood.

23.   In order to keep the large beams from springing outwards or in either direction, two or three of the middle joists should be let in with a dove-tail.

24.   Rafters should be firmly spiked—not pinned with wooden pins—to the plates; because wooden pins are very liable to shrink and become loose; and if the roof should project as far as it ought to in order to appear well, a violent gale of wind would lift the roof from the plates.   But fortypenny nails will hold it in place.

25.   Reference should be had, in erecting a large barn, to the most proper and economical disposition of the room.   The joists, which extend from one large beam to another, should be loose, so that they can be removed until the mow is filled up to them, when they should be put in their places, and a few loose boards laid on them.   Now the lower part of the mow may be threshed out; and then the upper part can be threshed, and the straw deposited in the lower part of the mow.   Should more room be needed, the horse fork may be used to pitch a lot of straw into the upper part of the mow.

26.   Every good barn should have a basement story, and a water channel of tile should be laid around the entire foundation, as recommended for a cellar, paragraph 11, in order to render it as dry as possible; and the barnyard should be so constructed that no manure will be wasted.

27.   Eaves-troughs should conduct all surplus water into the tile, for the purpose of keeping them open.   Basement and cellar walls are often ruined by allowing the water to fall from the eaves and soak into the ground along the walls.

28. When a carriage-house, hay-barn and stable are erected under one roof, the posts may be eighteen or twenty feet high, just as well as ten or twelve feet to the roof. When the posts are short there is but little room for hay. It will cost but a few dollars more to erect a carriage-house with twenty-feet posts than with twelve-feet posts.

29. I have erected a carriage-house the past summer. with eighteen-feet posts; and I regret they were not twenty feet long. The roof is one-third pitch, and on the top, at the middle of the ridge, is a hole five and a half feet square; and a square cupola, with a door five and a half feet square on one side of it, is erected over it, into which hay is pitched with a horse-fork. The highest pulley is attached in the top of the cupola. With such an arrangement the loft can be filled with hay to the peak with no inconvenience.

30. As tie beams are always very much in the way in a hay-barn, in my carriage-house loft, braces, made of iron-wood poles six inches in diameter and seven feet long, were neatly fitted, *without* tenons, and bolted to the middle posts below the plats, and to the upper side of the middle beam with iron bolts three-fourths of an inch in diameter, as represented by Fig. 3. Such braces keep the beam from sagging, and the plates from spreading apart.

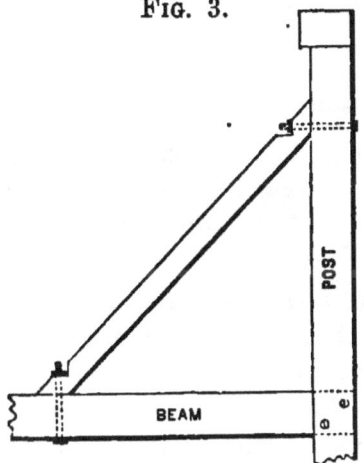

FIG. 3.

MANNER OF BOLTING A TIE BRACE TO BEAM AND POST.

SCARFING TIMBERS.

31. It is often very difficult to procure timber of a given length. For sills and beams that are well sustained with middle posts or studs, they subserve about as good purpose if they are neatly *scarfed* together, and keyed, or well bolted.

32. There are several different modes of scarfing, or "splicing," timbers; but some are very inefficient, while some others will render a stick almost as strong as

a whole stick.   Fig. 4 represents the best and strongest manner

FIG. 4.

STRONGEST MANNER OF SCARFING POSTS AND BEAMS.

of scarfing timbers.   This style requires more skill to make good
joints than either of the other figures.   This style is calculated
more particularly for beams and posts.   When timber is scarfed
like Fig. 4, iron bolts should be put through both ways, and the
feather-edged ends well nailed.   When two timbers are scarfed
like Fig. 5, if they are well pinned with wooden pins iron bolts

FIG. 5.

MANNER OF SCARFING SILLS.

will not be necessary.   The square hole in the middle of the
scarf or splice should be laid out with about *one-eighth of an inch
draw ;* so that when a wooden key is driven firmly in, the pieces
will be brought to a close joint.

CAUSE OF DECAY OF THE TIMBERS OF A BUILDING.

33. If the timbers of a building should be kept dry, they
would remain sound and serviceable during all time, even if they
were not made of the most durable kinds of wood.   When mortises for studs, or anything else, are made in the upper side of a
sill, or any other part of the frame; or when there are large checks
in the upper side of a stick, a hole should be bored in the side of
the stick, so as to intersect the bottom of mortises or checks, for
the purpose of affording a passage for any water to escape that
might find its way into such cavities.   I know it is argued that
when a house is erected it should be so well inclosed that no
water can ever find its way into cavities in the timber.   But

sometimes a driving storm will force the water through small cracks, so that it will be very difficult to determine from what source it comes. And may times, in cleaning house, some domestics will have every floor in the house completely deluged with water, which flows into mortises and checks, and soon causes decay. When my dwelling-house was erected, a hole was bored with a large bit in the side of the timber at the bottom of every mortice, and other cavities in the frame.

34. As there are so many manufactories throughout the country of window blinds, sash, and panel doors, the beginner will find it most economical usually to purchase such articles ready made ; because all such things when made by machinery are neater and truer than the majority of mechanics will make them, even if they have *ability* to do it as well. Panel doors should be allowed to season nearly a year before they are pinned together, and then they will not shrink after they have been hung.

VALUE OF BASSWOOD.

35. Whenever a man is located where pine lumber is scarce, and very costly, and other timber is abundant, such as basswood, whitewood, butternut, chestnut, and some other kinds of wood, they may be used instead of pine. For inside panel doors, basswood, for both stiles and panels, is equally as good as pine. When I built my house I used basswood for many jamb casings, and for the face casings, and for outside doors as well as inside. Basswood is better to paint on than good pine ; and will be as durable as pine if it is kept well painted. Some of the face casings in my parlor are basswood, some butternut, and some pine. They are painted white ; and nearly every stick of pine can be selected, because the coloring matter in the pine has struck through the paint, notwithstanding it has been well painted four times. Basswood siding is now coming into very extensive use ; and if I were to build a house, or any other building, and had good basswood on my own land, I would not hesitate to use it for siding, doors, and all kinds of casings, and for floors.

36. *Basswood Shingles.*—In localities where pine and hemlock

are scarce, and basswood is abundant, the beginner need not hesitate to use basswood shingles, providing they are well coated with coal tar once in two or three years. They may be sawed, cut, or shaved. I have laid several thousands of sawed basswood shingles during the past season, and I have great confidence in them. It is necessary to use nearly twice as many nails in nailing them on as is necessary for pine and hemlock. If basswood shingles are from eight to ten inches wide, each shingle should be nailed with at least five nails; otherwise, when they become a little wet, they will expand, and the middles, or edges, will rise or "bulge up." If well nailed they will make a neat roof; and if kept well coated with tar, will be serviceable a hundred years. (See PAINTING ROOFS, next Vol.)

WALLS AND LATH.

37. When the sides of a room or that part overhead are lathed with lath of ordinary length, wherever the lath break joint for a foot or two, there will be a crack in the wall. In order to remedy this cracking of the walls, the strips of lath should extend entirely across the room. When a house is lathed in this manner, there will be no cracks in the plastering across the lath.

38. The lath for my house were all sawed with a two-horse railway power, with a circular saw one foot in diameter, out of basswood plank, which was about an inch and a quarter thick. The lath were sawed, about three-eighths of an inch thick, very true; and there is not a place in the entire house where the lath break joint; and, consequently, not a crack to be found across the lath. This is a very economical way to procure lath; and they are usually much better than those that are purchased. Have the logs sawed into plank an inch and one-fourth thick, as long as the width of the widest room; and let them be sawed up into lath before they are seasoned, as they will not saw so hard. Such work should be performed when the business of the farm does not demand attention.

39. *Mortar.*—No one can reasonably expect to have good walls unless they are made of the best of mortar; and good mortar

cannot be obtained, however good the materials may be of which it is made, unless it is most thoroughly worked over and over again for a number of successive months, before it is laid on the lath. It is a very laborious job to work over the mortar for a large house, when it is performed by hand labor. When lime and sand are mingled together, and in a few days laid on the lath, the plaster will shrink and the wall will be covered with cracks, and the plaster will soon crumble off. But if about two bushels of clean, sharp sand is mixed with one bushel of unslacked lime, and the mass is worked over once in two or three weeks for a few months, a wall that is made of it will appear like slate ; and will not crack unless the building or some parts of it change their position, as is frequently the case by seasoning. In order to have good mortar, that may be spread like good butter, it must be mixed and worked over often enough to have the lime slack most thoroughly, and "*to work the shrinkage out.*" If mortar should be worked over once in ten days for a year, it would be all the better for it, and would make a better wall.

40. To facilitate the labor of mixing mortar so frequently as is desirable, when my house was erected I constructed a rude

FIG. 6.

MACHINE FOR MIXING MORTAR.

machine for mixing it with horses, which subserved an excellent purpose, and which is represented by Fig. 6. It is a very cheap concern, and will pay for itself in one day. It consists of a post, *a*, about six inches in diameter, very firmly set in the ground, not less than three feet deep, and about two feet high. Put an iron band on the top to keep it from splitting. An iron bar, *b*, (a small crowbar will answer,) passes loosely through the sweep, *c*, into the centre post, *a*. Next, lay a floor—water level—on the ground, and nail the side boards, which should be sixteen or twenty inches wide, to stakes driven into the ground. The side boards should be placed in· an octagonal form, as shown in the figure, although if the sides were circular it would be preferable. The floor should be about fourteen or sixteen feet in the clear. The sweep, *c*, should be six inches square in the middle, twenty feet long, and the ends may be made smaller or not. The paddles, or legs, should be made of hard wood, two by four inches square, firmly inserted in the sweep, *c*, with a two inch tenon, about six inches apart, and so disposed that those on one side will not traverse in the tracks of those on the opposite side, but between them. The form of the legs is shown at E. They are made similar to the wings of a wind wheel, with the two corners, which are in a diagonal direction from each other, dressed off smoothly, so that each knife-like leg will work the mortar towards the centre. They should be not less than three-fourths of an inch thick after they are dressed out. If they are too thin they will break in mixing stiff mortar.

41. Let the lime and sand be put in, and hitch a horse at each end of the sweep, and commence mixing as the water is poured in, until it is so soft that it will flow slowly, and the surface become level. Shovel the mortar from the corners into the middle every time it is worked out. When a large quantity of mortar is necessary, two or more places may be made, and the same sweep used for all of them. When the sun shines, the mortar should be covered with boards. Keep the surface of the mortar covered with water, when not working it; and if there should be too much water when it is to be worked over again, let it be dipped off. It should be worked over at least once in ten days, and should never be allowed "to set" or become so hard that it cannot be readily worked over with a trowel. It is better to have a horse at each end, because the strain will not be

as hard on the post in the centre, as it would be if the power is all applied at one end. Let the mortar be first mixed in the spring, and keep it well worked all summer; and if there is as much lime in it as there should be, it will spread like butter, and make walls as smooth and hard as stone. These directions were followed, to the letter, in mixing the mortar for my present dwelling-house; and some of it was worked over, once in ten or twelve days, for more than six months before it was used; and my masons affirmed that they had never before handled mortar that spread so neatly, and made such firm walls.

42. The hair should never be put in until a few days before the mortar is to be used, because the lime will destroy it. In separating the bunches of hair, some prefer to put it in a large tub, and allow it to soak for a few days, and then have it well stirred until there are no bunches; and some prefer laying it on a floor and whip it to pieces with an elastic whip.

MOVING BUILDINGS.

43. Buildings are very frequently located very inconveniently, both in regard to each other and to the fields of the farm, and removing them to a more desirable location, and arranging them more conveniently, appears, to most men, almost as impracticable as removing a mountain. I have known instances in which the task of removing a certain building, or cluster of buildings, seemed to the proprietor such a vast and expensive undertaking, that he has been almost ready to offer four times as much to have the job well performed, as the actual cost would be. When out-buildings are scattered here and there, if they are not erected on a substantial wall, the arrangement would suit the fancy of most men to have them conveniently arranged in a cluster, on sub-stantial foundations.

44. The machinery for moving buildings has become so well perfected at the present day, that it costs comparatively but a few dollars to load a large building, and haul it fifty or a hundred rods, up hill or down, without injuring it in the least. If the sills are sound, a building can be loaded in a few hours; and if the

ground is firm and smooth, it can be hauled along with all desirable rapidity. When a building is so long that it would sag down in the middle when loaded, it can be cut in two, and the parts moved separately and placed together on the foundation. Many times when a building was not erected in one part, but in two or three united together, by putting timbers under the sills, and by balancing it correctly when loading it on the trucks, it may be removed with ease and safety.

45. Proprietors of moving machines usually ask from four to six dollars per day for the machine, and one hand to work it. But they often work by the job; and if the owner of a moving-machine is a faithful laborer, and a man of honest principles, it will always be the cheapest to employ him by the day. When a man has buildings to move, and he is not at all posted with regard to the time and expense of moving a certain building, un-principled fellows will often ask four times as much as would be a fair and honest price for a given job.

46. I once built a good machine for moving buildings, and worked it a few years very successfully; and with four good hands and one horse, could load a large barn and move it eight or ten rods *in one day*. But small buildings can be moved with much greater facility. When a man has buildings of any kind to move, he should do it when the ground is dry and hard, as it costs nearly twice as much to move them when the ground is soft. If there is any manure around a building, it should all be removed; and the ground over which the building is to be moved, should be levelled. One or two day's work in preparing the way and clearing up the rubbish, will often save a man ten dollars in moving one building. I have known some farmers to move their barns when all the manure which they had made in two years remained about them, which always proved a great obstruction in moving the buildings, and cost three times more than it would have cost had the manure been first removed.

47. The art of moving buildings of all kinds has been so per-fected, that in most of our large cities there are those who possess sufficient skill and machinery to move with safety, not only the

heaviest wooden buildings, but those that are built of brick, and which are computed to weigh *three hundred tons.*

MANNER OF FRAMING THE MIDDLE BENTS OF A LARGE BARN.

FIG. 7.

48. The importance of having large buildings framed in such a manner that the sides will not be thrust laterally by the rafters, has already been alluded to in par. 17. Fig. 7 represents a style of framing the middle bents, which is very convenient and efficient; and I have never seen it laid down in any treatise on architecture. As purline beams are many times very much in the way,

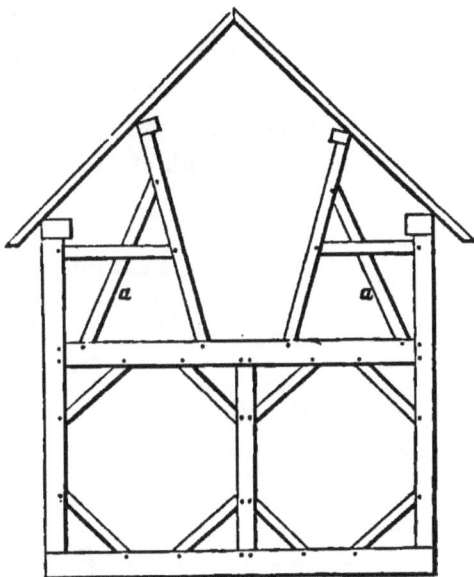

MANNER OF FRAMING THE MIDDLE BENTS OF A LARGE BARN.

they may be dispensed with entirely. The girts which connect the tops of the middle post to the purline posts, should be of strong timber; and the tenons should extend through each post; and one edge of the tenons be fitted to a dove-tail mortise, and keyed tight instead of being pinned. The braces *a a*, at the foot of the purline posts, should be nearly as large as the purline posts; and should face on the opposite sides from the girts. Should the purline posts be not less than twelve feet long, a beam might be framed in; and there would be sufficient room to pitch with a horse pitch-fork, both under and over the purline beam. If the doors are so arranged that teams are driven length ways of the barn or across it, the framing will be nearly the same in both cases. Very large buildings may be framed in this manner; and if the work is well performed the sides will not spread one-fourth of an inch. When a barn is framed in this manner *with purline beams,* the boss must remember not to pin one of the outside posts when raising the building, until *after* the purline posts have been put up ; because the girts which connect the purline posts with the main posts, cannot be put in after both of the main posts have been pinned ; unless one end of one of the girts is framed *without a shoulder,* so that it may be run through one post and then brought back to its place and pinned. If the barn is very wide there should be two middle posts instead of one, placed far enough apart for the width of the floor.

MANNER OF FRAMING A CORN-HOUSE.

FIG. 8.

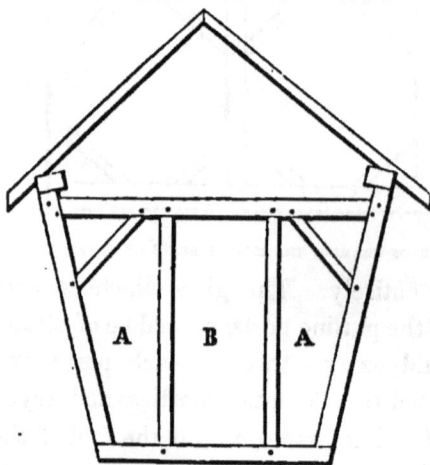

MOST IMPROVED MANNER OF FRAMING AN INDIAN CORN-HOUSE.

49. Fig. 8 represents a very good style of framing the bents of a corn-house. The figure represents one of the bents. *A A* are the spaces for cribs; and should not be more than three feet wide at the bottom, and as high as may be desired. · The bents should be placed about three feet apart, with girts between them not more than three feet apart, to which the slats are to be nailed. The space *B* is for the door or threshing floor, which should be tight for holding shelled corn. This space should be not less than seven feet wide with doors at each end of the building, so that a wagon loaded with corn ears can be driven through it. The upper floor should be made of slats or narrow boards, laid half an inch apart, for holding the poor corn. If the corn is not sorted in the field, it can

all be shovelled on the second floor; and the best corn thrown into the cribs from above. The most convenient way to get the corn out of the cribs is, to have a little door *at the bottom* of the cribs, on the inside, when the ears will come out as fast as they are shovelled away; and not more than two or three bushels will come out at one time. In dry weather, let the doors be kept open for the purpose of drying the corn. The frame may stand on a smoothly-built stone wall, or on stone pillars, or on pillars built of brick, or on wooden posts, covered with tin or zinc, to prevent the rats and mice climbing up the posts. Rats will jump sometimes three feet high; and if there is nothing but stone, or zinc, or tin, for them to ascend upon, they will not be able to enter a building. When an abutment is made at either or both of the doors, it should be at least four feet from the building; and a plank bridge, hung on hinges on one side, and the other side kept turned up against the building by a weight attached to one end of a rope, which passes over a pulley, and the other end attached to the bridge. The lower end of a flight of stairs may be kept up in the same manner.

BALLOON FRAMES.

50. In localities where hewn timber is scarce, every expedient must be resorted to in erecting buildings, in order to save un-necessary expense. Necessity and economy are the ostensible authors of the well-tested principle (which is no longer looked upon as an experiment which will most certainly fail) which has been for a score or more of years, successfully applied in erecting buildings of every description, which have received the sarcastic and technical appellation of " *balloon frames.*" They are erected without a stick of frame timber, or posts, or beams; without mortises, or tenons, or braces; and if erected in a workmanlike manner, the most incredulous need not hesitate to adopt this mode of building a most elegant house; for they will stand as firmly in a violent tornado as any framed building; and could be

moved from one place to another, or turned up on one side, without any more danger of injuring them than there would be if they were framed. I am aware that those—even good mechanics—who have always been accustomed to nothing but heavy frame timber, will scout at such a building, and, without any hesitancy, prognosticate that it would go to the winds before it could be half finished. But any good engineer who is at all acquainted *with the strength of materials*—if he has never before heard of such a mode of building, will unhesitatingly pronounce it a most complete triumph over the costly manner of building with heavy frame-timber; and that such buildings may be safely "*taken up by the hair*," and tumbled about like a huge box.

51. Such buildings require just as much siding, and lath, and roofing materials, and joists, and it will cost just as much to inclose them, and finish them off; but any mechanic who can make a window frame and hang a door, and nail two pieces of timber together at right angles, can erect such a building without the assistance of a *boss*.

52. The lumber for a balloon frame may be sawed of any desired dimensions; but for an ordinary building, the studs should never be less than four inches wide; and the joists should be not less than eight inches wide if sixteen feet long; and for twelve-feet joists seven inches wide is sufficient; and for rooms eight feet wide joists six inches wide will be sufficiently wide. The foundation must be as permanent and substantial as for a brick building. Now, lay a joist on the foundation walls on every side for the sills, and halve the corners together, and nail them well. Joists two inches by eight will be sufficiently large, although there can be no objection to using sills of timber or larger joists. Now, if the rooms are to be nine feet between joints, and the upper and lower joists eight inches wide, and the building is to be two stories or more high, make a pattern for the studs of a half-inch board, just ten feet and four inches long, with a gain cut in it, just at the under side of the upper joists, an inch deep and four inches wide. If the building is to be covered with vertical siding, gains must be cut in the outside of

the studs an inch deep and four inches wide. Fig. 9 represents
a stud pattern with two gains in the outside and FIG. 9.
one in the inside of it. Now, mark off all the
studs like the pattern, marking the ends with a
right angle or square mark. Now, with a horse-
saw saw off the ends square, and saw the gains,
and split out the blocks, and saw the joists of a
given length. Now, take two¯studs and two
joists—one joist for the lower floor and one for
the upper floor—and ·nail the studs and joists
together at right angles. Now, raise it as a bent
of a framed building is raised. Plumb it and
" *stale-aft* " it, so that it will keep in a perpendicular position. One man and a boy is all that is
needed. Now, nail two more joists and two
studs together, and set them up about one foot
apart in the clear. See that the studs stand
plumb both ways, before they are nailed ; and be
careful to have the edges of the joists exactly
even with the ends of the studs, and the upper
end of the *inside* gains even with the under edge
of the joists over head. After the studs and

A STUD PATTERN FOR
BALLOON HOUSES.

joists have been set up, fit ribs in the gains on the outside for the
purpose of nailing the siding to, and on the inside for sustaining
the joists of the upper floor. The ends of the lower joists will
rest on the top of the foundation sticks, into which nails should
be driven diagonally through the corners of both studs and
joists. If a building is to be but one story and a half high, the
studs may extend to the roof, and the joists be nailed to the sides
of them, as before. Now, nail a joist on the top ends of the
studs for a plate, and put up the rafters, being careful to have
the rafters rest directly over the studs. If a two-story house is
to be erected, erect one story as already recommended, having
the upper ends of the studs even with the top of the joists.
Nail a piece as wide as the studs on the tops of them, and erect
another story, nailing the lower ends of the studs into the strips

on which they stand.   On each side of the doors and windows studs four inches wide should be used.   If a building is erected with an attic story, *collar joists* should be nailed to the rafters near the lower ends, to keep the building from spreading.   If the studs should not extend more than one or two feet above the attic floor, collars on the rafters will not be necessary.   The rafters should be notched on the plate, and should extend beyond the side of the building; and the lower ends may be planed and painted; and the under side of the roof-boards planed and painted; or the rafters may be ceiled on the under side of them; or finished with a plain projection or cornice, as shown by Fig. 10, which

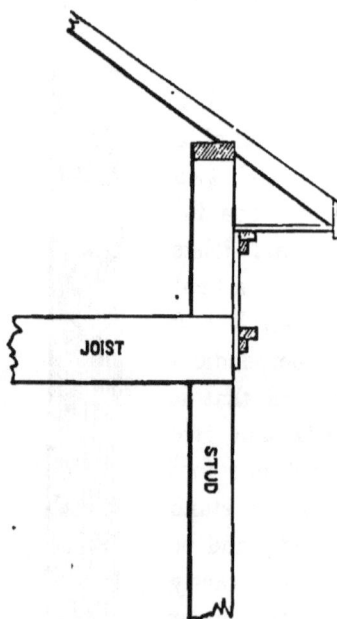

FIG. 10.

JOIST

STUD

A CHEAP CORNICE FOR A BALLOON HOUSE.

will require less than half the amount of lumber and labor; and in the eyes of many people, present a more desirable appearance as a cheap cornice.

53. Some builders line or ceil such buildings on the inside with rough, second or third quality of lumber; and then lath and plaster, which gives a building additional strength, but it is by no means necessary.   Where vertical siding is used, some ceil or line the outside of the studs.   Some place the studs just twelve inches apart, and fill between them with brick laid in lime and mortar.   But when good clay can be obtained, it will subserve about as good purpose as lime mortar.   Some tenon the ends of the studs, and mortise the sills and plates; but it is useless, as they will never move if well nailed.   If the timber is hard wood, holes, just large enough for the nail to drive in tight, and not split either studs or joists, should be bored for the nails through

one stick only. Use nails just long enough to extend through the studs and joists, and drive in twice the number of small nails that would be necessary of large nails, which would protrude through two inches.

54. When a balloon frame is not built on a substantial wall, the superstructure should be erected on sills eight inches thick. No young farmer need hesitate to build after this style; for there are more than thirty thousand of such buildings in the Western countries; and they give most complete satisfaction. Almost any kind of timber may be used for studs and joists; and if a man is possessed of but a small amount of mechanical skill, he can get his frame timber all sawed in the winter, and dress out the siding, &c., when he cannot labor on the farm, and if he is a good economist, his house or building will not cost three times more than it ought to cost for the labor alone.

55. When such a house is erected by the job, the young farmer should not neglect to see that not less than five good nails are driven in at the junction of each joist and stud; and that every other part of the frame is well nailed.

HOW TO INCREASE THE HEIGHT OF ROOMS WHEN THEY ARE
TOO LOW.

56. It is frequently very desirable to make the rooms, both below and above, one foot or more higher between the joints than it was originally made. When the attic story is to be made higher, if the roof is a poor one, it would be the best and cheapest operation to take it to pieces and raise the sides to the desired height; and then erect the roof as when a new house is built. But when a roof is a good one, and it is desirable to raise it any number of feet, let collar pieces be spiked to the rafters to keep them from spreading, and then raise it bodily with screws, with or without the plates, to the desired height. If the rafters are spiked very tightly to the plates, it will be better to raise the plates with the roof, and then put another set of plates in the place of the first ones.

57. I once performed a job in less than one day, by the as-

3

sistance of two men, of increasing the height of all the lower rooms of a two-story house. The lower rooms were eight and a half feet between joints, and it was desirable to make them ten feet high. Four screws were paced under the side sills of the house, two of them a few feet from one end, and two others about the middle of the building. One end of the house was elevated about twenty inches, when it was sustained on shores, placed under the beams, and girts. The sills and floor were then lowered with the screws to their original position, when the ends of the post and studs at one end of the building were all scarfed, or "spliced," and the sills were then raised again with the screws, and the shores were taken out, and the building was then lowered on the foundation. Then the two end screws were paced near the other end, and that end was elevated and sustained on shores, and the floor lowered, and the remainder of the posts and studs were scarfed, and the shores were then removed, and the house lowered to its original position.

58. Barns and outbuildings which are too low, may be raised, in a short period of time, ten or more feet higher; and the posts scarfed at an expense of a few dollars. If the spaces below the main beams of a barn are about right, let the roof only be raised; but if the arrangement of the timbers is about as one desires, above, and not below the beams, raise the superstructure and scarf the posts, or put a part of a new frame beneath the old one. (See PAINTING BUILDINGS in the next vol.)

CHAPTER II.

FENCING.

"Swift from the rural shades, O Muses, bring
Your wonted aid, while of the Fence we sing !
And let the fence our fathers built of rails,
With stakes and posts and boards, or logs or pales,
Close up the long-neglected gaps."—INGERSOLL.

59. IF there is any one thing more than another which is a source of constant anxiety and unremitting care to the farmer, it is the erection of suitable fences for enclosing his own grounds for the purpose of excluding lawless intruders, or keeping his own animals within proper bounds. Wherever a farm may be located, or whatever may be its productions, *fence, fence, fence,* is the first, the intermediate, and the last consideration in the whole routine of the operations of the farm. Erecting new fences and repairing old ones, and laying up a rail here, and fastening a loose board there, is something that demands the vigilance of the farmer, from the commencement to the close of the year. If there is a day, or a number of days, when the laborers of the farm have arrived at a point when they do not seem to know what to do to advantage and profit, they can almost always find something connected with the enclosures of the farm, the performance of which will be a work of some profit and economy, and sometimes of very great convenience. In the winter and spring, in summer and in autumn, on stormy days and leisure days, and parts of days, if all the plans of the farm are wisely laid, something may be done at fences or gates, or bar-posts or bars. But few farmers have any proper idea of the expense attending the fencing of a

(57)

farm of one or two hundred acres, when performed in an efficient and workmanlike manner; and could they see at a glance, in dollars and cents, the amount expended in their fences, they would be disappointed beyond measure. As a general rule, so changeable and perishable are the materials of which fences are built, that the expense of keeping them in good repair, from year to year, consumes a much greater amount of the income of the farm than we feel willing to appropriate for that purpose. But fences must be erected åt all events, and any thing that will reflect light on the subject of fencing the farms of America, in the most systematic and permanent manner, will be welcomed by every one who is experimentally acquainted with the enormous expenses which attend enclosing the fields of a farm, before it would be prudent to commence the cultivation of the soil.

60. Fencing is a branch of labor, in the operation of the farm, which requires the exercise of a good deal of wisdom and judg-ment in selecting, preparing, arranging, and disposing of the materials which are to be made use of in building fences in the most economical, workmanlike, substantial and durable manner; and as economy, durability and substantialness are the most im-portant considerations, as a general rule, in building a fence of any kind, and as there is a variety of materials to be worked up into fences, the preparation of materials demands our first atten-tion. It cannot be denied that there is a vast destitution of eco-nomy, not only in preparing the materials for fencing, but in working up those materials. The very best of materials, when improperly prepared, fail to make an economical and substantial fence; and, also, the best of fencing materials, when unskillfully arranged and worked up, make a fence far inferior, in almost every respect, to a fence made of materials of a very inferior quality, which has been well made. As economy in preparing timber for fencing is an object of the first importance, when the materials are of wood, we shall speak of the best and most suita-ble time for cutting timber, in order to secure its greatest dura-bility, when it is to be split into rails, as well as when it is to be split into posts and stakes.

THE BEST TIME TO CUT TIMBER.

WHEN autumn comes, and leaves are dry,
  And rustle on the ground,
And chilling winds go whistling by,
  With moaning, pensive sound,
Cut timber then for posts, and beams, and rails,
For tongues, and thills, for whippletrees and stales."

61. Late autumn is the best time for felling timber for almost any purpose; and it is particularly so when timber is to be worked up into rails, or stakes, or posts for fencing. At that season of the year, the new wood has arrived at its most complete maturity, and there is less sap and albumen in timber then than there is at any other season of the year, which albumen, when exposed to the influence of the weather, hastens the decay of timber. If timber be cut and split out in the latter part of autumn the seasoning process is much more gradual and perfect, because the grain of the timber contracts more equally and uniformly, rendering the timber firmer and less porous, and less cracked and checked than when it is cut at many other seasons of the year. Besides this, timber that is cut in late autumn and split out or sawed out before spring, will not "powder post," nor be injured by the worms working in it, nor be injured by the dry rot, as is the case with timber many times, which has been cut at some other season of the year. Fence posts and stakes particularly, no matter what the kind of timber may be, when felled and split out in late autumn, will outlast other posts and stakes of the same kind of timber which may be cut at a different season of the year, by several years, according to the time when it may be cut. Reason teaches us that this is so, and the experience of the most successful experiments in timber furnish the most indubitable testimony to substantiate this fact.

62. The treatment which timber receives immediately after it has been felled, effects its durability, and also its firmness and tenacity, to a much greater degree than many are wont to suppose. For this reason many farmers in experimenting on the durability of timber, have failed, almost entirely, to allow this consideration

to have any influence at all. If timber which is intended for rails, stakes and posts be felled in late autumn, and allowed to remain in the log for six or eight months, or half that length of time, with some kinds of timber, its durability will be more or less affected, according to the kind of timber; and no after-treatment will make it as durable as it would have been, had it been split out immediately and placed in a favorable situation for seasoning. Timber for posts or stakes ought always to be split out and seasoned nearly or quite one year before they are set in the ground. A post or stake which is set in the ground when it is green, will not last half as many years, as a general rule, as it would have lasted if it had been seasoned well before it is set in the ground. The first thing, after timber has been felled, is to split it out into rails, posts and stakes; therefore, as a very important branch of fencing, we shall treat of

SPLITTING RAILS, STAKES AND POSTS.

63. It requires the exercise of a little good skill to split timber *economically* into rails, stakes or posts. Any one who can handle a beetle and wedge, can split fire-wood, for it matters little how that is split; but if a man *does not know how to split timber straight*, he will be very liable, and, indeed, very *likely* to spoil a vast deal of timber when splitting up a tree. The truth is, if he does not know *how* to stick the wedges, and *where* to stick them, he will be very apt to make bad work, even in the best of timber, for splitting well. When we split fire-wood, we cleave it the best way that we can, and if it slivers to pieces, so much the better. But there is a regular rule for splitting rails, stakes, posts, wagon spokes, staves, and every thing else, and if one does not observe this rule, he will, most assuredly, spoil much timber. If in splitting any thing for fences, some pieces have huge ends at one end, and are run out to a mere splinter at the other end; or if they are not all of about a uniform size, if the operator does not understand his business, and if he makes many short pieces, it would be the wisest policy to employ some one else who will not waste so much timber.

64. In splitting timber for anything, it is best to set the wedges always at the smallest or top end of a log, should there be any difference in the ends. If there are no large checks across the end of a log, take the axe in one hand, and the beetle in the other, and make a crack entirely across the end of the log, so as to split it into two equal parts. If there is a large crack a part of the way across the end, drive in the axe a little with the beetle, so as to make a crack entirely across the end. Generally speaking, timber splits the best and wastes the least, by setting the wedges in an old crack or seam. But sometimes a log will separate much the easiest directly across the old check. Now, set two iron wedges in the end of the log, and drive them both together, and when the end is opened sufficiently, drive in gluts; if the wedges have been set in the middle of the end, the log will separate usually in the middle. Should it vary a little from following the middle of the log, it is better to let it go where it will than to undertake to open it at the other end, so as to meet the operation, which is attended with doubt and difficulty. Sometimes it is almost impossible to split a log through the heart. This is the case many times with black ash, and elm, and buttonwood. Logs many times have a seam entirely around the heart. When this is the case, it will require a vast deal of unnecessary pounding to split it through the heart. Such logs can be worked up far more easily and economically by slabbing them, following the old seams; and many times when a log has a very tough heart, even if there be no checks nor seams, it is best to split them by *slabbing off* about one-third of the log at once; this will leave, in a log thirty inches in diameter, a heart piece about ten inches square. If, now, the timber be very tough and stringy, this may be worked up by slabbing it. In splitting ordinary timber, the builder must keep in mind that a round stick or a square stick cannot, very well, be split into three equal parts; because, if we attempt to split off one-third of it at a time, the smaller part is very apt to run out before the split reaches the other end. Therefore, if a square stick be about large enough for three rails, it is best to split it through the centre, and then split the two halves of it in

the centre again, even if the rails should be a little too small, than to undertake to split it into three equal parts; or if such a stick, when split into four rails, would make them too small, it would be best to make but two of it, even if they were a little larger than we could desire. We cannot always have every rail, stake or post exactly of the size we may wish, but the aim should always be, in splitting rails, to have the smallest rails equal to a stick two and a half inches square, and increasing in size, so that the largest rails will be equal to a stick four inches square. This is a very good rule to split by, but if thought to be exceptionable, it is very easy to split in two those rails which A says are of the right size, and which B thinks are too large for one rail, and just right for two. A rail about three inches square, or equivalent to that size, will be pronounced by the great majority of farmers to be a more desirable size, so far as economy and convenience are concerned, than a rail of any other size. When a man has a saw-mill of his own, and timber does not split very well, it might be good policy to saw out his rails, making them about three inches square ;—but the same timber would build twice as much fence if it were sawed into boards.

65. Sometimes rails are split out of poles, which will make from two to eight rails each; and it often occurs that a pole would make about three good rails, and if split into four they would be too small, and if split into two rails they would be rather large. As it is very difficult, and usually impracticable, to split a pole into three, or five, or seven equal parts, on account of their liability to run out in splitting, if a pole be too small for four rails, it is best to make but two of it, even if they should be rather large. When a pole is about the right size for six rails, the best way is to split the pole into quarters, as nearly as we can, and many times one of the quarters will be large enough for two rails. The idea should be always kept in mind, that the rule which is observed in riving staves, wagon-spokes, and such like, is, *to split a stick through the middle*, and then take a smaller piece and split that through the middle, and so on until every piece or bolt is reduced to its desirable size. When a log or rail cut will make about

eight good rails, the true way is to quarter it first, and then split those quarters in two. If we attempt to split off of one side one rail, in most timber it would be sure to run out before it would split half the length of the log. The following cuts will furnish the learner with a more correct idea how a large log is to be split into rails, stakes, or posts. In the first place, split the log into quarters, if practicable, whether it is to be split into rails, stakes, or posts. Fig. 11 represents one of those quarters split into rails. After a log has been split into quarters, split the quarter in two again, as nearly in the middle as may be. If the workman cannot stick his wedge within half an inch of the centre of a quarter of a log at sight, he had better measure the distance. Now split these pieces, first in the direction a a a, then split off the heart rail b b, then split c c, and we have three rails. Split the other heart piece, like the first, into three rails; split the sap pieces at d, and split each piece at e e. Sometimes it is better to set the wedge in the middle of a stick, half-way from each end, then to set it at the end, when splitting a piece that will make two rails, as at c c, for example. When a wedge is set half-way from each end, in the middle of the stick, if the crack does not run in the middle, each way from the wedge, sometimes a blow or two with an axe will start it, so as to make it split in the middle ; and sometimes it is necessary to set another wedge half-way between the middle and the end. A little practice will enable the builder, if he has a little good skill, to split timber very accurately, without spoiling but few pieces. The same rules are observed in splitting stakes as in splitting rails; only it is necessary, first, in splitting a quarter, to make a little estimate how many pieces a quarter or an eighth of a log will make. In splitting fence posts it frequently occurs that a piece is too large for one post, and too small for two posts. In such a case, if a stake cannot be split off without its running out, it is best not to attempt to split it again, lest both pieces be spoiled.

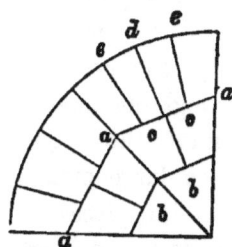

FIG. 11.

QUARTER OF LOG SPLIT INTO RAILS.

3*

66. In splitting bar-posts, or any pieces that are required to be thin and wide, first split the log in two, and if it is a large one quarter it. Make calculations how many posts a quarter will make, splitting from the heart to the bark. If a quarter will make four, split it in the centre, and these pieces again in the centre. If they are wider than necessary, take off a stake from the heart side, as at Fig. 12. If half a log will make about six posts, it is not best to quarter it first, because each piece then would contain timber enough for three posts each, and there would be danger of spoiling a post in attempting to split only one post from a stick which is large enough for three; therefore, divide the half log into three equal parts, and first split off a piece large enough for two posts, and then split the pieces in two in the middle. The

FIG. 12.

MANNER OF SPLITTING BAR-POSTS.

workman would do well, after opening the end a little, to set a wedge or two in the side of the stick, to prevent its running out, and drive all the wedges at once, or drive that wedge the most which seems to split the truest and straightest. When timber is not inclined to split exactly straight, by tracing it with the axe and beetle the whole length of the stick it can be made to split tolerably straight. In splitting a log eight or ten inches in diameter into bar-posts, or any other wide posts, make an estimate how many a log will make; if it will make four, split it through the centre, and then, by tracing or starting it a little with

FIG. 13.

MANNER OF SPLITTING A LOG INTO FOUR POSTS.

the axe and beetle on the side, the two halves may be split in two again the wide way, as represented by Fig. 13. Fig. 14

shows how a log may be split into three bar-posts by tracing on the sides as the wedges are driven in the end. We first take off a slab, and if the timber does not split rather freely it is very lia-

FIG. 14.

MANNER OF SPLITTING A LOG INTO THREE BAR-POSTS.

ble to run out and spoil a post. It is very impracticable to give a perfect idea on paper of splitting timber correctly.

THE LENGTH OF RAILS AND STAKES.

67. The most common length for rails is twelve feet, although many farmers make them ten, eleven, and even fourteen feet in length; but when we consult convenience and economy in splitting and handling, as a general rule twelve feet for rails is tho best length. If timber should split very freely, there is no objection to cutting them fourteen feet long; on the contrary, if timber should not split well it might be a matter of good economy to cut them ten or eleven feet long; but there ought to be a uniform length for rails on every farm, because when rails are of different lengths there will be more or less disadvantage in making them into a fence. Large logs should be sawed in two, just twelve feet long, and smaller logs may be cut with an axe; and as every rail cut should be measured with a pole just twelve feet long, each cut should be measured from the middle of the chip, or axe-cut, and the top end of each cut should be left square; this will make the heart rails a little longer than the outside rails. But in laying the foundation for a fence, if there should be a little variation in the length of rails, it should be remembered to select first the sap rails, and if the heart rails project a little more than is necessary at the joints, it will do no harm,

68. *The length of stakes* should always be regulated by the

height of the fence. They are usually cut from seven to nine feet in length; but whatever length may be adopted, it should be kept in mind that stakes should be cut long enough to admit of being set the second time, after the end which has been set in the ground has rotted off. The part of stakes out of the ground will usually last twice as long as the part in the ground, no matter what the timber may be. Therefore, if stakes be cut just long enough to be set but once, after one end is decayed, so that they need re-setting, they are worthless; but by cutting them long enough to be set again after a foot or so has rotted, it is much more economical than to make new stakes as often as the ends rot or decay enough to render them too short for the fence.

69. Some farmers deem it a matter of economy to cut their fence posts, and particularly bar-posts, long enough to admit of the other end being set in the ground after one end has decayed. But there are very plausible objections to this practice. Fence posts which extend from two to three feet above the fence present an unsightly appearance, and, besides, the longer the post is the more liable it is to deviate from standing erect. Bar-posts which extend three feet higher than they ought to are a nuisance, because they are always in the way, especially when one is passing with a load of hay or grain.

PEELING RAILS AND STAKES.

70. This should always be done when they are split out, so that they may season the better. It requires but a little time to peel them when splitting them, and as rails and stakes are often split by the job, at so much per hundred, a man will usually split them, peel them, and stick them up, for a few cents more per hundred than he will ask for simply splitting them, providing one insists on it when negotiating about splitting. When timber is cut in the fall, it is true, it does not peel as well as when cut in the summer, but as a general rule it will peel tolerably well after it is split out, even when cut in autumn. When the bark is thick and heavy it will peel about as well from small pieces, like rails and stakes, as it will when the timber is cut in the summer. But

the bark should be taken off at some rate; and when it adheres so tightly that it is necessary to *cut* it off, it may be cut off at each end about a foot or so and laid in the fence, with the bark *downwards*, and during the summer it will usually become so loose as to drop off itself; but if it is not held in the joints of the fence, it may be stripped off very readily after one end is loosened a little, and if the rail be laid with the bark down it will become loose by the drying of the rail. When rails are made of timber having a very thin bark, like iron-wood, for example, the most expeditious way of peeling them is to lay the rail to be peeled on a couple of benches, and then with a drawing-knife shave off the bark while the workman is sitting on it. When small poles are used for rails, if they are not peeled entirely a strip of bark should be taken off on two sides opposite to each other, and one of the peeled sides laid upward in the fence; by this means the bark will become loose during the season, and many times drop off itself. Rails, stakes, posts, and timber of every other description, will be very much more durable if peeled, unless it is buried in the ground. When a stick is two feet or more under ground, it will last much longer if the bark be left on; but if the bark be left on a fence post, the part of it two feet below the surface will be more durable with the bark on than if it were off. But that same post will rot off at the surface of the ground many years sooner if the bark was left on than if it was peeled before it was set. Bark preserves timber when it is alive, but after it has been cut down it hastens its decay, when it is exposed to the influences of the weather, wet and dry. When the bark is not taken off, worms damage rails and posts of many kinds of timber. Allowing rails to soak in a pond of water for a few days will generally loosen the bark so that it may be peeled off very quickly.

DISTRIBUTING RAILS FOR FENCE.

71. It is a very common thing for many farmers, in hauling rails and stakes where a fence is to be made, to distribute them, as to number, entirely at random, without any calculation at all how many will be needed for a fence of a given number of rails

high, and therefore in some places twice as many rails are un-
loaded as are necessary, while in other places there are not half
enough. Sometimes there may be just enough to build the fence,
but they have been distributed so unevenly that many of them
must be carried too far. When a man is obliged to go twenty
or thirty feet for every rail, it will take him twice as long to lay
up a fence as it would were the rails left within a few feet of the
place where they will be needed. It is a very easy matter to
distribute rails for a fence so that there will be just enough to
build it, and it argues a little stupidity and want of calculation to
see one distribute rails in such a manner that after the fence is
finished there are several loads to haul away. That is all lost
labor; and it will consume several hours to haul and unload, and
reload and haul away, two or three loads of rails.

72. In distributing rails for a fence, in the first place set a few
stakes where the fence is to be built. Now calculate how many
panels there will be in five or six rods. We will say there are
thirty paces in six rods. If the foundation is not laid, the rails
may be laid for thirty paces or so, in a straight line, or zigzag,
like a worm fence, and then, by counting the number of panels
in thirty paces, and by multiplying the number of panels by the
number of rails in one panel, we shall know how many rails are
wanted in a distance of thirty paces. Now, let the number of
rails required in thirty paces be distributed close to the place
where the fence is to be made, and put them in small piles, with
not more than ten in a pile, so that they will be near at hand,
and be well spread out, so that small rails can be selected, if necessary, without tumbling over half a load. Never leave them with
nearly a load in a pile, nor in the place where the fence is to be
built, lest they have to be removed; nor a rod or two distant,
for fear they may be in the way. Now pace off thirty paces
more—it can be done in less than one minute—and drop as many
more rails, and in the same order, and proceed in this manner
until a job is finished. When the foundation, or the first rail is
laid, it is a very easy matter to make calculations for hauling just
enough to make a fence.

73. Rails of one kind of timber should always be left to-gether, and rails of another kind of timber, unless they are equally durable, should be kept by themselves, because, when oak and basswood are laid together, the basswood will decay long before the oak, and the result will be, the entire fence must be repaired; whereas, if the oak had been kept together, and the basswood together, no part would need repairing but the basswood. For the same reason, new rails should always be kept together, when repairing fence; and take old ones to supply the place of those which have decayed. When one is hauling rails which are to be laid in a fence immediately, it is much quicker to take the rails from the wagon and lay them in the fence, than to throw them on the ground and then pick them up again and lay them in the fence.

74. When the stakes are to be hauled let them be placed near each joint of the fence, with one on each side of it; because it will save the time of picking them up. When the foundation is not laid, if we know how many panels there will be in a given distance, it is easy to calculate that two stakes will be required for each panel, whether the fence is to be zigzag or straight.

FENCE BLOCKS.

75. These are a very important item in building fence. It is very poor policy to place rails on the ground or on perishable materials which will soon let the fence down to the ground. Bowlders, from ten to twenty-five inches in diameter, make the best blocks. When one is a little too large, let a hole be dug a foot or so deep, and roll it in. When one is a little too small, put it on the top of a flat stone. A small pile of small bowlders, or little stones of any kind, will make a very good block for a corner to rest on. When wood is used for blocks, always place the bark side down, if possible, because they will last many years longer than if the bark side is up. When a round stick is used for a block, let it be peeled, if practicable; but, if not, cut off a strip of bark, three or four inches wide, on one side, and

lay that side up, and then, as it seasons, the bark will usually become loose, but if the bark be left on the *top* of blocks it will always hasten their decay. Sometimes a couple of good pieces of broken rails will make a very good fence block. Flat stones, a foot square, or more, laid on the top of a little mound of earth, or on the top of two or three sods, will make capital fence blocks. When one has a plenty of small stone, it is good policy to make a ridge of stone, a foot or so high, and lay the fence on the top of it. This will answer both for a straight fence and for a zigzag fence. Where no stone can be found, and wooden blocks are scarce, make a fence block with square sods, and lay on a piece of board, or slab, or two or three short pieces of old rails. *Let the fence be kept well up from the ground, at all events.* When a foundation corner is made of earth, or sods, the sides should be covered with sods, to prevent them from washing away in heavy showers.

MAKING A ZIGZAG, OR WORM FENCE.

76. In making a zigzag fence of rails, there are two modes of laying the bottom rail, by stakes, which I shall lay down, in order to have the fence straight. And when a fence is to remain for a number of years, or is to be a permanent fence, it ought always to be straight; but in making a temporary fence, if a man is mechanic enough to give the fence the necessary worm, he may lay the bottom rail by guess. But the beginner had better have some stakes to guide him; because, if he does not, he will be sure to give some parts of it much more worm or crook than is necessary, and give other parts so little worm that it will barely stand alone. When a fence has too much worm, or crook, it is a good fault; it will stand more firmly,—but it requires more rails. But when it has but little worm, it requires less rails; and the first driving storm may throw it from its foundation, and prostrate it.

77. The first step, then, will be, to set a number of small, thin stakes, six or seven feet high, in a line, where the middle of the

fence is to be made. Now make a fençe rule, Fig. 15, which consists

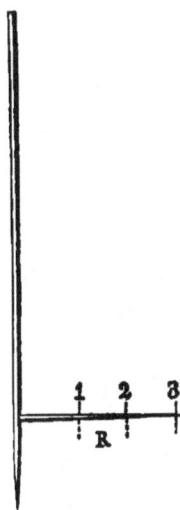

FIG. 15

of a stick, either round or square, about seven feet in length, as large as a fork handle, and pointed at the lower end. If the ground be stony and hard, the lower end ought to be fitted to an iron socket, pointed. Bore several half-inch holes through it, for the rod R, which should be made of a very tough piece of wood, about as large and elastic as a good whip-stalk. This rod should be about three feet long; and then it may be graduated, by making a mark for two feet, and for two feet three inches, six, and nine inches. This rod should be merely pressed into a hole, without fastening it, so that when laying a foundation on very high or low blocks, it may be raised or lowered, as may be necessary. Always work up hill, in laying any kind of rail fence;

A FENCE RULE.

because, when we begin at the bottom of a declivity and work upwards, the rails will lay more level than the inclination of the ground; and, if we work *down* a declivity, the rails will be *more inclined* than the ground, and will not stand as firmly as if it were made by working up hill. When a string of fence extends over rolling or undulating land, the proper mode of making it is, to lay the bottom rail the whole distance, and then go back and change those corners in that part of the fence which was laid by beginning at the top a declivity, so that in laying up more rails the operator can work up hill, both ways, from a valley. The next thing in order will be to decide upon

THE AMOUNT OF WORM, OR CROOK, FOR A FENCE.

78. The *length* of rails must usually determine the amount of worm for a fence. Long rails require much more worm, or crook, than short ones, in order to have the corners of each kind of rails of the same angle. Suppose, for example, that rails are nine feet long, and we wish to give the fence which is made of them three feet worm, *i. e.*, the fence will occupy, measuring across the fence,

three feet of ground, from the centre of one joint to the other. Now, if rails are fourteen feet in length, in order to give the corners the same angle of the nine feet rails, we must give these rails a crook of four feet eight inches, measuring from the centre of one joint to a point opposite it, in a line with the joints on the other side of the fence. Where fence is to be staked, the rule for the amount of worm which is most commonly adopted is, that it be equal to one-third the length of the rails. . This is enough for any fence that is well staked; and where a fence will not be exposed to furious winds, it may answer just as good a purpose to give it *less* than one-third the length of the rails. But where a fence is not to be staked, and the rails are rather light, the worm should be increased so as to be at least five-twelfths the length of the rails, and sometimes even more than this.

79. If the stakes are all stuck in a line, plant the fence rule (Fig. 15) in a line with the stakes, where we are to commence laying the foundation, having the rod R standing at a right angle to the right or left of the line which would cut the fence rule staff and the stakes. If the fence is to have a worm of four feet, which is about right for rails twelve feet in length, place a fence block under the rod R, so that the centre of the block will be just under the two feet mark, from the rule staff. Lay on a good straight rail, and carry the rule forward; and plant it down, in a line with the stakes, nearly opposite the other end of the rail, with the rod R extending in the opposite direction. Place a block beneath the two feet mark on the rod R, and lay on the end of the first rail, and then lay on another rail and carry the rule along, and lay another block in a line with the first block, and so on.

80. Many fence-makers, in laying up rails, have the ends of the rails extend beyond the points of conjunction at the corners about one foot. . But this practice uses up more rails than is necessary to build a fence a given number of rods in length; and, besides, when the ends of the rails extend beyond the joint from ten to twelve inches, a fence does not look as well, and is far more liable to be thrown down, by the whippletrees catching it, or cattle rub-

bing against it. If the ends of the rails extend three or four inches beyond the joint, a fence is no more liable to be thrown down than if the same rails extended a foot beyond the joint. It is very important that all the rails should lie, at the joints, one directly above the other. The smallest rails should always be laid at the bottom of the fence; and the largest ones, if there be any difference in the size of them, should be laid on the top, as heavy rails on the top render a fence, whether it is staked or not, much more substantial than if the large rails were in the middle of the panels, with small ones on the top. If there should be any difference in the size of the ends of the rails, the large end should be laid at the lowest corner. When there are many crooked rails, make a panel or two of crooked rails, placing those together that are of nearly a uniform crook. If there are but few crooked ones, reserve them for the top of the fence. After a fence is laid three or four rails high, if flat stones, three or four inches thick, are at hand, it is a good practice to lay one on each joint, as they will make the fence about one rail higher, and, at the same time, it will subserve just as good a purpose as if a rail was in the place of the stones. And another advantage is, flat stones laid on the joints will turn the water from the joints, and render them more durable, as rails often rot at the joints in consequence of the wet finding its way there and not drying out. A large flat block of wood will answer for this purpose, in the absence of flat stone. Roundish stones in such a place would be liable to throw the fence down. Low corners of a fence may be brought up level with the others by laying on a flat stone between every two rails.

81. Another mode of laying the foundation of a worm fence, which some people prefer to laying with a fence rule, is, to set two rows of small stakes the whole distance where the fence is to be built, with the rows just as many feet apart as there is to be given to the worm of the fence. If the worm is to be four feet, set the rows four feet apart; if the worm is five feet, set the rows of stakes five feet apart. Now lay a fence block in range with one of the rows of stakes, and lay on a rail diagonally from one row to the other; then lay another fence block in range with

the other row under the other end of the rail, and so on. In order to ascertain whether the block is in range with the stakes, stand in range with the stakes, and set a stick, about as large as a common fork-handle, *perpendicularly*, on the top of the block before you, and if when it stands in the middle of the block it is in range with the stakes, the block is in the proper place. By placing the trying stake, or stick, in range with the rows, the workman will readily perceive which way the block, or corner, must be moved, in order to bring the corner in range with the stakes.

82. There are other modes of laying the foundation by stakes, but they are so inferior to those already mentioned that we shall omit to notice them.

83. A common worm fence may be staked and capped, staked and ridered, staked and wired, locked and ridered, or it may merely be laid up without either stakes or riders or locks; but whichever mode is adopted, the operation of laying the foundation and of building the fence several rails high is the same in each kind of fence, with the exception that a staked fence does not require as much worm as one that is not staked.

LOCK AND RIDER FENCE.

84. Fig. 16 represents the manner of finishing a worm fence with locks and riders, which will resist the wind as well as some staked fences. The fence is first laid as many rails high as is desired; and then the largest rails are laid in a straight line, from panel to panel, as in the figure. The locks may be good stakes, or pieces of rails, placed in the nook of the fence formed by two panels, and inclined into the corner formed by the top rail and rider. The

FIG. 16.

LOCK AND RIDER FENCE.

dots in the figure show about where the foot of the locks should be placed. The locks are not usually set in a hole in the ground, although if they were the fence would be stronger. Sometimes the riders in this kind of fence may be long poles, extending the distance of several panels. Long poles are much better than rails for riders.

85. Another mode for locking a fence is shown by Fig. 17. The fence is first made as high as it is to be made, and then the locks, which may be of good rails, or stakes, or pieces of rails, are

FIG. 17.

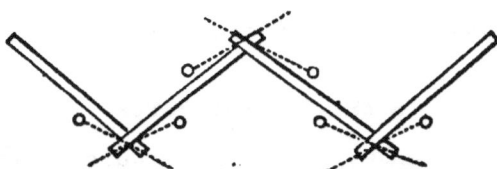

A LOCK RAIL FENCE.

stuck in the ground, as shown by the dots, or circles, and leaned on the corners, as shown by the dotted lines. In locking in this manner the builder must exercise a little skill, if he has any, in regard to setting the locks so as to *bind well*. If they are not placed on the correct side of each other, they will not lock the fence, by wedging, any more than their own gravity will lock it. It is not very convenient to show on paper which lock should be on the outside, and which on the inside. If the builder has any skill, he can alter the position of a pair of locks until they seem to wedge, or bind, more than they will in any other position, and then let the position of those locks be carefully observed, and let him endeavor to set the rest as nearly like them as is practicable. They should not be set too perpendicularly, nor too slanting, because if set too slanting they will not resist as great force as if they stand more perpendicularly ; and if they be set too perpen dicularly, the lock is not as binding ; and if the locks extend several feet above the fence, the wind is very liable to blow them over. If the locks be small stakes, or small rails, the foot of them must be placed almost close to the side of the panel which it locks; but if they be large, they must be placed farther away from the panel. Locking a fence is adopted more for a temporary fence than for one which is to remain for a number of years; and when stakes are at hand for locking, and a fence encloses a field of grain, it is more safe for the security of a crop to stake it, even if it were to remain but one season. A locked fence is always getting down; and when a fence stands in a very bleak situation, where the wind is liable to prostrate it, it is folly to attempt to keep it up without having it firmly staked. Locking a fence according to the first mode of locking may be adopted with safety, providing the last rails, which extend from panel to panel, are very heavy, and the locks well rammed into the ground.

STAKE AND CAP FENCE.

86. Fig. 18 represents two different modes of staking a zigzag fence. The black dots show the situation of the stakes. After the foundation has been laid the stakes may be driven, or the fence may be made four or five rails high before the stakes are stuck. In either case the holes should be made with a crowbar,

FIG. 18.

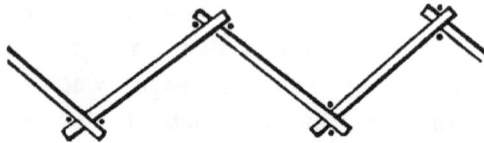

STAKE AND CAP FENCE.

at least twenty inches deep; and then, as one man stands on a bench, and drives them with a sledge-hammer, another man should keep them erect. In order to expedite setting the stakes, let the holes all be made first; and then let one hand get the stakes and place them in the holes, and hold them while another man lays his sledge hammer on his bench and carries them along, from joint to joint, and drives the stakes. Let the stakes all be sharpened for driving, and the top ends dressed off, so that the caps will go on readily before they are brought on to the ground. The most expeditious way to sharpen a lot of stakes is, to have a large flat block of wood for the stake to stand on, while it is held erect with one hand and sharpened with an axe in the other hand. Cut a little hollow in the top of the block so that the stakes, when being sharpened, will not slip off the block. The stakes must be sharpened true, or else they will not drive well. (See SHARPENING POSTS, paragraph 79.) When the fence is made four, five, or six rails high, as may suit the caprice of the builder, the caps are put on, and then one or two rails more are laid on the fence. If stone can be obtained of sufficient size, one may be put between each pair of stakes under each cap, and one above each cap, which stone will carry up the fence the height of two rails. Some farmers put on two caps to each pair of stakes, when the fence is to be unusually high, but when stakes are driven twenty inches, or more, in dry ground, and a cap put on three or four feet from the ground, two caps are not necessary. In lieu of caps many farmers use wire for holding the stakes together, which, by many, is considered preferable to caps. Good annealed wire is used—about 9 or 10 is the right size (see Fig. 30)—and after being put around a pair of stakes, and cut partly in two with a file and broken, the two ends are either hooked together or twisted together. If the wire be large and stiff it is best to hook the ends together, as they can readily be taken off the stakes when it becomes necessary to repair the fence. Wire is cheaper than caps when one must advance cash for making them, and by drawing it up tight around the stakes it will bury into them, and the weight of all the rails above the wires will rest on the stakes, thus tending to keep the stakes in the ground when the frost has lifted them upwards. A fence, with the stakes set at each joint, one on each side of the fence, will resist a greater force than when they are set in the acute angles *on each side* of the joint, as shown in the figure.

MAKING FENCE CAPS.

87. The cheapest and most expeditious way of making fence caps, when a saw-mill is near at hand, is, to have the logs sawed into stuff about two by seven inches, or one and a half inches by

seven, and then, with a circular saw, cut them off the length desired, and bore them.   But, when timber will split freely, more caps can be made of a log by riving them out than by sawing, when the log is about twice the diameter of the width of a cap. The logs are sawed off the length of caps and split into quarters with a beetle and wedges, and then with a cooper's froe, (Fig. 19,) an instrument used for riving timber, and with mallet, the the caps are split out, by setting the froe in the middle of the stick to be split. (See SPLITTING TIMBER, 63 and 64.) When caps are split out, one side of them will usually be thicker than the other.   The average thickness of the caps is a matter of fancy.   Some make them one inch, some two inches, some three or four inches thick.   The thicker

FIG. 19.

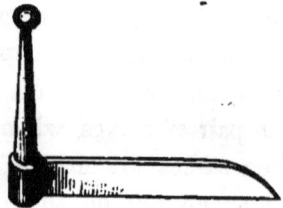

A COOPER'S FROE.

the caps are, the more they will aid in carrying up the fence to a given height.   If caps be made as thick as a rail, they carry up the fence as much as one tier of rails, and at the same time sub-serve the purpose of caps, and make a fence stronger than thin ones, which are liable to split very easily.   There is nothing lost in making caps four inches thick, for it requires much less timber to make such a cap than it does to make a rail; and a man can split out four times as many caps in a day as he can rails; and if they be thick as a rail, they will save one rail to a panel the entire length of the fence.

88. The length of caps must be determined by the size of the rails, the size of the holes in the caps, and the amount of worm in the fence.   These three considerations combined, will enable the builder to cut his caps of the correct length.   It is necessary first to ascertain, if we can, what is about the average size of the rails.   If they will average from three to four inches in diameter, the worm of the fence being from three and a half to four feet, the holes in the caps should be from five to six inches apart. Now, six inches between the holes, added to the size of the holes, which are usually about four inches in diameter, makes fourteen

inches, which, added to three inches at each end, between the holes and the ends, will make twenty inches, the length of the caps. Slabs which are cut from logs, at saw-mills, will make good caps, and, as they can usually be purchased at a low price, they will make very cheap caps.

BORING FENCE CAPS

89. Is often done by hand, in the winter season, when farmers have but little to do. Two hands can bore one hundred or more in an hour when they are not more than two inches thick.

90. There are various kinds of augers for this purpose. The kind which may be worked with the least power is a hollow auger, which cuts a circular ring through the cap, of the size of the hole, taking out a core from the centre of a hole. This kind of augers is not capable, generally, of boring caps which are more than about two to four inches thick. Their cost is from four to ten dollars, according to the work expended in fitting them up and making a bench for one. But when caps are to be bored by hand, an ingenious mechanic may get up an auger, bench and all, for about two dollars, which will perform well, and bore all the caps which will be required on one farm. When an auger is driven by horse power, or steam, or water, the mandrel which holds the auger must be of iron, having its bearings turned and polished; but when boring is done by hand, the mandrel may be turned out of a very tough and hard piece of wood, with a kind of large centre bit firmly fixed in the end of it for the auger, with a crank at the other end. An ingenious blacksmith will make for fifty cents a centre bit, with a square shank six or eight inches long, for fastening it in the wooden mandrel. The caps are placed on a slide, which is made to move towards the auger by a strap being attached to it, and passing over a pulley and fastened to a foot treadle. After the hole is bored, the slide and cap are pulled back with the hands. The whole of it is so simple as to hardly require a description. Sometimes the cap is fed towards the auger by a screw, working in a stationary part of the bench; but feeding with a strap and treadle is the quick-

4

est and most convenient way to bore caps. (See BORING MA-
CHINE, Fig. 122.)

BUNK AND CAP FENCE.

91. Figure 20 represents a bunk for fence, similar to stake
and cap fence, with the exception that the stakes are set in a
block about four feet in length, instead of in the ground. These

blocks may be as large as one man can
handle, or they may be small as a rail of
the largest size. The larger they are
the more substantial the fence will be.
The holes for the stakes should not be
less than three inches in diameter, and
should be bored entirely through the
pieces, in order to allow water to work
out at the bottom. When a stake is a
little too small, it may be made tight by
a wedge on one side of it. This kind of

FIG. 20.

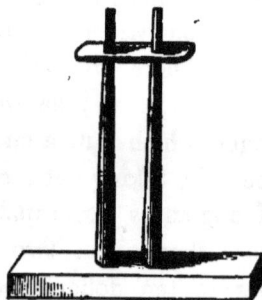

BUNK FOR RAIL FENCE.

fence may be straight or zigzag, and all the advantage it possesses over other stake fences is, it can be removed more easily.
It requires more timber and time to make it, and is not worthy
of adoption generally, excepting in localities where stakes cannot
be driven in the ground. When this kind of fence is made
straight, the ends of the rails in the bunks may lie side by side,
or one above the other. When they lay side by side, pieces of
rails must be sawed just long enough to lie between the stakes,
for the purpose of raising the next tier of rails several inches.
When this mode is adopted it will require as many short pieces
as there are rails to carry it up to the caps. This fence possesses
one good quality over a stake fence—it will not be lifted by the
frost, and is more easily kept erect.

STRAIGHT RAIL FENCE.

92. Figure 21 shows a section of a rail fence, built with the
rails in a straight line. The stakes are first set just far enough
asunder to receive a rail of medium size. Then turn two furrows

with a plow, towards the fence, on each side of it, and throw up the second furrow with a shovel, so as to form a ridge one foot or more in height, leaving it one foot broad on the top, so that the rain will not wash it down too much. Let grass seed be sown on this ridge. By throwing up a ridge the stakes stand more firm, and are less liable to heave by the frost, and cattle do not have so much advantage in endeavoring to get through it,

FIG. 21.

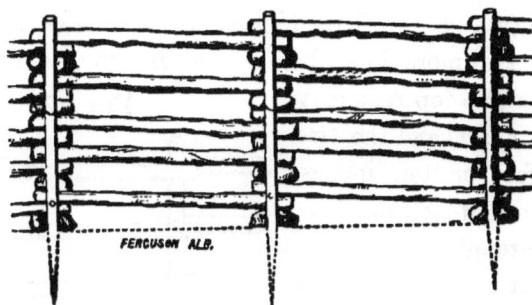

FERGUSON ALB.

A STRAIGHT RAIL FENCE.

or over it; and besides, it saves twice as many rails as a man could split while he is casting up a ridge. Blocks of wood or stone many now be placed close to the stakes, on the ridge, for the fence to rest on, or an inch pin, of durable and tough timber, may be put through both stakes for supporting the rails. When the fence is merely to stop horned cattle and horses, the pin may be one foot above the ridge. Lay the fence two or three rails high, laying between the stakes stones or blocks of wood, at pleasure, and then put in another pin, or put on a wooden cap or a wire. When a rail is too large, cut it away with the axe so that it will fit tightly between the stakes. Reserve the largest rails for the top, and keep the crooked ones in a panel by themselves.

93. This is the most economical rail fence that can be built for every kind of stock; every one likes it, and it possesses all the commendable qualities that any fence can claim; it occupies but little space, requires but few rails, is strong and substantial,

and looks neat and farmer-like. It may with propriety be denominated *the farmer's own fence.*

94. Which is represented by Fig. 22, is a straight fence,
constructed of posts, rails, and wire, in the following manner:
The posts are first set firmly in the ground, as far apart as the
length of the rail, allowing the rails to extend by each post two
or three inches; a line is then struck on the posts, as in building
board fence (see par. 152), as high as the top rail is to be placed;
then strike two more lines below the first one, as far apart as
desired; the two top rails may

FIG. 22.

be one foot apart, and the two
next one foot or ten inches.
Now, with a half-inch bit, bore
the holes through the posts at
cach mark at right angles with
the fence; then have two light
benches, just high enough to
set under the bottom rail, when
it is raised as high as it should
be on the side of the posts;
let the benches be placed so as
to hold the rail about where it

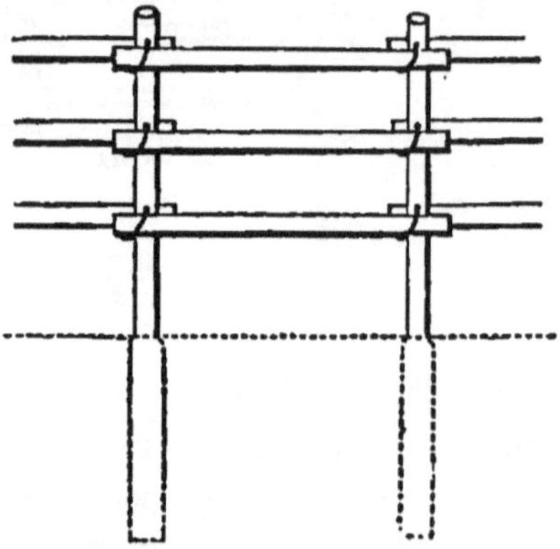

THE HORSE, OR SKELETON FENCE.

is to be fastened, and, with a wire running through the posts,
fasten it around the end of the rail, by twisting the ends of it
firmly together. Carry the first bench forward to the next post
and lay up another rail, and put a wire through the post and
around the ends of the two rails, a rail being on each side of the
post, and twist the ends together. Carry forward the next bench
and lay up another rail, and so on until the lower rails are all
put up. Put up the second rail, letting one end rest on the bottom rail while the other end is being made fast. When more
than one hand is at work putting up rails the benches may be
dispensed with, but one hand alone will find it very difficult and
inconvenient putting up the first rail without a bench to hold up

one end while he is fastening the other. It will be understood that the wire passes through the post and clasps the rails; and on the under side of the rails the wire is on the outside of the post.

95. Some men prefer having two holes bored through the post for every tier of rails, and having a hole in each end of the rails, and the wire put through one rail, then through the post, then through the rail on the opposite side of the post, and then through the post again. But it requires far more labor to make the fence when two holes are made through the post for each tier of rails, and a hole in the end of the rails also, and it makes a fence no better, in any way, than when but one hole is made through the post for each tier of rails; and, besides all this, when the holes are made through the rails as well as through the posts, they must be bored very exact, or it will be difficult putting the wires through. When the wires pass entirely around the rails, if they are twisted up tightly the rails cannot be got out without breaking the wires. This is a very cheap and substantial fence, and will turn horses and large cattle about as well as a fence seven rails to a panel. It is a great improvement to cast up a ridge along this kind of fence, as neither cattle nor horses can push against it with as much force as when the ground about it is all smooth and level. If the rails be unusually large, the holes in the posts may be bored farther apart than one foot.

96. The principal reason why many fail in building this kind of fence is, they do not use posts sufficiently large. Many use only stakes, driven eighteen or twenty inches into the ground. But in order to have such a fence stand well, the posts should be as large as for an ordinary board fence, and should be set as deep as for a board fence; then if an unruly animal thrust his head through he cannot throw off the top rails, nor push away the bottom ones; he must necessarily break the wires or rails, or demolish the fence, in order to get through, and any animal that will do that should not have his liberty in an open field.

97. Fig. 23 shows the mode of building a fence with logs, or large poles or rails; they may be cut as long as they can be handled conveniently. When a fence is made of logs, one end of them should be spotted with an axe, so that they will not roll off at every touch of an animal. When one has lots of timber that is of but little value, it may be worked into a fence in the logs, at very much less expense than to split it into rails. Logs thirty feet in length may be used for the two first tiers, and may be rolled to their places on the fence with a team. When it is one or two logs high it may be finished with heavy poles.

FIG. 23.

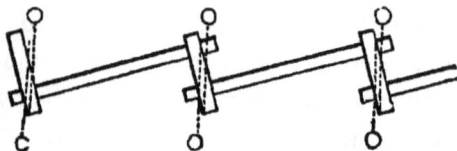

LOG, OR POLE FENCE.

98. When this kind of fence is made entirely of poles, the cross panels may be made of the sound pieces of old rails, or of pieces of poles. In either case the corners should be spotted, so that they will not roll.

99. When one has a large lot of sound pieces of old rails, they may be used up to an advantage in building a rail fence in this manner. When such a fence is made of rails, in order to have it straight, stick a row of stakes, and lay one corner of the fence in a line with the stakes, and cut the lower sticks, for the short panels, about two and a half feet long and place the next corner as far from the first as it will admit of, and lap a few inches at each end, laying the short panels at a right angle with the rails. As the tiers of rails are laid on, the ends should be laid inwards a little, every tier towards each other, so that when the fence is about five rails high the top rails will lay in a straight line, with their ends side by side. The pieces for the short panels should be shorter in length at each tier, and the top ones may be not more than one foot long. This kind of fence should always be staked, and after it is staked the ends of the rails will

touch the under side of the stakes from the bottom to the top of the fence. The place for each stake is shown by the preceding diagram. The heaviest rails are laid between the stakes for riders, and if large poles, as long as two rails, can be obtained for riders, the fence will be much stronger than if it were made entirely of rails. This kind of fence is to be staked with stakes not sharpened, but set in holes dug with a pick, or mattock, whose blade is about two inches wide.

100. I may be allowed to remark here, that but few men know how to dig a stake hole correctly. We often see the man stand facing the fence when digging the holes; this is decidedly wrong, because when standing in this position, the earth, which should all remain unbroken and solid, to keep the stakes from tipping up when the riders are laid on, is all broken up, and the stakes tip up very readily; but if the digger will stand with his *side* to the fence, and dig a long deep hole, leaving an unbroken bank for the end of the stake to raise against, it will be almost impossible to make the ends tip up by laying on any amount of heavy riders. It matters not how long the hole is dug in the direction of the length of the fence, but it should be dug to fit the stake. It should slant in the direction of the stakes when the riders are on the fence, and be just wide enough to admit the end of stake when it is thrust into the hole with a man's whole force. When the stakes are large, and the rails also, the stakes must be set more slanting than when the rails are very small. If stakes be set rather straight up and down, they may be in the correct position for a small rail, but if the riders were large there would be too much space between the rails and riders. Two riders are usually laid in such a fence, although many farmers use but one. The under rider is laid with one end in a pair of stakes, and the other end under the next pair of stakes. The upper riders, of course, are laid in the stakes, with both ends above them.

THE ROD FENCE,

101. Is a great favorite among some farmers because of its substantiability. This kind of fence is made like the zigzag stake and rail fence, with an iron rod passing through all the rails at the joints. Iron rods, from three to four-eighths of an inch in diameter, and about four and a half feet long, are set in a fence block two or three inches deep, and then a hole about three-fourths of an inch in diameter is bored through each end of all the rails, after which they are slipped on the rods. To save rails, pieces of rails may be sawed up about four or six inches long, and bored and put on the rods. It is not necessary that the rods be made very tight in the fence blocks, for the force of anything against the fence is merely in a horizontal direction, and when all the rails are laid up the fence will resist quite as great a force if the rods enter the blocks loosely, as when they are made tight.

102. When boring the rails, some eight or ten of them should be laid on two benches, and the holes made at an equal distance, measuring with a thin strip of board, or the like. The holes should be at least one-third larger than the rods, and care and skill must be exercised in boring them, and have them true with each other. If one hole slant a little one way and the other hole be straight through, or slant a little in another direction, it will be very difficult getting the rails on the rods, on account of their binding on the rods. If it were desired, a head could be made on the lower ends of the rods and a nut and screw on the upper ends, and they could pass through the blocks and rails and be screwed up tight. Let a small hole be drilled in stone blocks for the end of the rod.

THE SIDE HILL, OR GUN FENCE.

103. A section of which is represented by Fig. 24, is made with small stakes and short pieces of rails, or it may all be made

of stakes only, four, five, or six feet in length, pointed and driven in the ground. The rise of the ground where the fence is to be made will deter mine the length of both rails and stakes. Where the ground is so steep that an ani-mal—horse or ox—can scarcely ascend or de-scend, the horizontal pieces may be only four feet in length and

FIG. 24

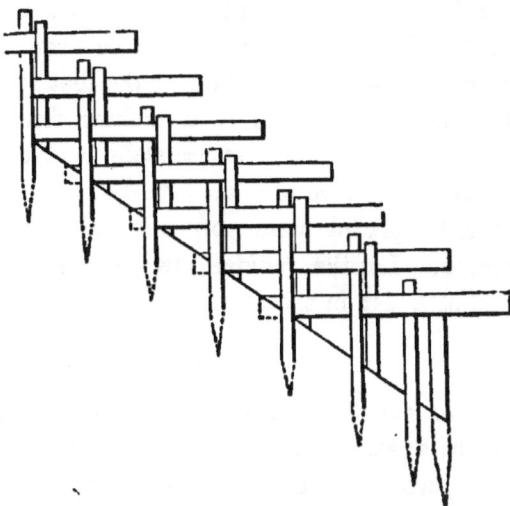

SIDE HILL, OR GUN FENCE.

the stakes four feet. Two stakes are required for each rail. Slabs placed edge ways in the stakes, will lay up much faster with a given number of stakes than pieces of rails or stakes.

104. The first step in building such a fence on level ground or up an acclivity, is to plow a narrow trench, from eight to twelve inches deep; and where the ground is too steep to be plowed, a narrow channel may be dug with a pick or spade. Commence at the foot of the hill and lay one end of the slab or piece of rail on a large stone or block of wood, or a short post driven in the ground, and the other end in the trench, and stamp the dirt on each side of it to keep it on its edge. Set a pair of stakes so that they will rest on this slab, as shown in the figure, and then lay another slab in the crotch of the stakes, with one end in the trench, and stamp in the dirt with the foot, as was done with the first one. When this kind of fence is built on level ground, slabs of almost any length may be used. Long ones must be placed more nearly horizontal than the short ones. When slabs are of various lengths, those of one length should be placed together, in order to make the fence of a uniform height. Whatever may be the length of a slab, the end of the

4*

first slab above the ground should be elevated just as high as the fence is to be made, and as the other slabs are laid in the crotch of the stakes, care must be exercised to keep them all of about the same inclination as the first one that was put up. If, for instance, one has been making fence of slabs sixteen feet long, and wishes now to use slabs twelve feet in length, in order to have the fence of a uniform height, the slabs twelve feet long must be placed more perpendicularly than those sixteen feet in length. Let the builder always remember to place the largest end of a slab in the ground.

THE PARK FENCE.

105. Fig. 25 is a representation of a fence which will turn almost anything that ought to have its liberty in the fields. This fence, where timber is cheap, is the cheapest fence that can be built, for a high fence. The first step in building it is, to plow a deep trench, and then make holes with a crow-bar in it, as far apart as the stakes are to be stuck. Have a long plank bench, standing by the side of the fence, and let one man put the stakes in the holes and hold them perpendicu-larly, while another man drives them. The stakes may be from three to eight inches apart, in the clear, according to the size of the animals to be turned. One side of the tops should be kept in perfect range, so that a narrow strip of board may be nailed to each of them. At the distance of about every ten or twelve feet, a stake two or three feet longer than the rest should be set, for holding wires, which may be fastened to the stakes with staples, or they may pass

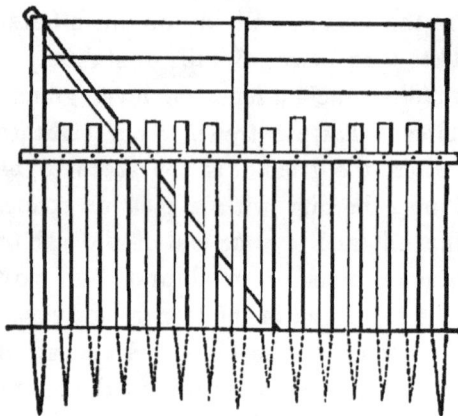

FIG. 25.

PARK FENCE.

through the stakes in holes as in the figure. Wire as small as number twelve would be sufficiently large for this purpose. After the stakes are all driven, there should be two or three furrows plowed on each side of the fence and cast up against the stakes with a shovel, and grass seed sowed on it. When such a fence is made of durable timber, well seasoned and well made, it will need no repairing, ordinarily, for a score of years.

STAKE AND RIDER FENCE.

106. At Fig. 26 the ordinary mode of finishing a worm fence with stakes and riders is shown. The stakes are set about one foot deep in the ground, the holes having been dug with a pick, about from eighteen to thirty inches from the fence, according to the size of the rails and the height of the fence, before it is staked, and the

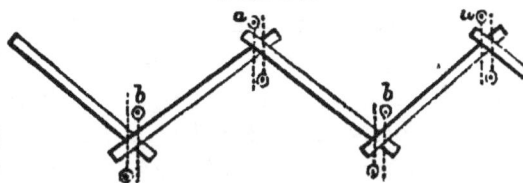

FIG. 26.

STAKE AND RIDER FENCE.

amount of worm which is given it in laying the foundation. The higher the fence is before it is staked, and the larger the riders are, and the more worm there is, the farther the foot of the stakes must be set from the fence. The dotted lines show the position of the stakes; and it will be discovered, that at every alternate corner of the fence they are placed with the *opposite sides together.* This is a very important consideration in staking a fence of this style, which men of experience well understand, but which the beginner does not always perceive very readily; and those who do not understand the practical importance of it place every pair of stakes alike, and the consequence is, the spaces between the riders are very much too wide. We will suppose, for instance, that in making a fence like the figure, we commence at a certain point and work west. The stakes on the north side of the fence *a a a* must be placed on the east side of those on the south side, and the stakes at *b b* must be placed on the west side of those on the south side of the fence. This is important only when the lower rider is placed with one end in the crotch of one pair of stakes and the other end under the next pair. For the lower riders, rails of small size should be used. When no cross rider is used, the first or lowest rider being laid, with both ends in the stakes, each pair of stakes may set just alike. Let the outside stakes all be set in a line, as nearly as may be, so that in plowing the plow may be run straight along by the foot of them. Set the foot of the stakes at a right angle with the fence, and not diagonally, either way, because, when set so as to lean on the fence in a diagonal direction, the spaces between the riders will often be rendered wider, and a fence will not stand as firmly as if the stakes were standing at a right angle with the fence. The *height* of this style of fence, before it is staked, must depend on the size of the fence blocks, the size of the rails, and the ultimate height of the fence. When the fence blocks and rails are of a good size, and animals orderly, and riders heavy, four rails high before staking, and two after staking, will make a good lawful fence, and any animal that would pass it by leaping over it, or by demolishing it, should be hampered without delay, or placed in a field which is fenced with a

DOUBLE STAKE AND RIDER FENCE.

107. Fig. 27 represents the manner of staking and ridering a fence in a twofold manner. The fence is first made like Fig. 18, and then long poles or rails are laid on the top of the riders, and staked as shown in the figure, and heavy rails or poles are laid in the stakes.

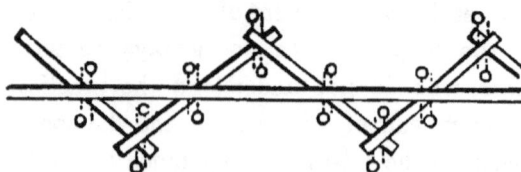

FIG. 27.

DOUBLE STAKE AND RIDER FENCE.

It is very convenient sometimes to have a yard or small field enclosed with such a fence, where a bull or stallion may be turned loose without any fears of his getting out of his proper place; and if it is enclosed with such a fence, any animals that are let loose within such an enclosure are obliged to remain there until they are allowed to go out at the gate.

THE GUARD FENCE

108. Is sometimes one of the most economical rail fences that can be erected. When one has but few rails at hand, and a temporary fence is needed for a few weeks, the guard fence is a very economical and convenient mode of fencing. It not unfrequently occurs that it is necessary to fence a narrow way across the end of a field, where the cattle are to be driven to a distant field every day to pasture or to water. Sometimes, also, it is very desirable to have a temporary fence through a field, for the purpose of allowing a team to graze for a few hours where there is good pasture, while there may be grain in one part of the field. This style of fence is not designed to turn cattle only while the eyes of some one is on them. It is made two or three rails high, zigzag or straight. Stakes, or crotches, are driven into the ground, so that the bottom rail, when resting on them, will be about two feet from the ground. Stake them with anything that will not decay while the fence is needed, and lay on one rider, or two, as may seem best. If two riders are used, the lower rider should be laid with one end in the crotch of one pair of stakes, while the other end is under the stakes. This style of fence will often subserve as good a purpose as one which would cost four or five times as much as this.

POST AND BAR FENCE

109. Is a style of fence which many farmers seem to admire more than almost any other, but it is not economical, as a general rule, because of the great amount of labor required to build it. The posts are mortised similar to bar-posts, and the rails are split from five to six inches wide, and about two inches thick; and the ends of two bars, one on each side of the post, are dressed off so that two of them will enter one hole. There can be no objection

to this fence save the expense of labor in building it. When a post and bar fence is built of durable timber, and in a workman-like manner, it will stand without any repairing as long, and perhaps longer, than almost any other rail fence.

POST AND RAIL FENCE

110. Is made similar to post and bar fence, only in this style: A round tenon is made on each end of all the rails, which are well driven into round holes in the posts. When a fence is built in this manner, the tenons should be well smeared with coal tar or paint, to exclude the wet, as in such places they would be very liable to decay in a few seasons if unpainted.

A post and rail fence may be made a self-sustaining fence by boring the holes in round sticks for corner posts, at such an angle that the rails of each panel will be about the same angle of an ordinary rail fence. But we would not advise the builder to attempt to erect such a self-sustaining fence, for he would most assuredly wish, in a few years, that he had never seen such a fence. There are several other styles of rail fence, which we have not adverted to, because we do not consider them worthy of adoption.

BARS AND BAR-POSTS.

111. Bars should always be made of light timber when they are made to be let down, so that children can put them up without difficulty. The lightest rails should be selected for bars, when the rails are being overhauled, so that no time may be lost in searching for them when they are needed. The neatest bars are made by having a log of some light timber sawed into bars about an inch and a half thick by four or five wide; one log will make a large lot of them. Bar-posts should be not less than eleven or twelve feet apart, as that amount of space is none too great to allow a load of hay or grain, or some of the implements of the farm, to pass through freely.

SLIDING BARS,

12. Represented at Fig. 28, are the most convenient style for bars, especially where bars are used very often. Three bar-posts are set so that the bar-holes will exactly range with each other. Two of them should be set about four feet apart, and two about eleven or twelve feet apart. The bars should be sawed true

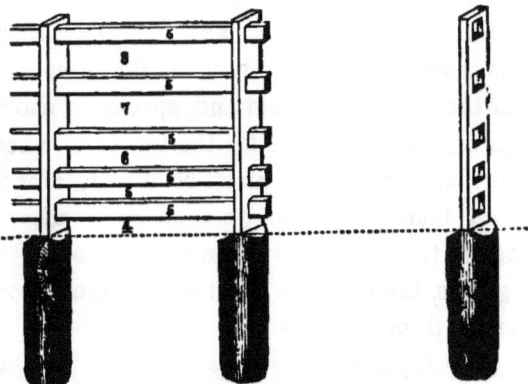

FIG. 28.

SLIDING BARS.

and straight, and in opening the bar-way they can be pushed back, as shown in the figure. Such bars are much more convenient than those which must be let down or taken out when anything is to pass through.

113. Cattle, horses, and some other animals, sometimes acquire the vice of letting the bars down, and thus opening the way to forbidden ground. This may be prevented by boring a hole in the bars on each side of one of the posts through which the bars slide, and by putting in pins. This is better than to wedge the bars in the mortises.

114. Bar-posts (see SPLITTING BAR-POSTS, Fig. 12) should be hewed out straight, as they are sometimes winding; and all the mortises should be parallel with each other. If the sides of a bar-post are winding, an unskillful workman is very liable to make the mortises crooked, or not parallel with each other, and the consequence would be that the mortises in the different posts would not range with each other. Good slabs, which are cut from logs at saw-mills, will make good bar-posts.

115. Fig. 29 represents the manner of making a bar-post so as

to connect a fence with it.   If the post is ten or more Fig. 29.
inches wide, it will be wide enough for the bar-holes
or mortises, and a row of round holes for the ends of
rails.   In case the post is not wide enough for a row
of holes for the ends of the rails, a stake may be set
on one side of it, with pieces of boards firmly nailed
on from the post to the stake, for supporting the rails.
The mortises should be not less than two inches wide;
and the length of them and spaces is shown by the
figures.   The mortises for the top bars, when bars are
made to be let down, must be a little longer, up and
down, than the bottom ones, so as to allow the other
ends of the bars to go down to the ground.   For sliding bars, the mortises need not be much longer than
the width of the bars.

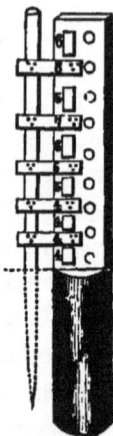

BAR-POST.

116. *Repairing bar-posts* is something that is seldom thought
of by those who have lots of bar-posts which have rotted entirely
off at the surface of the ground.   The tops would last many
times fifteen years longer, but the lower ends of them have decayed.   Let such posts be pinned firmly to a strong stake or two,
and an old bar-post will subserve the place of a new one.

117. Bar-posts should be made on stormy days and in the winter, when the forces of the farm are not engaged in the operations
which demand attention at some particular season.   To aid the
beginner in laying out the mortises for a bar-post, take a narrow
strip of thin board and cut notches in it, so that it may be laid on
a post and the mortises and spaces marked off correctly and alike
on all the posts.   The length of the mortises and width of spaces
must first be laid out correctly on the marking board, and then
there will be no danger of mortising a post wrong.   The mortises
and spaces may be made according to Fig. 29.

E. NASH'S IMPROVED FENCE.

Fig. 29½ represents a new style of straight rail fence, which has but recently been invented by E. Nash, Auburn, N. Y. It may be constructed of rails or of boards. If made of rails, flatten the ends a little, and cut them of a uniform length, and nail

FIG. 29½.

NASH'S IMPROVED FENCE.

pieces of boards four feet long, and five or six inches wide to the ends of the rails, as shown in the cut, allowing them to extend *beyond* the ends of the rails half their width. Two boards are required at each panel, one at each end, and on opposite sides. Set the panels erect on flat stones, or other blocks, and put a small carriage bolt through the upper ends of the braces, and through the uprights, or nail them, and set the braces, which may be made of pieces of rails, in the ground with a pick or spade. Drive small stakes, if necessary, near the foot of the uprights, to keep the bottom of the fence from being moved sideways. This fence may be used for *hurdles*, or fencing stacks, or for making pens for stock. When used for either of these purposes long staples, passing through one of the uprights and fastened by a wooden key, will hold the panels at the corners more conveniently than bolts. It may be erected on rolling land, or up and down slopes, as well as on level ground; and is very cheaply constructed, saving more than one-third the number of rails, and is as durable as any other style of rail fence, and is not liable to be displaced by the frost. The only portion liable to rapid decay are the ends of the braces, which may be cut off after the ends have rotted, and bolted to the uprights lower down from the top. Board fence may be built after this style, of any desired height or width of boards, and it will be difficult to displace or knock off the boards, as they are well battered on each side of the fence. The foot of the braces need not be more than twenty inches from the blocks. The cost of such a fence will depend upon the value of timber. In my locality, good fencing can be obtained for seventy cents per hundred square feet, and about thirty square feet will make a rod in length. The labor of erecting will not amount to more than six cents per rod. This is the most permanent and substantial straight fence for the surface of the ground, that I have met with; and I have no hesitancy in recommending it to my brother farmers.

SECTION 2.—BOARD FENCE.

" Where towering pines and rugged oaks abound,
With pales or boards the fields are circled round :
The royal oak supplies both posts and rails ;
Hemlock and tulip furnish boards and pales."—EDWARDS.

118. There is no limit to the different styles of board fence. Boards of all widths and lengths have been worked into fence; and in half the instances, the builders have never stopped to inquire whether they are using up their timber in the most economical manner or not. I have no apprehensions of being charged with making a random assertion, when I affirm, that were all the boards which are worked up through the country, in building board fence, sawed in the most economical forms and sizes, just twice as much fence could be made with them, and the fences would be just as permanent, efficient and durable as they now are. There is not half the economy exercised in preparing the materials for a board fence, that there is in building fences of other descriptions. Farmers too often trust to a sawyer to saw their fencing of the different sizes, which *they* (the sawyers) may think most convenient and suitable ; and in too

many instances it is sawed into *boards*, and that is all. Now, if a board four or five inches wide will subserve as good a purpose in building fence as one seven or eight inches wide, there is a manifest want of economy in preparing the boards for fence ; and if two posts will subserve as good a purpose for every sixteen feet in length of fence, as if they occupied only twelve feet, then there is a lack of economy in using up posts, and nails, and in digging the holes, and in performing most of the other work required to build a board fence. If the builder desires to build a *tight* board fence, *i. e.*, one with no spaces between the boards, it will require just about so many feet of boards for a rod, whether they are placed horizontally or vertically. But when an open board fence is to be erected, where economy in lumber and labor is a consideration of any account, the idea which should influence the builder is, to have the boards as long as will be most profitable, and as narrow as will be most consistent, with suitable strength and symmetry, and the spaces between the boards as wide as possible, and turn those animals which the fence is designed to stop from getting on forbidden ground.

119. Many farmers, and experienced fence-builders, also, have imbibed the notion that the bottom board must of necessity be a foot or more wider than the others, and the second and third still narrower than the bottom board, until the top board is arrived at, which must be narrower than any of the others. We might, with the same propriety, contend that the bottom rail of a rail fence should be preposterously large, while the top one should be the smallest. There would be just as much consistency in the latter as in the former. I know it is contended that a board fence *looks better* when the bottom board is about twice as wide as the top board. But we have all followed in the train of custom in this respect for so long a time, that we have come to think that a board fence looks " odd " and not tasty, if the boards are all of one width, being as narrow as would be consistent with their strength to turn animals. Had we been accustomed to see all the boards of a uniform width, it would appear still more odd and deficient in taste, to see a fence built with the

bottom board twice as wide as the top board. Sometimes the
bottom boards are from twelve to eighteen inches wide, and the
top boards of the same fence only four inches. There can be no
plausible reason whatever, to justify the use of such a wide
board for the bottom of a board fence. It cannot be argued that
greater strength is necessary near the bottom of a fence, for
the reverse of this is true. Swine and sheep do not require as
strong a fence as horses and horned cattle; consequently, if a
wide board is necessary, matters of taste and strength argue that
it should be placed at the top of the fence, where the greatest
resistance is needed. If a board four or five inches wide possesses sufficient strength to turn horned cattle and horses, most
assuredly a board of that width is sufficiently strong to turn
swine and sheep. If, for instance, a board were fourteen inches
wide, and placed three inches from the ground, it would make
the fence seventeen inches high. Now, if that board were slit
into three boards of equal width, being about four and a half
inches wide, with the first board three inches above the ground,
and the first space three inches, and the second space four inches,
that same board would make a fence $3+4\frac{1}{2}+4+4\frac{1}{2}+5+5\frac{1}{2}=$
$26\frac{1}{2}$ inches high, and sufficiently strong to turn any kind of
domestic animals. Again, fence boards are often sawed twelve
or fourteen inches wide for the bottom board, the next nine inches
wide, the next eight, the next seven, the next, or top board, six
inches. The spaces often are two inches below the bottom board;
first space two inches, second space three inches, third space four
inches, fourth space five inches, which will make a fence five feet
high. The boards used would be equal to a board forty-four
inches wide, with spaces amounting to sixteen inches wide. It
is granted that such a fence would be a strong and substantial
one; but, if the boards were all of a uniform width, (four and a
half inches wide,) with wider spaces, but still sufficiently narrow
to stop pigs and lambs, a fence five feet high, and far more tasty,
in my estimation, could be made with six boards four and a half
inches wide, equal to a board twenty-seven inches in width, with
spaces three, four, five, six, seven, eight inches in width. But

we would not be understood that we consider such a fence an economical one, or worthy of adoption as a general rule; because, for ordinary purposes, all timber that is used in building a fence above four and a half feet high is useless, and the labor of building no better than thrown away. And, again, there is no necessity for having so narrow spaces between the boards. A space of three or four inches wide between the first and second boards at the bottom is narrow enough; and any small animals, pigs or lambs, that will go under the bottom board when it is three inches above the surface of the ground, or through a space four inches wide, above the bottom board, will seldom do any damage on the other side of the fence. An animal must be very small to be able to pass through horizontal spaces only four inches in width. Allowing, then, a space of three inches below the bottom board, and four inches between the first and second boards, when they are not less than four and a half inches wide, the space between the second and third boards may be five inches wide, without any danger of pigs or lambs passing through it; for any pig or lamb that can go through a five-inch space, cannot possibly get through such a space when it is seventeen inches above the ground on which the animal is standing, *unless* it should be a descendant of the illustrious tribe of swine denominated "*land pikes*," or "*alligators*," or some mountain ranger of the sheep race. After a fence is built thirty inches high, if the spaces are just narrow enough to prevent cattle and horses from thrusting their heads between the boards, there will be no apprehensions that sheep will be able to get through them. There is no necessity whatever in making any of the spaces, which may be above two feet from the surface of the ground, *less* than seven inches wide; for no sheep nor swine can get through a space of seven inches, when it is above two feet from the ground. And there should be no space more than ten inches wide, or eleven, at the most. The upper space is often made one foot wide. But that is too wide; for horses and horned cattle of many kinds will thrust their heads through the fence in a space of twelve inches. But in a space of ten inches there is not room for the heads of ordinary cattle and horses. The builder, in building a board fence, can always calculate for himself on the width of spaces. If cattle more than one year old, and horses, only, are to be fenced against, it will be entirely safe, unless animals are quite unruly, to make all the spaces ten inches wide. In fencing against calves, the spaces below thirty inches from the ground should not be ten inches wide; because calves, and even most yearlings, can thrust their heads through a space of ten inches.

119. We will now show by illustration what we consider as *economical, substantial, symmetrical,* and *tasty* a board fence as can be erected, when there is no ridge of earth along the fence. We never consider a fence the most economical that can be built, when it is necessary to build a fence from the surface of the ground, that has not a ridge of earth below the boards; because a ridge of earth twenty or more inches high may be cast up at less than half the expense of purchasing other materials for fencing to such a height, making no account of the labor of putting them up. But as it is not always desirable, and sometimes very objectionable, to have a ridge of earth beneath a fence, we will calculate it from the surface of the ground. In all localities where animals of every description are allowed to roam, lawlessly, in the highway, a fence along the sides of the highway is usually required to be a little better than the ordinary fences of the farm. Along the highway it is often necessary to fence against all varieties of disorderly animals which belong to the dumb brutes of the fair creation, saying nothing of fencing against bipeds, which are most stupendously stupid, which run in the highways; and consequently a fence is needed which will offer a resistance fully adequate to the exigency of the circumstances.

120. A board which is sixteen feet long, four and a half inches wide, and not less than one inch in thickness, if it is of sound timber when made into fence, as it ought to be, will not give way beneath the weight of a heavy man when he is climbing over the fence, and it will resist a much greater lateral thrust than we would ordinarily suppose; and if the top board be covered with a cap board four inches wide and an inch and a quarter thick, if

of good timber, a horse or steer may mount on it and hang there until he becomes satisfied that his weight will not break down the fence; but the timber must be free from knots and curls, and places where the grain runs crosswise of the boards. If a board four and a half inches wide will sustain such a weight and resist such a thrust as have been mentioned, it cannot be considered as the best economy to saw boards for fence over four and a half inches in width, and sixteen feet long; and it cannot be denied that boards of these dimensions are sawed up in the most economical manner for fences; but if the timber be full of knots, and is "cross-grained," it would be more economical, and wiser policy, to saw some of them at least eight inches wide. With these considerations, the builder will be able to determine with propriety what sizes, length, breadth and thickness, will be

THE MOST ECONOMICAL DIMENSIONS OF FENCE BOARDS.

121. In order to save fence posts, the logs for boards should be cut sixteen feet long, besides the stub-shot. With this length the posts should be set just eight feet apart, from centre to centre. There can be no objection to cutting logs for fencing eighteen or twenty feet long; but with that length of boards, it would be necessary to have more than two posts to each panel, for a distance of more than eight feet between posts, when the boards are only four and a half inches wide, would be rather too great; but if boards were sawed proportionally wider—and in no case should fence boards be sawed *less* than a plump inch in thickness—there could be no objection to cutting the logs eighteen or twenty feet long, and in setting the posts nine or ten feet apart. It would be far better policy to saw fence boards that are four and a half inches wide, one and one-eighth or one and one-fourth inches thick, instead of sawing them one inch or less in thickness. Fence boards, when not well painted, become thinner every year by the wearing away of the grain, caused by the influences of wet and dry weather, and consequently every board becomes less strong year by year.

122. Fig. 30 represents a style of board fence which will turn, most effectually, horses, horned cattle, sheep, lambs and swine, if they are not incorrigibly unruly, and which, in the judgment of our civil fence law, would be considered a lawful fence, either along the highway side or between the adjoining farms. Some of our great sticklers for wide boards at the bottom may take some exceptions to it; but if fields are inclosed with such a fence, the proprietor, and all the force of the farm, may lie down to rest without entertaining any fears that any of their animals will get on forbidden ground through or over such a fence. It will be seen by the figure that it is fifty-three and a half inches high, including the cap board, and if that were one and a half inches thick, which would be economy, the fence would be four and a half feet high. The posts are set eight feet apart, from centre to centre, perpendicularly, and a line struck on the sides of the posts for the top board, according to the manner shown at paragraph 152; and if but one workman is employed in building the fence, to aid in holding up the ends of the boards he will find it very advantageous to use two gauge boards, like Fig. 31, which are very important in building a board fence, in order to prevent mistakes in the spaces. When two such boards are used, the lower ends can be set on the ground, and the top fastened near the top of a post, by driving in a nail a little, just sufficient to hold it while all the boards of one panel are being put up; two such boards would be of far more practical utility to a good workman, than any two boys from the Emerald Isle, because the gauge boards would always hold them in the right place. The boards should "*break joint*" on every alternate post, because it renders a fence stronger

FIG. 30.

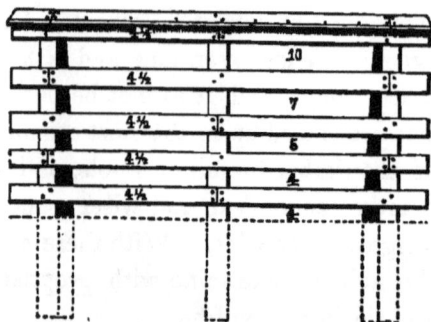

HIGHWAY SIDE BOARD FENCE, FOUR AND A HALF FEET HIGH.

than to have all the joints on one post. Not less than two eight-penny fence nails should be used in a place. The whole fence may be planed and painted, or not, as desired; but in either case, the face sides of the posts, and those parts of the boards which come in contact with the posts, should be painted, or smeared with coal tar, to prevent their decaying. After the boards are all nailed on, the efficiency and strength of the fence will be much increased by nailing on battens, four inches wide, over the boards on each post. The insides of the battens and the fence boards, where they are nailed, should be painted. Much care should be exercised in nailing on the battens, lest the large nails split the ends of the fence boards. If the nails are very large, holes should be bored through both battens and boards for the nails. Some fence makers consider it very important to fit pieces of boards in the spaces between all the boards, and nail them to the posts; but if a fence is well battened, and if the nails which hold the battens are driven near the lower edges of the fence boards, pieces in the spaces will not pay for the labor of fitting them and putting them in. After the battens are all nailed on, let the tops of posts be sawed off square, and the cap board firmly nailed on. This should be four inches wide, so as to cover the top ends of the posts and the top board and the batten. If it should be desirable to case all the posts of such a fence, or every second post, the manner and style of doing it may be seen at Fig. 32,

123. Which represents a style of fence which is almost universally admired, especially by the farmers' wives. The fence is designed to be planed and painted, and a part or all of the posts cased. The face casings are eight inches wide, and extend ten or eleven inches above the top of the fence. The tops of cases are finished with square pieces of plank, or with a pyramidal top, made of inch boards. The boards are all nailed on the posts, and then the face casings to posts are nailed on, as if they were battens. The side casings are then fitted by cutting gains in them for the fence boards, and they are nailed to the face casings.

The side casings are six inches wide. This makes a case eight inches square. If every alternate post is cased, the remainder should be battened, as shown in the figure. There is no economy in casing posts, and it is done merely to please the fancy. For

FIG. 32.

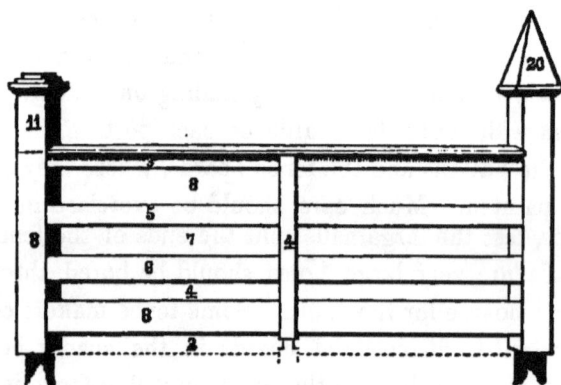

LAWN FENCE.

my own part, I do not approve of casing but few posts; and I may be allowed to say, that the majority of people are quite as well pleased with the appearance of such a fence, when only the gate posts and those at the corners of the yard are cased, as when every post or every second post is cased. It increases the expense of a fence very much to case all the posts, and they are by no means ornaments of good taste and of rural beauty. For a fence which encircles a huge cathedral of the Corinthian style of architecture, cased posts for a board fence would seem to be in better taste and harmony than around a plain country residence of a farmer. The fence, as represented by Fig. 32, is forty-five inches high, including the cap board. There is one objection to it, however, and that is, it is not high enough to suit most men. But the eight-inch space might be made two inches wider, and the bottom board might be slit in two, and a space between the two pieces three inches wide. There is a width of boards, aside from the cap in this fence, of twenty-two inches, and in Fig. 30

there is a width of twenty-two and a half inches, but about a foot difference in the height of the fences. The builder can choose either, or reject both, or make the spaces a little wider or narrower, to suit his caprice.

DIVISION FENCE.

124. Fig. 33 represents a style of board fence which almost every farmer likes, because of its *efficiency* and *cheapness* and *durability.* It is four and a half feet high, with boards sixteen

FIG. 33.

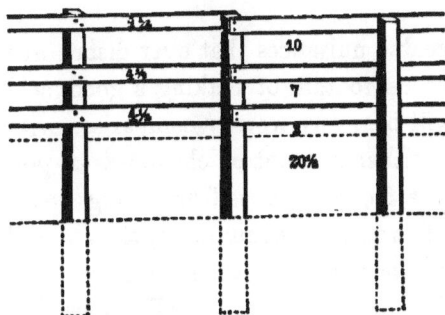

DIVISION FENCE.

or more feet long, and four and a half inches wide, and only three to a panel. The spaces are the same as in the fence at Fig. 30. There are no cap boards to this fence. The great excellence of this fence consists in its permanence, and the facility with which it can be made. The posts are set as shown at Fig. 34; and any one can see at a glance that such a mode of setting posts will render a fence far more substantial, and much less liable to be made to lean either way by any influence which causes a fence to deviate from a perpen-

FIG. 34.

MANNER OF SETTING FENCE POSTS FOR A DIVISION FENCE.

dicular position. The boards of each panel are independent of each other; they may all be put up without any sawing off. In making a fence of this style, all the posts at the ends of the

boards should be set on a line with each other; and then the
posts, at the middle of the boards, should be set about half an
inch on the other side of the line.   There is no face side to such
a fence, both sides being alike, and there are no joints to make,
nor to break, as in fences of other styles.   After the boards are
all nailed on, a ridge of earth, twenty two inches high, should be
cast up under the boards, and seeded with grass.   As the grass
seed sometimes all washes from the top of such a ridge, a row of
sods should be laid on the top of it, beneath the bottom boards.

SELF-SUSTAINING BOARD FENCES

125. Are the most disagreeable nuisances that ever dishonored
a farm.   It is perfectly ridiculous to talk of making a good self-
sustaining board fence that will bear any worthy comparison with
a good post and board fence, either in point of cheapness or permanency.   I have never seen a model of a self-sustaining board
fence (unless it had as much worm, or even more, than a rail
fence) which was fit for any other purpose than to entrap the
credulous, or to be kept in the museum.   I am well aware that
there are several styles of self-sustaining patent board fences,
which have been extolled to the clouds, and which, at first sight,
appear to be a great improvement in fencing.   They look well,
and seem to stand permanently; but after a few—yes, very few—
years of exposure to the influences of the weather, they begin to
twist and warp, and give way in important places by decaying
or shrinking, so that they soon become as "shackling" as a
rickety old wagon.   When it becomes necessary to give much
worm to a board fence, in order to save posts, any good arithmetician can show by figures, in a few moments, how many more
feet of boards it will require to build a zigzag fence than a
straight one, and it will be easy to show how many feet of boards
will be used up in making locks and cleats, and such like, for
the purpose of holding the fence erect.   He can then calculate
how much that redundant lumber is worth, which is required to

build a zigzag board fence, over and above what is required to build a straight fence. After this, calculations may be made for posts; and the cost of posts for a straight fence compared with the cost for a redundant quantity of lumber for a zigzag fence. A zigzag, self-sustaining fence cannot be made without using up lumber of some kind for locks and cleats, nearly as many feet as there are in a post. And so with a straight fence: there must of necessity be about so many square feet of lumber for the standard, and cross-pieces and sills, or locks and stakes, as the case may be; and there is more or less waste in working up such material, and by close calculation it will, in most instances, equal the amount of lumber in the posts required for a panel. If self-sustaining fences would continue to be permanent for as many years as a post fence, there would be some good encouragement for adopting that style of fence, but the standards will shrink, and the locks will become loose, and if the cross pieces are not painted where they are joined together, they will soon rot away; and the stakes, or pins, unless of the best of timber, and nearly as large as a fence post, will soon become loose and rotten, and the first heavy gale of wind will scatter the fragments as if it were a little boy's cob house. Patentees of self-sustaining fences will denounce me as a ninny for such words against their fences; but unless there shall a style of fence appear, which has never come under my observation, entirely different from any that is now in use, what has been penned will prove true to the letter in the experience of every one who may give such fences a fair trial. A good post and board fence is the fence for thrifty farmers; one that will stand firmly and erect, without repairs, for a score of years; and one that will not crouch, like a sneaking cur before a bullock, when he shakes his horns at it. When fence posts can be purchased for ten or twelve cents each, it will be the wisest policy and the cheapest, and infinitely better in the end, to make post and board fences, instead of being perplexed with such vexatious appendages as self-sustaining board fences.

126. But as there is such an insatiable thirst in many Americans for new things, I deem it best to furnish some specimens of

self-sustaining fence; and those who choose can adopt them in fence building, if they prefer either style, to a post and board fence. There are a number of patents on self-sustaining zigzag board fences, which, when they are *new*, appear quite substantial and efficient; but I consider them a poor apology for a fence. If a self-sustaining board fence is needed of a zigzag style, the best way is, to nail the boards to pieces of scantling as long as the height of the fence, having the corner standards, to which one end of two panels is nailed, standing on flat stone. But such a style of fence requires one-third more lumber than a straight fence, although it will be almost equal to a post fence in point of permanency and durability; and it will occupy a large space of ground, too much for an ordinary fence. It is poor economy to build a zigzag board fence. All self-sustaining fences that I have ever seen, were very deficient in point of durability for a number of years. But there are several styles of board fence which are not exactly self-sustaining, although they pass under that name. For a permanent fence, let me have a good post and board fence, even when a self-sustaining fence can be made for about half the expense of it; and, at the end of twenty-five or thirty years, if the expense is not in favor of the post and board fence, I am no arithmetician.

FIG. 35.

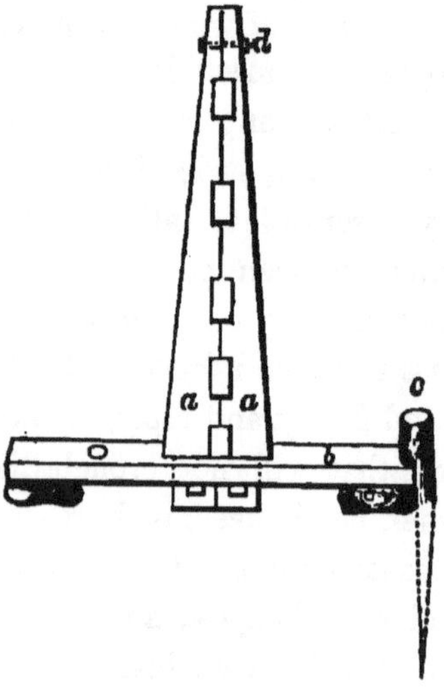

STANDARD FOR SURFACE
BOARD FENCE.

127. It is very convenient, many times, to have what is called *a surface fence;* and in some localities, where the soil is not deep enough to set fence posts on account of rocks, it is desirable to have some device by means of which the standards of a fence may be kept erect. At Fig. 35 is a representation of a standard for board fence, which subserves a very good purpose for that object, and many prefer it to posts.

a a are two standards, made of 1¼ inch lumber, about seven inches wide at bottom and three at top, with gains sawed in the edges for receiving the ends of the fence boards. *b* is a sill, about three feet long, two inches thick, and four inches wide. The two standards pass through the sill, and are fastened with keys on the under side of it. Keys are preferable to pins, because, if the standards shrink a little, they can be tightened a little with keys; but with pins through the sills, they could not be tightened so readily. The tops of the standards are fastened with a band, or small carriage bolt, after the boards are put in the gains. The ends of the sills are supported by flat stones, or blocks of wood, and kept in place by stakes well driven into the ground, as at *c*. The gains in every alternate standard may be just wide enough to receive the thickness of each board. Notches are sawed in one side of the boards to prevent their sliding endwise. This style of fence is made without any nails, and it can all be made in the workshop, and carried to the field, and put up in a short period of time. If it is preferred, stakes

FIG. 36.

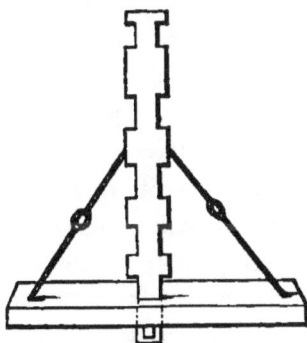

STANDARD FOR SURFACE
BOARD FENCE.

FIG. 37.

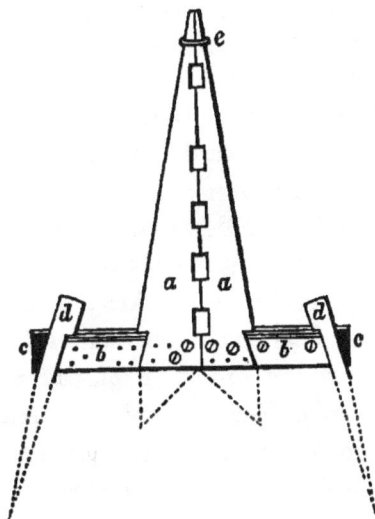

GABRIEL'S PATENT PORTABLE BOARD
FENCE.

can be driven through holes near the ends of the sills for holding them in place.

128. Fig. 36 represents a different style of standard. The sills may be about two by four inches square, with the standards passing through and keyed on the under side. Each side is braced with wires, twisted together to hold it firm. When wire braces are used and twisted up tightly, there is no need of keying or pinning the standard. The gains may be sawed in the standard with a circular saw, about half an inch deep, and the boards nailed to it. Large flat stones may be used for sills; or, the standards may be set on a rock, and the bottom kept from moving by drilling a half-inch hole one inch deep in the rock, and two inches deep in the bottom of the standard, and putting in a half-inch iron dowel pin. Holes are drilled for the wire braces, and made fast in the rocks by melted lead, and the wires afterwards twisted together. Or a heavy stone may be placed on each end of a sill, to keep the fence in the proper position; but it will require nearly as much timber for the sills and standards as it would for posts; and it will require more labor to make the standards, than it would to set the posts three feet deep.

129. Fig. 37 represents Gabriel's patent portable board fence standard, which appears to meet with much approbation by most farmers. a a are standards made of inch boards, fastened to the top after the boards are put in the gains by a wooden yoke, or a little band of iron e; c c is a horizontal strip of board, about thirty inches long and five wide; and the standards may be nailed or screwed to it at the bottom. b b are two pieces of boards fitted neatly between the stakes d d and the standards, and firmly nailed to the board c c. The stakes d d are one inch thick. Another board of the size of c c must be nailed on the opposite side of the standards. The standards may extend below the sills, as shown by the dotted lines, and the fence rest on these points; or the ends of the sills may rest on stones. The standards for this fence may all be made in the workshop; but if the fence is to be set up where it deviates from one direct horizontal line, the gains in the edges of the fence boards should not be made until the time when the fence is to be put up. In making such a fence up or down a hill, the standards should all be set perpendicularly, and not at a right

angle with the surface of the ground.   Many farmers like a style
of fence called

HALF WIRE AND HALF WOOD FENCE,

130. Or, a board and wire fence.   The posts for such a fence
may be set, as shown at Fig. 34, paragraph 124, and a top board
and bottom board be nailed on above the ridge of earth, and two or
three wires fastened on the posts, between these boards, with
staples.   Three wires between the bottom and top boards, when
there is a ridge of earth along the fence, will turn sheep.

131. I have a fence four and a half feet high, thirty rods in
length, with only a top sugar maple-board four inches wide, and
three number eleven wires below it, with a ridge of earth twenty
inches high, which has turned most effectually, ever since it was
built, (four years since,) calves, cows, oxen, horses and colts; and
they have never broken a wire, although crops were always on
the other side of it.   I own a young bull, which made many
desperate efforts to get through it, without any success.   The
posts are eight feet apart, and the wires were never strained as
they ought to have been, because it was my first experiment in
using wire; and I see no reason, at present, why that fence will
not remain permanent, as it now is, for ten or fifteen years to
come.   I state this to show what three small wires and one narrow board have done.

132. Fig. 38 represents a substantial barn-yard board fence.
As such fences should always be tight, i. e., no spaces between
the boards, on account of shielding animals from cold winds when
they are not in their stalls, the best, neatest, and most economical
manner of building them is, to set the posts three feet deep, and
frame the rails, which should be of scantling, not less than three
by three inches square, from post to post, as in building picket
fence, and nail the boards to the *corners* instead of the sides
of the rails. (See Fig. 49.)   Such a fence should be about
six feet high.   In that case the top rail should be about four
feet from the ground, and the bottom rail about twenty inches
from the ground.   It looks better and is better, all things

5*

considered, to allow the boards to extend nearly to the ground, instead of nailing on a bottom board, horizontally, below the vertical boards, as is often done; and, more than all this,

FIG. 38.

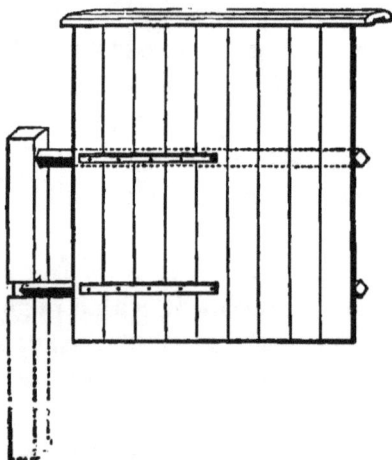

SECTION OF BARN-YARD FENCE.

boards will not wear out as soon in the weather, when placed vertically, as when in a horizontal position.   It is a good idea to place a row of flat stones under the bottom of the boards of such a fence, in order to keep them dryer, by keeping away weeds and grass.   After the boards are nailed on the yard side of the fence, battens two inches wide, portions of which are shown, should be nailed over the boards, into each rail, with large nails.   A line should then be struck at the tops of the boards, and all sawed off straight, and a *cap* nailed on the top of the boards, which is made of strips of two-inch plank, two and a half or three inches wide, and two inches thick, with a groove half an inch deep, and an inch wide on the under side of it, for receiving the tops of the boards.   The corners of the cap are to be planed off before nailing on.   This cap keeps the tops of boards dry, and prevents their springing, and warping in and out, and makes a fence much stronger, besides adding very greatly to its workmanlike appearance.   If it is preferred to cut picket points in the top ends of the boards, it can be done most expeditiously by marking them all out with a pattern, and cutting them with a circular horse saw.

THE RIB FENCE.

133. Fig. 39 represents a kind of fence which suits the fancy of some men better than any other style of fence. The posts are about five or six inches square, and three-inch holes bored in the sides, two inches deep, for the ribs. The ribs are about two and a half inches square. They may enter the posts by mortise and tenon, although that style increases the labor of making it. The ribs, if square, should be put in as shown in the cut, with one corner upwards and one

FIG. 39.

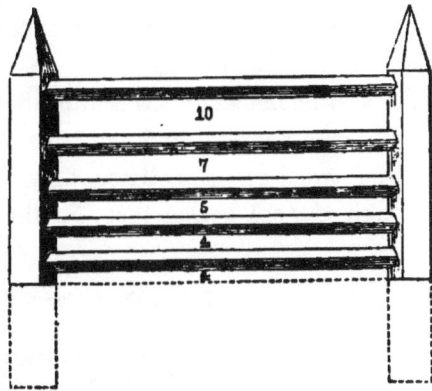

RIB FENCE.

downwards, as they will make less space between them than if they were placed with a flat side up. The ribs should be about eight feet long, and with the corners cut off a little the ends will enter a three-inch hole. (See BORING POSTS WITH BORING MACHINE, Fig. 122.)

134. By adjusting a three-inch auger by the side of a railway horse-power, so as to make about as many revolutions in a minute as the band wheel, with one horse a man could bore a large lot of posts in a few hours. And as the ribs are put up when the posts are set, one workman would be able to put up a long string of it in a day. A line should be stretched, when setting the posts, parallel with the top rib, so that one panel will not pitch down nor slant up too much. When the ribs are put in place the ends should be well painted. This is a very economical and substantial fence, requiring no nails, pins, nor wires. Should a rail or rib get broken at the middle of a fence, dig one post loose on one side of it, and lean it to one side of the fence and put in a new rib, and then set it up and fasten the post in its former

erect position. Five ribs in that position will give a width of
nearly eighteen inches, and the spaces thirty inches, which makes
a fence four feet high; but the two lower ribs may be left out
and a ridge of earth thrown up in their place, which would be
as effectual as a fence five feet high. A two-inch round tenon at
the ends of the ribs would be proportionally stronger than the
middle of the same stick, eight or ten feet long, when of the size
mentioned. Where the timber is all hard wood, it would be
quite as economical to saw it into ribs two and a half inches square
as into inch boards; and put them up with nails, because boards
of hard wood are, sometimes, ugly and hard things to drive nails
through without boring them for the nails.

SECTION III.—WIRE FENCE.

"Glorious triumphs wire brings !
Wire fences, wire springs !
Wire into "hoops" is curled !
Wire soon will span the world."—INGERSOLL.

135. The time has been, and it was but a few years ago, too,
when wire fences were considered by the great majority of people as an unwise experiment, which could never possibly be
attended with success; and, even in the last decade of years, wire
fences have been decried and condemned by many able corres-
pondents of agricultural journals, which were sound on all the
other ordinary subjects connected with the operations of the farm;
and in some instances the editors themselves have imbibed the false
inspiration, and have coincided with their respected correspond-
ents in their views with regard to the certain failure of wire
fences, and have denounced wire fence from beginning to end as
an "exploded humbug." For many years wire fences were
laughed at by almost every one who passed by; and every old
fogy would wag his head and denounce the inventor, and builders also, as "incorrigible ninnies," and would utter all sorts of
most direful prognostications against wire fence, and everything
else that resembled it.

136. It cannot be denied that there have been scores and hundreds of instances in building wire fence, in which it would seem that the experiment was a most complete failure; and many farmers, who have ever entertained a very favorable opinion of wire fences, when they have come to see the report of those who have experimented (very superficially) in building such fence, "that wire fence could not be relied upon for protecting cultivated fields from unruly cattle," have been fully deterred from ever attempting to build a fence of wire, notwithstanding their own good judgment has always seemed to be in favor of such a fence as a most complete success. If a substantial, permanent, and impassable fence can be built of wire, what mean so many failures in building it? Why so many rods of worthless, inefficient obstruction between adjoining fields, denominated wire fence, which animals of all kinds pass and repass at pleasure? The reason is plain, and the remedy is very obvious and simple, and the failures may all be expressed in one short sentence—*imperfect construction.* Because one or two, or one hundred, individuals have failed in building an impassable wire fence, it affords no plausible reason why a most permanent and impassable fence may not be erected of the same materials. We have no hesitancy in affirming, that the failures have always been, without one single exception, attributable to imperfect construction, and not to any deficiency or imperfection of the materials used for such a purpose.

137. But fences of wire are no longer viewed as an object of doubtful utility by men of enterprise and of practical common sense, in building fences of any kind. Wire fences, with posts of durable wood or of iron, are among the most permanent, impassable, and economical fences which can be erected, especially in localities where materials, in the shape of stone or wood, cannot be obtained at a fair price. It argues a great destitution of the knowledge of the strength and efficiency of materials, to admit that a wire fence cannot be erected, which will turn, most effectually, the most unruly animals that any one has no fears of giving their liberty in the open fields.

138. The chief difficulty, which has been almost invariably the cause of failure in the permanency of a wire fence, is, the snapping of the wires by animals bounding along, and plunging, when in full speed, against them. It is an unusual thing for wires which are destitute of flaws, to be broken by the simple pushing and hooking of an animal. A bullock, or any other animal, will not thrust very powerfully with his nose or neck against a bare wire, consequently a small wire will resist effectually all the force that an animal is disposed to apply to it. But when an animal plunges against a wire with rapid fury, something must give way, or he will be, perhaps, a little harmed by such an unceremonious rencounter. If we stretch up a lot of wires, and animals have nothing to admonish them that they are approaching an obstruction, when running at full speed, a wire fence is a dangerous obstruction to place in a field. When a wire fence is built thus, it is very imperfectly constructed; and if the wires should be snapped asunder, or the fence completely demolished, or animals seriously injured, we need not be filled with wonder, because something of that nature would be only a natural and certain result. When a wire fence is erected in a proper manner, animals will very soon learn where it stands, and they will no sooner plunge against it than they will against a rail or a board fence. When a wire fence is built across a field where the ground is entirely smooth on both sides of it, and also where it stands, if the posts are some ten or twelve feet apart, and nothing but bare wires from post to post, colts and young cattle, when running, unless they have learned that there is an impassable obstruction along the line of posts, will be very liable to attempt to pass between the posts, when running at full speed. But if a ridge of earth, from one to two feet high, be thrown up along the posts, or if a narrow board be nailed on the posts at the top, or even at the bottom, they will never plunge against it when running. It is always best to have a narrow board at the top of the posts, when it can be obtained readily. But in case boards are not at hand, a ridge of earth along the posts is a consideration of the first importance in building wire fences, because, if animals do not see

the wire they will see the ridge of earth, and will quickly learn
that wires are above it.

WIRE.

139. Wire is obtained at the manufactory or at hardware
stores in large coils; and sometimes the wire of a large coil will
be several hundred feet in length, and sometimes there will be a
score or more of pieces in one coil.   In purchasing wire for fences,
the builder should see to it that the coils are not all *pieces* of wire,
because it is much more convenient to make fences of long wire
than it is of a lot of pieces, the ends of which must be firmly
united before they can be used.

140. Wire for fences is usually annealed at the manufactory ; but
when it is not annealed before it is to be used, a whole coil or more
may be thrown on a brush heap when it is burning, or a small
fire may be kindled of wood for the purpose of heating it.   Wire
should not be thrown into a fire where it will become heated to a
white heat, lest it become materially injured.   All that is necessary is, to place it in a gentle fire that will heat it all to redness ;
and then, by allowing it to remain in the fire until it has all
burned down, and the wire has become cool, it will be as pliable
almost as lead, and very tenacious ; and the ends may be twisted
together without danger of breaking them.

141. The different sizes of fence wire are usually distinguished
by numbers.   The following, Fig. 40, will give a very correct

FIG. 40.

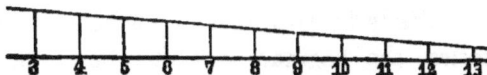

SIZES OF FENCE WIRE.

idea of the diameter of the various sizes, from three to thirteen,
which diminish regularly in size.   No. 3 wire is exactly one-
fourth of an inch in diameter ; No. 6 is about three-sixteenths in
diameter ; and No. 11 is about one-eighth in diameter.

142. Fig. 41 represents the most common mode of uniting the
ends of wires.   In uniting the ends of large wires, it is advisable
to have a small fire at hand in order to heat the ends when they

are to be twisted. An iron kettle full of burning coals will subserve a good purpose. It is not always an easy job to unite the ends of large wire when they are cold : but by heating them to

FIG. 41.

MANNER OF UNITING THE WIRES.

redness they may be bent very readily without danger of breaking them.

143. When a coil of wire is uncoiled, the coil should be rolled along like a hoop, or hung on a reel, until it is all uncoiled; because, if it be uncoiled by allowing it to run off at the side, the wire will be twisted just as many times around as there are rings in the coil. And twisting wire very often produces a kink or a number of kinks in it, and causes it to break before it has been strained to half its proper tension for a fence. When wire is to be coiled up, instead of winding it around anything as we do a cord or a string, the coil should be rolled over and over like a hoop, in order to avoid twisting it, or wound up on a reel.

144. The most expeditious manner of separating a wire, either large or small, is, to file a groove with a triangular file on two opposite sides; and if the wire be a large one, file entirely around it, and then bend it back and forth a few times, when it will separate very readily. It is by no means an easy matter to break a piece of annealed wire simply by bending it back and forth, unless it is held firmly by two pairs of pinchers or tongs.

145. Doubtless the beginner will often be in doubt as to the most proper size of wire for fences for ordinary purposes. One man will recommend No. 3, or 4, or 5, or some other number, as the most suitable; but he must exercise a little judgment of his own in this respect. As a general rule, those farmers who have built wire fences, and have reported their success in the Agricultural journals, have used twice or thrice as large wire as was necessary. Many have insisted on Nos. 3 and 4 as the only suitable sizes. There can be no disadvantage in using a large wire;

but when a wire two-thirds smaller, which costs only two-thirds as much, will subserve the same purpose as a larger one, the small one is to be preferred. There is no propriety whatever in using No. 3 or No. 4 wire in building ordinary fences. Wire of such a size would hold to draw out all the posts to which it might be attached, without breaking. Hitch a span of horses to one end, and let us see if, by fair drawing, they can separate it. By no means, if there are no flaws in it. There can be no consistency in using wire for fences which will resist three or four times as much as the posts to which they are attached. It is much better, and more economical also, to use a larger number of wires of a medium size, than to use a few very large ones. Wire should be strong enough to resist the force of the animals which it is designed to fence against. For fencing against small, peaceable animals, like sheep, No. 12 or 13 wire is sufficiently large and strong; and for horned cattle and horses, No. 9 will turn any-thing that wears horns; and any animal that will thrust into a fence, when it is properly made, with force enough to break a sound No. 11 wire, should not have liberty in an open field.

146. The manner of fastening the wires to the posts is a very important consideration. Bending the wires around sharp cor-ners of the posts should always be avoided, as wires are very liable to break when drawn tightly across a sharp corner. The ends of the wires may be fastened to the end post of the fence, by being passed entirely around it, after the corners have been rounded off a little; or they may be put through the post in a half-inch hole, and the ends of two of them twisted together; or, after the ends have been put through the post, they may be wrapped round a rod of wood, and the ends twisted round the same wire; or the ends, after having been put through the post, may be turned into holes in the post, and plugged up tightly with a hard wood plug. The wires may be fastened to the inter-mediate posts by driving staples over them, or by sawing gains in the sides of the posts for the wires, and nailing a strip of hard wood on every post, to keep the wires in the gains, or gashes.

Strips one inch by two square are sufficiently large; but if the posts should be square, they should be about as wide as the posts. But the best way of fastening the wires is, to bore half-inch holes through the posts for the wires, and, if thought best, pins of hard wood may be driven into each hole, which will hold them firmly. A little care and skill are necessary in boring the holes, in order to have them straight with the wires. If they should be bored crooked, or not in a line with the wires, the wires will bind on the sides of the holes with so much force that it will be very difficult, in straining them, to bring them up to the desired tension.

147. A pair of pliers for holding the wire, and a pair of pinchers for twisting it, are indispensable in putting up the wires, and a triangular file to aid in separating them.

148. Staples can be obtained at the hardware stores much cheaper than they can be made by hand. In driving them, if the posts are very hard, holes, a little smaller than the staples, should be bored in the posts, about half the length of the staples; otherwise the posts will be split, or the staples "stove up" before they are half driven in so as to hold the wire.

149. *The size of the posts* is another very important matter. It is not necessary to have posts for wire fence as large as they are for a board fence, providing they possess equal strength. One very common defect in wire fences have been posts that were too small. It is necessary to have posts which possess as much strength for a wire fence as for a board fence; otherwise a fence will be very deficient in fair proportion and symmetry. Many farmers have recommended posts for wire fence *only two inches square*. What a lack of common sense! Half a thrust by a heavy horse or ox, unless such posts were of the very best timber, would break them off at the surface of the ground; and, more than that, posts but two inches square are too small on the score of economy. It is true, that the wood of a small post may not decay sooner than a large one; but, allowing that they decay alike, when a half-inch or more of the outside of a small post is gone, there will be but little remaining; whereas, a half-inch of the wood

of a large post may decay, and it will be injured but little. Intermediate posts for wire fence should never be smaller than three by four inches at the lower end, and one and a half by three inches at the upper end. But if they were one inch or more larger than this each way, they would last many years longer, provided they have been cut at the best season of the year for cutting timber, and seasoned a year or more previous to setting them in the ground.

THE PRINCIPAL MANIPULATIONS IN MAKING A WIRE FENCE.

150. Suppose, for example, we wish to make a wire fence thirty or forty rods, more or less, in length : let a stake be set at each end, and then set a dozen or more stakes in range with these, one or two feet high ; plow a furrow where these stakes are standing, as deep as practicable, and straight as a line; by using a double team and a large plow, very much of the labor of digging the holes may be saved in a little time, by plowing a furrow twenty inches deep, or more (see DIGGING POST HOLES, 226). Set the straining-posts, Fig. 42, three and a half or four feet deep; they should be made of good timber, not less in size than three inches by six square, with two-inch auger

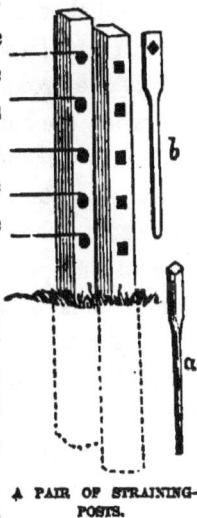

FIG. 42.

holes in one of them, and holes two inches square in the other. In order to have the holes correspond exactly with each other, the square holes should be made before the post is set, and after they are set the auger can be run through the square holes in order to bore those in the opposite post. These posts should be set at least three inches apart.

151. The *strainers* are represented at *a*, which should be made of the most firm and tenacious wood, about one foot in length, with four inches of one end four square, and the remainder turned round. The wires are put in a small hole through these strainers, and wound up with a wooden wrench *b*, three

A PAIR OF STRAINING-POSTS.

feet long, fitted to the square end of the strainers. When the wires are sufficiently tight let the strainer be driven into the square hole, and the wrench taken off. When a wire is to be loosened, drive the strainer a part of the way out, and let it unwind.

152. Set an anchor-post firmly at the other end of the fence. The anchor-post and straining-posts should never be more than forty rods apart. In making a long line of fence, straining-posts should be set every forty rods, in which case they will answer for both anchor-posts and straining-posts. They should also be well braced. Let them be set perpendicularly on the work side. Set one post about six rods from the straining-posts, perpendicularly, and then stretch two lines from this post to the straining-posts, one at the top, and one near the bottom, and set the posts by these lines. By having two lines, a workman will be able to get the posts more in a line than when only one line is used, with the plum rule (see Fig. 105) to keep them perpendicular. When all the posts are set between the anchor-post and straining-posts, let the top wire be attached and strained in part, or nearly as tight as it can be. The aim of the workman now is, to strike a line on the sides of the posts near the tops of them, which shall be parallel with the surface of the ground, were it even and smooth, and free from depressions and little knolls. If the surface of the ground is level, there will be no difficulty in doing it; but when the surface is undulating, it will require a little skill to do it in a workmanlike manner. Let the workman stand at the straining-posts, and look forward along the posts to a point where the ground begins to rise or descend. On the post which is nearest that point, raise the wire or fence line as high on that post as it is at the straining-posts, and support it with a nail. From this post cast the eye forward to the next point which deviates from a direct line, and support the line or wire on a post there with a nail. Let the top wire be adjusted after this manner throughout the entire length of the fence. Let the workman go back, and where the wire does not seem to be parallel with the surface of the ground, let it be adjusted by sticking a nail

under it where it seems to need raising a little, and a nail or two above it where it seems to be a little too high. Fig. 43 will give the builder some correct ideas on the sub-
ject, by which the
top wire or line is
properly adjusted,
parallel with the gen-
eral surface of the ground. Sharp angles in the rising and falling of the fence, as shown at *a b* of the preceding figure, should be avoided as much as practicable. After the top wire or line is adjusted as correctly as may be, let the workman stand away from it three or four rods, and walk the whole length of the fence at that distance from it; and if it appears all right, the next operation will be to mark off the distances on the sides of the posts, by means of a board six or eight inches wide, with notches made in it, like Fig. 44, as far apart as the holes are to be bored, or the wires to be fastened. The upper notch of the marking board should be placed even with the top wire, and then there will be no liability to mark some posts wrong.

FIG. 43

FIG. 44.—MARKING BOARD

153. Let the holes be bored with a good auger bit instead of an auger, as a man can bore more than twice as fast with a bit as with a small auger, and with much less fatigue. When the holes are bored, the wires may be put in and fastened at one end, and drawn up as tightly by hand as they can be, and then attached to the strainers, (see Fig. 42). It is a good practice to hitch a horse to one end of the wires, and draw them up as tightly as practicable before attaching them to the strainers. When it is necessary to unite a wire where it is in two parts, the junction should be midway between two posts, lest it should be too large to go through the hole in the posts. If the wires are to be fastened with staples, the staples should all be driven almost in before.

STRAINING THE WIRES.

154. Let the ends of the wires be firmly secured in the strainers, after having greased them with a little lard to make them turn easily, and draw them up as tight as possible without breaking the wrench or the strainers. About ten or fifteen rods from the straining-posts let a man step on the wires, and spring up and down on them; and if they stretch any let them be drawn up tighter. In warm weather the wires should be drawn up tight, as they expand in warm weather and contract in cold weather, about one inch in a hundred feet. As the cold weather comes on the wires may be loosened a little, as there is some danger of their breaking by their tendency to contract. There is but little danger, however, of their breaking by contracting.

155. When wires pass through the posts, some fence-makers prefer to drive a pin into each hole to keep the wires from rendering when anything presses against them; and when they are fastened by staples, some prefer to drive the staples tight on the wires. The most advisable way, probably, is, to fasten the wires at posts nearly a hundred feet apart, and then, if it is necessary to loosen or tighten them, it can be done at less expense than if they were fastened to every post.

156. The top board (see Fig. 46) may now be nailed on, and if desirable, the tops of the posts may be sawed off and a cap board put on. Or, what would be still less work, lét a scantling about three by three inches square be firmly nailed on the tops of the posts. It will add very much to the durability of both wires and boards to have them well painted with paint or coal, tar, or Japan, especially where they touch the posts and where the wires pass through the posts. By using a very small brush, paint can be worked into the holes on each side of the posts.

157. When posts are more than eight or ten feet apart, stay wires may be used to prevent an animal from thrusting his head between the wires of the fence. For this purpose No. 12 wire is sufficiently large, but should be well annealed before it is used. It is attached, first, to the top or bottom wire of the

fence, by wrapping one end two or three times around it, and then by passing once around each of the other wires, being careful to keep them at their proper distance apart.

158. The final operation now will be, to cast up a ridge of earth along the fence, twenty or more inches high, and seed it with grass seed. A wire fence should seldom be made without such a ridge.

159. Another mode of building wire fence, where posts of wood are scarce, and iron and stone abundant, is, to use *iron* posts and *stone* sills for the intermediate posts. Figure 45 represents an iron post, which is made of wrought iron, about three-eighths of an inch thick at the lower end, and three-six-teenths thick at top, and three-quarters *wide* at top, and an inch and a half *wide* at bottom, with shoulder on each side of the tenon, which is passed through the sill and fastened with a key, or nut and screw. A shoulder one-fourth of an inch deep on each side is sufficient, and the tenon may be tapered from the shoulder to the lower end of it, when a nut is used to fasten the posts; but an iron key is the best and cheapest, in the end of tenon, and is, usually, more convenient. The best way to obtain such posts would be, to give the dimensions of them to the proprietor of some manufactory of iron, and have them rolled out,

FIG. 45.

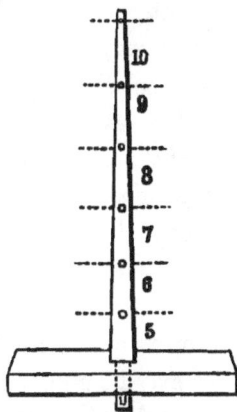

IRON POSTS FOR WIRE FENCE.

and holes punched for wires and keys, where machinery for such purposes is used, and then the expense of them would be but one cent or so on a pound more than for ordinary bars of iron. The sills may be made of almost any kind of stone. A sill six inches wide and four thick, and three feet in length, is a good size. Stone for flagging, which are not more than two inches thick, may be used for that purpose, providing they are not less than three feet long and eighteen or twenty inches wide. Bowlders and blocks of square stone, weighing several hundred pounds each, may be used by drilling holes in them three or four inches deep, and by placing the iron tenon in the hole, and by pouring in melted lead to make it solid.   Such posts may also be fastened into blocks of wood, or into plugs of wood driven into the ground as deep as for fence posts.

160. In making a wire fence with iron posts inserted in sills of stone, it is best to form a ridge of earth where the fence is to stand, about twenty inches high, and three feet wide on the top, and seed it with grass seed, allowing it to settle one season; and then place the sills in which the iron posts have been set, on the *surface* of the ridge, in a line with each other, as in setting posts of wood. Bowlders, into which posts have been set, may be sunk a few inches into the ridge in order to make the holes in the posts stand in range with each other.   Posts set in this manner may seem to some people like a very superficial fabric, possessing little permanency, but after such posts have been placed a few weeks, let a man move them, if he can, by taking hold of the iron posts. Such posts may be placed thirty feet apart on the ridge, and two or three stay wires put on the main wires, between the posts. In order to prevent swine from lifting the bottom wire, the stay wires may be first fastened to the stakes driven into the ridge, and then passed around the other wires to the top wire. After the wires have been put in and strained, the holes may be plugged with hard wood to keep them from rendering back and forth when the wires are pressed sideways. A fence made after this plan will remain permanent, without doubt, as long as one man usually wants a fence. If the posts should ever become a little inclined, they may be readily set erect by raising one end of the sills.

THE NUMBER OF WIRES

161. In a fence will always depend upon the size of the animals to be turned by the fence. No sheep, cattle, or swine, of a hundred pounds weight, will be able to pass between the wires of a fence like Fig. 46, when the wires are well strained. In merely

fencing against horned cattle and horses, there is no
necessity of having any of
the wires less than eight or
ten inches apart, and they
should never be *more than
ten inches apart.* The bottom wires, which are de-
signed to turn sheep and
swine, may be no larger
than number twelve or
thirteen, as no sheep nor

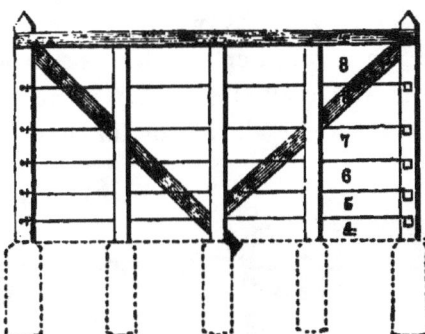

Fig. 46.

SECTION OF WIRE FENCE.

swine will be able to break a wire of that size. The strongest wires
should always be placed about as high as the shoulders of horned
cattle and horses.

162. There are several modes of straining the wires of a fence
besides the one noticed in paragraph 154, but for convenience,
cheapness, efficiency and practicability, they are inferior to this.
Straining wires by having a small iron screw and swivel in each
wire is a good way, but is usually too expensive. There are
modes of having all the wires pass through holes in an upright
roller, and then with an iron lever the roller is turned round, and
the wires are strained from the ends of the fence towards the middle of the fence, by being wound up on the roller from each way.
But this is a very inefficient manner of straining wires, and he
who adopts it will be glad to abandon it before he has been able
to bring all the wires to a uniform tension. There are several
other very neat modes of fastening wires to the posts, but some
are too expensive, and others are not worthy of adopting.

THE LOWELL WIRE FENCING.

163. Fig. 47 represents a style of wire fencing which cannot
fail, ultimately, to supersede every other style of wire fencing.
Wire of every size is woven into cloth, or network, by machinery, with the meshes of various sizes. The meshes are usually
about eight inches wide. After the wires are woven, the whole

6

of it is well coated with Japan, which is made from asphaltum, which prevents its rusting. About 20 or 25 rods in length of it are then rolled up in bales, as shown by the figure, which weigh from 200 to 300 lbs.; when it can be transported to any locality, and put up by almost any farmer. The very efficient manner in

FIG. 47.

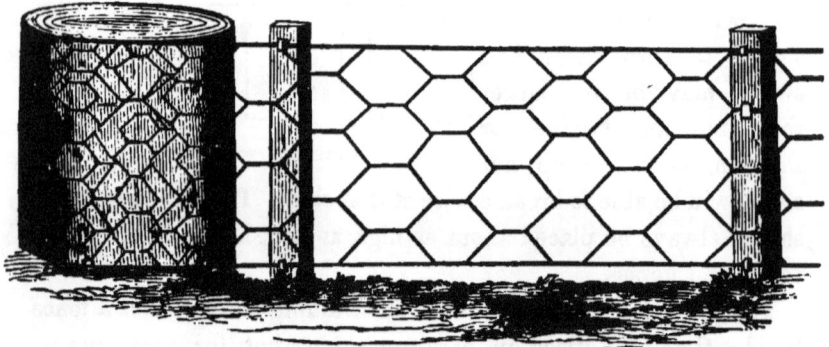

A BALE OF LOWELL WIRE FENCING.

which the meshes are formed by the weaving of the wires, is represented by Fig. 48. It will require the application of a force almost equal to the strength of the wires to separate the meshes, by drawing on two of them which are twisted together.

164. The COST of such fencing depends on the width of the cloth and the size of the wire, varying from 75c. to $2.50 per lineal rod. The cut represents a strip of network thirty inches wide, with eight-inch meshes, made of Nos. 10 and 12 wire, weighing five and three-quarter lbs. per rod, and is sold for 75c. per rod. W. J. Johnson, Boston, Mass., manufacturer, will send an illustrated catalogue of the various kinds and sizes which he manufactures.

165. *How to make the fence.*—Set the posts from ten to twenty feet apart, according to the size of the wire and weight of cloth per lineal rod. If the cloth is narrow, cast up a ridge of earth along the posts. Set the straining-posts, which are represented at Fig. 42, and attach wires to the cloth, and wind them up with the strainers. When there are a number of straight strands of

wire in the cloth, they may be wound on the strainers. Fasten the cloth to the posts with small staples driven over the wires.

166. In putting up such fence where the surface of the ground is undulating, the young farmer will meet with a difficulty which will puzzle many experienced mechanics to obviate. The wider the cloth is, the greater will be the difficulty. When a portion

FIG. 48.

MANNER OF WEAVING THE WIRES.

of such cloth is put up on a straight course, and then the ground rises abruptly, the *bottom* of the cloth will be tight, and the top, or upper edge, will be very loose. In such cases a strip of cloth may be put up in a horizontal position, or at a given angle, and another strip put up at another angle, with a pair of straining-posts between them, so as to tighten the strips on both sides of the straining-posts by one set of strainers. In any instance when either the lower or upper side of the cloth cannot be made tight, in consequence of the inequalities of the ground, cut one side of the cloth and take out a gore, or set straining posts, as already directed.

SECTION 4.—PICKET FENCE.

"The good old picket fences there surround
The garden, vineyard, and the furrowed ground,
To turn marauders, and nocturnal prigs,
And roaming curs, and pesty, rooting pigs,
And chanticleer, with majesty and pride,
Strutting along, with partly by his side."—EDWARDS.

167. There is probably a larger number of different styles of picket fence than of any other variety of fence, and the most fastidious can always find some style, among so great a variety, that will harmonize with his taste and fancy. There is greater adaptedness in picket fences to many purposes than in any other kind of fence; and in some instances picket fence will subserve a purpose which could not, practically, be accomplished with any other kind of fence. As picket fences may be built of so many different styles, he who aims to erect a picket fence which shall be in good taste and harmony with his grounds and buildings, if he knows exactly what he most desires, is not compelled to search a great length of time to find a style of fence which will come fully up to his ideas of what a picket fence should be. There is an appearance in picket fence which almost always affects surrounding objects more or less; and not unfrequently a picket fence of correct style, to harmonize with surrounding objects, imparts a beauty to the scenery which a board fence of the neatest style, or a stone fence, or hedge fence, would never impart. Picket fences have all the excellencies which can possibly be combined in any style of fence; they may be strong or fragile, costly or cheap, neat and tasty, or awkward and homely, or ornamental, or plain, to any desirable degree. No style of fence, in my own estimation, adds more to the beauty of a spacious dooryard, or lawn, than a tasty picket fence. Although a board fence may be made as ornamental and tasty as such materials will admit of, still a picket fence seems never to fail to satisfy the caprice of the most fanciful.

168. There is also an efficiency in many kinds of picket fence which no other kind of fence possesses. A picket fence will not only stop fowls from roaming on forbidden ground, but will often be the means of keeping the productions of the fruit-yard and garden in safety from pilfering interlopers, who would climb over a board fence and carry off, without difficulty, the delicious booty. A picket fence is usually a difficult, dangerous fence to climb over; and for this reason, when orchards and fruit-yards and gardens have been encircled with a substantial picket fence, the pro-

prietors have feasted on their own fruit and vegetables, which they would never have tasted had their grounds been enclosed by any other kind of fence. When a fruit-pilferer is passing a fruit-yard which is enclosed with a board fence that he can hop over at any place, he is sure to glut his swinish palate with anything within his sight; whereas, had there been a picket fence he would have passed on, and found his booty somewhere else. Horses, horned cattle, and almost every other kind of animals, fowls and other bipeds, which belong to a higher order of creatures, not excepted, which need to be fenced against, are usually more shy of a picket fence than of any other style of fence. Dogs will many times run many rods around a picket fence rather than jump over it, when, if a board fence of the same height were there, they would have bounded over it without any hesitancy. This is particularly the case if the tops of the pickets are pointed. Fowls, in flying over a picket fence, generally aim to perch on the top of the pickets, as they are accustomed to do on other fences ; but, as pointed pickets are not very convenient for them to stand upon, they soon learn that it is best to fly over without touching it, which they seldom do, or keep on their own side of it. Filching marauders, in quest of good fruit, fear the points of pickets, lest they, by an inadvertant hold or step, should meet with their merited deserts.

169. In point of economy in dollars and cents, a picket fence may cost more than a board fence, or it may not cost as much. The height of each fence being the same, there will be little, if any, difference in the cost of the rough materials; but the labor of building according to a given style will increase or diminish that cost, according to the amount of labor bestowed upon it. The style of casing and capping the posts, or not casing them; the style of rails and bottom boards; and the style of the tops of the pickets, all affect the expense of a fence, in proportion to the amount of labor required in dressing out and preparing the materials. There is often an unnecessary amount of labor expended in making the tops of pickets very ornamental, by cutting them of different forms, which only increases the expense, without

adding at all to its beauty or efficiency. The plainer the work is, in making a picket fence, and the less cut work in the shape of gains and moldings there is about it, the neater it appears.

170. *The width of pickets*, and the width of *spaces between them*, is a consideration which affects the symmetry and expense of a fence far more than most people are wont to suppose. Pickets are often made one-third or two-thirds wider than is necessary for strength, to say nothing for or against their beauty; and the spaces between them are too frequently twice or thrice as narrow as they might be, without detracting at all from the efficiency of the fence, or from its real beauty. Pickets are often four inches wide, and the space between them but two inches; in which case a width of pickets eight inches wide is required for every foot in length of a fence. But if the pickets were two inches wide, which is sufficiently wide for ordinary fences, with two-inch spaces, there will be a saving of just one quarter of the lumber for the pickets required for a rod in length. But when pickets are a plump inch thick, and not more than four feet long, a fence will look quite as well when the pickets are an inch and a half wide, with spaces two and a half or three inches in width. It is a thing of rare occurrence, that pickets of the size last mentioned are ever broken by animals thrusting against them, or by attempting to pass them in any way. When pickets are an inch and a half wide, and the spaces between them two and a half wide, only a width of four and a half inches of pickets is required for a foot in length of fence. Spaces two and a half inches wide are narrow enough to stop any kind of fowls, or pigs and lambs.

171. Fig. 49 represents a neat, cheap, durable and substantial lawn fence, and may be three and a half to four and a half feet high, to suit the fancy. The top of the pickets should extend not less than eight inches above the top rail; and if the fence is four feet or more in height, they should extend not less than ten inches above the rail. The rails should be about three inches square, in which case the posts may be twelve feet apart, and should be fitted to the posts as shown in the figure, so that the pickets may be nailed to a *corner* of the rails instead of the side.

Rails are much stronger, both laterally and vertically, when placed in this position, than when they are placed with one *side* up. And besides this, the surface of conjunction between the pickets and rails is so small, that there is little or no liability to decay, as is the case when pickets are nailed to the flat side of rails. Every

FIG. 49.

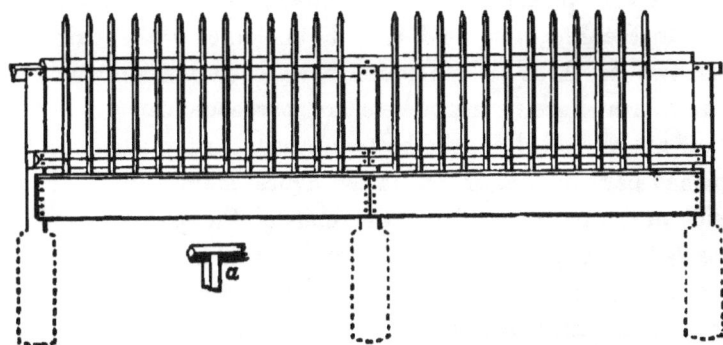

A LAWN PICKET FENCE.

one who has had any experience in picket fence, knows that when pickets are nailed to the flat side of rails, water will often get between them and cause them to decay in that place in a few years. The bottom rail may be halved and let into gains in the posts, or attached by mortises and tenons; and the strongest mode of putting up the top rail (unless by mortises and tenons) is, in sawing off the tops of the posts, to saw from each side of the posts, with cut slanting downwards, so that the top rail will fit the cut neatly, as shown at *a* in the figure. The top rails may then be nailed, as shown at the top of the posts. Where the rails and posts touch each other, they should be painted to preserve them from decay.

172. The pickets may be sawed out of inch boards with a power circular saw, as it is difficult to saw pickets of so small a size from logs at the saw-mill. After they are dressed out, the tops may be sawed off in a mitre-box with a hand saw, or with a small circular saw. In nailing them on the rails, let a chalk-line be stretched as high above the rails as the tops of the pickets

are to extend, supporting it in the middle, if it sags a little, with a picket slightly tacked to the rails. Dress out a space-board as wide as the spaces, and be particular to have both ends of an exact width. Drive a long nail in one side of it, near the top, so that it can be hung on the top rail; now nail on the first picket, and plumb the edge on one side. Hang on the space-board, and put up another picket to the side of the space-board, with the top barely to the line, and hold it with one knee while nailing it. After two or three pickets more have been put up, apply the plumb-rule and see if the pickets are perpendicular. After the pickets are all nailed on, the bottom board, the top edge of which is planed bevelling, as shown in the figure, may be nailed on the outside of the pickets. The lower ends of the pickets need not be sawed off even, as they are not in sight; and the bottom board may be nailed to the lower rail, subserving the additional purpose of a batten or ribbon; or it may be two or three inches below the rail. A ribbon about one inch by an inch and one-fourth square may be nailed on the pickets into the upper rail. But if each picket is nailed with two sixpenny nails to each rail—four nails in a picket—if the rails are of hard wood, a ribbon will be of little utility. A half round ribbon would look better than a square one. Near the middle of the bottom boards a few pickets may extend to the bottom of the board on the inside, and be nailed to it to strengthen it. The bottom board may be from eight to ten inches wide; or there may be two narrow boards four and a half or five inches wide, with a three or four-inch space between them, which is in quite as good keeping with a picket fence as one wide board. If it is desirable, the posts of such fence may be cased. But if the gate-posts and posts at the corners of the yard be cased, like those at Fig. 32, the fence will probably suit the majority of people quite as well as if every post were cased.

SELF-SUSTAINING PICKET FENCE.

173. Fig 50 represents a style of fence but little different from the one shown at Fig. 49. The pickets, bottom boards, rails and

ribbons, are all alike; but instead of posts, standards are used, one of which is shown at Fig 51. The sills *a* are made of scantling, not less than three by four inches square, and thirty inches or more long; and the standards, *b*, after the mortises have been

FIG. 50.

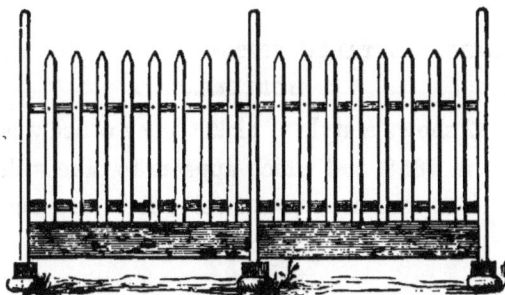

SELF-SUSTAINING PICKET FENCE.

made for the rails and bottom boards, are firmly united by mortise and tenon to the sills. Braces *c c* are then nailed on, or wires twisted together, as at Fig. 36. The standards may be of one and a half or two-inch plank, and may extend above tops of pickets, for holding one or two wires to prevent fowls from flying over it; or they may extend no higher

FIG. 51.

than the tops of the pickets. If preferred, the standards may be in two parts, like Fig. 35, or 37. The ends of the rails are halved together at the standards. The longer the rails and bottom boards are, the less will be the expense for the labor of building, as they may be run through one or two standards without having a joint at each one. When they are made in two parts, like Fig. 35,

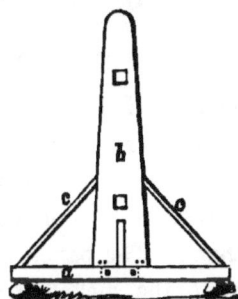

STANDARD FOR SELF SUS-
TAINING PICKET FENCE.

instead of fastening the tops with bolts or bands, a wooden yoke, made of two-inch plank, with a long mortise in it, is fitted to the standards, about half way from the tops of pickets to tops of standards. The ends and sides of the yokes are rounded a little, and give a very tasty appearance to the fence. The sills may be staked to the ground, or large stones

6*

laid on them, to keep them from being moved; or it will stand very firmly itself. But if fence posts of cedar, or yellow locust, or of some other durable timber, can be obtained for twelve or fifteen cents apiece, it will be the most economical, in the end, to build a fence like Fig. 49, with posts, instead of a self-sustaining fence, like Fig. 50, unless a portable fence is desired.

SELF-SUSTAINING PORTABLE ZIGZAG PATENT PICKET FENCE, OR HURDLES.

174. Fig. 52 shows a style of picket fence which was secured by letters patent in 1858, and which appears to take well where it is introduced. The rails are about twelve feet long and two inches

FIG. 52.

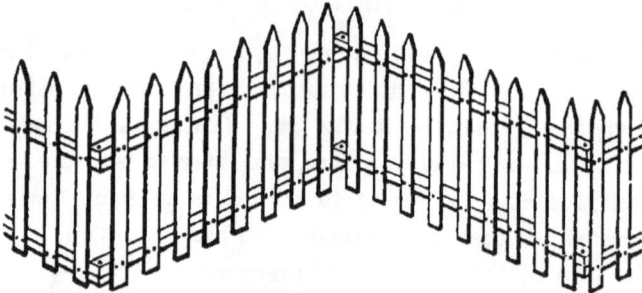

SELF-SUSTAINING PORTABLE PICKET FENCE, OR HURDLES.

square, of hard timber, and the pickets are two inches wide, pointed or not, with spaces to suit the builders. Each picket is nailed on with four nails, and the ends of rails are fastened together by pins of wood or iron, which are driven through two of them. The panels are all made in the shop, and care is taken to have the pickets nailed on at a right angle with the rails. The holes at the ends of the rails are bored straight through, in order to correspond with each other. If the pins are of iron, a rod three-eighths of an inch in diameter is large enough, or a three-quarter wooden pin. The panels are set up in a zigzag manner, with a worm of three or four feet, with flat stones under the corners; and if it does not warp and twist, and settle off sideways in a few years, or if the wind does not turn it topsy-turvy, and inside outwards, it will stand firmly until it rots down where it was set up. In the event of a hurricane, stakes might be driven in the ground at each corner, and the fence wired to them. It is a very good design for hurdles. When such a fence is made up and down hills, there should be a brace nailed from one rail to the other, to keep the panels in their proper shape.

POULTRY YARD FENCE.

175. Fig. 53 represents a very good style of picket fence for inclosing the kitchen garden or poultry yard. It may be built of any desirable height. It is best, usually, to have a bottom board,

FIG. 3.

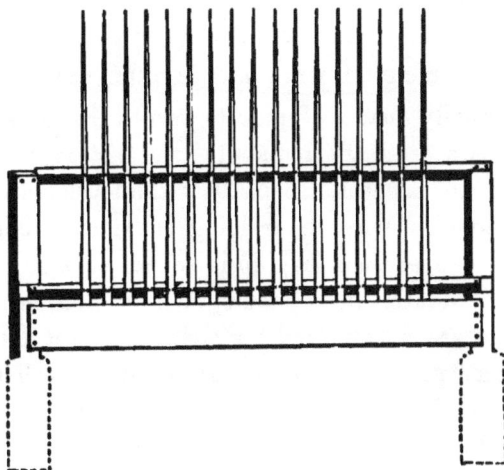

POULTRY YARD FENCE.

nine or ten inches wide, close to the ground, or a little ridge of earth may be thrown up under it, to keep chickens and ducklings, and such like, within the inclosure, and to exclude skunks and other "varmints" from the yard during the night. There is no necessity whatever, of building such a fence more than six feet high. Our domestic fowls do not need wings any more than they need fins; and if they are disposed to fly over the top of such a fence, let two or three inches of the end of one wing be clipped off, and they will soon make no effort to fly. The pickets for such a fence should be sawed tapering, as shown in the cut, about two and a half inches wide at the lower end, and not more than half an inch wide at the upper end; the space board should be (see 172) about two inches wide at the lower end, as a space of two inches is narrow enough, and the upper end must be enough wider than the lower end to correspond with the taper of the pickets. The space board need not be as long as the pickets. The object of sawing them tapering is, to save lumber, as the spaces can be much wider at the top than at the bottom of the pickets. It is always best, when it is not inconvenient, to nail on the pickets on the inside of the yard, so that fowls cannot fly on the top rail, and then fly over, or get through between the pickets.

THE FIELD, WIRE AND PICKET FENCE

176. Is usually made of pickets turned round and pointed, although square ones are frequently used instead of round ones; but they are not as neat, especially if the fence is to be painted, because the loops of wire, in straining, cut into the corners of the pickets much deeper than they do in round pickets. The pickets are cut out in a lathe in the same manner that broom handles and rakestales are cut out, and the ends are thrust into an instrument called a "pointer," holding cutters, which will sharpen the end of a picket in a second or two. They are from four to five feet long, and an inch or more in diameter. One inch in diameter is rather too small for a fence where cattle and horses run. Instead of wooden rails for holding the pickets, two wires are used, bent into loops, like Fig. 54, which represents a wire about the size of No. 10 or 11, ready for the pickets. It is very important

FIG. 54.

MANNER OF BENDING THE WIRE RAILS FOR A PICKET FENCE.

that the loops be bent with as much uniformity as possible; because, if both the upper and lower wires are not bent into loops as nearly alike as they can be conveniently, the pickets will not all stand in a perpendicular position. I have noticed fences made in this manner, where the pickets in some parts of the fence would lean more than the width of one space.

177. To aid the workman in making the loops, an instrument like Fig. 55 is necessary, which is made of cast-iron, and screwed fast to a work-bench, or held in a vise. The projections *a a* should be as large in diameter as the pickets, and FIG. 55. just as far apart as it is desirable to have the pick-ets when they are worked into the fence. In forming the loops, have the wire in a close coil, and after winding it around one of the iron pins

INSTRUMENT FOR BENDING THE WIRE.

a a, carry it to the other pin, winding the wire around that also. Now slip both loops off the tops of pins *a a*, and put the loop which was made last on the first pin. Again, slip off the loops and carry them back, making one loop every time they are slipped off. Great care should be exercised to carry the coil, in bending every loop, just so far forward, and to have the last loop put on the pin with the straight part of the wire between the loops at just such an angle with the pins; other-wise there will be a variation in the spaces, so that the pickets will lean a little in some places, and then will be perpendicular in some places, and then they will lean a little in other places in an opposite direction. An accurate workman will bend the loops with two pins; but the beginner had better have three pins instead of two, and then there will be no liability to make variations in the spaces. When three pins are used, all three of the loops must be slipped off the ends of them every time a loop is made. The wire should not be wound around as a string would be, but *the whole coil must be carried around the pin.* If this is not done, the wire will be *twisted* once around at every loop, which weak-ens its strength.

178. The posts for such a fence may be set as far apart as thought best, say from eight to twelve feet, with one side of them on a line with each other; and then the wires may be laid on the ground, and the pickets put in the loops, with the tops all in line.

When the ground is level, after the pickets have all been put in the loops, they may all be set up, and the wires strained (see Fig. 42) and fastened to each post, with staples driven over the wires into each post. Where the ground is undulating, it is a most difficult job to adjust the wires in such a manner that the pickets, up and down slopes, will all stand in a perpendicular position. Suppose, for instance, a fence is to be made fifteen or twenty rods on a level, and then to rise up a slope from ten to twenty rods. Let the wires be fastened to the post at the bottom of the slope of ground, and have a set of straining-posts at the top of the slope, and another set at the end of that part of the fence on level ground; and let the wires be strained from both ways. If either of the wires should seem to be looser than the other, and straining it more would incline the pickets from a perpendicular position, it would be best for a man to step on the wire which is the *tightest*, in several places, in order to bury the wires deeper in the wood; and then they can both be strained up to the desired tension.

179. The cost of such a fence will be easily estimated, and the fence very quickly made. The pickets, in this region, can be obtained, turned and pointed, for one dollar per hundred, four feet long. If they are one inch and a quarter in diameter, which is as small as they ever ought to be, with four-inch spaces, it will require about thirty-seven pickets for one rod of fence. The cost of the wire will depend on its size; and the cost of posts will depend on the locality, and the kind of posts used. Posts similar to Fig. 45 may be used for this style of fence, by passing a wire around the wire which holds the pickets, and through the holes in the post, and twisting it up tight. Instead of having the pickets four or more feet long, a ridge of earth two feet or so high may be cast up, and the pickets be made correspondingly shorter, which will lessen the cash cost, and at the same time increase the efficiency of the fence by means of the ridge of earth. When such a fence is put up in a workmanlike manner, and well painted, it harmonizes with the taste of many individuals better than almost any other style of fence.

180. Fig. 56 represents one of the most expensive kinds of

picket fence which can be built, but which harmonizes quite
well with the style of archi-
tecture of the buildings which
it is designed to surround.
The pickets are turned round
and pointed, and every alternate one passes through three
rails. The rails should be
bored with precision, and
with an auger or bit that
will cut a clean, smooth hole,
so that the pickets will fit
water-tight. If they are

FIG. 56.

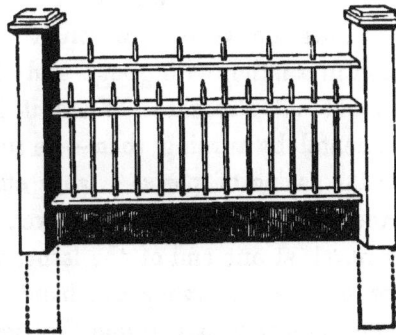

ORNAMENTAL ROUND PICKET FENCE.

painted, there will be no danger of their rotting in the rails on
account of the rain getting in the joints.

181. In making this or any other style of picket fence up a
slope, the rails for one panel must be fastened in the position of
inclination in which they are to be placed, when the fence is
built, and then, with the plumb rule, make a perpendicular mark
on the edges of the rails; after which it will be easy to adjust
the table on which the rails are laid when they are bored, in
order to have the holes of the desired angle. When the fence is
built on level ground, the holes for the pickets must be bored
through the rails at a right angle; but if bored at a right angle
when the fence is not on a level, the pickets will all lean in proportion to the steepness of the slope, which would look awkward
and very unworkmanlike.—I should not have mentioned these
particulars, had I not seen fences which were made by inexperienced workmen, with the pickets leaning down the slope at
about a right angle with the surface of the ground.—A modification of this style of

AN ORNAMENTAL LAWN FENCE,

182. A fine specimen of which may be seen encircling the
grounds of Mr. Andrus, of Ithaca, is made with turned posts
with acorn tops, and turned pickets with acorn tops, with two

rails through which the pickets pass, and a bottom board from eight to twelve inches wide. The fence last mentioned is about the neatest fence which I ever have seen for a lawn fence, and as durable as the wood of which it is made. The acorn tops are turned in a lathe, with gouge and chisel, after the other part has been cut out straight. When it is desired to make the posts ornamental by turning them—as turned posts are much cheaper than the casing of posts—a very efficient lathe may be fitted up for the purpose, without a mandrel, by having a point instead of a mandrel at one end of the lathe, with a screw and point at the other end, and allowing the band from the speed-wheel of the driving power to pass round the post instead of a pulley, on the mandrel. Or the posts might be mounted with a large wooden acorn, whether they were cased or not, or with any other orna-ment turned out of wood. But a turned post would be in better keeping with the pickets than a square one; and a man who understands turning, would turn out three posts sooner than he could case one. As we cannot drive such pickets in the rails, they should be just large enough to fill the holes, and so that they can be worked in by hand, without driving them. The pickets should be thoroughly seasoned; but the rails through which they pass may be green or half seasoned; because, when they shrink, they will hold the pickets tighter than when they have been seasoned before boring the holes.

AN ORNAMENTAL LATTICE FENCE

FIG. 57.

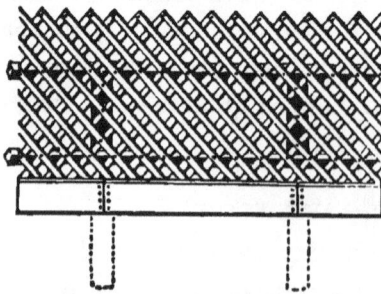

LATTICE FENCE.

183. Is shown at Fig. 57, which is often built between the gardens of adjoining own-ers, or on the back side of lawns or gardens. The rails and posts are put up in the same man-ner as for ordinary picket fence, with bottom board or not, as preferred; and the lattice is made of half-inch stuff, an inch

and a half or two inches wide, put up at a right angle to each other, or at an angle that will make the meshes or open spaces of a rhomboidal form, as in the illustration. The spaces may be of the width of the lattice strips, or from three to four inches wide. The tops of them should be screwed together, instead of nailing them, as screws will hold much better than nails. In putting on the strips, they should be kept at just such an angle; and the surfaces of conjunction, between the two courses of lattice, ought to be painted before the second course is nailed on.

THE FORMS OF PICKET TOPS

184. Are as numerous as the different styles of fence, and may be varied to suit the taste of the most fastidious. Many men like the plainest form possible for picket tops; and others, again, think a fence very incomplete and tasteless without ornamental tops of some style. The style of architecture in which the buildings are finished should determine, in a measure, the style of picket tops for the fence which encircles them. Figs. 58, 59, 60, represent turned pickets, and are particularly adapted to rural residences, with spacious dooryards, or lawns, beautifully embellished with a variety of shrubs and evergreens. The top of Fig. 58 is turned in the shape of an egg. The top of Fig. 59 is of any oblong conical form. Fig. 60 is of the form of an acorn.

FIGS. 58, 59, 60, 61, 62, 63, 64, 65, 66, 67, 68.

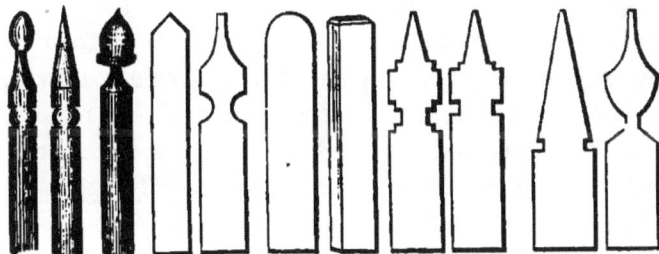

FORMS OF TOPS OF PICKETS.

If it were desirable to have the acorns larger than the main parts of the pickets, they might be turned separately, and a half-inch hole bored in the lower ends of the acorns, and tenons made no the upper ends of the pickets. When this mode is adopted, the acorns should be put on tight with good paint. The tenons can be cut with a tenon auger fitted to the mandrel of a lathe, and the acorns bored in a lathe, so that the expense of fitting them up in this manner would be quite small. The ends of round pickets are many times cut off square, or a little rounding, or pointed in a conical form, like those shown at Fig. 56. Fig. 61 represents one of the plainest styles of tops for square or flat pickets, with the corners sawed off. Fig. 67 is particularly adapted to inclosing buildings of gothic order of architecture. When buildings are of the very plainest order of architecture, Figs. 63 and 64 would correspond quite as well with the work on the buildings as any other style. Figs. 62 and 68 would be in good keeping with the architecture of a country villa, where the balconies and verandahs are encompassed with a balustrade of turned balusters. When buildings are finished with a heavy box cornice, with roof rather flat, and square columns with bevelled mouldings, instead of a bead, or ogee, or ovals, Figs. 65 and 66 would be in good keeping with the workmanship of them.

185. The most expeditious manner of rounding the tops like Fig. 63 is, to put fifty pickets or so in a gripe, with the top ends all even, flat sides together, and set them up by the side of a work-bench, letting them stand on the lower ends, and shave the corners nearly round with a drawing-knife, and then a few strokes with a joiner's hollow plane will make them all true. When all the corners are to be cut off, like Fig. 64, a lot of them may be put in a gripe, or they may be cornered with a drawing-knife while they are held in a vise, or they may all be nailed on the rails of the fence, and cornered with drawing-knife and bench plane. Figs. 62, 65, 66, 67, and 68, are usually put in a gripe with top ends even, and laid on the work-bench, and some parts cut with a back-saw and rabbet-plane, or a joiner's dado, or with planes called hollows and rounds. A joiner's dado, for such work, is a very useful tool. There are many other forms for picket tops, but these must suffice for a work of this character.

SECTON V.—STONE FENCE.

" Let me but place one stone within the wall,
While the stout masons, with great plumb and line,
Are laying the foundations broad and deep."—T. B. READ.

186. Stone fence or stone wall is about the best and most durable and efficient fence that can be erected, when it is properly built; but some farmers, who have an abundance of stone, have no confidence in stone fence, because it tumbles down so frequently in places, making gaps for the ingress or egress of hogs or sheep. But the difficulty is almost always attributable to imperfect workmanship in building. Stone walls are usually built by jobbers, who itinerate through the country in search of labor; and who sometimes understand the business well, and will lay up a good wall if their employer understands what constitutes a good wall, and insists on having his work done to order. Jobbers often will slight their jobs all they possibly can; and if they discover that their employer does not know when the work is well done, they will toss the stones together any how, and pocket their wages and be off. But if they have their orders how to lay up a wall, and these are insisted on at the time of negotiating, and the overseer watches the builders, there will be little danger of stone walls tumbling down in consequence of having been laid up in an unworkmanlike manner. Jobbers will often insist that it is just as well to lay the foundation stones on the surface of the ground, as it is to lay them eight or ten inches below the surface. If the foundation stones were always flat on the bottom, and large enough to extend entirely across the bottom of the wall, it would be just as well to lay them directly on the surface of the ground, because the entire wall would settle bodily and evenly, and, if the frost gets under it, it will be raised evenly. But when the foundation consists of small stones, either flat ones or bowlders, they will not settle perpendicularly. Large bowlders, when laid on the surface of the ground, will seldom settle straight down; because, when more rain runs off of one side than the other, the soil in one place will become softer than it is in others, and if

.

the stone rests on that point it will be very liable to slide a little sideways in that direction. And when the foundation is a part small bowlders, and another part large flat stones, and another portion something else, the wall will not all settle alike, and the frost will not lift it all alike; and, by constant lifting and letting down, here and there, the wall will begin to spread out in places, and in a few years will tumble down. A wall may often have the appearance of being well laid up, when in reality it has been very imperfectly done. It requires the exercise of good skill and judgment to place every stone in the best position, so that it will not roll or rock about at the slightest touch. Almost every stone has one side a little broader and flatter than the other sides; and the best side should be always laid down, so as to keep the stones from rocking about. If a stone has one good face side, and will lie more substantially with that side down, let it be laid in that position rather than to set it on the edge for the sake of having the face side outwards. It is desirable to have a straight and smooth face to the stones in a wall; but when this object cannot be secured without detracting from the permanence of it, it is best to place the best sides down, even if the wall is not quite as even and smooth as we could desire. A wall may be just as strong when the stones all have a rough and uneven face, as if those rough and uneven corners were all knocked off and a smooth face made on them. When jobbers lay up a wall, the stones of which are mostly small bowlders, if they are not watched closely they will lay up a row for each face, and then throw in small stones without any order at all, to fill up the middle. But such a wall will stand but a few years, because the sides will bulge out in a short time, and it will fall flat to the ground. The stones of a wall should all lie flatly, and lap on one another clear across the wall. Such a mode of laying stone will keep the wall from spreading or bulging out in places.

187. Stone walls are usually built by the perch or by the rod, running measure, with the foundation and top of a given width, and the wall of a given height. A perch of wall is sixteen and a half feet long, and a foot square, or sixteen and a half cubic

·feet. A rod of wall may be two feet wide or ten feet wide, and almost any given height, but always sixteen and a half feet long. When walls are laid up dry, the faces or sides should be laid battering, as they will stand much more permanently than when the sides are built perpendicularly. When the stones are mostly small and round, the faces should be laid more battering than when nearly all flat stones are used. If the stones of which a fence is to be made be nearly all large and flat ones, it is quite as well to lay the faces perpendicularly, as battering. The most important idea to be kept in mind in laying up a stone wall is, to have all the stones laid in such a manner as to bind the wall together, from face to face, so that the faces will not separate. The following figures will enable the farmer to know, if he is not a practical stone layer, whether a wall is laid up in a workmanlike manner, or whether it is performed in a slighty, job-cheating way. Fig. 69 represents a transverse section of a fence or stone wall which is laid so as to bind the two faces together, and which is done in a workmanlike manner. It will be perceived that there are no large holes between the stones, and that they are all laid flat, and not pitching this way and that way, and are laid so as to bind from face to face.

Fig. 70 shows a section of the same wall, and of the same size,

FIG. 69.	FIG. 70.

A SECTION OF WALL WELL LAID.   A SECTION OF WALL IMPROPERLY LAID.

and having faces equally as good as Fig. 69, but which is laid up very slightly, with merely a row of stones for each face, while the middle of the wall is filled with stones thrown in promiscuously, without being placed so as to lie firmly, and without having the face stones chocked on the *inside*. It is always very important to have the face stones well chocked on the inside. It is of little or no importance, usually, to chock stones on the face side. But if face stones are not well levelled up, and chocked up on the inside, especially in erecting a wall with a single face along a bank of earth, a wall is sure to bulge out and fall in a few years. This explains, in a great measure, why walls under a house or barn often bulge into the cellar and fall: the face stones were not well chocked on the inside; and a small force, produced by the superincumbent pressure of a heavy building, or by the freezing and expansion of the bank against which the wall is erected, will thrust the walls into the cellar. When long stones are laid in a stone wall, and the ends or sides within the wall do not rest one on the other, if they are not chocked clear to the ends, (not back six or eight inches from the ends,) the superincumbent pressure of the stones which rest on the ends of these long stones will tend to bring the ends together, and to separate the ends at the *face*, thus bringing them into a position to be forced or thrust easily from the centre of the wall.

MANIPULATIONS IN BUILDING A STONE WALL.

188. The first thing in building a stone fence usually is, to haul the stone; and they are usually thrown in a long row, exactly where the fence is to stand. This is always wrong. If stones are gathered from year to year, and hauled to a given place for the purpose of making a stone fence, the place where it is to stand should be staked off, and no stone should be dropped within four feet of the point where the face of the wall is to be, on both sides of it. If the wall is to be made six or eight feet wide on the bottom, no stone should be dropped nearer than six feet, especially if they are mostly large ones. It is a great fault with most farmers who build stone fence, to get their stones too close to the wall. It is but the work of a few moments to tumble a large stone six or eight feet; and it is far better to have a stone

one foot too far away than to have it a foot too close, to obstruct the progress of workmen.

189. When a stone wall is to be erected directly on the surface of the soil, the stones may all be dropped in a long pile where the fence is to be built, and then the workmen can commence at one end and carry the stones back and lay them up; and if they should not be abundant enough without carrying them too far in some places, they can be hauled along the side of the wall where they are needed. But we do not advocate the practice of erecting a stone wall on the surface of the ground, because it will not settle alike, unless the soil is of a uniform quality; and as the frosts of winter will raise it whenever it freezes beneath the foundation stones, it is very liable to freeze in freezing weather on the windward side *first;* and perhaps it will not freeze on the leeward side at all under the foundation stones. When this is the case, when one side of a stone wall is lifted by the frost, and the whole of it does not go up bodily, the stones will most of them be displaced a little. And again, supposing that it has all been lifted bodily and evenly, when the ground comes to thaw it is not at all likely to thaw evenly and settle uniformly. This will displace the stones a little, and a large number of such little displacements will soon produce bulges in the wall; and as soon as a wall commences bulging here and there a little, it is very liable to fall in a few years. In order to build a wall that will stand as long as any man will need a fence, the soil where the fence is to stand should all be thrown out, to a depth which will insure safety from settling, or from heaving by frost. In some localities the necessary depth will be only four inches, while in other places, perhaps in the same field, a depth of from eight to fourteen inches will be necessary. The foundation stones should be well laid, and chocked up all round. If a large stone, for instance, has but one flat, or smooth side, and has more the appearance of half of a globe than anything else, it is best to dig a hollow in the hard ground which will correspond well with the round side of it, and place it with the smooth or flat side up.

190. The width of the wall on the ground must be determined

in part by the size of the foundation stones. Should there be a good number of large bowlders, from four to five feet in diameter, it will be best to have the wall about that width. Between the bowlders let a row of good stones be laid for each face; now fill up the middle, and level it off entirely across the wall. Then if a large flat stone, or a number of them, can be obtained, lay them on the long way across the wall, and chock them well, so that a man may step on them without rocking or moving them. If there is a number of ill-shapen, rough-looking bowlders, let them be laid on such places as the tops of the large flat stones, and chock them well. Let the workmen be particular to break joints well, *i. e.*, let a stone be laid directly over the joints of the two below it; let long stones from each face of the wall extend inward as far as possible, and if a few can be obtained which will extend from face to face, they will render the wall doubly strong. When there are more large bowlders than can be laid in the foundation course, if two or three men cannot lift them two or three feet high on the wall, place a strong bench by the side of the wall, and lay a couple of plank, with one end on the bench and the other on the ground, and roll the large stones up this inclined plane with a cant-hook, and lay them carefully on the wall. In this way one man may handle stones with ease, and place them on the wall three or four feet from the ground, which three or four men could not lift directly to that place. When there is stone enough to build a wall, we will say three feet wide on the bottom, and two feet or two and a half on the top, and three feet high, if there should be enough bowlders about two feet in diam- eter to form a single row the entire length of the fence, they should be left till the wall is finished, from three to four feet high, as the case may be, and then these bowlders should be laid care- fully *on the top of the wall*, close together, and chocked up well all around. Such bowlders will be more efficient in building a fence when placed in such a part of the wall, than they would be if they were placed near the bottom; but they should be assorted, and those of a given size should be placed together. If we would make a fence five feet high, for example, it may be made three feet high as far as the bowlders, which are two feet in diameter, will extend; and then, if a lot of bowlders are but twenty inches in diameter, let the wall be laid a few inches higher, so that the tops of all the bowlders will be of a given height. It is a very great help, in putting on these *cope* stones, to lay two strips of boards, about three inches wide, and the longer the better, *on the top of the wall*, with their edges even with the faces of the wall, and then lay on the cope stones, letting them rest on these strips of boards. A board or plank as wide as the top of the wall is often laid on the top for the cope stones to rest on; but two strips of boards, I think, are preferable, because they are cheaper, and they do not require so much chocking on the sides, and any corners or points of the stones will set down *between* these strips much better than they would rest on a wide plank.

What has been penned in the preceding paragraphs has particular reference to walls which are made of all kinds of stone. We shall now notice the best mode of building

COBBLE-STONE FENCE.

191. When stone fences are made of small stones only, where there are no flat stones to bind the wall together, small strips of wood, called *binders*, about an inch wide and one-fourth of an inch thick, which are usually split out of cedar or some other durable wood, are laid between all the courses of stone as thickly as thought proper; but one binder extending entirely across the wall to every six or twelve inches will be sufficient. If the stones are all quite small, it would be well to use more binders than if the stones were larger. The stones will settle a little into these wooden binders, and keep the sides from bulging out and falling down. The binders should not extend beyond the face of the wall far enough to allow cattle to move them; they should be cut of different lengths, when the wall batters on both faces, so as to be just as long as the wall is wide, as the wall increases in height. When any of the binders extend beyond the face of the wall, the ends should be sawed off even with the stones.

7

This mode of building refers more particularly to walls about thirty inches wide on the bottom, and a foot wide at the top, and from three to four feet high. This kind of wall is sometimes covered with a row of square stones, sometimes one foot square; and sometimes stones from two to six feet long, and from four to ten inches thick, and as wide, or even a few inches wider, than the top of the wall, are placed carefully on the top. Sometimes a stick of timber is placed on the top of the wall, and the top of it dressed in the shape of a roof of a building, and cased and painted. Sometimes, again, when such a wall is from three to four feet high, the top is levelled off, and a board of some durable timber is placed on the top; and stones of a given size, which were reserved when the workmen were carrying up the wall, are placed on the top close together, and chocked up well on both sides. It will require the exercise of a little skill to place these cope stones in the most firm and permanent manner. A large stone should be placed at the end to keep them from moving readily, and the others should be placed in the best possible manner for laying firmly and wedging the entire length of the wall. Sometimes such walls are finished with two or three rails in height, or, what is much better, long poles staked and ridered.

192. Throwing a bank of earth against each side of a wall about two feet high, and sowing grass seed on it, is highly recommended by some, and equally denounced by others. When a wall is resting on a good foundation, below the influence of frost, there can be no advantage in banking up the sides of a wall, excepting this: it prevents stock from approaching as closely to it as they could do if it were not banked up, and consequently they are thus deprived of the advantage they would otherwise have, to rub, and hook, and displace any of the stones. Many farmers contend, and with very plausible reasoning, too, that when a wall is banked up the dirt finds its way between the stones, filling all the spaces so completely that a frost affects a wall just as much, and sometimes even more, than it would if it were built on the surface of the soil. If a wall is properly laid up, a bank of earth on each side will not make it stand any longer than if it were not

there. The farmer can do as his own judgment may dictate in reference to banking up the sides.

193. Another thing of no little importance in building stone fence is, to lay all the stones as nearly level as may be practicable. In making a wall up or down a slope, the workmen should always work *up hill*, laying the stones level, instead of laying them parallel with the surface of the ground. When stones are laid sloping in a wall, they are moved much more easily than when they are laid in a level position ; consequently, a wall built in such a manner would not be as strong as it would be were the same stones laid level.

194. Whenever a wall is built along the hillside, and the dirt is hauled down against it, the face of the wall should be more battering than are the faces of a double-faced stone wall. It is a very great error to lay up a wall in such places with the face perpendicular; because the earth will freeze and expand *behind* the wall, and, unless it is several feet in thickness, it will thrust it over in a very few years. Stone walls that are erected along the sides of abutments should always be laid battering, lest the sides bulge out in a few seasons, and they fall. The face of such a wall should be laid battering not less than one foot in three. For example, if a wall be three feet high, it should be laid battering one foot; and if six feet high, two feet battering. And there is another very important consideration in laying up such a wall, which is almost always entirely overlooked, or not even thought of, which is this: the stones, especially the flat ones, instead of being laid level, as in other kinds of wall, should be laid *pitching inward* towards the bank or hill above, with their surfaces at a *right angle* to the face of the wall. When a wall is laid up in this manner, if the frost should ever thrust it over any, it would settle back again to its original position as soon as the earth behind became all thawed out. When a wall is built along a side-hill, as has been mentioned, it should never be less than two feet thick clear to the top. It should be as thick, and even thicker, at the top than at the bottom. The wider it is, the less liable it is to be thrust over by the frosts of winter. In localities

where there is an excess of water in the soil, arising from springs, a good ditch should be made, and well tiled or stoned two or three feet *above* the foundation of the fence, in order to receive the water before it should saturate the earth under the foundation of the wall. This precaution will keep the dirt about the wall more dry, and consequently less liable to heave by freezing.

DITCHES UNDER STONE WALLS.

195. It is a very common practice with some farmers to throw out the earth, where a stone fence is to be built, to the depth of thirty or forty inches, and from two to four or five feet wide, or as wide as the wall is to be built at the surface of the ground, and then fill this channel with small stones, thrown in promiscuously. In this operation they have two or three objects in view—draining the soil, preparing a good foundation for the fence, and a place for the surplus stone. But this is a very expensive way of disposing of surplus stone of any kind. It would be far more economical to lay them up even on the top of a wall that is already high enough, than to bury them beneath the soil. We do not approve of nor advocate the practice of forming a channel for water beneath a stone wall, by simply allowing the water to percolate between the stones, because dirt will keep working towards the bottom, and mice will haul in dirt in places, so as to stop the passage of water entirely. When it is desirable to have a passage for water under a stone fence, the earth should be thrown out from one to four feet deep, to suit the judgment of the proprietor; and then a channel should be dug in the bottom of this trench from six to twelve inches deep, and a good throat laid, as in an ordinary ditch, and well chinked with small stone, and then filled with the kind of earth that was taken from it, and well trodden down even with the bottom of the large trench. If there should be much water, it would be necessary to make a large throat; but, whether a large or small throat be made, the workman should exercise unusual care to do every part of the work in such a manner that mice cannot possibly find their way into the throat of the ditch. If the ditch be well chinked

with small stones, and then about six inches of hard earth be well trodden down on these stones, mice will never try to burrow in it, and the water will have a free channel as long as water runs. A row of tile laid beneath a stone fence would be the most complete manner of making a permanent channel for water; but where stone is abundant, economy dictates that *they* should be used for this purpose. When stone walls are built up and down a steep slope, with a stone drain beneath them where there will be much water, flat stones should be laid in the bottom of the ditch to prevent the water from gullying the bottom of the ditch, and thus undermining the wall. Where there is much flood-water, make a deep furrow on each side of the wall in the former part of summer, and seed it, so that a stream of water will not wash it away. (See MANNER OF STONING DITCHES, Par. 422.)

DITCHES ON BOTH SIDES OF A WALL.

196. Many farmers seem to prefer to have a deep ditch usually open on both sides of their stone walls, to having a ditch directly *beneath* the wall, as has been recommended. The method pursued in such cases is, after the wall is finished, to cut a large open ditch on both sides of the wall, say three or four feet wide on the top, according to the depth of it, and about one foot on the bottom, leaving sufficient space between the ditch and the wall to receive all the dirt, so that when the ditch is finished the embankment on each side of the wall will correspond with the slope of the sides of the ditch. The sides are then sown with grass seed.

197. Although this style of stone fence is very common and much admired, it is decidedly objectionable on account of the expense incurred in cutting two such large ditches, and also the amount of land occupied. If the two ditches are made three feet wide on the top, and the spaces from them to the wall be four feet on each side, and the wall three or four feet wide on the bottom, and as we cannot plow nearer than about two feet to a ditch, it will be perceived that the space occupied by such a fence will be about twenty feet wide, or more, when less than half that

space, with a ditch beneath the wall, would be much cheaper and subserve a better purpose.

HALF WALL

198. In localities where stone is not very abundant, and where there is some fencing timber, a very good, economical, and durable fence can be made by laying a stone wall two or three feet high, according to the amount of stone at hand, and then by staking and finishing with two or more rails, as may be necessary to make it of sufficient height to turn stock. Some farmers finish their stone fence by laying on the top of the wall long poles, say twenty or thirty feet in length, and then staking it, and afterwards laying on heavy poles for riders.

199. Another mode of building half wall fence is, to set the posts as for a whole board fence, and then lay up the wall about half as high as the fence is to be made, and then nail on the two top boards. If the boards should be nailed on before the stone are laid up, they will be very much in the way of the workmen.

200. Another manner of finishing a half wall fence is, to set the posts, and, after the wall is laid up, fasten rails to the posts with wires, as shown by Fig. 22, paragraph 94, skeleton fence. When this mode is adopted, rails may be used, or poles twenty feet long, instead of rails.

A CHEAP WALL OF QUARRIED STONE.

201. Whenever stone are quarried expressly for a fence, and they can be taken from the quarry from one to two feet wide, and from two to eight or ten feet in length, a small amount of stone may be made to build a long line of fence, in the following manner, which will stand firmly as long as one man will need the advantages of a good fence, and subserve as good purpose as those walls in which there are three or four times the amount of stone.

202. If the soil where the wall is to be built is at all inclined to be a little wet, let a ditch be made as directed (paragraph 195), and then throw up a ridge of earth over the ditch not less

than two feet high, and three feet wide on the top of it, and six feet or more at the bottom. Let it all be smoothed off level, and grass seed sowed on it. Allow it to settle for one year or more, and then lay the stone wall directly on the top of this ridge.

203. The object of the ridge of earth is, to save stone; and the object of seeding with grass seed is, to prevent the rain from washing it down; and the object of letting it settle one year or more before the wall is laid on it is, to have the earth the entire length of the ridge of a uniform density, so that the whole wall will settle uniformly. Other advantages of such a wall will be readily perceived without mentioning them.

HON. A. B. CONGER'S STONE WALLS.

Hon. A. B. Conger, President of the N. Y. State Agricultural Society, has forwarded me his mode of building stone walls, which has been very successfully adopted by many other farmers in various parts of the State.

"I cast up a ridge with plows and shovels about eighteen inches high, one foot or more wider on the top than the bottom of the wall is to be made. This is done at any time before frost, as opportunity offers. The bottom stone are then hauled on, even in the winter, and placed in a line, without the usual filling in with small stones, so as to have the benefit of being thoroughly bedded in by the following spring, when they can be readjusted, if necessary, to the line, and filled in; and the "seconds"—stones of a smaller size than the bottom ones—are placed upon them, and the wall raised to three and a half feet high, without levelling. After the foundation has been laid, the wall may be left to undergo another settling by the next winter frosts, and early in the succeeding spring can be topped off and finished. In all cases thorough draining of the ground where the wall is built is very necessary for the security of the wall, otherwise water will be absorbed and remain late in the season under the bed of the wall, and so tend to its upheaval.

"It may be added, that the strength of the wall and its durability will be materially assisted by the care of the builder in chink-

ing in all the interstices between the large stones, and especially
by a careful binding of the sides together, as only in this way
can displacement be prevented under the action of our severe
winters. In passing across gullies, or over undulating fields, it
may be well, in order to give the wall when finished a more uniform top-line, to lay a lower wall of the rougher stone of a height
to correspond with that of the ridge on which they are placed.
The width and height of a wall will necessarily vary with the
quality, size and character of the stone.   If large bowlders exist
in abundance, they must be blasted when they are larger in diameter than the base of the wall.   It will be sufficient to build the
wall four feet wide at the bottom, four feet eight inches high, and
twenty inches wide at the top.   If the stone are of a smaller size,
and cobbles mostly, or of slate, the width at the bottom may be
two and a half feet only.

"It is understood that a wall is considered of a lawful height if
it is four feet six inches high.   But I have thought best to con-
struct my walls four feet eight inches high, so as to allow for
settling."

Some farmers cut an open ditch on both sides of the wall, and
throw up the dirt on the top of the ridge against each side of the
wall, so that animals cannot approach the wall.   But such ditches
take up too much land, and increase the expense of a fence to an
unnecessary amount.   (See par. 196 and 197.)

QUARRYING STONE.

204. The first step in taking stone of any kind from a quarry
is, to remove the dirt from a large surface.   Sometimes this may
be done with a team and scraper; and sometimes, when a stream
of water is near, it may be turned out of its natural course and
made to wash the dirt away; and sometimes it must be removed
with shovels.   When the surface of the stone is all laid bare, if
the stone is found with regular, vertical, and horizontal seams, at
the distance of a foot or so, it will be very easy to get them out.
It requires the exercise of a little judgment and skill to quarry

stone, or the operator will make bad work by damaging many good blocks of stone, that might, by a skillful workman, be taken out of the quarry of a very desirable size and form. Stone are not very elastic, and the operator should bear in mind that he cannot drive in wedges in the seams of stone as carelessly as he may in a block of wood. Stone will break before they will render, or give but little; therefore it will not answer to drive in wedges all in one place.

205. A workman in a quarry needs a half score of wedges many times. They should be about four or five inches long, one inch and a half wide, and about three-eighths of an inch thick, of the very best iron, and steel-pointed. These should be driven in the seams not more than one foot apart, and all driven at one time, by striking them alternately one or two blows at a time. This will open a seam uniformly, without danger of breaking a stone. But if a wedge be driven in at a corner, for example, unless the stratum is very thick the corner will be very liable to break off. Where the courses are laid bare, having vertical seams from two to four or five feet apart, and the strata from four to twelve inches thick, the surface should be marked off in a square form, of the size of which it is desirable to have the stone, and then a row of holes may be drilled eight or ten inches apart where the stone is to be broken, and iron wedges driven into these holes until the stone separates. Two pieces of half round iron should be placed in each hole, leaving a space in the middle of each hole for a flat wedge to enter between the two pieces of half round iron. When the strata are not very thick, and the stone are such as may be broken with fire, the strata may be broken *by fire* instead of drilling holes and separating with wedges. It is usually best to drive most of the wedges at the end in lifting a stratum of rather thin stone, although some wedges may be driven on the side; but if the wedges should be driven mostly on one side, a stone will seldom break square across the stratum. When the strata are rather thin, by cutting a groove with a cold chisel about an inch deep where it is desirable to break the stratum, if the wedges be driven in the side opposite the groove,

7*

the stratum will break very true where the groove has been cut.

206. In addition to a good crowbar or two, and hand-spikes, a good canthook, represented by Fig. 71, is a very useful and

FIG. 71.   **A CANTHOOK.**

convenient implement for handling bowlders which two or three men could not handle with crowbars without much difficulty. But with a good canthook one man can roll along a bowlder of six or eight hundred pounds with ease, and by using a couple of plank he will be able to load such a stone on a sleigh or stone-boat in a very few minutes.

207. The handle of the canthook is almost always made too large and clumsy. It should be about six feet in length, and of a uniform taper from the mortise where the hook enters it to the end, which end need not be larger than the end of a fork handle. The other end may be tapered off, as shown in the cut. At the mortise it should be about two by three inches square, or even smaller if the timber be of the best quality, otherwise it must be larger. The hook should be made of the best iron, about an inch and a half wide and three eighths of an inch thick, with half-inch holes every two inches, and from twenty to thirty inches long, according to the size of stone or logs to be rolled with it. At the hook end it must be made much heavier and stronger than the other part of it. The curvature of the hook is a very important feature of it. If it is curved but little it will hook on a large stone or log very readily, and will not hook on a small one. But if the curvature of it will admit of its hooking to a small stone, it will usually hook on a larger one, except it is *very* large. The bolt which holds the hook should work easily in and out, and be fastened with a leather key.

208. The grapple hook, Fig. 72, is used for hooking on to large stone with a team, in rolling them over and over, or in lift-

ing one end of a stone, so that a chain can be passed around it, when one end of it is in the ground. It is very convenient in a quarry, for hitching a team to a corner of a large stone, when it

FIG. 72.   FIG. 73.

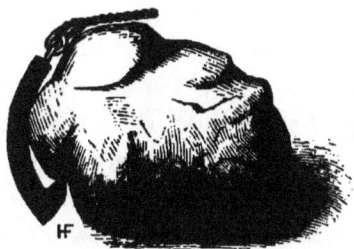

A GRAPPLE HOOK HITCHED TO A LARGE BOWLDER.

A WINDLASS FOR LOADING STONE ON A WAGON.

is desirable to slide it a little. With three or four such hooks, a stone may be slung up, when it would be very inconvenient getting a chain round it.

209. The grapple hook should be made of about the same curvature as the iron part of the canthook, Fig. 71, with a link and ring in one end, as shown in Fig. 72, for the purpose of hitching a chain to when in use. It should be made from eighteen to twenty-four inches long, of the best iron, with the point of the hook laid with steel. The hook should be large enough to retain its shape without bending, even when two teams may be hitched to it. At the hook-end, where it is exposed to the greatest strain, it should be about three-fourths of an inch thick and two inches wide. The other parts need not be half as heavy as this.

210. Fig. 73 shows a portion of a platform to a wagon or sleigh, with a windlass attached to the hind end, for the purpose of loading stone which would weigh from one hundred to three or four hundred pounds. One man can roll a stone, which three or four men cannot lift, on the wagon; and by having a windlass on the hind end of the wagon, one man can raise a large stone on the wagon in one minute, with ease. In loading a stone, the fore end of the platform should

be fastened down, so that it cannot tip up without raising the forward wheels of the wagon. Hitch the chain around the stone, and raise it as high as the top of the platform, and then let a board be slid under the stone, with the two ends resting on the sills of the platform. The stone can then be rolled forward on the platform, and another raised in the same manner.

211. The windlass should be about three inches in diameter, of good timber, and about thirty inches above the sills of the platform. The sticks for turning the windlass should be at least four feet in length, and if the timber be very tough, one inch in diameter is large enough for ordinary purposes. The ends of the sills should extend beyond the cross-piece about eighteen inches, as shown by the figure. A small chain is best, although a rope would subserve a good purpose, for winding up on the windlass.

212. For loading stone on a wagon, which will weigh from four hundred pounds to a ton or more, a set of sheers and tackles, Fig. 74, is about as convenient and efficient as anything

FIG. 74.

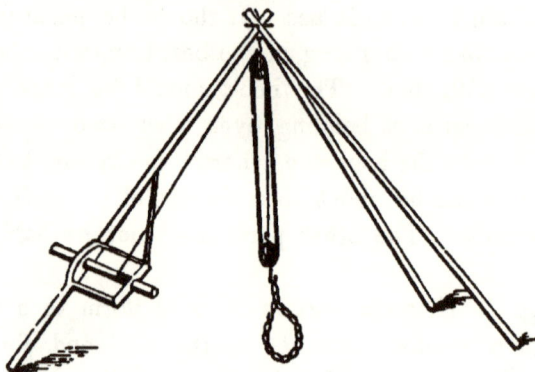

GIN FOR LOADING LOGS AND STONE.

in the line of cheap implements which can be made use of. Almost every farmer often sees the need of such an apparatus for many purposes besides loading stone. It hardly needs a description; but, to aid the beginner, we will give the chief dimensions. The sheers should be not less than sixteen feet in length, of light timber, and should be larger in the middle of the sticks than at the ends, to keep them from bending. The single sheer, or the one to which a windlass is attached, for winding up the slack rope, should be, in the middle, of a size-equivalent to a scantling three by four inches square. The other two sheers may be two and a half by three inches in the middle, and tapering to each end to two inches square, in order to render them as light as possible. At the upper end of the single sheer an iron rod, about seven-eighths of an inch in diameter, and twenty inches long, should be fastened, by passing through it, for holding the other two sheers, which should have an inch and a quarter hole in their upper ends for receiving the ends of this rod in the single sheer. The tackles may be made by almost any mechanic, with cast-iron sheaves. A rope an inch in diameter is large enough to hold one ton and a half, when the rope is three-double, or three sheaves in the upper block of pulleys.

213. Such an apparatus is very convenient in hoisting large stone on to any part of a stone wall, and especially in placing large stone on the top of a wall. It may be used also very advantageously in loading logs and timber, and such like, on a wagon. In extensive quarries a crane will be found to be more efficient and convenient than almost any other apparatus, for hoisting the stone from their bed on a wagon or other vehicle. As cranes may be seen in every locality where stone quarries abound, we do not think it advisable to give, in this place, a cut and description of one. When the farmer has a quarry of any kind of stone, if he has not in his employ a man who has a good share of practical experience in quarrying stone, he will find it very much to his interest and convenience to visit some extensive quarry, and spend a day or so in witnessing the manipulations of the workmen, and in making inquiries of the foreman and proprietor in relation to the business, and in examining the tools used in quarrying. A day or two spent in this manner may be worth hundreds of dollars to an individual, in enabling him to start in his operations in the most efficient manner. Scores of

men have been in the possession of excellent quarries, but who, for the want of getting *started right* in the quarry, and not knowing exactly what they really needed, have blundered along at a very great useless expense and inconvenience for a long time, or many times have entirely abandoned the operation as a non-paying business, when a day or two spent in examining the machinery, &c., of an extensive quarry would have enabled them to *start right*, and progress with all desirable rapidity and efficiency.

BREAKING STONE WITH FIRE.

214. Many kinds of stone may be broken very readily and very expeditiously with fire. Large bowlders, when a fire is built on them, will, in a short time, separate into small pieces; and many times these pieces will have straight edges and smooth and true faces, and may be used in a foundation for a building, or in stone fence, with no little economy. When a large bowlder is mostly *below* the surface of the ground, let the earth be thrown away from it all around as low as the middle of it, and then pile on a lot of old rails or pieces of stumps, or even good wood, and it will soon crack into pieces so that they may be pried out with the crowbar. Should it not be broken clear to the bottom, apply the fire again after the broken pieces have been removed. Sometimes, after the fire has been burning for a few minutes, the top of the bowlder will be covered with large scales of stone, which should be immediately removed, in order to allow the fire to come in contact with the unbroken stone. Some kinds of stone that are taken from the quarry may be broken very straight and true into almost any desired shape. In many quarries stone are often taken out ten or twenty feet in length, and from six to ten or twelve inches in thickness, and sometimes from one foot to three feet in width, with straight edges and true and smooth sides. Now, in order to break them in pieces of a desirable size, let little fires be made with hard, dry wood, across the stone where it is desirable to break it, and in a few minutes a seam will be

formed so that a crowbar will easily separate them. We have often broken large flat stone, very true and straight, with fire, by laying a scantling about four inches wide on the place where it is to be broken, and then shovelling dirt on both sides of the scantling, about an inch in depth. Take up the scantling, and make a fire with short pieces of dry wood, split very fine, the whole length of the stone where it is to be broken. Small hard wood chips are the most convenient article to make a fire with in such a place. The dirt is to prevent the fire from heating the stone on each side of the line where it is desirable to have it broken. If the fire burns uniformly entirely across the stone, it will require but ten or fifteen minutes before it will crack, when the fire should be immediately removed lest it should injure the edges of the stone. Small thin stone may be broken very readily by heating a large bar of iron and laying it on the stone where it is to be broken.

215. Some kinds of stone will not break at all with fire, and some kinds will crumble to pieces before they will break in two parts. The beginner can soon learn, by a little observation and experience, which kinds may or may not be broken with fire.

SECTION 6.—FENCE POSTS.

216. There are several considerations of first importance in making fence posts, which should not be overlooked. One is the *length* of posts. Posts are cut, many times, nearly one foot longer than is necessary. If all the logs of a tree be cut one foot longer than necessary, there will be waste of timber enough in one tree, many times, to make a cut for posts. The farmer should calculate how deep he intends to set the posts, and how long they are to be above ground, and then cut them but three or four inches longer than that length.

217. Another thing is the *size* of posts. When timber is good and well-seasoned, a large post will always outlast a small one; therefore, it is not a bad fault, so far as durability is

concerned, to have posts large; but, on the score of economy, it is not best to have them *very* large. It is much better to have them *too* large than *too small.* A post six inches square is much better, and will last longer, than one four inches square; but it would not be an economical manner of working up timber to make ordinary posts six inches square. For ordinary fence, sawed fence posts may be about four inches square at the lower ends, and two by four inches at the upper ends; but some prefer to have them sawed five by five at the lower ends, and five by two or three inches at the tops. For a high fence, like Fig. 39, this last size would be better than a size smaller. In splitting fence posts, when a portion of a log is rather large for two posts, and too small for three posts, it is much better to make them a little too large than too small. It is much more economical to have posts sawed out than to split and hew them, when a saw-mill is not more than two or three miles distant, providing the timber is large. It is not practicable to split as many posts out of a log, even when it splits well, as can be sawed from the same amount of timber. By sawing the lower ends large, and the upper ends proportionally smaller, there is always a saving of timber, and the posts are of a much better form. If timber is very small, and will split good, it might be best to split them out, instead of sawing them. Sometimes, when small timber is winding, four posts, worth fifty cents or more, might be sawed out of a small log which could not be split into posts, and which, if not sawed, would make only one post.

218. Another thing, which seems almost superfluous to mention, is, the *kind of timber* for posts. Red cedar and mulberry are, perhaps, more durable than almost any other kinds of timber; yellow locust, oak of different kinds, butternut, red elm, red beech, and many other kinds not mentioned, will make good posts. The butt-ends of trees, when the trees are sound and healthy, are usually more durable than cuts near the *tops* of the trees. It is always very poor economy to make fence posts, and especially gate posts, of perishable kinds of timber, such as sugar-maple, or

bass-wood, and such like. All kinds of posts should be seasoned at least one year before they are set in the ground.

219. *Hewing posts.*—When posts have been split out, the most convenient mode of scoring and hewing them is, to lay the post to be hewed on two large blocks or logs, and then drive in two stakes or pins, about six or seven inches apart, in one log, and let them extend beyond the surface of the log eight or ten inches, and key the post with a wedge in the desired position between these two stakes; then line it and hew it. Some men prefer hewing their posts after they have been set in the ground, but the practice is not a good one, because it loosens them.

220. *Sharpening posts.*—When the ends of posts are to be sharpened, if they are so large that a man cannot hold them erect with one hand, with the post standing on a firm block, while he sharpens it with an axe in the other hand, they may be fastened with a wedge in a gain cut in a heavy log, in a device similar to the one for holding posts when they are to be hewed, as shown by Fig. 75. It requires the exercise of a little skill to

FIG. 75.

A POST CLAMP FOR HOLDING WHILE SHARPENING.

sharpen a post in a proper manner for driving well. The bevel or slant should be of exactly a given angle on each side of the post. The following figures will give some correct idea on the subject: Fig. 76 represents a post sharpened in the most proper manner. A post sharpened thus, when it is being driven, will go straight down, if the point does not hit a stone. Figs. 77 and 78 represent two posts improperly sharpened. Although they may go straight down, when sharpened like Fig. 78, they

will drive very hard, because

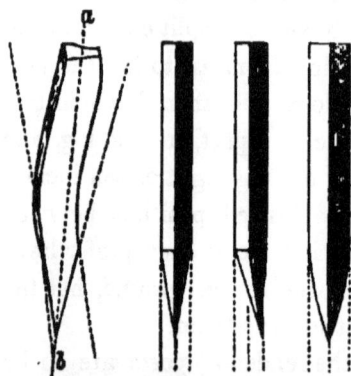

MODE OF SHARPENING FENCE POSTS.

they are *too blunt.* When they are sharpened like Fig. 77, it is almost impossible to keep them, when driving them, in a perpendicular position. Sometimes, when posts are not entirely straight, the sharpening must all be done on two or three sides of it only, as the case may require. Fig. 79 will furnish a very good idea of the most proper manner of sharpening a crooked post, in order to have it drive true. The dotted lines will show on which side the post should be sharpened. The idea to be kept in mind in sharpening a crooked post is, to work by a line drawn from the centre of the top of the post, Fig. 79, at a to b, and then bevel the end on both sides of this line, so that the angle of the bevelling will be nearly the same on both sides of the line a b. It will be perceived by the figure that the sharpening is almost all done on one side, at b; but a thin chip only was taken from the other side. A workman who has a mechanical eye, will sharpen posts with all desirable accuracy without a line. He will cast his eye from end to end of a crooked post, and at a glance observe about how much must be cut off on each side, in order to make it of a true taper, and then will snatch up his axe and cut it off while another man would be getting ready to sharpen it. . In sharpening straight posts, a workman must calculate to have the point at the centre of the post, and to have the cut on each side of the post of a true taper, from fifteen or twenty inches from the end, according to the size of the post, to the point, like Fig. 76. If these rules, which may seem trivial to some, are · observed, the beginner will soon be able to sharpen his posts with necessary accuracy. If the ends of posts are of a true taper from the points to that part which is at the surface of the ground, they will enter the ground much easier; but they will not stand as well as those which have a short taper. Pointed posts are far more liable to be lifted out by the frost than those which are of full size clear to the end, and we would not recommend the practice of pointing fence posts; but as farmers will persist in doing it, we have thought proper to give some practical hints on the subject, to aid the inexperienced workmen in doing the job in a workmanlike manner. Let the farmer avoid sharpening posts like Fig. 77.

JENKINS' PATENT CAST-IRON POST.

221. Fig. 80 represents a cast-iron fence post for board fence; but the pattern for it may be made shorter, with holes in it for receiving the ends of the rails for picket fence. The entire length of this kind of post is six feet. The breadth is three and a half inches. The length below the *flange* or cross-pieces is eighteen inches, tapering and terminating as shown in the figure, in a barbed or spear-head end. The flange is two inches wide, eighteen inches long, with a mortise in the middle of it, through which the post is inserted,—the flange being put over the top of the post, and resting on little shoulders or projections, eighteen inches from the lower end. The main part of the post, through which the mortises are made, is one-fourth of an inch thick, with a flange around the margin, from half an inch to three-fourths of an inch wide, to give strength to the posts. The mortises for the boards are two inches wide, and of any desirable length.

Fig. 80.

JENKINS' CAST-IRON FENCE POST.

222. The object of the flange or cross-piece is, to aid in keeping the fence erect, and to prevent the frost heaving it. Holes are made with a crowbar for the posts, when a piece of hard wood plank is thrust through the lower mortise, and the posts are driven in by striking on the edge of the plank. Afterwards the cross-piece is put on; and a ridge of earth is thrown up along the fence to save one board, and to cover

the cross-pieces, and thus keep the posts in their places. The posts should receive a good coating of pitch and gas tar, applied hot, which will keep them from rusting. If this is not done, in some

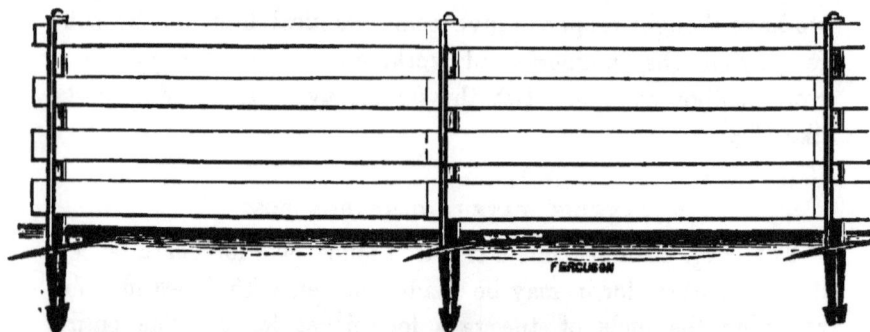

SECTION OF BOARD FENCE WITH CAST-IRON POSTS.

soils such posts would corrode or rust so rapidly, that in less than twenty years the wind would blow them over. But by smearing them they will last for ages.

223. The *weight* of a post will be according to the pattern and style of fence. For ordinary board fence, if they weigh from twelve to fifteen pounds they will be sufficiently strong. If a goodly number were ordered, they could probably be obtained for about three cents per pound in most of our cities. One such post is worth two posts of the most durable kinds of timber.

224. In making a board fence with such posts, stretch two lines, one a few inches above the surface of the ground, and the other near the tops of the posts; and drive every post so that the top mortise will exactly coincide with the line. Now, put in the boards, and smear the ends, where they come in contact with each other, with paint or coal tar. No nails are required in building such a fence; no post holes are to be dug; and the posts may be set twelve feet or more apart, and the ends of the boards driven into the mortises. If the boards are not very stiff, nail a narrow strip across all of them at the middle of each panel. A fence built with such posts in a workmanlike manner, is worth all the portable board fences in America. Alex. S.

Rowley, Hudson, N. Y., holds the right for these posts, who will sell farm or State rights for them.

REMEDY TO PREVENT POSTS BEING LIFTED BY THE FROST.

225. When posts having a straight end of uniform size are set in the ground, unless they are set three or four feet deep in the ground, they are very liable to be lifted out of the ground in a few years by the influence of the frost. In dry localities, however, the freezing and thawing of the ground has little or no effect on them. Setting very deep in the ground is the usual remedy against their heaving out in the winter, but a more convenient and cheaper one is to bore a two-inch hole through the bottom of each post, and drive in a hard wood pin, allowing it to extend beyond the surface of the post about four inches, and then in setting the posts place a stone on each end of the pin, and let

FIG. 81.

the dirt be well rammed down on the stones. Another and better remedy is, to cut a notch on each side of the bottom of the post, about four inches from the lower end, and ram the dirt well into these notches, or place stones in them, as shown by Fig. 81, which represents a post with stones placed in the notches. Posts may be cut on both sides, if they are of good size, so that in the thinnest place they will be not more than one inch and a half thick, without injuring their strength or durability, because at the bottom of a post, which is from two to three feet below the surface of the ground, but little strength is necessary; and at that depth in the ground a post decays very slowly. It should be remembered, that posts decay most at the surface of the ground. When posts are rather small, a notch may be cut only on one side of them for receiving the stone. This is a most effectual remedy for the heaving of posts by frost.

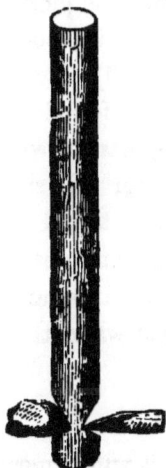

MODE OF PREVENTING FENCE POSTS BEING LIFTED BY THE FROST.

DIGGING POST HOLES

226. Is a part of fence building which may be performed at "odd spells," and may be done by the forces of the farm which are very awkward and unskillful in everything they attempt to perform, providing the work is all laid out for them, so that it will be barely possible to do anything wrong. In the first place, set two stakes and plow a deep trench, as stated, if the saving of labor is any object, and then stretch a line four or six rods long, and have a little pole as long as the distance is to be between the posts, from centre to centre, and measure along the line, and stick a little stake exactly where the centre of every hole is to be made. With the spade cut a circle in the sod or dirt around these little stakes, and throw out the dirt with the spade for one foot or so in depth, if the earth is not too hard to be spaded with facility. Let the digger be careful not to work the holes so far on one side of the centre that the posts cannot be placed in range with each other. There is no necessity of digging the holes for ordinary fence posts more than one foot in diameter. If the ground is very hard and dry, it must be picked up with the crowbar or spud, and taken out with the dirt-spoon. If the ground is not stony, the post-hole augur (Fig. 99) may be used to great advantage, especially after a hole is two feet deep. In digging large holes for gate posts, or straining-posts for wire fence, which are to be four feet deep, an expert digger will sink such a hole much the quickest by stepping down into it, and by making it at least thirty inches in diameter at the top and nearly two feet at the bottom. The hole for fence posts should be large enough to admit the rammer freely all round them when they are being set.

SETTING FENCE POSTS.

227. Let the post be placed in the hole so that it will almost touch both the upper and lower line, (see mode of adjusting the lines, par. 152,) and throw in a little dirt, say enough to fill the hole around the post not more than two inches after it is well rammed ; put in as much more and ram it, and the post will stand without

holding it. , Be careful in ramming not to move the post by ramming too hard on one side of it. Be very particular in making
the bottoms of the posts firm. Let the dirt be well rammed in
at the top of the holes, by filling in a little at a time; and let the
earth be raised around each post a little above the level of the
ground, with the hardest kind of dirt. This will keep the posts
from becoming loose. When small stones are used for filling
the holes around the posts, they should be placed with care, and
in such a position that, by being rammed a little, they will hold
the post very securely. When there is water in post holes, it
must be bailed out, as it is not practicable to make a post stand
firmly when there is water in the hole. Posts are somtimes set
in grout, which is made of good sand and water-lime, and poured
among the stones which are placed in the holes around the posts.
This renders them very firm, but the frosts of winter are very
liable to injure it as deep as it freezes.

228. Posts are often set by driving them in a hole made with a
crowbar; but as a general thing I never could like it as well as setting them in holes that have been dug. I have often practised
driving posts in the bottom of the holes after they have been
dug two feet deep, and I have always found that this práctise
saves much digging; and the posts are more solid and quicker
set than when the holes are dug as deep as the posts are to be set.
By digging two feet, and driving one foot or more, posts will be
sufficiently deep for ordinary fences.

229. In driving square posts a wrench is very necessary to keep
them from turning from a right line when they are being driven.
For this purpose an iron wrench, large enough to fit on the
post, may be used, or a mortise as large as the post may be made
in a piece of tough plank, or a gain may be sawed in the edge
of a plank, and the posts held in the desired position by one
workman while another drives them with a sledge. When
posts are driven without any digging, the workmen are too apt
to drive them only twenty or twenty-five inches, instead of thirty-
five and forty inches deep, as they should be. It is no easy job
to drive a post three feet into the ground in some localities, while

in others a post may be driven clear down with comparatively few blows. In such places driving posts is preferable to setting them in holes which have been dug.

CHARRING POSTS,

230. With a view to render them more durable, has long been commended by men who ought to pass for good authority on such subjects; but the beginner may rest assured that the practice is by no means a good one, as a post will last longer when *not* charred than when charred; and this is particularly true of green timber. I am fully persuaded, that if posts of green timber be charred it hastens their decay. Charcoal, we all know, is very durable in the ground, but posts which have been charred are not all converted into charcoal. Simply a small portion of the outside, by being charred, is rendered more durable. But this does not exclude moisture from the wood inside or *beneath* the charred portion. There is a thin portion of wood just between that which has been converted into coal and the remainder of the post which has not been affected by the fire, which has been heated almost to a burning point, which will quickly decay, when the whole charred portion will afford no more protection from the influences of the weather than so much loose charcoal placed around a post. Posts are charred usually around the part that will come, after they have been set, just at the surface of the ground, because posts always decay first near that point; and if that part could be rendered as durable by any artificial means as the other portions of the posts, they would last as long as we could desire. When posts are charred they are almost always burned too much. It is necessary to form only a thin coal on the outer surface, which is just as efficacious as if coal an inch thick were formed around the posts.

231. In order to place the matter beyond a doubt, let two posts be taken from the same log, and from the same portion of the log, and let them be seasoned for one year; and then let one be charred, and both of them set in the ground where the soil

and moisture are as nearly equal as they can be, and if the charred post outlasts the uncharred one, the result will be in favor of charring them.

STEEPING FENCE POSTS

232. In different kinds of antiseptic liquid, for the purpose of rendering them more durable, has been often practised with very good success. The process has been denominated Kyanizing and Burnettizing timber, from the names of the inventors. Kyan used corrosive sublimate, and Burnett used chloride of zinc. A tank or vat is prepared, or a molasses hogshead will subserve a good purpose, and about one measure and a half of the dry chloride of zinc to about one hundred measures of water are put in the tank and well stirred together, when the posts are set in this liquid, and allowed to remain ten or fifteen days, or until they become thoroughly saturated with the liquid. They should then be taken out, and allowed to dry, under cover, until they are entirely dry. It is necessary to saturate only that part of the posts which is set in the ground, and a few inches above the surface of the ground.

233. Dr. Boucherie, of Paris, France, has used for this purpose about one pound of sulphate of copper to one hundred pounds of water. It is contended that timber thus treated is rendered more firm, and will endure three times longer than if it had not been submitted to the process of steeping it in the liquor of an antiseptic character. In some localities there are companies having suitable apparatus for impregnating large quantities of wood with an antiseptic liquid, for bridges, ships, &c., and it is considered to be a process which pays exceedingly well.

234. The practice of boring a hole in posts near the surface of the ground, and filling it with common salt, is but a modification of steeping. The salt soon becomes dissolved, and is absorbed by the wood, and thus preserves a small portion of the post for a short time. All these processes which have been mentioned are *chemical* processes of preserving wood. There are *mechanical* modes of preserving posts, of which I will mention but one,

8

which is, smearing the parts of posts near the top of the ground, for a few inches above the ground and several inches below it, with melted pitch or coal tar, or anything else which will exclude the moisture. A mixture of equal parts of pitch and coal tar, applied hot to posts, is far more effectual in rendering fence posts durable, in my own estimation, than any chemical antiseptic liquor that has been used for that purpose. A good coat of such materials will protect posts much longer than we are wont to suppose, until we have tested it in a practical manner.

THE TOP END OF TIMBER UP, AGAINST TOP END DOWN.

235. Almost every man who has ever set fence posts, and many who have never set a post, will recommend setting them with the *top end* of the wood in the ground, affirming that they will last many years longer than if the butt end was set in the ground. But we have never seen nor heard of a philosophical reason *why* they will last longer when the top is in the ground; and we never had one atom of confidence in the theory, and we never expect to have, until it has been fairly and honestly shown that the theory is a correct one. It is a most palpable absurdity to affirm that a post will last longer when placed in a reversed position from that in which it grew. This is not the place to show, by extended argument, that the theory is a false one, but those who are anxious to investigate the matter may find an article on this subject from the pen of the author, in the *Country Gentleman* for 1858, page 323. It is sufficient to say, in this place, that posts well seasoned before they are set in the ground will tell infinitely more on their durability than the position in which they may be placed.

SECTION 7.—GATES.

" Opes the gate that hung for ages,
Rustling in its old repose,
Which, once swung upon its hinges,
There's no giant hand can close."—READ's NEW PASTORAL.

236. A gate closes a passage or opens a way to an enclosure, and consists, usually, of a rectangular frame, made of wood or of

iron, or of both these materials, and is so adjusted on hinges or rollers that the force of a child can open and close it at pleasure.

FIG. 82.

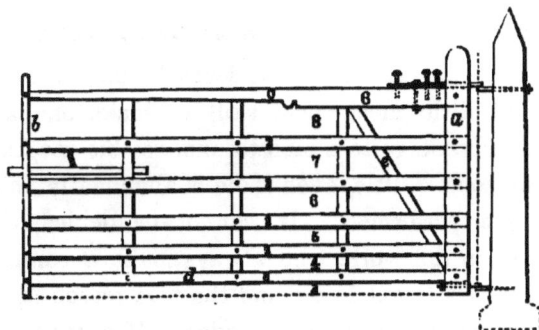

A SUBSTANTIAL FARM GATE.

237. The essential and very important parts of a gate are, a *heel-post* or *stile a* (Fig. 82, inserted at the head of this article); the head or *latch stile b ;* the top bar or *arm c ;* the *lower arm d ;* the *slats* or the filling, which extend from the heel stile to the head stile ; the *stay* or stays, or those pieces which èxtend across the middle of the gate vertically ; and the *struts,* or those pieces which extend diagonally in the direction from the bottom of the heel stile towards the top of the head stile. *Ties* extend from the upper end of the heel stile to the lower end of the head stile, or in that direction. The struts operate as *supports* to the gate to keep it in an unchangeable position and shape. The *strut* of the gate operates as a pillar, and the force applied to it is a *compressive* force. The *ties* operate in an opposite direction, and sustain the gate by *suspension.* Struts are more effectual in keeping a gate in position and shape when they are made of wood than when made of iron, unless they are made of a bar heavy enough not to be bent by the weight of the gate. *Ties* are more frequently made of wood, in wooden gates, but large wire, with a nut and screw on one end, and a head on the other, makes a tie which will keep a gate in shape and position as long as the wood remains sound. *Stays* are very important in a gate ; and every gate that is long enough to allow a load of grain or of

hay to pass, should have not less than one stay. The slats frequently pass through mortises in the stays, but, as a general
rule, the stays are nailed, riveted, or bolted to the slats.

INSTRUCTIONS TO AID IN MAKING A GATE.

238. Every young farmer should learn to make his own gates.
It requires but little mechanical skill to make one, and it will
not be any disadvantage to a man to exercise his mechanical faculties in using tools a little, even if he is abundantly able to hire
every such job performed. It cannot be denied that there
are a few men in the world who always make a complete *botch*
of every job they attempt to do, and the true reason is, they lack
the exercise of energy and perseverance. If a man will go to
work with a determination to succeed in performing a job well,
he seldom fails, after a few trials. There are thousands of young
farmers who could, with the instructions we shall give in this
place, make gates for all their fields, and they need only occupy
the hours which they squander in idleness. Come on, then,
my good friends, and make a gate, and hang it in the place of
those bars which you have taken out and put in a hundred and
one times during the busy season, and see if you do not detect a
smile on your countenance every time you go through it; and
listen, and you will, doubtless, hear the proprietor soliloquizing
thus: "This is truly more convenient than those old bars. I
wonder I did not have one years ago. I shall soon save time
and strength enough to make a gate; and, more than this, Eddy
can open and shut it, and turn away the cows, and bring them
up." Don't be disheartened because you cannot make one quite
so neatly and quickly as I can. I can make a gate like any one
of the cuts given here, and plane it, paint and hang it in a day, and
dig the holes for the posts; and can make six such gates in a
week, in a workmanlike manner, and hang them, too,—and I
never had one single word of instruction about any part of the
business. If you will make as good a one in two days, we will
give you a meed of praise, of "well done."

239. In the first place, have a log of good oak timber for

gates, like Fig. 82, sawed into stuff, a part three by six inches square, for the heel or hinge stiles, and a part into slats, one by three, and a part into upper arms, *c*, three by six at one end, and three by three at the other end, and have the sawyer saw the upper arms at the mill like the arm in Fig. 82, as far as the jog in it. At the jog in the arm it should be about three by four inches. The piece that is taken off will make a good head or latch stile. As soon as the timber is sawed out, let it be stuck up, *very straightly*, under shelter, where it can season not less than one year. If any of the pieces are sprung after being sawed, if the pile is stuck up straight put a lot of stones or timber on the pile to bring all the pieces down straight.

240. The next thing will be, to have a few tools in order to work with. The planes must be sharpened after they have been ground, on an oil-stone, which will give the irons a fine, keen edge (see EDGE TOOLS). Let the chisels be well sharpened, for it is impossible to make a good mortise with dull chisels. Let the hand-saw be well filed and set. Saw off a piece of scantling for the hinge stile, as long as desirable, and plane off the smoothest and truest side of it, and mark it with a pencil as the *face* side. It is very important to have the face side not only straight, but true, *i. e.*, not winding. Fig. 83 represents a hinge stile laid out ready for mortising; *a* is the face side and *b* the work side. If the face side of the stile should be a little winding, it may be the means of making the whole gate winding. Therefore, to ascertain whether the face is winding, lay it on the bench face side up, and lay on the square at one end and the jointer planet at the other end, and look over the edge of the square to the jointer; and if the edges of the square and plane coincide with each other, the face is true. If the face is not true, the mortises will not be true. Apply the try-square, and see if the work side is at a right angle with the face. Plane this side straight and true, and mark it (see HOW TO PLANE). Now, with the rule and scratch-awl, prick off the spaces

FIG 83.

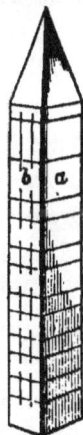

GATE STILE.

for the mortises (see Fig. 82), and then, with the try-square
and scratch-awl, make marks across the *work* side, *b*, as in
the figure.   Place the square against the *work side always*, not
against the side opposite the work side, and make the marks across
the *face* side of stile, as in the figure.   Then, from these marks,
with the square against the *face side*, draw the marks on the
side opposite the work side.   Have two points in the gauge
just one inch apart.   (I would not recommend to purchase a
mortise gauge, for they cost too much.   A common gauge,
costing fifteen or twenty cents, with two steel points for marking, will answer a good purpose.)   Run the gauge along against
the face side, and mark the sides of the mortises, both on the work
side and on the side opposite to the work side.   Lay the stile on
two benches as high as a man's knees, and have it lay level.   One
cannot work as well when a stick does not lie level.   Bore the
mortises half through from each side, and dress the sides of the
mortise to the mark.   Or the stiles may be bored with the boring
machine (Fig. 122).   Be careful and not break the wood over
the mark.   With mallet and *corner* chisel, head down the ends.
If the farmer has no corner chisel, let him procure one, for it is
worth a score of straight chisels for making mortises.   See that
the mortises are true clear through the stile.   If they should be a
little winding, and if the tenon is made to fit tightly, the stile will
most certainly split when the gate is put together.   Now plane
out the latch stile, and lay it by the side of the other stile; and
lay out the mortises, and see if they correspond with each other.
After the mortises are made, bore the holes for the draw-pins
in the *stiles*.   Half-inch or five-eighths are sufficiently large.
Dress out the arm of the gate, having a face side and a work
side.   Let the face side on the arm be on the face side of the
stile, and the work side of the arm upwards.   Lay out the tenons
with the gauge, and make them a sixteenth of an inch *wider*
than the length of the mortise, so that they will be tight when
driven in.   If the tenons are a trifle *too thick*, they will split the
stile.   Make the tenons on the slats, and have a little shoulder

on one edge at each end. See that the tenons on the slats are not too thick, but have them a sixteenth of an inch wider than the mortise. Drive stiles and slats firmly together, and mark the tenons in the holes of the stiles with the bit. Drive the stiles partly off, and bore the holes in the tenons about a sixteenth of an inch *nearer* the shoulders than they are in the stile. Give all the tenons a good painting, or smear them with coal tar, and drive them together and pin them, painting the pins when they are driven in. A gate usually decays first in the joints, and if they be well painted, and the draw pins, which should be made of oak or yellow locust, well painted when they are driven in, a gate will last forty years. Put on the stays by cutting a gain on one side of the arm, about half an inch deep, and halve the ends of the stays, and paint the joints, and fasten them with carriage-bolts. If it is thought best, lay out the mortises for the slats in the stiles half an inch on *one side of the centre,* and then make mortises in the *under side* of the arm two inches deep for the stays. Put small carriage-bolts through the lower ends of the stays and bottom slat. A wrought nail will answer through the other slats and stays. Let in the strut in the hinge stile and upper arm, by making a gain half an inch deep. Make the strut first, and then mark off the gains, and have it fit tightly. If the upper hinge is not bolted to the arm, as in Fig. 82, put not less than three draw-pins through the tenon of the upper arm, because there is great strain on this arm, which tends to draw the tenon out, while the strain on the lower arm or slats is inward. I have mentioned the most important considerations in making a gate. Space will not allow me to give all the minutiæ.

HANGING GATES.

241. The first step in *hanging* a gate of any kind is, to decide how it is desired to have it hung. One must decide whether he will have it hung so as to open both ways, or but one way only, and whether it is to be so hung that it will remain at rest at any point which it may pass in opening it; or whether it shall be so

adjusted on its hinges that it will shut of its own accord when
it has been opened at any angle, in one-fourth of a circle.   Gates
may be so hung that they will immediately open when unlatched,
and swing back to a right angle; or they may be hung so as to
shut themselves when opened at a right angle.   Many farmers
seem to think it very important that a gate should be hung so as
to *shut* of its own accord; while others prefer to have it hung so
as to swing *open* when unlatched, and remain open; and others
choose to have a gate hung on an *even balance*.   Hanging a gate
according to one's fancy may sometimes not be practicable, on

FIG. 84.

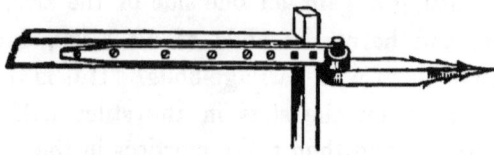

STYLE OF GATE HINGES CALLED HOOKS AND STRAPS.

account of the kind of hinges.   With hooks and straps, like
Fig. 84, gates may be hung so as to open or shut of their own
accord, or to remain at rest when opened
wide or opened but little.   But with such
hinges they cannot be opened both ways.
With hooks and eyes, like Fig. 85, they
may be hung to open both ways, and at the
same time they may be hung so as to be
self-opening or *self-closing*.   The most proper
and expeditious manner of *drawing out* a
gate hinge from a post is, to bore a hole
close to the hinge, above or below it, a little
larger than the hinge, and then with a cold-
chisel crowd it down or up into the hole
bored.   A large nail or spike may be taken
out in the same manner.

FIG. 85.

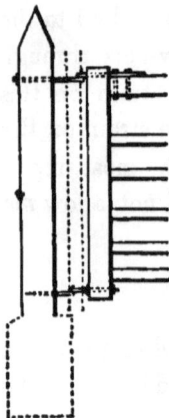

MODE OF HANGING A GATE SO AS TO BE SELF-SHUT-
TING WHEN OPENED EITHER WAY.

242. We will now show how the farmer may hang his gates,
no matter what may be the style of hinges, so as to suit his wishes.

And should one mode of hanging them not seem to coincide with the fancy of his fastidious neighbor, we will lay down rules which will aid *him* in hanging his gates to his mind. If Mr. A. wants his gates to swing *open* as soon as unlatched, exposing his crops, or offering an opportunity to cattle to leave their enclosure and run away, or to enter on forbidden ground, will he allow me the prerogative to hang my gates so that they will close *of themselves*, rather than swing open when unlatched. Gates are often left open by children; and indolent interlopers, wandering about the fields, are frequently too lazy to shut a gate. Therefore, if a gate should, by any means, get unlatched, if it is hung so as to shut itself, it may be the means of saving much damage to a crop, or the running away of animals. Vicious cattle and horses are often rubbing and hooking about gates, and if they happen to un-latch them and they immediately swing open, they are more in-clined to try their skill *again* in opening them. But if a gate is hung on an even balance, or so as to shut itself, they are obliged to learn, not only to *unlatch* a gate, but to push it open, before they can pass through. Now, if one unruly animal has succeeded in getting through the gate, if the gate closes after him, the others must necessarily learn the tricks of their leader before they can follow him.

243. It is important that the farmer should understand the *principle* of hanging gates so as to make them swing any way he may desire, or have them remain at rest, which is nothing more nor less than adjusting the *centre of gravity* in the gate. The centre of the turning points of the hinges, *i. e.*, the centre of the hooks and the centre of the eyes, are the two centres of motion. The whole gate, in swinging, is supported by and revolves around these two points. If, now, the higher point of the centre of mo-tion is perpendicularly *above* the lower centre of motion, a gate will be hung on an even balance, and will remain in any part of the circle which it describes, in opening and closing. It is no difficult job for a skillful workman to set the posts for a gate by the *square rule*, and attach the hinges, doing everything by meas-uring, so as to have a gate swing as he may desire. But the

8*

young farmer must first understand the *"cut and try"* mode of hanging a gate, which is the most practicable, and most generally practised, even by the best workmen.

244. We will run through with the operation of hanging a gate. Set the heel or hinge post firmly (see Fig. 82), with the inside, at least, perpendicular. (The inside of a post is the side towards the latch post.) If the gate is to be hung with hooks and eyes, like those represented at Fig. 85, it is best to hang the gate so as to swing both ways. After the heel post is set firmly, strike a perpendicular line on the inside of it. Put the eyes in the heel stile of the gate, square through the stile. If it is desirable to have a gate hung so as to shut itself, the upper *hook* must be about two inches longer than the lower, and the lower *eye* must be about two inches longer than the upper one. This subject will be made more intelligible by reference to Fig. 85, which represents the position of the hinges as just de-scribed. It will be readily perceived, that when a gate thus hung is swung around through a quarter of a circle, or more, it will not stand perpendicularly, but is inclined *towards the gateway.* This inclination tends to close the gate. If it is desirable to have a gate swing open itself, all that is necessary is, to *reverse the hinges,* having a long *hook* at the bottom, and a *short one at the top.* When a gate is hung in this way, when open at a quarter of a circle, or at a right angle, it will lean *from the gateway.* This inclination tends to keep the gate open.

245. When a gate is hung with hooks and straps, like Fig. 84, a gate can open but one way, and it may be hung on an even balance, or so as to swing open or to swing shut. The straps should be bolted first to the gate, and if it is desirable to hang it so as to swing shut, let the lower strap extend be-yond the heel stile of the gate about one inch and a half far-ther than the top one. Set the gate post, and plumb the inside of it, and also the side of it where the hinges are to be put. After the straps are bolted on the gate, set it up and hold it in the position it is to hang, and bore the holes for the hooks, observing to keep the bit or auger directly under the eye

of the strap. Drive the hooks partly into the post, and hang the gate on, minding to keep the latch end of the gate blocked up until the hinges are driven clear in. If the farmer would have his gate swing open, let the upper strap on the gate extend beyond the lower one about an inch and a half. Another way of hanging with hooks and straps, so as to have a gate swing open or shut, is to let both straps extend an equal distance beyond the heel stile of the gate, just as they do when a gate is to be hung on an even balance. Now, if the gate, when it is being opened, swings to the south, for example, set the heel post leaning to the north about an inch and a half from a perpendicular line. This slight inclination of a post will hardly be perceived by the bystander, and yet so slight an inclination will close a gate quickly when it is open a quarter of a circle; but when swung *beyond* a right angle, it will swing back the other way. In order to have a gate swing *open* when unlatched, when it is hung as last mentioned, let the heel post lean a little the way the gate swings open. It will then open at a right angle, and there remain, and if swung back through half a circle, it will return again, itself, to a right angle, when set free.

246. I have been unusually particular in the preceding paragraphs, in order to show the farmer what is necessary to make a gate swing to his mind which has been hung for a long time, and needs righting up a little. If, for instance, a gate has been hung on an equal balance, but will swing open one way, and swing shut from the other way, the heel post leans the way the gate swings open, and must be righted up a little, if we would have the gate remain at rest when open or partly closed.

247. When it is desirable to have a gate, when hung with iron hinges, open both ways, and shut itself from both ways, the gate should be hung with hook and eye at the top, as shown at Fig. 85, and with a forked hinge at the bottom, like Fig. 86. The forks rest against two staples which are driven into the heel posts, one of which is represented at Fig. 87. The staples are made of half-inch round iron, about two inches wide and three inches long, and the forked hinge may be made more or less

forked or branching. For ordinary purposes the forks should be about four or five inches apart from centre to centre. When the forks are six inches apart, the gate will close itself so rapidly, from a right angle, as to break the latch, or to split the latch stile when it closes. The true way to hang a gate on such hinges is, to put the hinges in the gate stile *first*, and then set the heel post perpendicularly *on the inside*, and strike a line on the

FIG. 86

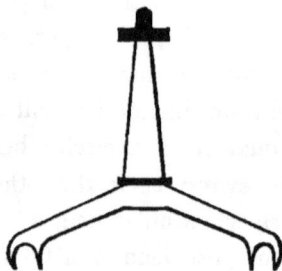

A FORKED GATE-HINGE.

FIG. 87.

A STAPLE FOR FORKED GATE-HINGES.

inside of the post, from top to bottom; and having driven the upper hook in the post, in the line, hang on the gate, and drive in the staples at an equal distance from the plumb line on the post. A gate hung in this manner may be made to *swing open* both ways of itself, by leaning the heel post *from* the gateway far enough to raise the latch end of the gate four or five inches above a horizontal line.

248. The advantages of the forked hinge over hooks and eyes, or hooks and straps, are: the latch end of the gate, in opening either way a quarter of a circle, *rises* from eight to twelve inches, more or less, according to the length of the gate and the width of the forked hinge, and the distance the hinges are apart. This is a matter of convenience when snow obstructs the gateway, or when the ground on one side of a gate would not allow a gate to be opened horizontally. When a fence runs down a slope, having a gate in it, if the heel or hinge post is set on the *upper side* of the gateway, the latch end of a gate will *rise* on being

opened, and allow the gate to be opened *wider* than with any other hinges.

249. Fig. 88 represents a cheap wooden gate, with wooden

FIG. 88.

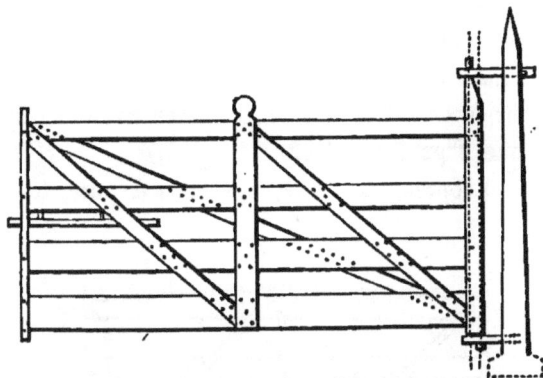

A SELF-SHUTTING GATE WITH WOODEN HINGES

hinges, self shutting, when opened either way. The dotted lines running up and down the heel stile, cutting the centre of the upper and lower hinge, which lines should be about two inches asunder, will show how to make the round parts of the stile. The round parts of the stile should be not less than two and a half or three inches in diameter. The bottom eye should be made of a good piece of hard, durable wood, about three by six inches square, and the mortise for receiving it should be not less than three by four inches square and six inches deep, and the tenon of the eye and mortise should be well painted or tarred before the eye is firmly driven in.

250. To hang such a gate with the greatest facility and dispatch, drive in the lower hinge and put the hinge post in its hole, and fill it just enough to keep the post erect; then put the gate on the lower hinge, and drive in the upper eye while it is hooked on the upper end of the stile. Block up the latch end of the gate on a level with the heel end, and plumb the side of the heel stile, keeping it in that position while the hole is filled to the surface. Afterwards set the latch post. Instead of having the *lower end* of the heel stile made round for a hinge, it may be

square on the end, and a piece of three-quarter-inch round iron driven into the lower end of the stile, and passing through the wooden eye which supports the gate.   In such a case the wooden eye need not be more than two and a half inches square, but it should always be made of the very best of timber.   Always keep wooden hinges well greased.   Never put on tar, because it will soon become hard and wear the hinges more than if nothing were used as a lubricator.   This style of gates will correspond well with fences like Figs. 30 and 32.

251. Fig. 89 represents a very neat board gate, to correspond

FIG. 89.

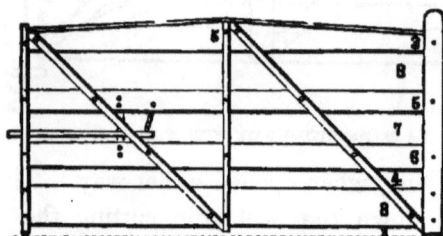

CARRIAGE-YARD GATE, THREE FEET SIX INCHES HIGH.

with the style of fence like Fig. 32.   The heel stile is about three by four inches square, and the latch stile two by three square, of oak, or other hard and durable timber.   The stay may be mortised for the slats, or halved on one side, and a ribbon of a corresponding width fitted to the other side and bolted with carriage bolts.   The *struts* are one inch by two, neatly fitted, one on each side of the gate, and bolted with carriage bolts.   Carriage bolts are much better than rivets, because they will draw the struts tighter than rivets, and are more easily put in; and they cost no more, and look much better than rivets; and in case a gate gets broken it can be readily taken apart, whereas it would be no desirable job to get out a lot of rivets after they have been firmly put in.   The latch plays in a mortise in the latch stile, and is suspended by a little chain near one end.   The gate may be from ten to twelve feet long, with boards one inch thick, and widths and spaces as indicated by the figures in the illustration.   The tenons should be well painted, and also the surfaces of conjunction between all other parts. The cap board is as wide as the stiles, with the ends let in them about half an inch, as shown in the figure. When such a gate opens into the highway, it looks quite as well to have it hung with hooks and strap-hinges, like Fig. 84.

A STRUT AND PICKET GATE.

252. Fig. 90 represents, in the eyes of many people, a very

FIG. 90.

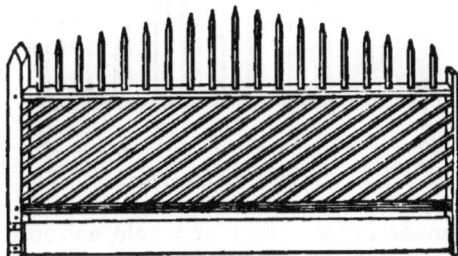

A STRUT AND PICKET GATE.

tasty and fanciful style of lawn gate. The heel stile is about two and a half by four or five inches, and the latch stile two and a half by two, and the arms also two and a half by two. The bottom board is about eight inches wide and three inches below the lower arm. The struts are one inch thick and two and a half wide, and the ends sawed off in a mitre-box. In nailing on the struts, commence with the shortest one, at the *heel* stile. The pickets may be of any desirable style, with or without ornamental tops, or the tops may be plain and tapering to a point. Such a gate ought to be hung with hooks and strap hinges, bolted to the stile and the upper arm. If such a gate is more than nine feet long, there should be a stay bolted to the arms and bottom board in the middle of the gate. When such a gate is used very often, it would be much better to have a double gate—two short ones—than *one* twelve feet in length. It may be fastened with a latch or hook. It would be well to have an iron *tie* on a gate

of this style, to keep it from sagging, as without one the arms
may bow upwards more or less.

A PICKET GATE FOR A LAWN ENTRANCE.

253. Fig. 91 represents a very good style for a picket gate,

FIG. 91.

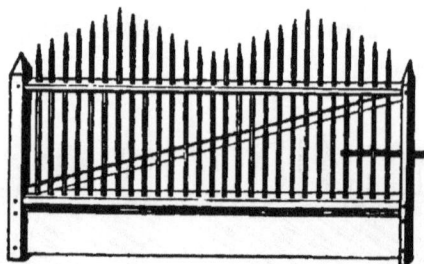

A GATE WITH SQUARE PICKETS.

and it may be made in two parts, or whole, as represented by the
cut. The hinge stile is three by four or five inches, the latch
stile two by three inches, the arms two by three, and the pickets
about an inch and one-fourth square. The arms are about two
feet apart, and the longest picket extends twenty inches above
the upper arm, and the shortest ones about eight inches above it.
The ends of the stiles are pointed also. The bottom board may
be close to the lower arm, or two or three inches below it.

254. In making such a gate, make the mortises in the upper
arm smooth and true *through* the arm, and dress out the pickets
one inch and a fourth square, and point them in the vise, with
drawing-knife and plane. Drive in the longest one first, and then
extend a line from the point of it to the point of the stiles, and
drive in the others. Let them be dressed so that they will fill
the mortise *water-tight*. When they are all in, nail them, and
saw off the lower ends, and drive on the lower arm, and it will
be then ready for the stiles and bottom board. Let the tenons
and parts of pickets in the arms be well painted, before putting
them together. Hang it with hinges, which may be bolted to the
stile and arm, like Fig. 84. I have been thus explicit on this

gate, because many workmen are at a loss to know how to put it together in the most advantageous manner.

WIRE GATES.

255. Fig. 92 represents a *wire* gate, with the heel or hinge stile and latch stile of wood, upper and lower arms of wood, with

FIG. 92.

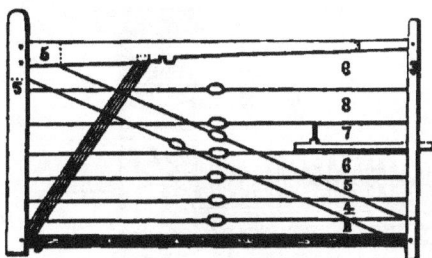

A WOOD AND WIRE GATE.

the wires passing through the stiles, and the two ends twisted together. The *hinge* stile should be at least four inches wide, although five inches would be better, and the latch stile should be at least three inches wide, and, for ordinary gates, about two and a half thick. Both the upper and lower arms should be tapering, as represented in the illustration, and the deeper, up and down, they are, at the hinge stile, the less liable a gate is to sag. At the other ends of the arms they need not be more than two and a half inches square. Wire as large as number twelve, (see Fig. 40,) well annealed, is sufficiently large for filling between the arms. Two wires are put at one place, and strained, by putting a short rod of iron between them at the middle of the gate, and turning it over and over until it is sufficiently tight. Before straining them, however, a stiff rail or pole should be placed parallel with the wires, between the stiles, to prevent the wires, when they are being twisted, from *springing* the latch stile *inward.* After all the wires are strained, this rail may be re- moved, and the wires will all remain of the same tension. Should any of the wires become a little slack they can be strained a little more, at any time, as two wires when twisted together will not untwist of their own accord.

256. Fig. 93 represents a very neat and cheap gate, made entirely of iron and wire, with posts of stone. The posts may be

FIG. 93.

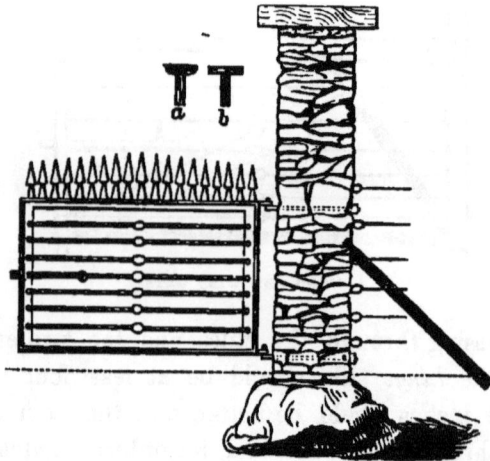

IRON LAWN GATE WITH STONE POST.

made of small stone, laid up in cement, with hinges for gates and staples for wires laid in the cement. The hinges should extend entirely through the posts; and the staples, for attaching the wires of a fence on each side of the gateway, should also be long enough to reach from side to side of the posts, with the ends bent like a square hook, to prevent their drawing out. The stiles and arms may be of cast or wrought iron, with holes in each side for the wires, which may be put in and strained by twisting them together, as recommended in Fig. 92. A very light pattern may be made of wood, with both sides of the gate alike, and gates cast after it. Two such gates swinging together may be used to close a drive or carriage-way. At a and b two cross sections of the stiles and arms are shown. The top may be ornamented with pickets of any style, and cast with the gate.

The hinges may be also cast with the gate. The pattern for latch stile may be made of stuff an inch and a half by three-eighths, and the hinge stile a trifle heavier. The posts should be of very small stone, with the joints pointed, and the top mounted with a square cope stone, with any ornament on the summit of these. Should a wire fence be attached, the post should be most substantially braced, so that the frost would not move the posts by lifting the ends of the braces.

257. Fig. 94 represents a very cheap but durable farm gate, which has one quality to recommend it, of which the other gates noticed are destitute, which is, it is adjustable on the hinges, and when snow obstructs the way it can be raised as high as the top of the hinge post, and fastened there by putting a small iron pin into the round

FIG. 94.

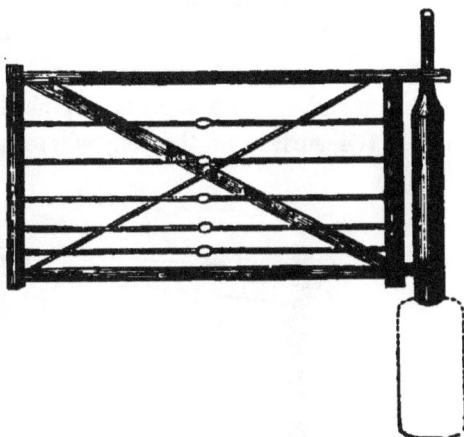

A CHEAP WOOD AND WIRE GATE.

part of the post, under the end of the *upper* arm. The top end of the post is turned round, not less than three inches in diameter, and, instead of passing through the upper arm, a strip of band iron may be bent around it, and bolted to the end of the arm. The lower hinge is made of a tough piece of hard wood plank, not less than two inches thick, of a form corresponding to the size of the post, with a gain in one side. The lower end of the heel stile is fitted to this gain, and the hinge is bolted to the stile, and plays on the outside of the post. A gate hung in this manner will swing entirely round the post. The slats of such a gate may be of narrow boards instead of wire, or pickets may be nailed on the arms. Let the hinges be kept well greased. Sometimes an iron pin is put through the end of the arm into the *top of the pos'*, instead of letting the post extend *above* the gate, as shown in the figure; but the stress at that point is so hard, that a small iron pin, if it were not turned smooth, would in a few years wear a large hole in the arm. This gate will open either way, and hangs on an even balance at whatever point it may be opened. It may be fastened with a latch or hook.

SELF-SUSTAINING GATEWAY.

258. Fig. 95 represents a gateway which some men prefer to all others, because it has many things to recommend it which are not available where nothing but bare posts are used. It is *self-sustaining*, and may be successfully used in localities where rock lies near the surface of the soil, where it would be impracticable

FIG. 95.

SELF-SUSTAINING GATEWAY.

to dig post holes. It may be made as ornamental as desirable by casing the posts *c c* and the plate *d*. One gate, or two, may be hung to the posts, and by having the hooks (hinges) go through the posts, and fasten with nuts and screws on the outside, the hooks can be taken out with facility and put into holes one or two feet *higher* in the winter when the snow is deep, which is a convenience of no trivial consideration in many localities where snow is liable to drift about the gate. The bed-piece *a* should be of durable timber, and extend a little on the outside of the posts and braces. The sills *b b* should be let into the bed-piece about two inches. The posts need not be more than six inches square, and the plate four by six. The gains, tenons and mortises should all be painted well, or smeared with coal tar. By attaching a piece of plank each post may be used as a straining-post for wire fence. The bed-piece *a* may be a round log, flattened a little on the upper side, with the surface not less than three inches above the surface of the ground. The sills should not be set on the ground, but supported with flat stones.

RAILWAY GATES.

259. It may be asked why I do not give an illustration of a *railway* gate, since there are so many different styles of them. If I had ever seen one that I truly admired as economical and convenient, I would not fail to give a description and illustration of it, but I have never seen one that I liked half as well as a hinge gate; and I never have known one instance where a man had used a railway gate for a few years who did not utterly dislike it, and wish a good hinge gate were in its place. An illustration of one looks well, and a new gate looks well, and if well made will *work* well for a few seasons; but if it is used very much the wheels will soon rub hard against the wood, and will make it run hard; and in wet and wintry weather the wheels will be frozen fast, and a man's strength will be required to open it; and, more than all else, a railway gate is *more expensive* than a hinge gate. A good stick of timber, more than enough for two gate posts, is required for the *track*, and as it is laid near the surface of the ground, it will not last but a few seasons. A man will make and hang a good hinge gate with less timber and in less time than a railway gate, and when it is finished it will outlast the railway gate by twice the number of

years, and be twice as convenient. A railway gate is always getting off the track, or something else, and the proprietor is always wishing that he had never seen such a vexatious nuisance.

SECTION 8.—HEDGES FOR FENCE.

" In rural shades, 'mong rural hills and dales,
The Osage Thorn supplies the place of rails.
The Yellow Locust, with far-reaching roots,
Of rapid growth, and thorny, numerous shoots ;
Or the Red Cedar, with its ugly arms,
Guards safe the way between adjoining farms."—EDWARDS.

260. On the subject of hedges I shall be unusually brief, because at the present day many writers, and experimenters, too, of unquestionable authority, pronounce hedges a total failure, while, on the contrary, others, of equally good authority, speak of them in the most approved terms. It cannot be denied that good hedges have been made in America, and that there are now hundreds of miles of hedges which will turn, effectually, every kind of animals that are allowed to have their liberty on the farm. It is granted that there have been very many total failures in making hedges, but the *cause* of failure could not be attributed to the *materials* employed, but to the manner of arranging and disposing them, and to the improper treatment which they received at the time of transplanting, and for a year or two afterwards. The *first steps* in making a hedge decide the question whether it will ultimately prove a failure or a success. Because one man has failed in his attempts to make a hedge, the beginner should not be deterred from exercising his ingenuity and skill, if he wishes to have a hedge, by endeavoring to produce one that will not disappoint his expectations. Hedges require care and protection, and sometimes a little skillful pruning and other treatment, in order to render the plants even, vigorous, and strong. There are miles in length of most beautiful hedges, in many of the older States, which have stood for years as an impassable barrier to every animal that it is desirable to turn on

a farm, besides being a most beautiful appendage to a well cultivated farm. And, without doubt, more than an equal number of miles of hedge can be found, which, on account of its having received improper treatment and cultivation during the first years of its growth, stand, not only as a complete failure, but as a *nuisance* on a farm, and an eye-sore to a skillful farmer.

261. The first step in making a hedge is, to prepare the soil where the hedge is to stand. If the soil be wettish it should be thoroughly drained. It would be folly to attempt to grow a hedge in a locality where it would be too wet to raise good winter wheat. But few kinds of trees will flourish well where there is an excess of water in the soil. If the soil needs a ditch where the hedge is to stand, a portion of the distance, or all of it, commence preparing the ground the season previous to planting the hedge, in order to have a deep, well pulverized soil for the roots to ramify in. The use of the ground need not be lost while the hedge is growing, but it will be an advantage to raise a crop every year, until the hedge is sufficiently large to turn animals. Stake off a strip where a hedge is to be planted, about sixteen feet wide, or wide enough to have, at least, two or three rows of potatoes on each side of the rows of hedge plants. It is better to have the strip unnecessarily wide than to have it *too narrow*, or so narrow that the ground on each side of the hedge cannot be cultivated with a horse and scarifier of some kind. Commence plowing this land early in the fall. If there is sod on the ground, commence in the spring. Plow it four or five times, at least, before winter, throwing the furrows outward at every plowing. This process will produce a *deep middle furrow*, and the deeper it can be plowed the better. After working the land as deep as is convenient with the plow, make a ditch in the middle so that it would be not less than three feet deep on a level. Tile it or stone it well, having a good outlet for the water. Fill the ditch with dirt, and let the whole remain exposed to the influence of the frosts and rains of winter, which will make the whole soil very mellow. This operation is very important, where the soil is inclined to be lumpy during the summer, and where

the subsoil is very stubborn. On gravelly soils, or on any other
soils where the roots of trees strike deep readily, where the subsoil has not been pulverized, this operation is not necessary.
The operator must exercise his own judgment, whether or not his
soil would be improved by such a process.   In many localities,
such a preparation of soil for a hedge would be injurious, and a
hedge would not flourish as luxuriantly on it as it would have
done had the subsoil been allowed to remain untouched.   Where
a soil can be benefited by fall plowing, such a preparation is very
necessary.

262. On the succeeding spring, as soon as the soil is dry
enough to plow, plow this strip of land by turning the furrows
inward at every plowing, until it is six or eight inches *higher*
over the ditch than it is at the sides.   Level it with a harrow
and mark out the rows with a plow, and it is ready for the plants.

263. When the soil is not of a uniform quality throughout the
whole distance, care and pains should be taken to make it so, as
far as practicable.   In crossing a field forty or fifty rods in width,
for instance, a portion of the distance may be a deep, mellow,
and very fertile soil, where almost anything would flourish rapidly,
while, perhaps, only a few rods from this fertile soil, on a little
rise of ground, for a number of rods in length, the soil is very
compact, stubborn and barren.   When this is the case, a few
loads of the good soil should be hauled, and well mingled with
the poor soil before the plowing is finished ; and there should be
enough spread along on the top to set the plants in.   Besides
mingling the different kinds of soil, some parts of the land should
be well manured, and plowed in at the last plowing.   The idea
to be kept in mind is, to have the soil, for the entire distance as
nearly as may be, of a uniform character, so that the hedge will
be of a uniform height throughout.   If the soil be barren in one
place for a few rods, and very fertile in another place, it will be
impracticable to produce a hedge that will be at all beautiful, and
efficient for the purpose of turning animals.   If the soil is not
sufficiently fertile to produce good crops of grain, it should be
well manured with *chip manure* where the soil is compact, if it

can be obtained, or with well-rotted barnyard manure. It would be great folly to transplant a lot of quicks in a soil where they would not make a good growth the first season. It is no uncommon thing to meet with barren spots in fields that are considered to be in a good state of cultivation, and whenever a hedge is to be made through such a place, it must be plowed and pulverized, and enriched thoroughly, or we may rest assured that in such places hedges will prove a complete failure.

HOW TO OBTAIN THE QUICKS.

264. When a farmer contemplates making a hedge, he should sow the seed in drills in the nursery, in a soil which is not in a better state of cultivation than the soil where the hedge is to be made. If quicks be taken from a nursery where the soil has been manured very highly, and transplanted where the soil is of an inferior character, they will not grow as much in a season, if they grow at all, as if they had been taken from a soil inferior to the soil into which they are now to be transplanted. The practice of taking plants from a rich, well-cultivated soil, and transplanting them into a soil *inferior* to the one from which they were taken, operates like taking a well-fed animal from his regular allowance of grain and good hay, and compelling him to subsist on *straw* only. In order to have the quicks grow well, the soil where the hedge is to be planted should be quite as rich, mellow, and fertile as that soil is from which the quicks are taken when they are to be transplanted. For this simple reason the farmer will succeed much better in his attempts to grow a hedge if he sows *his own seed* and raises his own quicks, than he will to purchase of professional nurserymen, whose grounds are kept in a high state of cultivation by an abundant supply of good manure. Farmers often purchase quicks—and the same thing holds good with fruit-trees—of men whose grounds have been made as rich as they could conveniently be made with manure ; and although they have transplanted them in the best manner, and have cultivated the soil on which they stand in the most thorough

9

manner, still, during the first season or two, many of them barely live, without growing two inches.

265. Does the beginner ask, Why not sow the seed where the hedge is to grow? One reason is, the quicks would not be as well protected from cattle, usually, as if they were in the nursery; and another reason is, it would not be *as practicable* to produce a hedge with the quicks of so *uniform* size and distance apart from planting the seed, as it would to grow them in a nursery, and then transplant them. Were it not for the fact that plants of almost every kind, when produced from the seed sown in drills, will in some places be very vigorous, while others will not grow as rapidly as they ought to in order to keep of a uniform size and height, and were it not also for the failure of some of the seed to grow, and the liability of the quicks to be of unequal distances apart, and to stand not in a line, as they should, it would be as well to sow the seed where the hedge is to be made. It will, as a general rule, be found to be the most convenient, economical, and best, to grow the young plants in a nursery, and transplant them where the hedge is to stand. The soil should be prepared as for carrots or beets, and sowed, with a drill or by hand, in rows from thirty to forty inches apart, to suit the proprietor. It is best to have them far enough apart to allow a horse and scarifier to pass between them. In clayey soils that are inclined to bake over the seed, the drills should be covered with black dirt or mould, or fine chip manure, tan bark, sawdust, or such like. The seed is usually sown thicker than the quicks should be allowed to stand, and must be thinned out so as to stand from two to three inches apart. Let them be nursed, and the ground kept clean and mellow about them; and remember, that weeds in some States will grow four times as fast as the young plants, and if not kept down the plants will soon be smothered.

TAKING UP THE QUICKS.

266. When the young plants are dug up, if dug with a spade, great care should be exercised by the laborers not to mutilate

THE YOUNG FARMER'S MANUAL.

the roots more than can be avoided. When there are many to take up, it can be performed very expeditiously with a plow and team. Let the tops all be cut off within about four inches of the ground with a stiff very sharp grass scythe; and then, if one has a subsoil plow, let the plow run about eight or ten inches deep, if the roots run as deep as that, on each side of a row, *about eight inches from the row;* and then a third furrow, with the handles of the plow leaning to the left, will loosen all the plants so that they can be taken up with the hands without any spade or mattock. When the roots run very deep, those who raise many thousands of plants have a plow made almost expressly for such a purpose, with a very wide wing to the plow point for the purpose of cutting off the *long tap roots;* but ordinary farmers may use any plow, and hitch on a strong team to plow up the row, and if half of them or more get covered up, let them be hauled out with manure hooks. After they are all taken up, they should be assorted, and no little care should be exercised to keep the roots from being injured by sunshine or drying winds while they are out of the ground. If thought best to take them up in autumn, and to keep them in the cellar during winter, as many prefer to do, the roots should be well covered with sand or loam to keep them from wilting.

ASSORTING THE QUICKS.

267. The object of *assorting* quicks for a hedge is, to have all those of a uniform size planted together. If they be transplanted without any regard to size, with the small ones mingled with the large ones, the large ones will most certainly overgrow the puny ones, making a weak place in the hedge. There will be many quicks which are not fit to transplant into the hedge row, and which should be rejected as worthless, or left in the nursery to grow another year. If such quicks be planted with others which have strong, healthy roots, the roots of the large quicks will spread all around where the roots of the small weak plants should be, thus robbing the small ones of their necessary nourishment; but by transplanting those of a given size together, *i. e.,* those having

roots and stems about of an equal size, the hedge will grow up of a uniform size and strength. If, for instance, there are quicks enough in one lot to make a hedge row four or six rods in length, let the smallest ones be set together in the best soil, if there should be any difference in the quality of it, and the largest ones in the *poorest* locations. Assorting the quicks properly is one of the most important parts of making hedges. It requires the exercise of keen and quick perception, and good discrimination and judgment. In assorting them the operator should select one of the largest and most vigorous quicks in the lot, and lay it by itself. Then select as small a one as is fit to be transplanted. Select one or two, if there be much difference in their sizes, of a size *between* those already selected. These will answer for a *common standard*. Distribute the quicks, with the large ones by themselves, and the small ones and those of medium size by themselves. One must be guided in assorting, not only by the size of the *stems* alone, but by the size of both roots and stems. Should a small quick have very strong and vigorous roots, it would be better to rank it with those having roots of about an equal size. If a large quick has but few roots, it should not be placed with the large ones because it has a large stem, but it should be placed with those having roots which correspond in size the nearest to it. The operator cannot be too particular in this operation, for not only the beauty and evenness of a hedge depend on a judicious assorting of the quicks, but their *efficiency* is involved in it. If quicks be transplanted without the foregoing considerations, gaps and weak places in a hedge will surely follow.

SECTION 9.—TRANSPLANTING QUICKS.

" Beneath the sunny, vernal sky,
Now scoop the mellow earth aside,
And bury in the fertile soil
The tiny rootlets spreading wide."—EDWARDS.

268. In the first place take the plow, adjusted to run about three inches deep, and turn two furrows *from* each other, where

the hedge is to be planted. Next, with a shovel, clean out the trench, three or four inches deep, and wide enough to receive the roots of the largest quicks, when they are fully extended from side to side, without their being bent sideways. The roots should spread out as far as they will reach, and all the little roots and spongioles should be spread out to their full extent, as they originally grew. Cut off all tap roots smoothly, and cut off the ends of those roots that have been mutilated in digging up the plants. Stretch a line about three or four rods long, about an inch on one side of the place where the row is to stand. Have it high enough so as not to be in the way when hauling in the dirt. Let knots be tied in this line, as far apart as the quicks are to be planted. Set each quick about an inch from the line, at every knot. When two rows are to be planted, the quicks of the second row should be placed opposite the *spaces* and not opposite the other plants. When three rows are set out there should be two lines stretched, one for each outside row, and the quicks in the outside rows should stand opposite the spaces in the middle row. When the stems of the quicks are cut off, the line may be stretched where the rows are to stand, and a quick placed under every knot of the line. If the dirt is not mellow and fine in every place, it would be well to have a load hauled by the side of the hedge row; and when one man places the quicks, let another man throw a few shovelfuls on the roots. Manure should never be applied directly to the roots. A few inches of mellow earth should be applied *first*, and then manure, and then more dirt, when manure is applied at transplanting. The quicks should never be transplanted, when the soil is too wet to be worked in for other purposes, lest it *bake* around the root.

269. When the quicks are all transplanted in a workmanlike manner, the hedge is by no means finished. Indeed, this is but a good beginning. From five to ten years, according to the soil, the kind of plants used, the kind of hedge to be made, and the training and cultivation it receives, will require strict care and protection, to render it an impassable barrier to stock. The first thing will be, if it has not already been decided, to determine

what style of hedges shall be adopted, as different styles of hedges require very different treatment.

270. Hedges may be made to grow in almost any form desired, but it is always best to imitate nature, as far as convenient and practicable; and, especially it is best, when greater efficiency is secured by adopting a given style. The tops of all trees and plants assume a conical form more than any other, in their natural state. If some other form for the tops of trees were more desirable, they would unquestionably assume that form. But, as a hedge cannot be trained in a conical form, we must adopt the style nearest to it,—that of a *pyramid*. The quicks are trained to a single stem, sometimes, for a few feet high, and then the top is sheared in the shape of a pyramid. Sometimes two or three rows of quicks are transplanted in a hedge row, in which instance they are trained to a thick mat, as it were, from the ground, with sides perpendicular, sometimes, for a few feet high, and then of a pyramidal form; and sometimes it is trained of a pyramidal form from near the ground to the top. Sometimes the sides are kept perpendicular, and the top is square across, or flat. But this style is considered objectionable by our best hedgers. Sometimes the hedge is trained or sheared in the shape of a sharp-pointed egg, with the point upwards. But whatever style may be adopted,

THE PRUNING AND TRAINING

271. Must be attended to in a proper season, or one may at once abandon the idea of making an impassable barrier for even small stock. We must not be afraid to cut off a fine growth of sprouts for fear it will require a year longer for them to attain that height again. Depend upon it, this is the most important operation in rearing hedges. The quicks need to be cut off, time after time, in order to give them size and vigor. If they are allowed to grow, from year to year, without being cut down, the hedge will be thin in places, and the sprouts will be tall, slim, and easily demolished by animals.

272. In order to make a thick, impenetrable hedge clear to the ground, the quicks standing in three rows, as has been previously stated, should all be cut off two or three inches from the ground, when they are one or two years old. It is desirable that they should be cut off with some instrument which gives a *drawing cut*, as a *crushing* cut is very liable to injure the stems. If they grow up again very soon, they should be cut off again, the same season, in the latter part of July, some five or six inches higher than the first cut. At every cutting a thick growth of sprouts is produced, which interlace each other so closely that it is difficult for a small bird to get through it. If any sprouts shoot off *laterally* several inches beyond the majority of the side sprouts, they should be clipped. The sprouts should all be cut off at least once every year, six or eight inches higher every year, until the hedge is four or five feet high, training the hedge in the form of a pyramid. (See TOOLS FOR PRUNING HEDGES, Par. 360.)

273. Another mode of training is, to have but a single row, and not cut off the tops until they are all about two feet high, when the limbs are all interlaced with each other, by hand, and the ends of those which grow at right angles to the hedge row are sheared off to an even length, making the body of the hedge from two to three feet through. This interlacing the limbs is continued, as the height of the hedge increases from year to year, until it is five or six feet high, when the top is simply pruned in the form of a pyramid.

LAYING AND PLASHING.

274. "The operation consists in first removing the thorns and prickles, and cutting away all the needless branches and stems, and leaving straight upright stems in the middle of the row. The best and straightest of these are left for stakes, and their tops are cut off at the height of about four feet. If possible these should be at equal distances of about two feet apart; but as they cannot always be had so regularly distributed, stakes may be driven in the ground to supply their places. The rough-

est stems are then cut out, and those that are left are bent over
to an angle of about forty-five degrees, and a hack is made in
them near the surface of the ground.   They are then woven
backwards and forwards in a slanting direction.   When a portion of the hedge is thus treated, long slender sticks are cut and
wattled in among the stakes, within an inch or two of the tops,
by twisting backwards and forwards, and crossing them on alternate sides of the stakes.   The live stakes, in consequence of
being surrounded by the hedge, are apt to send out shoots thickly
at the *tops,* and not below, unless prevented by being cut half
through at the ground.   Strong leather mittens, with long
sleeves, are needed by the man who does the work."—*Albany
Cultivator.*

CULTIVATING THE SOIL ALONG HEDGES

275. Must be thoroughly performed yearly, until the hedge is
large enough to turn cattle.   The soil should be plowed every
spring, just as if no hedge were there, and some hoed crop planted
by the sides of it.   If corn be planted there, a row of potatoes,
or carrots, beets, turnips, or the like, should be planted on each
side of the hedge *between the corn and it,* never nearer to it than
three feet.   Let a horse scarifier be run along the hedge row as
often as you can find leisure during summer; and keep the ground
mellow and level, and free from grass and weeds, during the
entire growing season.   Never allow plants of any kind to cast
their seed near the hedge row.   If weeds or thistles are allowed
to grow among the quicks, they will soon choke them, and produce a thin, weak place in the hedge.   If some parts of the hedge
do not seem to grow as fast as others, give the small parts of
stinted growth a liberal dressing of well-rotted chip manure, or
sawdust, or well-prepared compost, and work it in with a hoe.
If the soil in places seems to be so hard that they do not grow
as fast as other parts of the hedge, let mellow dirt be spread on
each side two or three inches deep.   There will be a great many
times during the growing season, when, for an hour or two, and
perhaps for half a day, the work hands will have nothing which

they can do advantageously. Let all such leisure hours be occupied with a hoe at the hedge. Let the farmer keep an eye on the hedge and see that it is not neglected in autumn, and that a lot of weeds do not go to seed, so as to keep one weeding for seven years. Remember, that

276. "One year's seeding makes seven years' weeding." Never think of making an impenetrable hedge in less than a decade of years, when only a little strip two feet wide on each side of the hedge is scratched over a little once or twice a year. If land is cheap, and it is no object to cultivate a crop by the side of a hedge, let the work of cultivating be performed with plow, harrow and cultivator, *without* a crop. Another thing which is too commonly neglected is,

PROTECTING HEDGES FROM CATTLE,

277. While they are too small to protect themselves. Young steers, especially, and bulls, delight to plunge into a hedge row to hook, and horses and sheep like to nip off the tender shoots; and, if it is not protected by a good fence, it is all folly to attempt to grow a hedge. Nor should we delay to fence a hedge row for the first year or two; for cattle are very liable at any time to get on forbidden ground, when they would quickly make irreparable breaches in it. Should there be no sheep kept on the farm, the expense of protecting a hedge would be trifling. A fence on each side of it, like Fig. 22, even if the posts were not of the most durable timber, would subserve a good purpose until the hedge should be strong enough to turn cattle without any protection. It is always advisable to keep cattle away from hedges, until there can be no risk in permitting them to hook into it to their satisfaction.

REPAIRING HEDGES.

278. Should a breach be made in a hedge, or should it become so thin and weak in places as not to be strong enough to turn cattle, if the stems are not healthy, it would be best to remove them entirely for a few feet in length, and commence *anew* with

9*

young quicks; or, if thought best, the stems should all be cut off
a few inches from the ground, when new sprouts will spring up,
which must be treated like a new hedge until the gap is securely
closed.   Wherever thin spots occur in a hedge, it is a pretty
sure indication that the soil is not as fertile as it should have
been made previous to transplanting, or that roots of the quicks
were mutilated, or that they did not have an equal chance with
the rest of the hedge.

HEDGES FOR WET GROUNDS.

279. It is frequently the case, that lands on the borders of
rivers and lakes, which are liable to inundation in the spring and
in autumn, are so wet that none but aquatic plants would flourish
well there.   In such localities an impenetrable hedge may be
made in a very few years with the branches of the *yellow willow*,
or of any other kind of trees the limbs of which will take root
when stuck in the ground.   The limbs should all be cut of a
uniform length, say five or six feet long, *with a saw*, as an axe is
very liable to split and sliver the ends.   The upper ends should
be *sawed* off *slanting*, for a slanting cut will heal over more
readily than a *square* cut.   The lower ends should not be sharpened by cutting off the wood all around them, because the ends
will be very apt to rot as far up as the bark is all taken off, and
sometimes farther, endangering the life of the plants.   But the
sharpening should all be done *on one side* of the limbs, and then
roots will start from the ends, and a portion of the lower ends
will not decay.   Take the limb in one hand, when it is to be
sharpened, and set it on a block, and make a clean slanting cut,
only on one side.   Limbs that are less than two inches in diameter should not be sharpened at all, because they will take root
all round better than if they were sharpened.   Let limbs of a
uniform size be planted together, and never stick *small* ones and
large ones indiscriminately together, lest the large ones *overgrow*
the small ones.   Let all the branches remain on them for interlacing, except such as grow on the parts which are to be *below*
the surface of the soil.

280. In sticking them, draw a line and make the holes with a crowbar, directly *under* the line, about ten or twelve inches apart. For large limbs let large holes be made, and for small ones do not make the holes so large and deep that the limbs will extend downward so that the lower ends will all decay. If they are planted ten or twelve inches in depth, unless the soil is very deep, they will flourish better than if they were planted twenty or more inches deep. Plunge them in the holes to the desired depth, with the hands, and never drive them. If, then, any of them do not seem to stand sufficiently firm, place a good sod on each side of them, and stamp it down well. After the limbs are all stuck let the branches on them be interlaced, by commencing at the bottom and weaving them back and forth, forming a kind of lattice work. Should the whole seem not to stand very firmly, let long slender branches from the trees of some other kind of wood, be interwoven at the tops. Such a hedge should be made early in the spring in preference to the fall; and it will require shearing at least once a year, to keep it even, and to prevent its growing too high.

WHAT KINDS OF PLANTS ARE USED FOR HEDGES.

281. "The selection of suitable plants for hedges depends, in a very great degree, upon the *locality*. In some localities one kind of plants will flourish very luxuriantly, and make the best of hedges, while only a few hundred miles distant from such location, that kind of plants will not succeed at all in hedge-making. Some species of plants are not at all adapted to the climate where they are to be used; while some others, which flourish well in a given climate, are so liable to be attacked by the borer or blight, as to be of no value whatever for hedges. The English hawthorn, for example, has been found entirely unsuited to most parts of the United States.* Some plants do not seem to be hardy enough to endure, without injury, the extreme cold of our northern winters; and such plants, although they may have a great reputation for

* Albany Cultivator.

making hedges, in some localities, should be tested with caution, where any doubts are entertained of their success.

282. In searching for information in regard to hedges in the agricultural journals of the present day, the young farmer will be puzzled, beyond measure, to know what to do in regard to mak ing a hedge of any kind. One article, penned by a man who professes to have been successful in making hedges, will state, in most unequivocal language, that "every farmer may raise hedges." Another writer, of very reliable authority, will assert, with the strongest confidence, that it is *by no means practicable* for American farmers to make hedges, with a view of enclosing and dividing their fields, which shall be cattle proof. One writer will recommend a certain plant for hedges, with the most confident assurance that it will ultimately be universally adopted for fencing the western prairies, where timber is not abundant, and that such a plant succeeds for hedges remarkably well; while, on the contrary, another man will declare, most positively, that such a plant can never make a good hedge; and that he will defy the world to produce a *solitary instance* where an efficient and impenetrable hedge has been made of that kind of plant. Amid such a conflict of opinions, on a subject apparently so full of doubt and uncertainty, the farmer must exercise a little good common sense, and let the bugbears and sharks go to the winds that brought them.

283. It cannot be denied that there are miles in length of the most efficient and impenetrable hedge, in nearly every State in the Union, through which an American bison could not pass, and which has been produced with but a small degree of expense and care. And, if a few enterprising farmers have succeeded in making a good hedge, the arguments and assertions *against* hedges, of a man who has failed to produce a good hedge, *from utter neglect,* or from local causes, should have no influence in deterring the young farmer from making a hedge, if he desires one.

RED CEDAR FOR HEDGES.

"On barren cliffs, the hardy cedars red,
Clinging to crevices, lift up their heads."—TUPPER."

284. The red cedar is acknowledged, by the most reliable authority, to be one of the best plants in America, for both ornamental and field hedges. It has more desirable qualities to recommend it than any other known plant which is used for making hedges. *If it only bore thorns*, it would be incomparably better for hedges than any other plant whose merits have been thoroughly tested as a hedge plant. It is extremely hardy, and adapts itself to both barren and fertile soils, although it flourishes on a rich soil as much better, as any other plant; and it attains a great age, is as highly ornamental as the most fastidious can desire; and is not liable to blight, or winter-kill, or to be injured by insects. No other plant bears shearing any better, or with less injury, than the cedar; and a hedge of this kind of plants may be sheared into almost any form with great facility.

285. The best mode of obtaining the young plants is, to gather the berries or seed as late in autumn as possible, before the ground freezes, and sow them in drills, covered about one inch deep with some very light mellow earth. But few seeds will vegetate the first season, but if the soil be kept well cultivated and free from noxious weeds during the growing season, the second season they will appear in abundance. If the soil be deep, mellow, and rich, they will grow from one to two feet in height the first season; if the soil is rather poor, and the little quicks are obliged to grow or die among weeds, if they grow six inches high the first season, it will be all that can be expected. The plants should be thinned out when they stand too thick, and transplanted in rows for a year or two. When they are from two to three feet high, they should be planted out for hedges, in soil prepared as recommended, as early in the spring as it will answer to work in the soil. If they are set in only one row, they should be not less than twenty inches apart, and if in two rows, two feet apart, with the plants of one row

opposite to the spaces of the other row.   Let all the limbs on all the insides of the trees be interlaced, as neatly as may be; and let the limbs on the *sides* of the hedge row be sheared to a uniform length, from six to twelve inches in length, according to the length of the limbs.   During the first and second seasons, or perhaps longer if necessary, let the *tops* be sheared of a uniform height. As the hedge grows higher, let the inside limbs be interwoven from tree to tree, backwards and forwards; and do not fail to keep the soil well cultivated on both sides of the hedge row, for at least six or eight feet on each side.   If everything is performed in a workmanlike manner, a complete lattice-work, impenetrable by any domesticated animal, will be formed in a few years.

286. As the red cedar bears no thorns, and as cattle are so much inclined to hook and thrust about in evergreen plants, the red cedar may, upon trial, succeed better by training the young trees to bare stems about four feet high, and then allow the tops to branch out, so as to be sheared in the form of a pyramid, or in the shape of an egg, with the little end upwards.—(See paragraph 270.)   In this style of training the inside limbs should be interlaced, from a point two feet above the ground to the top of the hedge.

287.   A little skill and judgment, and the exercise of a little common sense, are indispensably requisite in pruning the young cedars.   If the trees are two or three feet high it will not answer to cut off all the limbs the first season, and leave but a little bush at the top.   The first season that they are transplanted in the hedge row, the lower limbs, for about six inches along the bottom of the stems, may be cut close with a sharp knife; and if the limbs *above* this point be more than a foot long, the ends may be clipped off to a foot in length on each side.   The next spring trim off the limbs a few inches higher, close to the stems. If the plants have grown six inches or more in height, it may answer, if there is an abundance of limbs, to cut off smoothly all the limbs for six inches more.   The growth of the plants upwards will usually determine how much of the limbs may be cut off *below* in one season.

THE YELLOW AND HONEY LOCUST FOR HEDGES.

"The fair Queen of Spring, as she passed down the vale,
Quaffed the nectar of locusts in every mild gale :
Its fragrance and odor replenished each breeze,
And lily-white glory environed the trees."—CAMPBELL.

288. The yellow locust and honey locust are *indigenous* in the United States, and flourish luxuriantly in almost every locality where there is not an excess of water in the soil where they are planted. They are among the most beautiful ornamental trees, and when in full bloom the yellow locust seems most delightful. Both of the kinds already mentioned are very hardy and great feeders, the roots of the yellow locust growing to an almost incredible length in one season. The *honey* locust bears bunches of long and sharp thorns, from two to three inches in length, presenting such an ugly appearance as to deter almost any animal, man not excepted, from climbing up into it; but the thorns of the *yellow* locust are small and short, and *deciduous* on the main stem and limbs of the trees when they are a few years old. The honey locust is said to be a very common tree in the forests of some of the Western States, and when found on rich bottom lands, it attains a growth equal in height to most other trees which surround it. The *timber* of the honey locust is somewhat hard, and rather porous, and is sometimes made use of for cabinet purposes, and sometimes for posts and rails for building fences. The timber of the *yellow* locust, of thrifty trees, is remarkably tough and firm, and durable when exposed to the influences of the weather. On account of its excellence in resisting the action of moisture, it is used in preference to almost any other timber for *pins* and *wedges*, and such like, in ship-building. For fence posts it is not inferior in point of durability to white oak, and for carriage hubs it is not inferior to the best of birch. In some localities the yellow locusts have been entirely destroyed by the ravages of the borer and the large green caterpillar. But the borer seldom attacks any other part of the tree excepting the *body*, for six or eight feet from the ground. But if the *epidermis* or dead part of the bark be *all scraped off* or shaved off, to the

live bark, once in four or five years, or as often as any signs of the borer are discovered, and the bodies of the trees smeared with a daubing made of three parts of pitch or rosin, and one part of tallow, melted together and applied warm with a brush, the borer will be most effectually excluded.

289. Neither the yellow locust nor honey locust have been tested satisfactorily for hedging purposes. It has been used to a limited extent in a few instances, and there are at the present day many young hedges of both kinds which promise to be in a few years most impenetrable barriers against any kind of stock. I am able to discover no good reason why the locust may not be used most successfully for hedges, with proper treatment and care. It grows quickly even on poor soils; is easily propagated; bears shearing extremely well; and is very tenacious of life. The locust will probably succeed better when planted in a single row and plashed, than in two or three rows and trained in a *mat* hedge. The locust flourishes best *solitary;* and when the art of hedge-making shall arrive to greater perfection, the locust will rank among the *first plants* for hedges.

290. Both kinds of locust bear seed contained in long pods, which may be gathered late in autumn and kept in a dry apartment until the succeeding spring, when, to insure their vegetation, the seed is put in a vessel of some kind and boiling hot water poured on them while they are stirred lively for a few moments, and then allowed to remain in the water for a day and a night, when most of them will be swollen to twice their original size. All such seed is sure to grow if planted in a soil that will produce good corn, and covered about as corn is covered when planted. Those seeds which have not swollen during the operation should be treated in the same manner the second time. The object of scalding the seeds is to *soften* the hard and tough skin which envelops the germ, so that moisture can enter the seed. If the seed is planted as soon as it has arrived to maturity early in autumn, before the skin on them becomes so dry and tough, most of them will vegetate in the succeeding spring, when they may be treated as has been recommended.

THE OSAGE ORANGE FOR HEDGES.

291. The Osage Orange, a cut of which is here shown (taken from the *Albany Cultivator,*) has been used extensively for

FIG. 96.

OSAGE ORANGE.

hedges, so that its success is no longer attended with doubt. It is found wild in Arkansas, Mexico, Mississippi and some other

States, where it grows from twenty to thirty feet high. It flourishes well in most of the States and Territories, and with proper treatment has never failed to make an impenetrable hedge. Many failures have been reported respecting the Osage for hedges, but in all probability the failures could be traced to improper management, such as neglecting to shear down and to keep the soil in good condition, or assorting the quicks and transplanting them properly. We need apprehend no failure in making a first-rate hedge of the Osage, if the course is strictly followed which has been marked out in the preceding pages.

We copy from the *American Farmers' Encyclopedia* the following description of the Osage Orange: " It is very branching, each branch being armed with numerous sharp thorns. The wood is remarkably tough and solid. The male and female flowers are on separate trees. The fertile, or female tree, bears fruit abundantly in a few years. These are round and rough, and greenish colored, resembling somewhat an orange, and weighing from twelve to eighteen ounces, containing from one hundred to one hundred and fifty seeds."

292. The best manner for any one to obtain the quicks for hedges is, to procure the seed in some locality where the Osage flourishes in a wild state, and sow them in autumn in well-prepared ground. The seed, like many other kinds of seed, will vegetate better after having been exposed to the frosts of winter in the soil. It is said that there are about eight thousand seeds in one quart, and that they may be obtained in Arkansas for the mere expense of gathering them. When they are obtained of nurserymen the cost is from two to four dollars per quart. It is recommended by some farmers to *scald* the seeds of the Osage in the spring, at the time of planting them. Hedges made of the Osage Orange require trimming twice a year, and some, who have experimented with it extensively, say that three trimmings are necessary in one season. The farmer must exercise a little judgment with reference to trimming a hedge. Should the growth be small, it would not be proper to cut off as much as if there were a very great growth.

BUCKTHORN FOR HEDGES.

"What a thorny maze we tread !
Thorns beneath and overhead !
How they pierce, and scratch, and tear !
Cursed thorns grow everywhere."—HAMLET.

293. The buckthorn is pronounced by some writers to be the most suitable plant for hedges that can be found in the United States. It makes an efficient and impenetrable hedge when properly treated, and grows very rapidly, is very hardy, and almost entirely exempt from disease and from the attacks of insects. There are hedges of the buckthorn in some of the older States, which have subserved the purpose of an impenetrable fence for more than forty years, and are now free from gaps and weak places. The buckthorn bears pruning very extensively without any apparent injury, and is never injured by the most intense cold of winter. It vegetates early in the spring, and does not cast off its verdure until late in autumn.

294. The figure here shown represents a branch of the buckthorn. The seed may be sown early in autumn in mellow soil, covered about one inch deep, when most of them will vegetate the next spring, if the seed is good. It is best to have at least two rows, or three, in a hedge row of buckthorn, and train them by shearing down, so that the hedge will be an impenetrable mat clear to the ground.

There are several other kinds of thorns, such as the Washington, Newcastle, Hawthorn, and some others, which have been used for hedges, and sometimes successfully; but they are so liable to be affected by blight, or insects, or something else which is very injurious to them, that it is not safe, except in a few localities, to experiment with them. The various kinds of thorn are propagated by gathering the haws or seed, and divesting them of the skin and pulpy matter, and sowing them in the fall, so that they may freeze and thaw during the winter.

FIG. 97.

BUCKTHORN.

RECAPITULATION AND GENERAL REMARKS.

295. After the farmer has fully concluded to raise a hedge, let him secure *good seed*, which is generally distinguished from an

inferior quality of seed by its *weight*. *Poor* seed is usually rather *light*, and feels dry to the touch, while good, plump, bright and heavy seed seems to be *colder*, when handled, than it really is. Let all seed that is more than one year old be rejected, and none but new seed sown. Bear in mind, that as seed advances in age it looses its vitality. Seed is many times injured, and often the vitality is entirely destroyed, in preparing it for use. The pulpy matter which encircles the seed is usually removed by placing them where they will rot gradually, and afterwards washing the pulpy substance from the seed, and then by spreading out the seed where they will dry. But they should not be allowed to become *too dry*, as that will injure the germ. If they are permitted to lie, while rotting, in piles so large or deep that they will *heat* and *mould*, the germs of such seed will be liable to be destroyed. I must be allowed to insist that it is important that every farmer *grow his own quicks*, on soil of about the same quality of that where the hedge is to stand. (See Par. 264.)

296. When the quicks are cut off in autumn it would be a good practice to have a vessel of equal parts of melted pitch or rosin, and tallow, and smear the ends with it, applied with a paint brush. The most expeditious mode of doing it would be, to hold as many in one hand as is convenient, and then apply the brush. Even after the quicks have been transplanted, a man with a small brush would smear the ends of a long row in a few hours. It would not be practicable to perform such an operation after the first shearing, or cutting down, on account of the great number of stubs, although such an application will be found very useful in preventing the stumps from drying and cracking, to the injury of the quicks. Any instrument, in pruning, shearing, or slashing, which cuts the stems *square off*, with a *crushing* instead of a *drawing* stroke or cut, is quite apt to shiver the butts or stumps of the quicks, so that they will not heal as readily as if they had been cut with a *slanting* and *drawing* cut. (See Par. 543.)

297. On the subject of pruning, too much care cannot be taken, for rules and practices which would be all-important for raising an efficient hedge in one locality, would be very deleterious to a

hedge in another region. In some regions the sprouts cf the Osage Orange grow so rapidly as to attain the height of four to seven feet in one season, while in other places they would not grow as many inches. Where they grow so rapidly the roots become proportionably strong, and shearing must be resorted to. But when the growth is very small, and the stems slender and weakly, it *might* be the wisest policy to allow them to grow un-molested for one season. It is not easy for one to tell, with pen and ink alone, whether a hedge should or *should not* be cut down at a certain stage of its growth. Sometimes it might be very advisable to trim or shear a hedge twice in one season; but the probability is, that in our climate it is best to clip but once a year, and the best and most natural season for this operation would seem to be *in the spring*. I know many recommend late autumn, and others the month of July, for this purpose, as being the best, but it appears to me that unless the ends of the quicks are smeared with something to prevent the weather from drying them, it would be best to do it in the spring, about the time the buds begin to enlarge a little. If some of the quicks grow too rapidly during the summer, the top ends may be pinched off a lit-tle. This will check the tendency to shoot upward tall and slim, and will tend to enlarge the stem and side branches. If it is desirable to have limbs clear to the ground, the side branches should not be clipped until they have grown, laterally, not less than two feet on each side of the row. In order to have the branches low, the quicks must be clipped near the ground the first time they are cut off. If they are clipped *high* the first time, it will be impossible to produce limbs near the ground, unless the whole top is cut down, when, if the roots are strong and healthy, many sprouts will start from the stumps, both upward and hori-zontally. (See Par. 301, 302.)

298. Hedges oftener prove a failure in consequence of *neglect* than from any other cause. Hedges cannot grow, they will not grow well *among weeds and grass*, and those who expect them to flourish will be most certainly disappointed. The soil on each side must be kept loose, mellow and clean, for at least half a rod

from the hedge row. When only a narrow strip of two feet or so on each side is scratched over occasionally, it would be no more beneficial, in many localities, than if the soil were not broken at all. On prairies and bottom lands, where the soil is deep, always mellow, and fertile, preparing the soil as recommended in paragraph 261 is not so very important as on stubborn, clayey and calcareous soils, in which localities the directions should be followed up to the very letter.

299. I have never, as yet, met with any writings in which it was recommended to transplant the quicks as suggested in par. 268. The more usual practice is to *dibble* them in with a kind of paddle, or to thrust in a spade where a quick is to be set, and, thrusting the handle forward, the quick is set *behind* the spade in a wedge-shaped hole, without any spreading of the roots. But it seems to me that, if it would pay in transplanting fruit-trees, which none will deny, to spread out the roots, it would be time profitably spent in transplanting the quicks for a hedge in the most workmanlike manner. According to the *modus operandi* in par. 268, a long line of hedge could be put out in a day by a faithful laborer and a small lad ; and in such soil as we find, for the most part, in central and western New York, and in some of the New England States, no one who is acquainted with their character, and with the most proper manner of working them, will wish to deny that this is the better mode of transplanting the quicks. It is most certain that the more the roots of a tree or quick are spread out, in transplanting, the better the tree is transplanted ; and the more they are crowded into a small compass, the less liable they are to flourish luxuriantly for the first year or two after transplanting. If a quick has side-roots, nature and common sense teach us that it is better to spread them and extend them in their full length, than to *double* them and crowd them into a small hole.

300. The proper distances apart for plants to be set, is a very important question in growing a good hedge. For my own part, I am fully persuaded that hedgers, as a general rule, plant *too close.* It is a most common fault, in transplanting all kinds of

fruit-trees, to · plant *too close together;* and, although *very* close planting is recommended, on good authority, for hedges, it is my candid conviction that if those hedgers who advocate and adhere to very close planting, and who succeed well in raising efficient hedges when planted *very* close together, would plant the quicks farther apart, they would meet with still better success than they do in very close planting.   No one will deny that quicks for hedges may be planted *too closely together,* and we all acknowledge, without any argument, that it is not difficult, in the least, to plant them *too far* apart.   Now, then, if there is a point beyond which, in one direction, it may be said the quicks are *too near together,* and, in the opposite direction, they are *too far apart,* that is the point which will determine most accurately the most proper distance apart for transplanting the quicks, in order to make the best and most efficient hedge.   The distance that might *properly* be called close planting when one kind of plants is used, might not be said to be too close for another plant.   The kind of plants used always should, in a great measure, determine the proper distance for the plants to be set apart.   We consider eight inches apart *too close* for any plants, and for any style of hedge, although some hedgers advocate a distance of only *four* and *six* inches apart.   ·But when plants are set so very close together, the shoots are very apt to be small and slender, with not sufficient space for the lateral branches to attain suitable size for consistent strength ; and, more than all else beside, when they are crowded so closely together they are quite liable to die, in consequence of being deprived, by those on each side of them, of their necessary nourishment at the roots.   We consider *one foot sufficiently close for any plants in a hedge row,* and for some plants one foot apart is just twice as close as they should be.   When plants are set *closer* than one foot, or even one foot and a half, let a few plants be placed in a row at such distances apart, and see how little space they have for branching out.   Look, for example, at the sprouts around stumps which stand very close to each other.

They are tall, slim, and not half as strong as they would be if they were not half as numerous; and, more than all else, their lateral branches, if there are any at all, are very slender, and will very soon decay; whereas, if the plants stood twenty or thirty inches apart, the lateral branches—which give the greatest efficiency to a hedge—will be large, strong, and not liable to premature decay, as in *close planting*. It is better to have one strong, healthy, lateral branch, than three, or even four branches in the same space, which are slender and liable to decay in consequence of close planting. Strong, stiff, lateral branches, with the ends clipped off, and having thorns on their sides, are very repulsive things for stock of any kind to plunge into. But when all the sprouts grow erect and slender and smooth, bullocks with very long horns will delight in the fun of thrashing them to the ground. Any one who is well acquainted with the habits of the red cedar, or the hemlock, or American arbor vitæ, will, I doubt not, fully coincide with me, that when planted very close together they could not be relied upon for making an efficient and impassable hedge; but if transplanted at about thirty inches apart, they will make, in some localities, a more efficient and impassable and *durable* hedge than any other plant which has as yet been successfully cultivated for hedges. Of these three plants last mentioned, the red cedar is most preferable. The honey locust, the yellow locust, the Osage orange, and, in fact, almost every other plant which has been and is now cultivated for hedges, will flourish best when standing nearly or quite solitary. Therefore, to close this subject, we lay it down as our candid conviction, that all the plants just mentioned will flourish better, be more durable, be stronger, less liable to premature decay, be trained with less difficulty, make an impassable fence sooner, be kept within the desired limits assigned for the width and height of the hedge, after the hedge is completed, and be grown at a much less expense, and by laborers possessing inferior skill in the business of hedging, when the plants are set from *sixteen to twenty inches apart*, in some instances *thirty inches*, than if they were set from six to twelve inches apart. I have

10

planted some red cedars for a hedge fence, and I place them thirty inches apart, believing that at that distance they will make a better hedge than if set any closer to each other.

PHILOSOPHY OF PRUNING.

301. Why do we prune trees and plants? Trees and plants are pruned for several reasons. They are pruned sometimes for the purpose of removing the dead branches, and sometimes to make a tree grow higher, and sometimes to make it grow *broader* and *lower;* and sometimes for the purpose of making the fruit grow larger and fairer, by removing the redundant branches. If the ends of all the limbs of a tree should be clipped off two or three times during the growing season, and they were not allowed to grow only so high and so far laterally, a tree would soon send out sprouts or suckers all over the limbs, and in a few years a tree would be a complete mat of brush. If all the topmost branches are clipped off about as fast as the ends grow, the greatest part of the sap will be driven or thrown into the lateral branches, and they will shoot off horizontally with great rapidity. On the contrary, if one bud or stem is allowed to *shoot up* in the centre of the top, and all the others are kept back by clipping off the ends as fast as they grow, there will be an unusual amount of sap flow- ing to this centre stem, and it will run up tall and slim. When young fruit-trees are inclined to grow slim and tall, we clip off the top buds, which will throw the sap into the lateral branches, and the trees will begin to thicken. Although pruning fruit- trees is not intimately connected with the subject of this section, still I cannot forbear to notice, briefly, some things connected with pruning trees.—(See Figs. 125 and 150, TOOLS FOR PRUNING.)

302. In forming a head to young fruit-trees, the young farmer should aim to have one stem run up in the centre of the tree, and then a system of two or three or four limbs extending horizontally from the upright stem, about thirty or forty inches apart, clear to the top of the tree. The first system of branches should be about five or six feet from the ground. If they should be inclined to

sag down too much, they might be well shored up, or tied up with wires extending from the top of the tree to them, during the growing season, when they would probably remain in that position.

303. It is bad policy to allow trees to grow at random for a number of years, and then give them a severe pruning. It injures a fruit-tree to cut off a large limb as much as it hurts a man to have a limb amputated. Fruit-trees should always be pruned so that a man can easily get around in the tops of them, without the assistance of a ladder. Small branches should be left all along large limbs, so that a person may go on them when plucking fruit. Many people have clipped off all the branches on the large limbs of their apple-trees, so that nothing but a bare limb is left for ten or fourteen feet, with the fruit branches all at the ends of the limbs. This is a very objectionable manner of pruning. The heads or tops of fruit-trees should always be formed as low as will be practicable, and not be too inconvenient getting around beneath the lowest limbs. It will be far better to have the branches low, than it is to prune them so that a man will need a sixteen feet ladder to get on the limbs. The higher the trees are, the more, by a great deal, will fruit be injured when it falls to the ground, when it falls on any hard substance or against each other. When trees are low, they will produce quite as much, and even more fruit than they would if the same tops were elevated on long limbs sixteen feet higher. When they are very high, much more of the fruit is blown off by high winds, sometimes before it is ripe; and a greater portion of it cannot be plucked when the trees are high; whereas, if the trees were *low*, almost every apple could be plucked.

304. Many good orchards have been almost ruined by employing a raw "bushwhacker" to prune their fruit-trees, who knew no more about the correct principles, according to which fruit-trees should be pruned, than the skillful paddy did whom a certain farmer employed to prune his young orchard, who, on being asked at noon how his pruning progressed, replied, "*And I have pruned none at all yet, but have cut them all down.*" Get J. J.

Thomas' Fruit Culturist, and learn to prune according to the most approved principles.

305. As soon as a tree has been pruned—the limbs having been cut off smoothly—a little kettle of liquid grafting cement should be at hand, and with a brush every wound that is as large as a man's thumb should be smeared, and a piece of coarse paper put over it before it becomes hard, and pressed into the wax. Have a little basket with square pieces of paper in it; and if the paper is a little larger than the wound, it will do no harm, for the rain and wind will soon carry away all that does not adhere to the wax. I have and do now practise these directions.

THE HEDGE COMPLETE.

306. "The following figure will give the young hedger the most approved manner of pruning a hedge, which is made to assume the form of a Gothic arch, as shown by the curved lines *o n* and *o m*, the apex of the hedge. The dotted line *c* represents the point where the hedge should be clipped the first season, if it is large enough. The dotted line *d* shows the place for the second clipping; *e* is the third clipping, *h* the fourth clipping, and *o* the hedge complete."*

307. Since penning the preceding thoughts on hedges, I have read "Warder's Hedges and Evergreens," a most useful treatise for every one who ever contemplates raising ten rods of hedge. When I penned this article on hedges, I did not know that such a book was in existence, and am much gratified to learn that our views on the subjects connected with hedging should coincide so well, especially in regard to the *distance apart* at which the quicks should be set. I have to acknowledge, with gratitude, my indebtedness to the *Country Gentleman* and *Albany Cultivator*, published by Luther Tucker & Son, for some of the ideas in composing this Section. When anything has been copied, due credit has been given.

* Dr. Warder's Hedges and Evergreens, price one dollar.

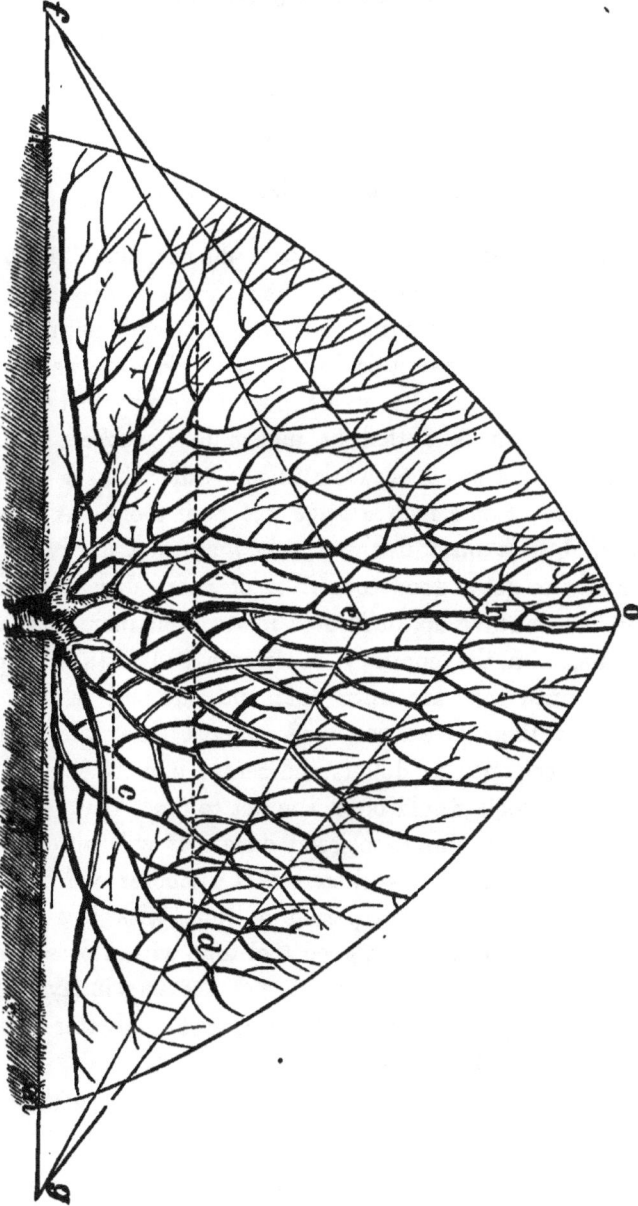

WARDER'S MANNER OF PRUNING A HEDGE.

CHAPTER III.

THE fencer comes, in order well arrayed,
His little kit, and saw, with glittering blade,
With piercing crowbar, spade and spud and rammer,
With plumb-rule, line, and auger, axe and hammer,
Not strewn in wild confusion in the track,
But neat and clean, supported on the rack.

308. It is a trite but usually true maxim, that "a workman is known by the *chips* he makes and by the *tools* he uses. A good workman, as a general rule, will not work with poor and awkward tools, because it is bad policy. He knows that with poor tools, he is required to exert much more physical strength in doing a given job; and that he makes little progress, and many times cannot do a piece of work in any other than a very ineffi- cient manner. Some men *always* use poor tools. A good tool of any kind, *with them*, is the *exception* and not the *rule;* and if they chance to get a good tool, it is of short duration, for it is soon broken or stove up, or injured in some manner, so that it is a poor one. On the contrary, other men will always keep their tools good until they are worn out; and one will seldom find a poor tool in their possession. *Good* tools, many times, cost no more than *poor* ones, in dollars and cents; and the loss sustained by using poor tools would often amount to more than enough, *in dollars and cents*, to purchase good ones. It will not be denied by the great majority of workmen, that a laborer will be able to do *twice as much* in a given period of time, with less force and fatigue to his powers, with a good tool than with a *poor* one; and many times the difference is even *four or five times* in favor of good tools. The best of tools are often rendered no better than very

(228)

poor ones, by neglecting to keep them in good order; and they are often allowed to be used in that unworkmanlike condition, because those who use them do not know how to keep them in good order. And good tools are often very much damaged by neglecting to take care of, and keep them fr(m the influence of the weather. This leads me to speak of

THE USE AND CARE OF TOOLS.

309. It is not always those who break and wear out the greatest number of tools who perform the most labor, but the opposite of this; for those who are in the habit of damaging, staving up and breaking the most tools, are usually those who do a very limited portion of labor. One-half of the laborers—yes, *more* than that proportion—do not seem to think but that they may *pry* and *lift* with a spade, shovel, or hoe-handle, as they would with a crowbar or handspike. For this reason, the handles of both spades and shovels become so badly sprung, if they are not broken, as to render them very inefficient, and almost worthless. The beginner should learn to exercise a little judgment in regard to the *strength* of the materials of which tools are made, and to *protect* them from the injurious influences of wet and dry weather, which will rust, warp, distort and rot them, to their injury more than all the wear of them when in actual service.

THE FENCE TOOL-RACK.

310. When laborers are digging post holes, it becomes necessary to use several different tools, at various times, in digging one hole, and when there is nothing to lean them against, a workman will spend a portion of his time in picking up his tools and changing them; and in some places, where the surface of the ground is covered with mud and water, tools will be falling into the mud, and then a laborer must spend time to wipe off the mud. All these little points of time will soon consume enough to dig a hole or two. A workman needs all his tools *close by his side*, where he can lay his hand on them without stepping away from his work. To aid him in having his tools all at hand, and for keeping them out of the mud, a tool-rack, Fig. 98, is a very

important implement in fence building. It should be made very light, so that one will not dread to move it when necessary.

FIG. 98.

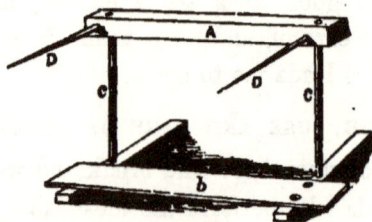

TOOL-RACK.

A is a piece of scantling, two inches square and two feet long; *b* is a light board, one foot wide and two feet long, screwed to the sills; *c c* are standards, round, two feet long and one inch in diameter; *D D* are guard-pins, one foot long and one inch in diameter, for keeping the tools, as they stand on the platform *b*, from falling on the ground. On this platform should be kept the shovel and spade, the auger and spud, the crowbar and spoon, and the rammer, and then no time will be spent in picking them out of the mud; and it should be borne in mind, that this little light bench is not strong enough to be used as a heavy *saw* bench.

THE POST-HOLE AUGER.

A Post-hole Auger here we view,
Without a pod, or worm, or screw.
See AUGERS, Par. 588.

311. Fig. 99 is an illustration of a dirt auger, which is a very useful tool in digging ordinary holes for fence; and when the stones are all so small that they will pass between the lips, a workman can bore a hole three times quicker than he can *dig* it with other tools. When the ground is very wet, one can make a hole three feet deep in less than five minutes, should the auger not hit any stone. When there are many stones, they must be taken out by hand. But few men know how to use such an auger. Many will insist upon having a large *screw* on the end, to draw it into the ground; but such a thing

would be impracticable, because the threads of a screw would immediately clog with dirt, and be worse than a small plain

FIG. 99.

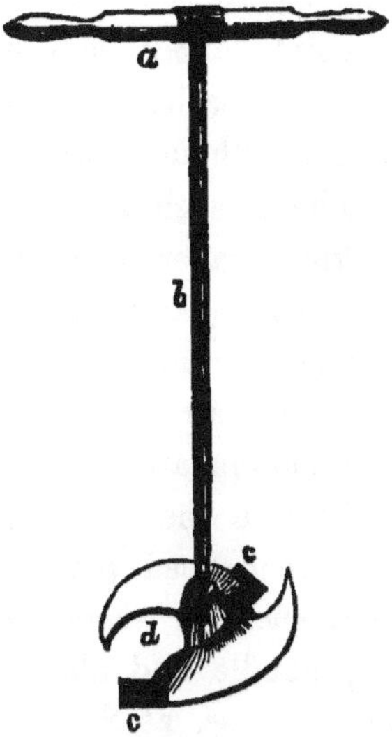

THE POST-HOLE AUGER.

point, such as they should always be made with. In using such an auger, dig a foot or so with the spade, and then with the crowbar make a hole six or eight inches deep for the point of the auger to turn in, if the ground is hard. When the ground is soft, a hole made with a crowbar will not be necessary. Bore in six inches, and with the rammer pack the dirt *a little* on the auger, so that when it is lifted out it will bring all the dirt with it. In *dry* dirt, if it is not rammed a little on the auger it will fall back into the hole when the auger is taken out. Make a hole with crowbar again and bore as before. Have a little paddle at hand to clean off the auger when the dirt adheres to it. Never strike an auger on a stone for the purpose of knocking off the dirt. It should be kept so bright that dirt will seldom stick to the lips. Bear in mind, that a post auger is not a *crowbar* nor a *sledge*, and when made as light as it ought to be it can be easily broken. When the lips hit a stone in boring, let the auger be taken out, and pry out the stone with the crowbar.

312. *Description.*—*a* is the handle, two feet long, which passes through an eye in the shank *b*, which shank is made of three-quarter-inch round iron, about three feet long, screwed into the socket of the auger. *c c* are the cutters or lips, which are all lips and point, which point cannot be seen, cast in one piece. The lips at *d* are from one and a half to two inches apart, according to the size of the auger, although two inches is large enough in the widest place. The lips should not be more than one-fourth of an inch in thickness, tapering to the edges, which should be *chilled* when they are cast (see paragraph 312). The point should not be more than two inches in diameter, terminating with a point about three or four inches long, made of a true, round taper. As such augers are seldom kept on hand, and where they are kept for sale the price is from $3 to $4, the farmer can employ an experienced pattern-maker to make the pattern, and he can get such an auger fitted up at a machine-shop for about $1 50, handle and all. Treman Brothers, of Ithaca, sell them, ready for use, at $1 25. The whole of the boring portion should be kept as bright and smooth as a plow, and never allowed to become rusty. When not in use it should be washed and wiped clean and dry, and kept where it will not rust, because if it becomes rusty it will not work well, any more than a plow that is not scoured so bright that the dirt will slip in plowing.

THE SPUD.

313. For digging post holes, a spud, Fig. 100, is frequently the most convenient and efficient tool that can be used. Where

FIG. 100.

THE SPUD.

there are but few stones, and the earth is too hard to spade it up, a spud is very useful. In digging holes twice as large as the dirt auger will bore, the spud is brought into use, and with it the sides of the holes are cut down and dressed twice as quick, and twice as easy, as it could be done with spade or crowbar. For digging up the earth in the bottom of post holes, when no dirt auger is used, a spud is far better than a crowbar. Any good blacksmith can make a spud, and the cost will be from $1 50 to $2 50, according to the size and weight of it.

314. *Description.*—*a* is the blade, from two and a half to three inches wide, and about half an inch thick and a foot long, and of the best of iron, and the edge or lower end of the blade, for two or three inches, all steel, properly tempered for cutting stone and gravel. The edge is bevelled from both sides like a crowbar. *b* is the socket, large enough to receive a handle two inches in diameter, and not less than four inches deep. The handle *c* should be round and tapering, and made of the firmest and toughest timber. If it is two inches in diameter at the socket, it will be of a fair proportion if it is made of a true taper to the upper end, which should be about one inch and an eighth in diameter. The whole tool is about six feet in length. Remember that a spud is not made to *pry* or *lift* with, like a handspike, but to *cleave* off the dirt, and to dig it up, so that it can be taken out of the holes with the dirt spoon. Let the edge be made as thin as will be consistent with sufficient strength. If it is *too thin* it will soon break or bend.

THE RAMMER.

315. The rammer (Fig. 101) is used for packing the earth firmly around posts. In using it workmen are too apt to

FIG. 101.

THE RAMMER.

pack the dirt close around the posts and leave much of it *untouched* with the rammer. The dirt should be well rammed from the post to every side of the hole. The rammer should be about five feet in length. The large part of it should be about four inches in diameter and twenty inches long, and the lower end mounted with an iron plate over the end, and a good band around it to keep it from splitting. It should be made of heavy, durable wood. The upper end of the knob need not be but one inch in diameter. Rammers are often made by boring a hole in a piece of scantling, and putting in a handle. But a *turned* one is a little . neater. A handle may be turned of the proper size, and driven firmly in the head, after which the head may be turned. Recollect that a rammer is not a tool to *pry* with, nor *to strike sideways* with.

THE CROWBAR.

"Behold here the crowbar, a lever for prying
And lifting stone, standing or lying."—EDWARDS.

316. Here we have something that you do not break and stave up without some extra exertion. This is not a shovel! lift

FIG. 102. with it as heavily as you please! It is not a spade! pry with it till you are tired! It is not an axe-helve, nor fork-handle! And now, friend, you who are always breaking and staving up tools that were never designed to pry with, when you have anything to pry, *get the crowbar*. A crowbar is a very useful tool, and its efficiency depends, in a great measure, on its form and size. For ordinary purposes on the farm, a crowbar of the following dimensions is of a fair proportion and good form and size, and as small as one ought to be. For handling heavy stone, crowbars may be heavier than this, but never lighter. It is better, for general purposes, to have the basil from *a* to the edge tapering like a wedge, instead of being pointed. From *a* to the edge, four inches, made of steel, and tempered as hard as it can well be and not break when punching on stone. From *a* to *b* eight inches, and one inch and three-eighths square. From *b* to the upper end, which is about one inch in diameter, *round*, it should be of a true taper. From *b* to *c* it is twenty

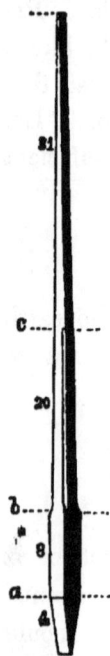

THE CROW-
BAR. inches, with the corners hammered, as in the figure.

From *c* to the end, thirty to thirty-four inches, round and smooth. The upper end should be laid with steel, so that it will not become battered up in hammering or driving stone with it. Let the edge of the crowbar be kept sharp, and it will not be difficult to work a hole in almost any soil.

317. The most efficient and proper manner of using a crowbar when making holes in the ground is, to clasp it with both hands close together, when it stands perpendicularly before the workman, with the hands about as high as the elbows, and then lift it perpendicularly, and plunge it down perpendicularly. By handling it in this way, it is easy to thrust it straight in a hole at every thrust. But when a man attempts to make a hole by taking hold of the crowbar as he would take hold of a pitchfork or spade, he finds it very difficult to thrust twice in one place. In digging up the earth in the bottom of a post hole with a crowbar or spud, first make a hole three or four inches deep in the centre of the post hole, and then thrust in the bar about three inches from this hole, and pry the dirt towards the centre of the post hole. Let the dirt be loosened all over the bottom of the hole, and then take it out with

THE DIRT-SPOON.

"There is a choice in spoons."—BARLOW.

318. A dirt-spoon (Fig. 103) is not calculated to shovel dirt, nor to spade with; its office is to *scoop out* the loose dirt in dig-

FIG. 103.

THE DIRT-SPOON.

ging post holes. It is better for such a purpose than a spade, or any kind of shovel, because it is not so pointed as some shovels, and has a deeper bowl, like a scoop shovel. They are seldom made to hang correctly, and the bowl is usually too long to do

good work.   The bowl is frequently made in a straight line with
the handle, whereas, there should be so much hang to it that
when it is full of dirt there will be no tendency to turn over in
the hands of the workman.   (See SHOVELS, paragraph 323.)
There should be so much hang (see HANG, in the next vol.)
or crook to it that, in filling it with dirt, it must be carried to
the opposite side of the post hole from where the digger is
standing, and then crowded down into the dirt, not by thrusting, but by the weight of the operator, and as it enters the
dirt it should be carried back to the other side of the hole.
Fig. 104 represents a side view of the dirt-spoon, by which it

FIG. 104.

SIDE VIEW OF DIRT-SPOON

will be seen what is about the correct shape for the bowl, and
crook of the handle.   Our old-fashioned ladles for scooping
boiled beans from the dinner-pot come nearer to a dirt-spoon
than any other implement, and when a ladle hangs correctly for dipping beans out of a dinner pot, it may be used
as a model for making a post- or dirt-spoon.   The *handle* of
the dirt-spoon may be of wood, and bent like a shovel-
handle; or the spoon may have an iron shank, a foot or so in
length, bent in proper shape, like Fig. 104.   Let the bowl be
kept bright, so that dirt will not adhere to it, and clean it with a
little paddle, instead of striking it on a stone or block to knock
the dirt off.   When it is struck on a stone to clean the dirt off,
the edges will soon become all stove up, and the dirt will not
slip off readily.

THE PLUMB RULE.

" From the zenith above to the nadir below,
A plumb in a vertical line will go."—GRAY.

319. The plumb rule, Fig. 105, is made of a strip of board

about four feet long and three inches wide, and scalloped or forked at the bottom, as in the figure, so that it may rest on the points, while the plumb c swings freely. The rule must be planed as straight as can be with the jointer, with the edges parallel, and

FIG. 105.

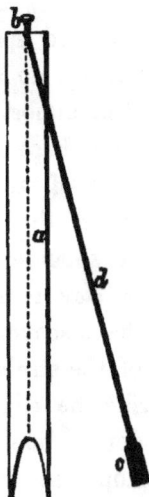

PLUMB RULE.

a mark made with the gauge along the centre, as at the dotted line a; b is a screw to which the plumb line d is attached; c is the plumb, made of lead, about two inches long and one inch in diameter. To make a plumb, bore a smooth hole in a hard stick of wood, and fill it with melted lead; as soon as the lead is poured in, hold a little wire staple in the melted lead, with the pinchers, until the lead becomes solid. Split the stick, and attach the plumb by the staple, to a piece of small cord d. Place the edge of the rule against the side of a post, and if it is *plumb* the cord will hang exactly over the dotted line a. Such a rule is usually quite as convenient as a *spirit level and plumb*, which will cost ten times more; and it is often far more correct, and will show any slight variation with more accuracy than many spirit rules.

THE SPADE.

"Hurrah for the spade, and a workman to use it!
It turns the black glebe into bright shining gold!
What could our fathers have done, boys, without it,
When the fields lay all bare and the zephyrs blew cold?"—DWIGHT.

320. Fig. 106 represents a good spade, in one sense, but because it hangs so awkwardly it is worthless.
It would be almost impossible to spade with
such a tool, because there is no *hang* to it.
The names of the principal parts of the
spade are, *b*, the handle, *a*, the hilt, *c*, the
stamp or shoulder, *d*, the blade. Fig. 107
shows a *side view* of a well-hung spade.
It will be discovered that a line cutting the
middle of the straight portion of the handle
will strike the edge of the blade, as shown
by the dotted line, and the upper end of the
blade should set *back* of this line about two
inches, in a spade about a foot long. When
the blade hangs in such a position that a
line cutting the centre of it would be *parallel* with a line cutting the straight part of
the handle, (see Fig. 108, OF SHOVELS,) it
will not work easily, because the laborer
will be obliged to make an extra effort to
prevent a spadeful from slipping off the end
of the blade. When a spade has as much
hang as a well hung shovel, a spader is obliged to reach *forward* with the handle so far that the motion is awkward, inefficient, and not easy. But when a spade has about as much
hang as is shown at Fig. 107, a workman is not obliged to use
up any of his energies in an inefficient manner. It is much
better to have a spade-handle *entirely straight*, without any
hang at all in a spade, than to have the edge and the blade
stand at such an angle as is represented by Fig. 106. A spade

FIG. 106, 107.

SPADE.

with a handle entirely straight, and straight with the blade, is not an awkward tool to spade with until one attempts to lift a spadeful, then we shall see distinctly the necessity of having a spade hung in the most proper manner. Manufacturers would do well to make *two kinds* of spades, one kind very neat and light, but sufficiently strong for skillful laborers, and another kind unnecessarily heavy and clumsy, for the special benefit of those stupid dolts who use a spade as if it were a crowbar, and who cannot use a spade a half day without bending the blade, or breaking or springing the handle, or staving it up into some unde sirable shape.

321. In using a spade, especially in spading sod, the operator should always remember to cut a spadeful loose on both sides before it is thrust in to take up a spadeful. When a spade is thrust in its whole length into hard soil, and the force of a laborer applied to the handle to loosen the spadeful as if it were a lever, if it is not made too heavy and clumsy for a skillful laborer, it must *break* or *bend*, so as to be unfit for use. In spading we cannot avail ourselves of any advantage by resting the handle across one knee, as in shovelling; therefore a spade should not be one ounce heavier than is necessary for consistent strength. The blade should be made of steel, because a steel blade is much stiffer than an iron blade of the same thickness. A man whose mind is enlightened with a knowledge of mechanical principles, will never bend nor break a spade; his keen perception will tell him, even if he were blindfolded, when the strength of the spade is unequal to the force applied to the handle.

322. In spading the soil in gardens, when a plow is not used, the laborer takes a spade-slice six or eight inches wide and spades clear across a given plot of ground, leaving a furrow about half as wide as the furrow made by a plow. The narrower the spade-slices are the more completely the soil will be pulverized. When manure is worked into the soil in spading, it should be spread in the furrow, and every spadeful turned upside down on the top of it; and if the dirt does not all fall to pieces, a thrust or two with the edge will pulverize it sufficiently for raking. When spading

soil of a clayey or adhesive character, after the spade has been
thrust in, instead of prying the spadeful loose by prying down on
the handle, the laborer should thrust the handle *from him, forward,*
so as to loosen the spadeful.   This operation will not require
half the force for spading that is necessary where the spading is
all done by *prying down on the handle* to loosen the spadeful.
A skillful spader will *wear out* his spade ; but an awkward Jonathan will *break* and *stave up* twice as many spades, and will not
perform half the amount of labor, as he who handles a spade with
a little skill.   In spading in ditches where the soil is quite wet,
ninety-nine diggers in one hundred will put their whole weight
on a spade-handle in order to pry a spadeful loose; whereas, if
they would loosen it by thrusting the handle *forward,* it would
not require one-fourth the strength, and it would be loosened in
less than half the time.   By *prying down* on the handle to loosen
a spadeful where there is water, a spadeful is not easily pryed
loose, because in separating the spadeful from the unbroken
ground there is a tendency to form a *vacuum*; but by thrusting
the handle *forward* enough to loosen the spadeful, air and water
will find their way *behind* the spadeful, and it may be easily
lifted from its place with the spade.   *Remember, that a spade is
neither a crowbar nor handspike.*   If the edge and blade of a
spade are made of steel, as they should be, and polished on the
grindstone, and the edge ground up sharp, if the edge has a good
temper, so hard that it will not batter when it touches stone, nor
break when thrust on a flint, it will not require much force to
drive in the spade when spading.   But when the edge is all battered up, and towards one-fourth of an inch thick, spading is a
very laborious operation.   A good steel spade should never be
allowed to become rusty, nor to be exposed to heavy rains, as
bent handles in spades are quite apt to spring straight when left
in wet places.   A few drops of oil will keep the blade from rusting, and it will not require half as much time to clean a spade
and oil it and put it under cover as it will to scour it fit for use
after it has become rusty.   If the edge of a steel spade is *too soft,*
it may easily be tempered again as hard as may be desired, by

heating about two inches of the edge.   (See TEMPERING TOOLS, 532.)

SHOVELS.

"O give me a shovel ! There's magic about it !
And the laborer skilled will teach us to use it."—EDWARDS.

323. The great excellency and efficiency of shovels, and the ease with which they may be handled, depend almost entirely on the correct hang of the handles and blades.   If a shovel or spade be made of the very best materials, and is defective in the *hang of the blade and handle*, it is a poor tool; and the intelligent farmer would find it for his interest to dispose of such tools to those who seem to contend that a laborer can perform just as much work with a tool having a straight handle as with a tool correctly hung, *providing he is only accustomed to using* such tools. Shovelling dirt, or manure, or anything else, is very laborious work, even when the very best kind of shovels is used; but when shovelling is to be performed with a *poor tool*, the laborer is sure to be greatly fatigued, while he performs but a light day's work; but when a shovel is made of good materials, is light and bright, and correctly hung, a man will be able to perform *twice* the amount of labor, with half the fatigue that he would experience with a shovel improperly hung.   Shovels are too frequently made unnecessarily heavy in order to be of consistent strength, because the materials of which they are made are very poor; but if they were made of good steel they might be often full one-third lighter, and sufficiently strong for any skillful laborer to use without fear of breaking.   When the blades are made of poor iron, it is necessary to make them nearly twice as heavy as if they were made of steel; and more than this, iron blades will not wear as smooth, and will not enter the dirt as easily, as a steel blade; and dirt is far more apt to *adhere* to an iron blade than to a steel one,— all of which require the exercise of more force in using a shovel. It is no uncommon thing to find shovels from one to two pounds heavier than is necessary.   Suppose, for example, a laborer will throw up ten shovelfuls in a minute; at that rate he will throw up six thousand shovelfuls in a day of ten hours.   If his shovel

be two pounds heavier than is necessary, he will in ten hours
exert a force, which is entirely lost in handling a heavy shovel,
which would have been sufficient to have thrown up twelve thousand pounds of earth, with no more fatigue than he experiences,
had he used a lighter shovel.   The laborer will discover from this
fact the importance of having shovels *as light* as will be consistent
with necessary strength; and the better the materials are of which
shovels are made, the lighter they may be, and the more a workman will be able to perform with a certain amount of force.   In
using a shovel, all the force which a laborer exerts should be
turned to the most efficient purpose.   It requires but little force
to shovel a ton of earth when a man handles a good shovel with
dexterity; but if a laborer must bend his legs and back very much
in order to bring his shovel in the best position to enter the substance to be shovelled with the least force, the fatigue produced
by bringing his body into such a position, and straightening up
again, will be *greater* than that caused by thrusting in the shovel
and lifting a shovelful.   For this reason it is very poor policy for
a laborer to use a shovel with a very *short handle*, like the handle
of a spade, for shovelling any length of time, because it is very
laborious and fatiguing.   A man may shovel with a short handle
for an hour or so as fast as he would with a *long* handle, and not
discover any difference in the fatigue produced or force expended;
but let him continue to use a shovel with a short handle all day,
and if he does an honest day's work, unless his powers of endurance are very great, he will pronounce shovelling very laborious
business.   In shovelling dirt or manure with a short-handled
shovel, the operator usually places the hand which holds the *hilt*
of the shovel against the inside of one thigh, and bends his knees
and body forward, and in this position, by no means an easy one,
thrusts in the shovel.   The simple act of bringing the body into
such a position, and bringing it again erect, will require the ex-
penditure of more force than the shovelling alone.   In order to
shovel with the least fatigue, a laborer needs to stand almost erect,
with his back straight and knees bent but little; and then, with
the handle resting across one knee, the shovel is thrust into the

THE YOUNG FARMER'S MANUAL.   243

dirt by a forward motion of the body; and by straightening the
knees and keeping the arms stiff, with the shovel across the knee,
the shovelful is lifted a few inches with the least possible fatigue.
Then, by making a fulcrum of the knee across which the handle is resting, and by thrusting the upper end of the handle
down with one hand, the shovelful may be raised nearly a foot
high with the greatest ease. It must then be lifted by the arms.
But a man's back should be always kept about straight in
shovelling, as he will be able to work much longer and with less
fatigue than would be possible when he is constantly bending
and straightening his back. The knees should always perform
the most laborious part in shovelling dirt, and the arms should be
kept as closely to the body as is convenient. My apology for
being so *particular* on this subject is,—few laborers, old or young,
know how to use a dirt-shovel with the greatest ease, and to
perform the greatest amount of labor with the least fatigue;
and they often labor very hard and accomplish but little, because they do not understand handling the shovel with dexterity
or because it is not properly hung. I shall now treat more particularly of

THE RULE FOR HANGING SHOVELS IN A WORKMANLIKE MANNER.

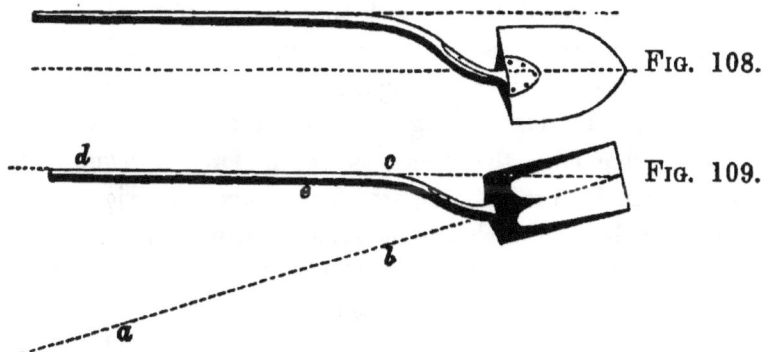

FIG. 108.

FIG. 109.

A SHOVEL WELL HUNG.

324. Fig. 109 represents a shovel well hung, and the dotted

lines show the angle at which the straight part of the handle and
the blade should stand with each other, in order to have a shovel
hang in such a manner as to work easily. When a man takes
such a shovel in his hands across one knee, as if he were about
to shovel dirt, the blade should lie nearly *flat on the ground*,
on a level with his feet. This will be readily comprehended
by the dotted lines. Every laborer who knows how to handle a
dirt shovel with dexterity, knows that the blade of a shovel
must lie nearly flat on the ground, in order to enter the dirt
with the least force of the operator. In Fig. 109, for example,
the dotted line *a b* represents the level on which the laborer
stands. The blade lies flat on this level. ·One hand of the workman grasps the handle at *c*, and the other hand at *d*, while the
handle rests across one knee at *e*. Now by a slight motion
of the body *forward*, the shovel is thrust in with the least
possible force, and by the motions then of straightening up and
thrusting down the hand at *d*, as already mentioned, shovelling is
performed with as little fatigue and force of a laborer as it is
possible to do it. With a shovel hung like Fig. 109, a laborer
can avail himself of some *mechanical advantage* in shovelling;
whereas, with a shovel exactly like it, which has a *short handle*,
like the handle of a spade, one hand must not only lift much
more than a shovelful, but it must operate as a *fulcrum* for the
other hand to pry across, so as to balance the shovelful. A
shovel like Fig. 109 is not designed to be used in ditching, or
for shovelling up ridges along a fence, because it is so wide
at the entering edge that twice as much force is required to
make it enter the dirt as is required for a shovel like Fig. 110 of
the same width. For shovelling sand or mortar, or for cleaning stables and such like, a shovel like Fig. 109 is preferable
to one like Fig. 110, which represents a round-pointed ditching
shovel, or the best kind of a shovel for casting up a ridge along
a fence. Fig. 111 represents a round-pointed shovel similar to
Fig. 110, with the sides turned up by a blacksmith, for working
in a narrow channel or ditch. Figs. 109, 110 and 111 are all
hung alike, as will be seen by the dotted lines, and hung ac-

cording to the most approved mechanical principles. A shovel that hangs just right for a tall man will not hang exactly right for a *short* man, when they both grasp the handle at the same

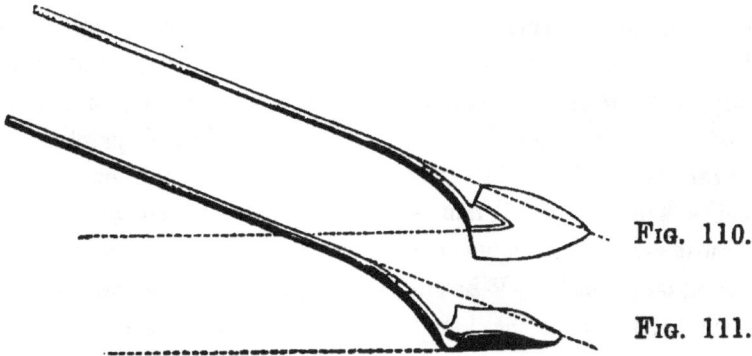

FIG. 110.

FIG. 111.

places; but a short man, by grasping the handle nearer the blade. may use a shovel that hangs just right for a *tall* man, and *vice versa.*

325. Fig. 108 represents a round pointed shovel very awkwardly hung, and it would be a very disagreeable and ugly tool to work with. There is curvature enough in the handle, but it will seen by the dotted lines that the straight part of the handle, and the blade of the shovel, are in lines parallel with each other. Whereas, if the point of it stood at the upper dotted line, as in the other figures, it would be a good shovel, and a laborer would be able to shovel with it with as much ease as he would with one hung like Fig. 110. With a shovel like Fig. 108, a laborer must bend *his whole body very low*, in order to bring the blade in a position to enter the dirt by the application of the least force. If he attempts to shovel with it across one knee, the blade stands up and down at such a sharp angle that it is difficult to keep a shovelful of dirt on it, and more than this, a laborer cannot thrust it into the dirt unless he stamps it with his foot, except the dirt i very mellow. Shovels are never made of this shape by skillful workmen; but by allowing them to be exposed to the influences

of wet and dry weather, and by *prying* with them, and other *rough* and *hard* usage, shovels that are correctly hung are often brought into a shape like Fig. 108 before they are one quarter worn out. The handles of such shovels ought to be made of timber having *a natural crook*, not bent, and then there would be little liability to spring out straight. Let the blades of shovels be kept *bright* by wiping them dry after using them, and applying a few drops of oil,—*not salted grease*, as many do, for salt will *rust* iron,—and keep the handles near the blade well painted, and never use a shovel for *spading* or *prying*, for it is not a spade nor a handspike. When a shovel is used to spade with, the almost certain consequence is, that the blade will be *bent directly across the middle*. What has been penned holds equally good with reference to the hanging of *scoop* shovels, and of forks for pitching manure.

BOOT IRON FOR SPADING.

326. In spading or shovelling, when it is necessary to stamp the spade into the dirt with one foot, the shoulder of the spade or shovel would, in a short time, wear the sole of a boot entirely through, besides making the foot tender or lame. To obviate all such occurrences, a boot iron, Fig. 112, is used for the purpose

FIG. 112.

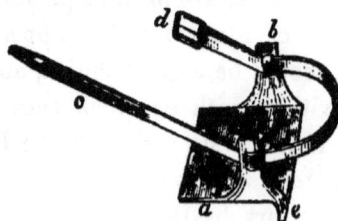

BOOT IRON FOR SPADING.

of protecting the boot, and for giving efficiency to the force of the laborer. *a* is the sole of it, made of iron, about three-sixteenths of an inch thick, as long as the boot is wide, and about two inches in width from the flange *e* to the forward edge of the iron at *a*. At *b* is one of the ears through which the leather strap c passes; d is a buckle in one end of the strap. The ears are a part of the sole iron, turned up, from two to three inches long, according to the size of the boot. The flange e is turned downwards, like a hook, to prevent the shoulder of the spade from slipping off it. The iron is placed in the hollow of the boot, with the flange e against the forward side of the *heel* of the boot, and the strap c is passed behind the heel, and through mortises in each ear, as shown in the figure, and buckled around the instep. An ingenious blacksmith will make the iron for ten or twelve cents, and the strap and buckle will cost eight or ten more. This is a very useful article in using the spade, and will save the wear of boots very much more than its cost.

THE RAIL FENCE JACK.

327. In repairing rail fence it is often necessary and desirable to put in a good rail near the bottom of a fence, where a rail is broken or rotten, without taking down the corners. When there are heavy riders on a fence, and the stakes are firmly set, it is no little task to take off the riders and loosen the stakes and let

Fig. 113.

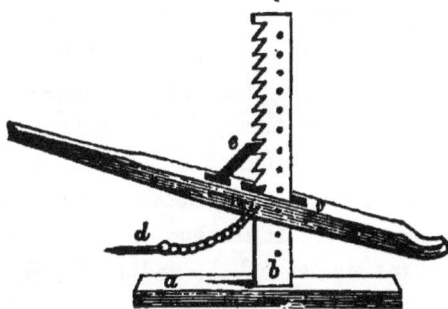

A RAIL FENCE JACK.

down the corners, in order to take out old pieces of a rail, and place a good one there. But by having a *fence jack* like Fig. 113, a man or boy can raise the corners of a fence, when it is staked and ridered with heavy rails, and take out the pieces and put in a good rail much quicker than he would be able to do it by taking the fence down and putting it up again. It is so plain

11

that almost any one can make it. *a* is the sill, about thirty inches long, of good timber, two by four inches square. *b* is the standard, about three and a half feet long, five inches wide, one inch and a quarter thick, with three-quarter inch holes bored in it about four inches apart. *c* is the lever of tough timber, not less than three inches square at the mortise where it plays on the standard. The mortise should be so long that the lever can play up and down freely. The short end of the lever should be six or seven inches *longer* than the end of the sill, and scalloped, as in the illustration, to prevent its slipping off the rails. The other end should be about six feet long, and of a true taper from the mortise to the end. The end need not be larger than a fork handle. *d* is an iron pin with an eye in the end, attached to the lever *c* by a small chain or leather strap. The pin is for holding the lever at the holes in the standard for prying across. *e* is a pawl, attached to the handle, and plays in the notches in the standard *b*. In using the jack for lifting the corners of the fence, put the end of the lever under a rail and raise the corner a little, and put a stone or block of wood between the rails to keep them apart. Now, carry the jack to the next corner and raise it up a little, and fasten the lever with the pawl, and then take out the pieces of the rail and put in a good one, and let the fence down again. When it is desirable to raise the corners of a fence so as to put larger blocks under them, the fence jack is much more convenient than a handspike, because one hand can work with it very advantageously, while with nothing but a handspike *two* hands are very necessary. If the end of the lever on which the rail rests extends too far beyond the end of the sill, the jack will *tip over* when a corner is resting on it. To obviate this difficulty, run the end of the lever under the rails so far that the weight of the fence will not be *beyond* the end of the sill. If the rails should be close to the ground, raise them a little and block them up, and then set the jack a little *under* the fence. Such a jack is a very convenient implement for raising one end of the axle-trees of a wagon, when the wheels are to be taken off. The notches for the pawl should not be quite as close together as they appear in the illustration. It would be a great improvement to have an *iron rack*—a straight piece of iron with teeth on one side of it—bolted to the standard, and an iron pawl playing in it; but for ordinary purposes, notches in a wooden standard and a tough piece of wood for a pawl will subserve a very good purpose.

A PICK MATTOCK OR GRUBBING HOE

" Let servant be ready with mattock in hand,
To grub out the bushes that cover the land."—TUSSER.

328. Is a very useful tool for setting stakes for a rail fence, when the stakes are not driven in the ground in a perpendicular position. The blade of a mattock should be not less than two and a half inches wide, and the handle should be of an *oval* form instead of round, so that a laborer can hold it more advantageously in the proper position when using it. When the handle of a mattock is round, it may turn half way over in the hands of a workman and he will not perceive it; but when a handle is of an oval form, the eye also being oval, a workman will perceive a slight variation of the mattock without looking to see if he is holding it correctly. (See HAMMER AND BEETLE, Par. 331 and 338.) The *handle* of a mattock should always be put through the eye from the *lower side*, and then it will not draw or work out, if the eye is made as it should be—a little the largest on the lower side. Remember, that a mattock or grubbing hoe is not a crowbar for prying stone, nor a mill-

FIG. 114.

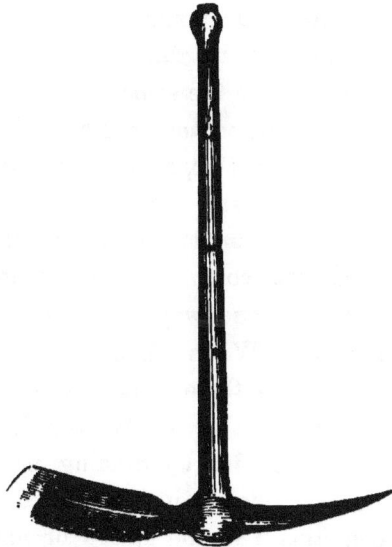

A PICK MATTOCK OR GRUBBING HOE.

pick for dressing stone.   Neither the handle nor blade is calculated for prying.   Mattocks and picks of all forms may be seen in the illustrated catalogue of R. L. Allen & Co., New York city. For digging up trees, and for setting fence stakes among *roots*, one edge of the mattock should be in the form of an *axe*, for the purpose of cutting roots and sprouts.   For ditching, or for picking up very hard dirt, a pick with a pointed end, instead of an edge like a mattock, is much the best, as in the figure.

SPOOL FOR CHALK LINE AND FENCE LINE.

"The twisted lines curl into kinks and loops."—Homer.

329. The majority of farmers, if they have any chalk line at all—and the same is true of many good mechanics—wind it up on a *corn cob* or a stick of wood, notwithstanding the very great inconvenience in letting a line off, and the injury it receives by being wound up and let off *over the end* of whatever it is wound up on.   Many mechanics have a little pocket spool to wind the line on, and let it off by holding it, as it revolves, with a thumb at one end and a finger at the other.   It is a fact which but very few people understand, that in winding up a line or cord, or rope of any kind, by *putting it over the end* of the stick or spool, if it is wound up the same way it was twisted when it was made, it will be twisted *harder* and *harder* every time it is wound up, and will soon curl up, running into all sorts of kinks and loops, while, on the contrary, if it be wound up in an *opposite* direction, it will soon be all *untwisted* and nearly worthless.   I have seen many good lines completely spoiled in this manner, by being always wound up one way, and then let off by allowing the spool to revolve.   When a line is wound up over the end of a stick, and let off over the end it does not injure it, providing it is wound up the way that will twist it *harder* as it is wound up.   If it is twisted harder by winding up, and untwisted by letting it off just as much as it was twisted, the line will remain in the same condition if wound up few or many times; but when it is wound up in the contrary direction, which will *untwist* it, as it is wound

up, it will not generally twist it as hard as it ought to be twisted by simply allowing it to run off. These few ideas will enable the farmer to understand and to appreciate the importance of having a spool like Fig. 115. It will be discovered by the cut that there are three flanges to this spool, which are about four inches in diameter, and two inches between them. A half-inch hole is bored through the spool, and it revolves easily on the part of the handle which passes through it, which should be made of very tough wood. In letting off the line, let the workman, as one hand grasps the handle, apply the thumb against one flange of the spool to keep it from unwinding too rapidly, and in winding it up let the spool be turned by taking hold of the *wrist-pin* or little handle, in one flange. By letting a line off such a spool, and by winding it up without passing it over the *end* of the spool, it will never become untwisted, nor twisted so hard that it will curl into kinks; and a line will last much longer when kept on such a spool than it will when kept on a corn cob or stick, and more than all besides, it is infinitely more convenient. A chalk line is kept in one gain and a fence line in the other. To keep the other line from unwinding when one is being let off, cut a gash in each flange with a saw about three-sixteenths of an inch deep, and after the lines are wound up draw the ends into these gashes. Always have a loop in the end of each line, for hooking on a scratch-awl or pin.

FIG. 115.

SPOOL FOR CHALK LINE.

330. *When chalking the line,* the line should not be allowed to run *across* a lump of chalk, cutting gashes all through it, but the chalk should be held in such a manner that the line will run *between the thumb and chalk, wearing down one side of the chalk.* A little skill will enable a workman to wear a piece of chalk all out on the line without cutting gashes all through it. Select soft chalk, as hard chalk will not *shed,* and will wear out the line. For black chalk, a billet of basswood, burned to a coal, and the

fire quenched by dipping it in water quickly, will answer a good purpose.

THE HAMMER.

> " Here view the hammer, glory of our nation ;
> The universal emblem of mechanics ;
> The boasted empress of civilization.
>   What thrilling, wondrous stories in dynamics,
> Are told of hammers, back in bygone ages !
> How oft its feats fine laurels crowned ! Wise sages,
> With their fair hands the chaplets round entwined,
> And statesmen, kings, with glory it enshrined."—EDWARDS.

331. Fig. 116 represents a claw hammer ; and the face should be of steel, so hard that it will not batter up, and not so hard that it will cleave off, and the claws should be of the same material. The handle should not be round, but of an *oval* form, so that it may be held in the proper postion, when in use, more

FIG. 116.

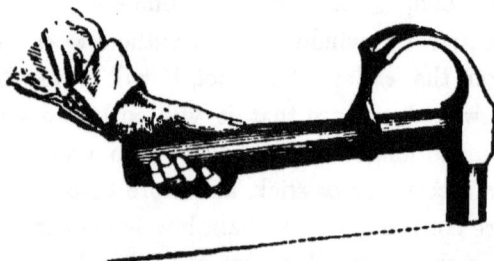

CLAW HAMMER.

advantageously than if the handle were round.   The *face* should be ground smooth and true on a grindstone, and should be parallel with a line cutting the centre of the handle, as shown by the dotted line. If the face stands *inward* too much towards the handle, or in an opposite direction, or if the face be convex or one-sided, or if the corners be knocked off, it will be a poor thing to drive nails with. The *face* of a claw hammer should never be used for pounding on chisel handles when mortising, because the corners are so sharp that it will soon split them or wear them out ; and it should never be used for hammering iron or stone, lest the corners of the face be broken off or battered up.   Make it a rule to use the claw hammer for nothing but driving nails and drawing nails. If oil or tar be on the face, it will be almost impossible to drive a nail with it until it has been removed. In drawing a nail out of hard wood with the claw, strike it one or two blows, enough to start it in a little, and it will come out much easier than if it had not been started in. When the hand grasps the handle, let the thumb lie lengthways of the handle, instead of clasping it as shown in the figure. With the thumb on the top of the handle one can strike truer and longer without tiring the wrist. In order to drive a nail true, place the hammer on the nail, and then keep the eye on the nail, when striking, instead of on the hammer. Never try to draw a nail with the claws if it will not start without starting the *handle* in the eye of the hammer. If one is always careful to put a little block or piece of iron *under* the hammer for a fulcrum, there will be little danger of starting the handle. If the hammer hangs correctly, and the handle gets bent, it will not hang right, and will bend a nail down before it has driven it in. If the face of a hammer is ground true, as it should be, on the grindstone, not one-sided nor convex, and if the face is in a line parallel with a line which would cut the centre of the handle from end to end, as in the figure, and if the handle is made of a true and oval form, there will be little danger of bending nails over sideways when driving them. When the handle of a hammer is *round*, a workman can-not perceive *by feeling* the handle whether a hammer is in the right position for driving a nail or not; but when the handle is of an *oval* form, and is put in the eye true, with the widest way of the handle in the direction *exactly from the claw to the face*, after a workman has become accustomed to a hammer he can snatch it up without looking at it, and the perception of the fin-gers and thumb will determine most accurately the correct posi-tion for driving a nail. If the face of the nail hammer were a little *concave*, it would be less liable to slip or glance off when driving nails. A good nail hammer is not a proper tool to drive wooden pins with, nor for driving any piece of work together with, because the corners are so sharp that they will split a pin very readily, and make deep dents in the sides of anything that is hammered with it. Should the face of a claw hammer become battered up, it should be tempered again, and made as hard as it will bear to be and not fly or break easily. The handle of a hammer should have a little bilge in it at the point where the hand grasps it, as in the figure. If the handle is made of a uniform size from end to end, a workman will be constantly losing his hold; whereas a little swell in a handle will prevent its slipping in the hand.

332. Sledge hammers are of various forms, and are made, when made properly, with a reference to the services which they are intended to perform. If a sledge is wanted simply to drive stakes and posts for fencing, the best form for such work will be a round cast-iron sledge, with two faces, similar to the beetle. The faces of such a hammer should be convex a little, and not have sharp or square corners like the face of a claw hammer, because, if the corners are square or sharp, if a workman does not strike exactly square when driving a stake or post, such sharp corners, will make deep dents in them; and they are far more liable to split a post than if the faces were a little convex. But it is not well to have the faces *too convex;* because, if they are too convex the efficiency of a blow, in driving wood, is partly lost, in consequence of the great convexity of the face, which bruises and indents the wood more than if the faces were square. When the pattern for such a hammer is made, the convexity of the faces should not exceed one-eighth of an inch across the face, and the sharp corners should be rounded off a little. About twelve to sixteen pounds would be the proper weight for a hammer of this description. But such a hammer should never be used for pounding iron, nor for breaking stone, because cast-iron hammers will break easily when hammering substances harder than wood.

333. The *handle* for such a hammer should be of an *oval* form, and of good timber, with a knob at the end of it similar to the beetle handle, with faces in lines parallel with a line cutting the

centre of the handle, as shown at the beetle, Fig. 117; and the *widest* way of the handle should be in the direction from one face of the sledge to the other.

334. When a workman attempts to drive a post, for example, with such a hammer, which has a *round* handle, if he is not skillful in using such a tool, he will not be able to strike true, and will split half the posts which he undertakes to drive. When the handle is round, such a hammer may turn one-fourth of the way around in the hands; and unless the workman can *see* the face of the hammer, he will not be able to tell whether he is going to strike with a *corner* or *side*, or with the *face* of the hammer. But if the handle be of an *oval* form, and the hilt oval, the perception of the hand will determine, very correctly, whether the face is in the proper position for striking a square blow or not. Such handles are almost always made round; and we often see laborers strike, many times, a half-dozen blows, without starting a post at all, simply because they do not strike true and straight; and they will strike with a *corner* of the sledge, when it will fly over and over in their hands, and they will be obliged to give it up with the exclamation, "*It can't be driven!*" when the fault is partly in the *tool*, and partly in the workman.

335. When a skillful laborer attempts to drive a post with such a hammer, he will set the sledge on the end of the post, on the face, *square*, and at once calculate how far to drop the hand that holds the hilt, in order to have the hammer strike *square;* and he will grasp the hilt of the handle firmly to prevent the sledge from striking on one corner; and every blow, when the face strikes square, will crack as sharply as the report of a cut rifle. But when an awkward, unskillful Jonathan attempts to drive a post with a hammer having a *round* handle, his blows sound as dull as if he struck a post of India-rubber; and he will hammer the end of a post all to slivers, before it is half driven into the ground. Let the farmer bear in mind, that in order to have the blows of a hammer most effective, the face must strike *square* against the substance to be driven. When striking heavy blows, he should observe how he holds the handle when he strikes an *effective* blow,

11*

and then endeavor to *keep* the hammer as nearly in that position
as possible at every blow.   A skillful laborer will usually strike
truer and more effective blows by grasping the handle at the hilt
with *both* hands, and swinging it at arms length over his head.
But this manner of swinging a heavy sledge-hammer is much
more fatiguing and laborious than to slide one hand towards the
sledge every time it is elevated.—(Read paragraph 339.)

STONE MAULS

336. Are sometimes made of cast-iron, for the purpose of break
ing stone ; and instead of a flat face, one end of the pattern is
rounded off to a kind of *conical* obtuse apex, while the other end
is rounded in the form of a pyramidal apex, not brought to a
sharp edge, but in the form of a blacksmith's swedge for making
a circular groove. A hammer of this form will stand a vast
deal of hammering without breaking, but it would be a worthless
tool to drive posts or stakes with, because it would indent and
bruise and split the end of a post, without driving it but little.
There are several other kinds of hammers, a notice of which does
not seem to come within the province of this work.   But as every
farmer needs a hammer, besides the claw-hammer, for riveting, a
few words with reference to

THE RIVETING HAMMER

337. May not be out of place, which for ordinary purposes
should weigh about one pound. If it be too heavy, rivets are
very apt *to bend* in consequence of too heavy a blow, when spreading the ends of them with the hammer. The *face* of a riveting
hammer should be a little convex, and the *edge* of it should be
acute enough to dent or spread the ends of a rivet readily ; and
it should not be so sharp as *to cut* the iron when riveting. Light
blows made with a light hammer are more effective in spreading
a rivet than a blow of an equal momentum made with a *heavier*
hammer. A riveting hammer should have a longer handle than
an ordinary claw hammer, in order to give a greater velocity to it

in striking. It is not very practicable to spread the end of a small rivet with a hammer that weighs two or three pounds, because a stroke with such a hammer would be so heavy as to *crush* or double a rivet before the end could be spread. Riveting hammers of almost any desirable size may be obtained at most of the hardware stores. (See MOMENTUM, in the next volume.)

THE MALLET AND BEETLE.

"The beetle, now twin-brother of the hammer,
Holds equal rank in pounding and for clamor ;
Unlike the hammer with its flinty face,
The beetle, in close impact, yields an ace."—EDWARDS.

338. A mallet should be made of some very hard wood; and if it be not made of a knot, the ends of it should be banded like the beetle, to keep it from splitting. That part of a tree, if it be tough wood, which grows just above the surface of the ground, which is called the *crook*, will make the very best mallets, which will require no hooping. I have a mallet which was made of the crook of a part of a white ash stump, which has been the only mallet in use for framing all my buildings, and doing all my shop work for sixteen years, and it is not half worn out as yet. A mallet should be turned out true, with the ends convex or rounding, not less than half an inch from edge to edge. The handle should be put in true, so that the faces will be parallel with the handle, as shown in the Fig. 117. Let it be well oiled to prevent its cracking. Never allow the faces of the mallet to be bruised and dented on iron bolts and the like, but keep it smooth for pounding on chisel handles only. A tough piece of apple-wood will make about as good a mallet as almost any other kind of wood. But if it is made of a round piece of wood, on account of its great liability to check, it should be treated as recommended for

BEETLES.

339. Figure 117 represents a farmer's beetle, made in a work-

manlike manner. Beetles should always be turned true, and the

FIG. 117.

handle turned of an oval form, (see SLEDGE HAM-MER, paragraph 332,) and *put in* very true, so that a line cutting the centre of the handle will be exactly parallel with lines continued square across the ends or face

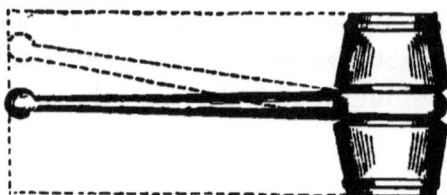

A WOODEN BEETLE.

of the beetle, as shown by the dotted lines, Fig. 117. The beetle should hang as nearly like the sledge hammer as possible; and the reader can refer to that paragraph (333) for the information which seems to be lacking in this place.

340. Beetles should be made of very firm, tough wood, such as the butt end of a small locust, iron-wood, or apple-wood. If a beetle is to be made of a round stick, which has the heart of the tree in the centre, when the timber is green, a lot of beetles should be sawed off, about eight or nine inches long, in late autumn, and an inch and a half hole bored *lengthwise* through the centre of the sticks; and they should be allowed to season during the winter, not in a stove room, lest they check badly, but under shelter. The object of the hole in the centre is, to allow the timber to settle together, without cracking or checking. When they are made of split pieces of wood, it will not be necessary to bore them, as they will not check like a stick with the heart in it. (See SEASONING TIMBER, in next vol.) When they are seasoned *thoroughly*, turn out a tough stick, just large enough to drive through the beetle, and turn out the beetle like the figure, with a shoulder two inches from each end, leaving the ends just large enough to receive the rings when they are red hot. (See EX-PANSIVE FORCE, in next vol.) By heating the rings before put-ting them on, and driving them down to the shoulder while hot, and then by cooling them quickly, before they have time to burn the beetle but little, they will, by contracting, become so tight that they will remain tight until the beetle is worn out, without

wedging. Should they become loose, let them be wedged well with wedges of hard, tough timber. (See paragraph 345.) Many men will wedge such things with wedges of *soft* timber; but every good mechanic who knows anything about driving wedges, will tell you, that anything can be wedged very much tighter with hard wood wedges than with wedges of *soft* wood. Use an inch framing chisel (see Fig. 156) for making checks in the ends of a beetle for the wedges; and make the wedges a sixteenth of an inch *wider* than the chisel, and then they will not work out. Some men prefer to have a beetle made *without* any shoulder for the rings, but my experience teaches me, that a beetle will wear longer, and the rings remain true longer, when it is made with shoulders, than when it is made of a true taper, *without* shoulders for the rings; because, if a laborer happens to strike mostly on one side of the end of a beetle, unless the rings are so tight that they cannot be moved by much pounding, one side of the rings will be driven on farther than the other, and the faces will soon become *one-sided*; and then it will be an awkward tool to strike with.   And if the rings are not very tight, when the wood begins to batter and spread over them they will drive on towards the middle of the beetle, and a beetle will be all stove up and worthless before it is half worn out.

341. The *size* of the different parts of an ordinary beetle is about as follows: *beetle* eight or nine inches long, *shoulders* two inches, *rings*, of the best of iron, one inch wide, about three-eighths of an inch thick, and about large enough to go on the end of a beetle, five inches in diameter, and *handle* about thirty inches long. For a strong man the handle should be longer than for boys, or men of inferior strength. Where the handle enters the head, it should not be less than an inch and a half in diameter. The hilt and straight part of the handle may be made to suit the size of the laborer's hands. A man with small hands and short fingers needs a smaller handle than he who has very large hands, with fingers of a corresponding length. Great care should be exercised in putting in the handle, lest it stand as shown by the dotted handle in the figure. It is no uncommon thing to see handles standing

at such an angle; and when they do, we hear those who use such beetles complain of having their hands hurt often by the jar, in consequence of not hitting the wedges true; and more than all else, beetles that are hung one-sided, wear one-sided; and as they usually in striking hit *one corner* or *one side* of the top of an iron wedge, they will not wear as long, nor will the force of driving, when the beetle is in use, be half as effective as if the *face* struck the wedge perfectly square. (See USING SLEDGE, paragraph 335.) After the rings have been but on and the handle driven in, make two plugs of hard wood, and drive them in the ends of the beetle very tightly, and saw them off even with the surface; it is then ready for use.

HANDLING A BEETLE.

342. It is often very amusing to see how awkwardly and inefficiently many laborers handle a beetle in splitting wood or rails, or anything else. One blow will be on one corner of an iron wedge, and the next blow will be on *another* corner, and the next one will be in such a manner that one corner of the wedge and beetle ring will come in contact, and the beetle will roll over and over, and very likely will fly half a rod; and when the laborer goes to get his beetle again, he will not unlikely find a ring broken. When beetle rings are put on as tightly as they ought to be, one or two awkward blows with the beetle, in such an unskillful manner that the iron wedge and beetle ring will come in contact, will snap a ring asunder instantaneously, unless it is of the very best iron; and even then rings will often break, especially in frosty weather, when the blow is not very powerful. Laborers ought to know—but I blush to say that one in fifty does not know—that when the face of a beetle is struck on the *corner* of an iron wedge, the blow is not half as effective as it would be if the face struck the head of the wedge *entirely square*. And more than all this, when all the blows are applied to a *corner* of the wedge, a beetle will be completely worn out before it has performed one-fourth of the service that it would have done had

the blows been applied in such a manner that the face of the beetle and head of the wedge came together *square*, as they should come. It is most surprising to witness how long a good beetle will last some laborers, and how much they will use it at hard pounding, while, on the contrary, it is still more surprising to see how very soon another laborer will use up a good beetle, before he has used it enough to begin to even *think* of its being worn out. The first alluded to always strike very true and square, while the latter deal their blows in every imaginable way but square and true. A laborer who handles his beetle with skill, will pound very hard on his wedges all day, and the faces of the beetle will be battered but little, while he who strikes awkwardly with a beetle just as good as the other, will use it up in one day, as if it had been in hard service for a week or more. It is all folly to use up beetles at such a rate, and a laborer ought to know better than to strike a ring on an iron wedge, or to strike a *corner* of a wedge with the face of the beetle.

343. In whatever position a wedge may be standing, place the face of the beetle and head of the wedge *square together*, then grasp the hilt of the handle firmly, and be careful to make every blow *square*, and not on *one side* of the face of the beetle, but as nearly in the centre of it as may be. If a wedge leans a little, or varies its position as it is driven in, let the position of the beetle be varied accordingly, so as to have the beetle and wedge strike each other *exactly square*. By exercising a little skill in this respect, a laborer will very soon find that he will be able to drive a wedge with *half* the number of blows, and not use up his beetle one-fourth as much as when he deals his blows *every* way *but square* on the head of the wedge and face of the beetle. (Read the paragraphs on the HAMMER AND SLEDGE, 331.) As beetle and wedges are used together, I shall now notice

THE WEDGE.——HOW TO MAKE WEDGES.

"The mighty power of the wedge to sever
Both flinty rocks and gnarls, exceeds the lever.
Impelled by force of oft-repeated blows,
In splitting, piercing, cutting, and in cleaving,
Or rending right and left, or in upheaving—
Unlike the screw its power no measure knows."—EDWARDS.

344. Fig. 118 represents a well-formed iron wedge, and *a* is the head, *b* is one of the sides, *d* is one of the edges, and *e* is the entering edge. A wedge will not rebound as readily when the corners at the entering edge are made flush, or square, like the figure, as it will when the corners are *rounded off* very much like the edge of an old axe, the corners of which are well ground off. Sharp corners of an iron wedge make it *stick* when entering.

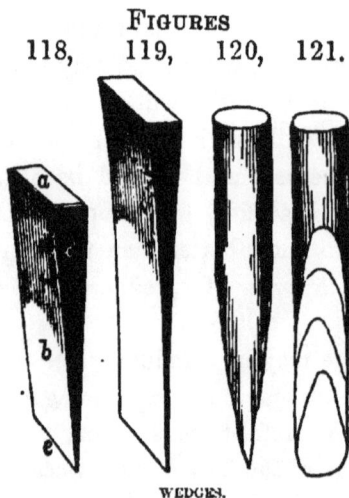

FIGURES 118, 119, 120, 121.

WEDGES.

345. Fig. 119 is a very ill-shapen wedge, but very like the iron wedges which many laborers use, and exactly like the wooden wedges which are often made with the false impression that they will be *more effective* of such a form than if they were like Fig. 118. But wooden wedges of such a form cannot possibly be as effective for any purpose as if they were like Fig. 118, because small wedges of such an ill form will be *crushed* at the entering point before they are half driven in; and if large wedges are made of such a form, it requires a greater number of blows to drive one in far enough to open a log two inches.

346. Every author whose writings I have consulted on the subject of the wedge has simple spoken of it in philosophical or *theoretical* terms, and the most important considerations which affect, directly or remotely, many of the operations of the farm, and which are all-important for the beginner to understand, have been entirely overlooked or rejected; and what has been penned

in reference to the wedge, if put into practice according to the strict letter of the various writers, will, in *practice*, lead the beginner into most egregious errors. The wedge has always been considered as a *double inclined plane*, and its *efficiency* has been spoken of as being in proportion to the *acuteness* and *length* of its sides. *Theoretically* speaking, this is all correct; but, in *practice*, no principle in philosophy proves to be more erroneous than this. *Theory* would teach the farmer to make his wedges, in order to be most effective when impelled by a given force, sixteen or twenty, or more, feet in length. But *practice* instructs us that there is a certain length for a wedge, and thickness for the head, which is much more effective, when impelled by a given force, than if it were longer or shorter. Every man who has split much timber knows too well, that a wedge of the proper length and thickness can be driven into a log with less force than one of the same thickness which is twice as long, to say nothing of a short and blunt wedge. Now this is what the beginner wants to know; he needs something *tangible*—some instruction in making wedges that will render his labor as light and effective as possible. Suppose, for instance, an iron wedge is two inches square at the head, and its sides of a true taper to the edge, and twelve or more feet long. *Theory* would instruct us, that a wedge of such dimensions could be driven with *less force* than one about ten inches long, of a . true taper to the edge, with the head of the size already mentioned. But, in *practice*, we find that such a long wedge would be utterly useless, because it would not possess sufficient *strength* to resist the force of heavy blows without being *crushed* or doubled up in places, and it would be very liable to twist and turn wherever the grain of the timber ran; and, more than all else beside, it would require *three times as many blows* to drive it up to the head at it would require to drive a wedge of the proper dimensions, and the friction would be so incalculably great in such a long wedge, that it is not at all probable that the force exerted by one man with a beetle would be sufficient to drive such a wedge clear to the head, even were it sufficiently strong to bear driving. And even if such long wedges were most effective, they would be most inconvenient and unwieldy tools. As the friction in driving wedges is usually so intense, the idea of an intelligent laborer always is, to have the most *economical* and *convenient* amount of surface in the sides of the wedge, which will prove most effective under a given number of blows. This leads us to speak of

THE MOST CONVENIENT AND EFFECTIVE DIMENSIONS OF WEDGES.

347. Iron wedges for splitting timber should always be so thick and strong that they will not bend nor twist, even when driven into the toughest knots and gnarls. The size which has been found in practice to be the most *convenient and effective* for ordinary purposes, is about ten inches long, two and a half inches wide, and about two inches in thickness at the head, and of a true taper to the entering edge, which should not be brought entirely to a *feather* edge; but the entering edge should be left about a sixteenth of an inch thick when it is tempered, and then ground off to a sharp edge, like the edge of an axe (see Fig. 152). The entering edge of, iron wedges should be made of steel, and tempered about as hard as for cold-chisels. Iron wedges may be smaller than this, or larger, if desired; but it is just as well, when a man has two wedges of the size just mentioned, to have *gluts*, as large iron wedges are rather costly, and are no better following in a check made by iron wedges than a good glut.

348. One very important consideration, which has been and is entirely overlooked by laborers, is, to have their iron wedges *in the most proper order.* The head should be a little convex, and the sharp corners on the edge smoothed off a little, so that they will not cut the face of the beetle. The two edges and two sides should be hammered as true as is convenient, and then they should be ground off on the grindstone as smoothly and true as the blade of a saw. After the sides are ground smooth, if they were polished they would enter their whole length with less than half the number of blows which would be required to drive the same wedge unpolished and all battered up, as wedges

usually are. Laborers are not aware how much unnecessary hard pounding they perform when the entering wedge is very dull and the sides uneven and rough; and they will not believe that there is really any difference, after all, in driving rough and smooth wedges, until they have some *ocular proof* of the fact. But let the beginner, or any one else, rest assured that it will abundantly remunerate him, in saving hard labor, to *polish* the sides of iron wedges, and to keep them smooth and the entering edge *sharp*.

349. Is it suggested that if well polished and sharp they will not *stick* as well as if left rough and uneven? I know, and any one can try the experiment, that a polished and sharp wedge will not recoil when splitting green or frozen timber, *half as often* as a dull and rough wedge; and with sharp and well-polished wedges a laborer would be able to split frozen timber many times when it would be impracticable to do anything with it if the wedges were dull and rough. Iron wedges should never be driven with an instrument of iron, because it would soon batter and spread the heads, and destroy their proper shape. When wedges are driven with an iron beetle, they soon become in shape like Fig. 119, with the head spread so that the sides are not of a true taper. When it is almost impossible to make a wedge stick in green or frozen timber, by having the wedge quite warm, or by driving a little wedge made of dry wood into the check, and then driving the iron wedge into the dry wedge, it will usually stick. Some laborers drive a little flat stone into the check where the wedge is started, and then drive the wedge into the stone in order to make it stick; but stone will usually make the sides of a wedge rough, so that it will drive hard.

GLUTS

350. Are large wooden wedges, and are not to be driven into the solid timber like an iron wedge, but into the checks which have been formed by the iron wedges. They are usually made of round sticks of timber, with two sides flattened at about the same angle of iron wedges. A lot of sticks ought to be sawed

of the proper length, and laid up under shelter in a safe place, where they will be seasoned and ready for use when gluts are needed. None but the hardest and toughest timber should be used for gluts, and if made when the timber is green, they will check less, and it is not half the work to make them that it would be to make them after they are seasoned. Laborers generally make no provision for gluts until they arrive at the woods, or where they are to labor, and then they will make gluts of the limbs of a green tree, which are very poor things for such a purpose, and spend time enough to no good purpose, to pay for half a dozen well-made gluts. And, more than this, gluts made of green timber will seldom last one quarter as long as if seasoned, and they require, many times, twice as many blows to drive them as if they were seasoned. And another thing of importance is, it is not at all practicable to make a glut in a workmanlike manner with the axe only. I know that they are usually made with no other tool but the axe, and they are made of every imaginable shape and form, like Fig. 119, or like Fig. 120, which shows an edge view of a glut which has been made with the axe alone. It will be discovered that the face sides of Fig. 120, which should be as true and smooth as the face of a plane, are very rough and hacked up, and not of a true taper, and will require more than twice as many blows to drive it than if it were true and smooth. He who wishes to appropriate all his strength, or the strength of his laborers, to the most effective purpose when splitting timber, will make his gluts at the *work-shop*, and have them well seasoned before they are used.

351. The most proper manner of making a glut is, to dress it off with an axe as true and smooth as practicable, leaving the entering edge never *less* than half an inch thick. In large gluts the entering edge should be three-fourths of an inch in thickness. Then, put it in the vise and plane it off true and smooth, and round the corners of the head and the corners of the entering edge with the drawing-knife, as shown at Fig. 121, which represents a view of the face side of a well-made glut. If the entering edge of a glut is reduced in making it to a feather edge, it

will be very liable to be split and shivered to splinters, when it happens to be driven on to, or among slivers. It may seem, too, unnecessary to finish the face sides of a glut with a plane; but let two wedges be finished, one with a plane, as directed, and the other with an axe only, and a laborer of keen perception will quickly tell which will drive the easier. If a glut is not smooth and true on the face sides, it will be far more liable to recoil, or "bound out," when opening a log. Wedges of every description should be smooth and true.

BORING MACHINE.

352. At paragraph 89 allusion has been made to a boring machine, for boring fence caps. But as there is so much boring to be performed in making the different styles of fence, I have thought best to give a cut of a very cheap and efficient boring machine which I have had in successful operation for several years.

FIG. 122.

FERGUSON ALBANY

BORING MACHINE.

353. Fig. 122 represents a perspective view of the machine, the frame of which is made of square scantling, 3 by 3, of

any desired length to suit the length of mandrel, length of · auger, and materials to be bored. It is about three feet wide, and from two to three feet high, to correspond with the stature of the workman who uses it. Fence posts, fence caps, bar posts, or anything else to be bored, are laid on the slide *a*, to which a strap of leather *b* is fastened, which strap passes around a pulley-roller *c*, and then is carried back under the slide *a*, over another pulley roller, as seen in the end of the frame, and is fastened to a treadle. The slide *a* has gains in the under side of it, which fit neatly to the top pieces of the frame, so that it can slide back and forth toward the auger. If it does not fit well, and one end is allowed to be moved *faster* than the other end, a post will not be bored at a right angle. (See RANGING SAWS, paragraph 679.)

354. *The way to bore with it.*—Place a post on the slide *a*, and stand at the end of the machine, having hold of the slide with each hand, and when the auger revolves place one foot on the treadle and press downwards with it, and push a little with the hands. As soon as a hole is bored, remove the foot and draw back the slide. When the stuff to be bored is small, lay some pieces of board on the slide *a*, in order to adjust the height to correspond with the auger. To bore holes *diagonally*, nail pieces of board *on one end* of the slide, to serve as a gauge to hold the material to be bored in a diagonal position.

355. This machine may be worked by hand, or it may be driven by any kind of horse power. Pullies of various sizes may be placed on the mandrel, and for boring small holes it may revolve as rapidly as the journal of a circular saw. When large holes—say four or more inches in diameter—are to be bored, the pulley on the mandrel should be so large that it will revolve about one hundred and twenty times in a minute. One horse turns my auger when boring four-inch holes in hard timber, and the auger revolves about one hundred and thirty times per minute. Now, if it were driven by a smaller pulley, that would make it revolve twice as rapidly, it would require *two* horses to turn it in order to keep boring constantly.

HOW TO OBTAIN SUCH A BORING MACHINE.

356. If you go to the machine shop and order such a machine, it will cost not less than about $20. I have cuts of patent boring machines which cost from $30 to $50. But farmers do not wish to pay $30 or $40 for a machine which can be afforded for six or seven dollars, which will subserve every good purpose, and last a whole life-time. It is all folly to pay mechanics an extortionate price for turning, filing and polishing a piece of coarse work, which will not add in the least to the durability or efficiency of a machine.

Fig. 123.

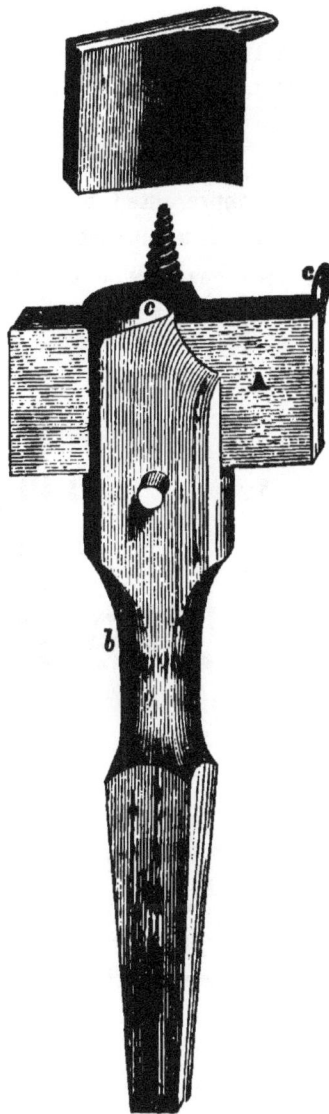

BORING MACHINE.

357. In the first place, if you are not mechanic enough to make the frame, employ a good joiner by the day, who will be able, if he can perform a faithful day's work, to make all the wood-work in a day and a half.

358. Next, write Wales French, 68 Beekman street, New York city, or to Westville, Conn., and procure a patent extension-lip bit, which is represented by Fig. 123, with which holes of any size larger than two inches may be bored with one bit. A is the adjustable extension cutter, which is adjusted in the mortise of the main part of the shank *b* by a set screw or key. Two spur cutters *c c* cut the shaving or chips, making a

clean, smooth hole. D represents an edge view of the extension
cutter, separate from the shank *b*. The entire auger should not be
more than one foot long. Order the end of the shank made
round, to fit a hole or socket in the end of the mandrel (see
Fig. 124), instead of having it square, because it can be fitted
to run true with less ¯work when the socket is round. The
next thing will be,

THE MANDREL,

which is represented by Fig. 124. Take a round bar of inch-
and-a-half iron, eighteen inches long, to the machine-shop, and
have two bearings *a a* turned and polished (see FITTING UP

FIG. 124.

THE MANDREL.

MACHINERY, next vol.), and fitted to two iron boxes; have the
shank of the auger fitted to the end of the mandrel, and have a
small hole bored *through the mandrel*, at the end or bottom of
the socket, so that a punch may be driven in to force out the
shank of the auger. The shape of the rocket is shown by the
dotted lines at the end of the mandrel. Have a fly-wheel *b* and
large pulley *c* keyed on the mandrel, and have a small bolt put

through the end of crank and mandrel. The bearing *a* nearest the crank should be turned an inch in diameter, in order to form a good shoulder; and the other bearing should be an inch and a fourth in diameter, as more strain will come on that when boring. A hoop of band iron may be put on the fly or balance wheel, about three inches wide, and may be used for a pulley in boring large holes. Always take off the crank when boring with a horse; because a crank will produce a tremulous motion unless there is a corresponding weight on the other side of the mandrel. (See BALANCING MACHINERY, in next vol.)

359. If one has a horse saw, or straw-cutter, or threshing-machine cylinder, have a hole bored in one end of the journal, for the auger, and make the frame of the boring machine to receive the shaft of saw or shaft of straw-cutter. This will save the expense of a mandrel. A hole may be bored for the auger in the end of the shaft for twenty-five cents. Then, the cost of auger, $2 50, frame and fixtures, $4 00=$6 50, will cover the whole expense, besides the mandrel, of as good a boring machine as any farmer can desire.

A GRASS HOOK, OR DUTCH GRASS SICKLE.

360. Fig. 125 represents an instrument for pruning or trimming hedges after they have grown too high to be clipped with a stiff, sharp grass scythe. They should be heavier than a

FIG. 125.

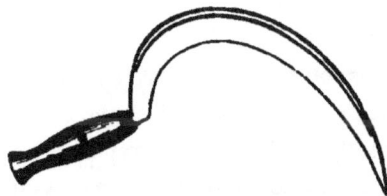

A GRASS HOOK.

common grain sickle, having a sharp fine edge—and not a *sickle* edge. They may be obtained at R. L. Allen's Agricultural Warehouse, 189 Water street, New York city.

361. For the first two or three seasons, the best instrument for

12

clipping a hedge is a good grass scythe. After this time there is no better instrument than such a sickle, according to the opinion of Mr. A. H. Ernst, Spring Garden, Ohio, who says: "In clipping hedges, if the sickle is to be used with *one* hand, the handle may be about six inches long; and, if *both* hands, it should be from two to two and a half feet long. For a hedge not over three and a half feet high, one hand is all sufficient. But when the hedge is higher than that, both hands are necessary. We have a fine hedge, of some two miles, around Spring Garden Cemetery, of Osage Orange, six feet high, for trimming which this instrument alone is used. Two men, one right-handed and the other left-handed, start at the same point, on opposite sides, and with a quick stroke *upwards*, make a clean sweep of all the straggling branches, trimming the hedge in the form of the letter A, which is decidedly the best form for a hedge, as it gives the greatest exposure to light and air, which is a very essential point to the health and duration of a hedge. I should prefer to have the borders of my hedges raised somewhat above the common surface of the ground, so as to admit a freer circulation of air and light to the lower branches."

THE AXE.

" The faithful axe, whose burnished blade
Stood gleaming in the old oak's shade,
In quick response replied, Who, tell,
Save me, the mighty forests fell?
Who clave the gnarly oaks and pines,
The thorn, the brambles, and the vines ?"—EDWARDS.

362. The axe is one of the most efficient implements of the farmer, and, when made of a correct shape and put in good order, when hung correctly and handled expertly, performs wonders, even when he who handles it is by no means strong. It is very poor policy to attempt to chop with a poor axe, because a laborer, in a very short time, with a poor axe, will lose time and expend strength—to no profit—sufficient to purchase a good axe. Choppers often feel too poor to purchase a new axe, and will *peck, peck*, with an old worn-out tool, year after year, very much dis-

satisfied with their day's work. If they had no other means of obtaining a new and good axe, it would be a matter of *economy* " to work out" a day or two, and earn each enough to get a good axe; and then with *half* the time and strength that would be required with the *old* axe, they would be able to accomplish enough more with a good axe to pay for it.

363. Figure 126 represents an axe with its different parts

FIG. 126.

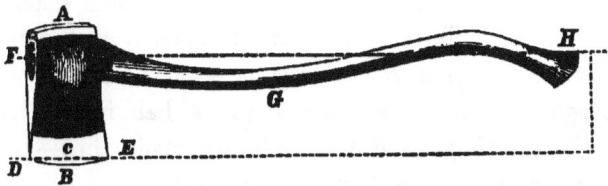

A CHOPPING AXE CORRECTLY HUNG.

lettered. *A* represents the heap or poll, which is sometimes made of steel; *B* the edge, *C* the steel, *D* the outside corner, *E* the inside corner, *F* the eye. The position of the axe, from the eye to the edge, is called the *bit* or *blade* of the eye. *G* is the helve, *H* is the *hilt* of the helve. The dotted lines represent the *angle* of the axe and helve, and will be referred to under the head of hanging an axe.

THE SHAPE OF THE AXE.

"A neat, symmetrical, becoming shape."

364. Nothing adds more to the efficiency of an axe, as a tool, than a correct shape of the bit or blade. Manufacturers often give a shape to the axe which defies and sets at naught every correct principle in mechanics. Some make them with a very small poll—with almost no poll at all—and with a very long blade, and very wide from the outside corner to the inside corner, with the edge about twice as long as the poll, and with almost the whole weight of the axe on one side of the eye—in the blade or bit. Some make them with a very heavy poll and a long narrow blade, with no corners to the blade, but almost *circular* on the

edge like an old axe with the corners ground off. It cannot be denied that an axe with no corners will enter farther into wood, at a given stroke, than one that has corners; but a man can chop much faster with an axe that is almost *straight* on the edge, than with one that is very *round* on the edge. The reason for this is, a chopper with an axe that is very rounding on the edge makes a great deal of *mince;* but with an axe that has but little rounding on the edge, he will make but little mince or fine chips. An axe of due proportion will measure about five inches from one corner of the edge to the other, and about three and a half inches the length of the poll, and about eight inches from the crown of the poll to the edge *A B, midway* between each corner. An axe, the poll of which is about two and a half inches long, the edge six inches long—and hundreds are made thus—is a very poor tool to work with, and an ill-shapen thing.

THE WEIGHT OF THE AXE

365. Is a consideration in regard to which choppers often disagree; but the majority of them will probably agree in what follows. If a chopper is naturally very slow in handling an axe, and is not disposed to exert much strength, he should have an axe which weighs from *five* to *eight* lbs., according to the strength of the chopper. If a chopper strikes *very quickly*, and raises his axe very quickly,—if he is a man of ordinary strength, he should have an axe weighing about four lbs. A chopper will cut off a log quicker with a heavy axe than with a *light* one; but when he comes to handle it all day, he will find he will be able to chop quite as much, and with less fatigue, with a four- or five-lb. axe than he can with one that weighs six or seven lbs. or more. It is better to exert the muscles a little in *striking* with an axe, than it is to exert all the strength in *lifting* an axe which is heavy enough to cut sufficiently deep at a stroke by its own weight.

366. Were a chopper to strike twenty blows per minute, he would strike twelve thousand blows in ten hours. With an axe weighing five lbs., in that time he would raise as high or higher than his head, an equivalent to *sixty thousand* lbs., or thirty tons,

—a good day's work aside from chopping. Chopping with a six pound axe, he would raise, at the above rate, in ten hours, thirty-six tons, of 2,000 lbs. per ton. For trimming the limbs of trees, cutting under-brush, and for other light chopping, an axe weighing four lbs. is preferable to a heavier one.

367. Boys should always have light axes to chop with, lest they make poor choppers, soon tire out, and imbibe an ever-lasting dread of and disrelish for chopping.

PUTTING THE AXE IN ORDER.

368. There are two things of great importance to be kept in view when one is putting an axe in order, which are, to have it of a shape which will *cut* the fastest, and *chip* the best. It may be seen, by referring to EDGE TOOLS, (paragraph 543,) that the axe cuts with a *crushing stroke.* Now, if nothing else were required of an axe but *to cut,* it would be wisdom to grind it as thin as possible, consistent with strength. But since an axe must *chip* as well as cut, it is important to give it a shape which will not only *cut fast,* but which will *chip well.* An axe ground very thin near the edge, will cut fast and deep at every stroke, but will not *chip* well; and a very thick axe, with a blunt edge, will *chip well,* but will *not cut* fast. If an axe is ground very thin, it enters the wood so far at a blow that it is apt *to stick,* especially in soft wood.

369. It is almost impossible to give a correct idea of the proper *shape* of an axe, in this respect, on paper; but Fig. 127 will give something of an idea. This figure represents a transverse section of an axe, at about two inches from the edge. A ridge should be formed on the dotted line of the angle of the axe, (see Fig. 126, *A B*,) which *should disappear towards the cutting edge,* and *towards* the *eye* of the axe. The object of this ridge is to *split the chip.* From this ridge towards each *corner,* it should be ground of a true taper, with a little swell.

370. When holding an axe on a grindstone, put the head of it in the gain of the Clamp, Fig. 128, which may be made of a piece of two-inch plank, about eighteen inches long, and put the

opposite end of the clamp against the abdomen of the workman who holds the axe. Such a little instrument will be found of very great service. In grinding up a new axe, make a gain in the end of a rail or scantling, and *sit on it* when grinding. The cutting edge at *B* should never be more than half an inch beyond a

FIG. 127.   FIG. 128.

A TRANSVERSE SECTION OF THE BLADE OR BIT OF A WELL-FORM- ED CHOPPING AXE.   A CLAMP FOR HOLDING AN AXE WHILE GRINDING IT.

line drawn from the outside corner *D*, to inside corner *E*. (See Fig. 126.) For scoring timber, an axe must be a little circular on the edge from *D* to *E*. If this edge is very circular, the timber will be badly hacked. After grinding, whet the edge with a fine gritted oil stone; and if the sides of the blade could be polished on a polishing wheel, it would enter the wood farther at a given stroke. (See OIL STONE, paragraph 572.)

THE AXE HELVE.

371. In order to chop well and easily, a man must have a *good helve;* and unless a helve is made of good timber, and of a good *shape*, it will be an awkward tool in the hands of a good chopper. A helve, in order to be a good one, must not be too

large, nor too small, at the hilt, nor midway between the hilt and the end that holds the axe. It should be made with a good *hang*—or, as some call it, *with a good deal of crook*—from the hilt to the other end. A helve should always be made so that the *hang* will be in the direction of the grain of the wood from the bark towards the heart. If a helve is made "*slab fashion,*" or as our backwoodsmen call it, "*bastard fashion,*" with one *side* of the helve towards the heart, and one side towards the bark, it will soon spring so as to be a worthless thing to chop with. If the hilt be too large, or too small, or of an improper shape, it will surely cramp and blister the hand. It should not be made round, but of an oval or elliptical shape. Without a good hang and an oval shape, it will be impossible to strike true. (See HANG, in next vol.) Some men, who know nothing about chopping, contend that if a man is accustomed to chop with a *straight stick*, he could chop as well as he could with a helve having a *good hang*. But no good chopper will ever make such an assertion. When a helve is round, an axe may turn half way round in the hands, and not be perceived by the chopper; but when it is of an *oval* shape, and has a good *hang* in chopping, an axe will adjust itself; and a little deviation will readily be perceived by the accustomed hand. (See Par. 331.) One who chops much with a straight helve, or with one that has a hilt too large or too small for his hand, is very liable to complain of lame hands and of lame wrists; and that he is not able to strike twice in one place. If a man has a very small hand, his axe helve should be correspondingly small; and *vice versa*.

372. Helves that are made by machinery, when they are made of good timber, with straight grain, and the right way of the grain, are usually superior to those which are made by hand; unless those made by hand are made by one who understands the business extremely well. It is a very difficult task for some good mechanics to make a good axe helve until they have practised by making a number of helves; and some *never can*, with ever so much practice, succeed in giving a helve the most correct *hang* and *shape* at the hilt, and at other parts of it. But if the

tyro be favored with a little ingenuity, the following directions, with a little practice, will enable him to make a very good helve.

HOW TO MAKE AN AXE HELVE.

373. Fig. 129 represents an axe-helve pattern of a very good shape. From *a* to *b* is two feet eight inches. This is too long for some men. If a pattern cannot be obtained from a helve having a good shape, a pattern can be made in a few minutes of the desired shape, out of a piece of thin board, as shown by the

FIG. 129.

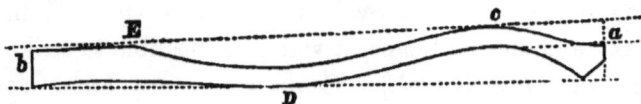

AXE HELVE PATTERN.

dotted lines. At *a* let it be made not less than three inches wide, and at *b* about two and a half inches wide. At *c*, about six inches from the end, near *a*, make a pencil mark for the most prominent point. At *D* make another mark, about two-thirds of the distance from *a* to *b*. At *E* make another mark, six or seven inches from *b*. Now, with a pencil, mark out the shape, like the figure, as nearly as possible; and then cut it out very exact and true. The dotted lines at *a* will show how much of the upper corner should be cut away in order to give the hilt a good shape.

374. Now, rive out a piece of tough hickory, and dress it with an axe or circular saw, four square, and as thick at the large end as the hilt, and wide enough to admit of marking out a helve with a pencil by the pattern. Now, with the draw-ing-knife, smoothing plane, spoke shave, and rasp, dress it down to an oval shape. This oval form should extend entirely through the hilt. Avoid a *round* hilt; because with a *round* hilt the best choppers cannot keep the axe in the correct position, with-out grasping the hilt so firmly that the muscles of the hand will soon be cramped. Avoid, also, making the edges of the

helve *too sharp;* and avoid a *very large hilt.* Such a hilt is sure to cramp the hand, and make a man's wrist lame, and the fingers stiff. Always lay the pattern on the stick, so that the part at *c E* will be towards the *bark,* and the part at *D* towards the *heart* of the tree. Then, if the helve should spring, it would spring with the curve, which will make an axe hang still better; whereas, should it spring *sideways,* it would be a worthless thing to chop with. (See SPRINGING OF TIMBER, in next vol.) Endeavor to make a hilt that will work easily in the hand, and not one so short and sharply curved that the third and the little fingers hold the axe, while the *first* and second fingers do nothing. A longish hilt is most desirable; because it never cramps the hand in chopping. Fig. 126 is an exact representation of helves made by the author, which have been pronounced by some of the best choppers in the Empire State to be exactly right in every particular.

HANGING THE CHOPPING AXE

375. Is a piece of labor which requires no little skill to perform correctly; and if it is not correctly done an axe will not work well. Good choppers usually know when an axe is correctly hung; but a great many excellent choppers cannot *hang* an axe correctly. And when an axe hangs wrong, or "bad," as choppers say, it is impossible to chop well.

376. The RULE for hanging an axe upon the most approved mechanical principles is, to *have it so fastened on the helve that the edge will range exactly in the direction of the centre of the hilt, and that the hilt, the centre of the eye, and the centre of the blade, will be at right angles.* By consulting Fig. 126, it will be seen by the dotted lines, showing the *angle of the axe,* that this line cuts the hilt, the centre of the eye, and the centre of the blade. When the eye of an axe is *crooked,* or not in range with the edge, which is often the case with even good axes, the edge may be made to stand in range with the hilt of the helve, by wedging the axe on *one side of the centre* of the helve. When the eye is true we insert a wedge in the centre of the eye, splitting the helve in the

12*

centre; but when the eye is *one-sided*, by splitting the end of the helve on one side of the centre, and inserting a wedge one side of the centre of the eye, the edge may be adjusted with all desirable precision. If, when the helve is driven into the eye, it should not touch on one side, and the edge stand correctly, it is best not to split the end of the helve in wedging, but to wedge on *one side*, with timber as hard as the helve. Have a thin, iron wedge made to fasten on the axe, with a *large flat head* that will cover the *eye* of the axe. This may be readily taken out in case of a broken axe or helve, when a *wooden* wedge could not be extracted.

CHOPPING.

"The sturdy feller, with his glittering axe,
Incessant plies the well-directed blows."—Anon.

377. Why can one man chop so much faster and neater than another? Why can a very small man, possessing but little strength, often chop twice as much as some large, strong, Goliah-like fellow? The reason is very obvious: it requires but little strength to chop well, and to chop fast, when a chopper handles his axe well and easily, and strikes as straight as may be, losing no strokes. But when a chopper handles his axe *awkwardly*— be he ever so stout—he is not likely to strike very straightly; and if he does not strike exactly in the same spot at every blow. he *loses his strokes;* and when he loses his strokes, and makes a great deal of *mince*, or fine chips, before he is able to bring out the chips, it requires many more strokes to *start* the chips than when there is but little or no mince made. A good chopper makes but little mince, and he always strikes so as to start a chip at nearly every stroke. The first thing, then, in order to be a good chopper, is, to learn

TO HANDLE THE AXE CORRECTLY.

378. When a chopper stands on a log which he designs to cut off with the axe, he should stand erect, straighten his back at every stroke, and, with one hand holding the hilt of the helve,

the other should grasp the helve eight or ten inches from the axe; bring the axe right up before the face, and thrust it up into the air as high as he can reach easily, letting the hand that held the middle of the helve slip down against the other hand as the axe rises. Now, the eye of the chopper should be fixed on the spot where he wishes to strike. Now strike straightly, and always look to the place where the axe cuts, *looking between the arms*, and not on *one side* of the arms. Let the arms be as limber and elastic as a leathern strap, but keep the hand that holds the hilt of the helve firmly grasped, so as to keep the axe in just such a position as it is in when it comes down.

379. Some choppers, in lifting their axe, give it a *side* swing, bringing it round near one shoulder; and some thrust it out forward of them, and raise it up.before them, with arms as stiff as a stake, to an angle of about forty-five degrees, before striking. But such are very awkward, feminine and inefficient ways of handling an axe.

Another consideration of great importance in chopping is,

THE SHAPE OF THE KERF, OR CHIP.

380. Fig. 130 represents a log cut off with an axe. At *A* the kerf, or chip, is shaped *badly*, and at *B* it has a *good* shape. The RULE, among good choppers, for the length of the outside chip, usually is, *not less in length than the diameter of the log*. Then, as we chip deeper into the log, the cut should be more. square across it, so that the ends that have been cut off will be *circular*, as at *B*. If a log be two feet in diameter, commence a chip, to take a log half off, two feet long. The tyro may then trace the *shape* of the kerf, with his axe, on the bark, until he can form a good kerf *by the eye*. In cleaving the *outside* chips, let three or four inches of the ends be cut off *square*, and it will be seen that a stroke of the axe will start a chip the end of which is *square*, when several

FIG. 130.

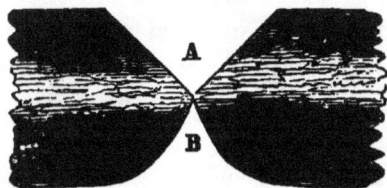

blows would have but little effect if the end were not cut off square. He who would be a good chopper must learn *to strike straight*, and not strike *too quick*, lest his strength fail, nor *too slow*, lest suitable progress be not made, and he must learn to shape his kerfs like *B* in the figure.

FELLING TREES WITH AN AXE.

" Loud sounds the axe, redoubling strokes on strokes ;
 On all sides round the forest hurls her oaks
 Headlong. Deep-echoing groan the thickets brown ;
 Then rustling, crackling, crashing, thunder down."

381. The first and most important consideration, when we have concluded to fell a tree, is, to decide which way it will fall most advantageously. When a tree stands perpendicularly, it may be felled just which way we choose. If, for instance, we wish to fell a tree to the north, let the north side be cut a little more than half off, and three or four inches *lower* than the south side, and it will surely fall towards the north, unless the wind is contrary. A tree that stands perpendicularly will always fall in the direction which the chips fly when it is being cut down. A tree will fall usually on that side of the stump which is cut the lowest. When a tree is large and valuable for timber, if a chopper does not understand felling trees, he is very liable oftentimes to damage a tree very much, and for some purposes spoil it entirely. Large trees, especially very tough timber, are very apt to *split, shiver* and *check* at the butt when falling, if they are not cut correctly.

382. We have often seen valuable trees split at the butt six or eight feet when falling; and sometimes splinters six or eight feet long are *drawn out* of the butt of the tree, and stand erect on the stump, damaging a tree very much.

383. A tree for timber should be cut as low as possible, as one foot in length of the *butt* of a tree is worth, in many instances, four times the cost of cutting down the tree; and each side should be cut *square across*, and not diagonally, with one side slanting one way, and the other side in an opposite direction. It is just

as easy, and far better for many reasons, to cut trees *low* than to cut them *high*. Let a chopper keep the hand that holds the hilt of the axehelve *well down*, (the length of the arm,) and bend his back a little—it will not injure him—and he will soon get accustomed to cutting trees low and *square across*.   In order to save timber, the kerf should be more straight *inward* than it is in chopping off a log.   It will require a little more time and strength to cut down a tree with a short chip; but, where timber is valuable, the amount saved by a short kerf more than compensates for the. extra time in cutting down.   When one is cutting down a large tree, and there is any apprehensions of its splitting at the butt, and the tree is cut off within eight or ten inches, the *heart* of the tree should all be cut off *first*, letting it stand as long as it will on a portion of the sap part of the tree.

384. My practice, in cutting down a valuable tree, is, to set two long braces against it, one on each side, in the direction where we intend to fell it, and brace it firmly until the tree can be cut entirely off. Then knock away one of the braces, and the tree may be made to go whichever way we choose to have it.

385. When trees *lean*, they should never be cut to fall in the direction they lean, because they will surely split or damage in some way.

386. Suppose, for instance, a tree stands near a precipice, and leans a little *towards* it, it may be made to fall in any direction we desire, by attaching a rope and tackles to it and fastening to another tree, or to a post set firmly in the ground, and then hitching a team to the slack rope, when the tree is nearly ready to fall. When a valuable tree is to be cut, when standing on an eminence, never allow it to fall *down hill*, but always *up hill*, or along the slope.

SAWING DOWN TREES.

387. Sometimes trees may be sawed down to good advan· tage. Before using a saw, however, for sawing down a tree, a kerf a few inches deep should be cut with the axe, so as to

steady the saw.   Let a tree be sawed about half off on one side, in the direction it is designed to fall the tree ; and then saw on the *opposite* side, and drive wedges into the kerf as fast as the saw goes in, to keep the tree from swaying and pinching the saw, and from falling in a wrong direction.   If a tree be large, three wedges should be driven in ; and the saw should be worked straight across the tree, and not all round it, lest it fall to one side and break the saw.

388. Let the tyro remember, before a large tree is felled, to take the team and haul three or four small logs or sticks of timber, fifteen or twenty feet long, for the tree to fall on.   Never trust to a few rails, or a little pole or two ; for a heavy tree will surely crush or bury such trash in the ground ; and then, before the tree can be sawed or worked up, there must be *tugging* and *prying*, and time enough spent *very disadvantageously*, to have got the team and hauled a *score* of logs for a tree to fall on. Let trees be kept *up well* from the ground ; because it is far easier to let logs *down* than it is to raise them a few inches after a tree has fallen.   When a chain cannot be put under a log to roll it over, hitch the grapple-hook to it.   (See Fig. 72.—See How to Handle a Cross-cut Saw, Par. 648.)

CHAPTER IV.

FENCE LAWS.

389. Our civil law in relation to fences, which appears to be founded on principles of strictest equity, provides, that where land is enclosed, and lies contiguous, and possessed by two different owners, each one must build and maintain a good lawful fence on one half the distance of the entire line between their land. *According to law*, A may not build his half of the line fence *exactly on the line;* neither may B. But each must erect his fence *on his own land*, as *near* to the line as he desires. But *neighbors* usually erect their line fences *exactly on the line;* while *waspish* owners place them as they choose.

390. If A refuses to build or to maintain one equal half of a line fence between his land and the land owned by B, by giving A thirty days' legal notice that he must build or repair his line fence, and A neglects so to do, B may build or repair such fence, and collect of A the expense of building the same as for any other indebtedness.

391. If A has land not enclosed, or "open to the commons," which lies contiguous to the land of B, if B desires to have his land enclosed, he must build all the fence between them. But after B has *enclosed* his land, if A should then enclose *his*, he cannot hold one half of the line fence. He must allow B to remove one-half of the fence; and he (A) must build a fence in the *room* of it; or he may *purchase* one-half of it. If he refuses to do either, B, the owner of the fence, may prosecute A and recover pay for half of the line fence.

392. B may not, in a fit of resentment or frenzy, remove his

division fence, and throw open his own fields to the commons with impunity, unless he give A ten days' notice of his intention to throw open his fields to the commons, between November and April. During the time from April to November, if a line fence is removed by A, and B is made to sustain any loss by such removal, A is responsible for the damage.

WHAT IS A LAWFUL FENCE?

393. There are three very important considerations which constitute a *lawful fence:* viz., *height, strength* or *substantiability,* and *tightness.* When a fence is four feet six inches high, and made according to the various styles of fence laid down in Chapter II, and built of good materials, our civil law would hold the proprietor of any animals that would get over it or through it, accountable for any damage which they might do. A fence that is three feet six inches high, *might be,* under certain circumstances, very lawful. Sheep and swine that would get over or through, by demolishing a substantial fence three feet six inches high, would be considered *as unruly animals;* and their proprietor would be held accountable for any damage done by them.

394. I have failed to bring out in the chapter on fences, *uncle Will's lawful fence,* which he testified in court was " a *lawful, buncombe fence :*" "*it was horse high—bull strong—and pig tight.*"

CHAPTER V.

" Each bog and marsh industriously drain,
Nor let vile ponds deface the beauteous plain."—ANON.

395. Notwithstanding there has been so much written on the
subject of underdraining with tile, stone, and wood, writers on
this subject have failed to bring out, with their suggestions and
directions for draining, many things which I consider of very
great importance, and which all good practical ditchers consider
of greater importance than almost any other part of draining.
There have been volumes written on draining which appear very
plausible while reading them, to those who have had but little
experience in thorough draining, but which in reality, instead of
imparting the desired information to the young farmer, *mislead
him.* It is attended with no embarrassments to pen a good chapter on draining, and to give diagrams of ditches, and to direct
how deep they should be cut, and with what materials they
should be filled. But let a beginner take the tools, and attempt
to follow up the directions which have been laid down by writers
on draining; and if he does not meet with some almost insuper-
able embarrassments, he will be an exception to the general rule.
Making a long drain in a manner to subserve the best purpose,
is a job which is not to be performed every year; but it should
be done so that it will work well for a life-time. A long drain
may be made in the best manner throughout its entire length,
with the exception of a few inches near the outlet, which will
render all that lies *above* it nearly or quite worthless. Drains
are often rendered worthless by having been improperly dug, or
by having been filled with poor materials, or by the improper

(287)

arrangement and disposition of *good* materials. If a drain is made of good materials, and those materials are properly disposed of, we may safely calculate that it will work well for ages to come, without any repairing.

396. The first consideration in draining wet land is, to ascertain with certainty from whence the water which renders a soil too wet comes. Land is often made too wet for cultivation by the superabundant water coming out of the earth, or by its being retained by a retentive subsoil. Where a very thin super soil lies on a very retentive subsoil, water will often collect in ponds in low places ; and so long a time will be required before it will disappear, that a crop would be about destroyed. In this case, if the young farmer desires to drain only such low, wet places, a good drain may be run directly through them. But if his aim is to drain the *entire field* in the most thorough manner, drains parallel to each other, about two rods apart, should be made across the field, *up and down the slope*, if the surface of the field is inclined, all of them intersecting with one large drain. . Sometimes the most proper place for the main drain will be across the middle of a field. But it is a minor consideration, where the water is turned, if a drain is properly made, and has *a good outlet*. When a low place is rendered very wet by water arising from springs, a drain entirely around it, between the wet ground and the dry ground, will cut off the source of the water ; and if the bottom of the drain is *lower* than the lowest place in the pond-hole, it will be well drained ; otherwise, a drain should be cut *through* the lowest place, and then *around* the outside of it.

397. When the surface of a field that lies sloping is too wet in places over the entire field, the most approved manner of draining it is, to cut the ditches *up and down the slope*, from thirty to forty feet apart. Then, if a spring of water should happen to be near the middle of two drains, which the main drains did not seem to affect, a *branch* drain should be made, diagonally, above the wet ground, two-thirds of the distance across the space between two drains. In cutting off the water from springs, it should always be borne in mind that the most proper place for a

drain is—in order to be most effectual *above the wet ground*—be-tween the wet ground and the dry. The *slope* of the field must determine how far above the wet ground the drain should be made. If the surface of the ground slope about six inches in a rod, the drain should be made not less than forty or fifty feet *above* the wet ground. The idea is, to have the diagonal drain far enough *above* the wet ground to cut off the veins of water which render the ground wet, so that they will be near the bottom of the drain.

398. There are veins of water all through the earth in most localities; and if a drain intersects any of these veins, the water flowing from them will find its way to the bottom of the drain, even if the drain should be filled with clay, well rammed in. But if the drain is not deep enough to reach a vein, the water in it will flow on, and come out at the surface, as it always has done, and the drain will be of little benefit. Sloping fields, which lie below large bodies of standing wood, or below large tracts of swamps or wet land, are very liable to be so wet as to need *thorough* draining; whereas, if the woods above them were re-moved, or the wet ground alluded to were well drained, those sloping fields would be sufficiently dry, in some instances, without drains. In such instances the water from above may, many times, be cut off by running a deep drain along the upper side of the field, to receive the water as it finds its way from the up land, and spreads over the fields below. One of the fields on my present farm slopes to the west about six inches per rod. About one-fourth of a mile above it was a tract of wet, swampy land, which was supposed to be the source of the numerous veins of water which *out-cropped* in this sloping field. The sloping field has been drained; and before the swamp above was drained, the drains in that sloping field emitted an abundance of good water, as long as there was water in the swamp. But now that the swamp has been drained, the water in those drains in the sloping field fails early in the season, showing very conclusively that the *source* of the water has failed.

399. Sometimes mill-races or canals are cut along hills, and the

water from them percolates through the bank, rendering a large tract of the land below the water very wet during the whole growing season. Now, if a deep drain is made along the race or canal, it *will cut off* the water that would render the soil too wet for cultivation. If, after one drain has been made for such a purpose, some of the water passes *under* the first drain, and renders the soil wet several rods below it, another drain nearly parallel with the first will effectually cut off all that would otherwise pass on and render the soil wet.

400. The young farmer need have no apprehension that he may cut a drain in some places where it will injure the soil by draining it *too much*. There is but little danger of draining a field so much as to injure it. Most soils operate like a sponge in retaining water. If deep drains were made at a distance of every ten feet across our driest fields, they would retain all the water, as it fell in rain, that is necessary to sustain healthy vegetation; and they would be *benefited* rather than injured by such a system of thorough draining. I pen these suggestions to show that if the young farmer should cut a drain in one place, and it should fail to drain the soil *thoroughly* on both sides of it, he need not fear to cut another drain, even within a few feet of the first one. Now that the most proper place is chosen for drains, and the stakes stuck for it, the next consideration which is of great importance is,

THE MANNER OF CUTTING DRAINS.

401. The young farmer will, very frequently, be so fortunate as to have in his employ some piece of stupid intelligence who professes to know more about thorough draining than all the world besides, and who will insist that a drain must be cut *here* or *there*, and that a given depth, which he may mention, is infinitely better than any other depth; and that he can excel any other man in laying out, cutting, and stoning or tiling a drain. But the truth is, too frequently, with such knowing ones, that they, in reality, know about as much as juvenile school-boys. There can be no impropriety in giving such knowing ones a hearing; but the beginner should consult some farmers who have had

no little experience in underdraining, and read attentively all that has been written on the subject, and then bring all the common sense that is in his possession to bear on the subject.

402. It is a consideration of very little consequence how rough and uneven the sides of a drain are, providing the *bottom is made true.* Therefore, when a drain is to be cut without the aid of a regular Ditching Machine, in order to facilitate and economize the expense of cutting it, if the soil is in sod, plow a furrow where the drain is to be made, about six inches deep, and then cut another furrow about six inches wide, very straight, and throw it beyond the first furrow, either with the plow or with manure hooks. Now drive back to the other end, and plow the subsoil as deep as is convenient, by going twice in the same place. Now shovel out the loose dirt, and plow again. By hitching the team two or three feet further from the plow, with a chain, than they are hitched for ordinary plowing, a ditch can be plowed two feet deep with a common plow. A strong double team and Michigan Sod Plow is much better than a single team. After the dirt has been shovelled out, if the drain is to be a small one, have a very long yoke for oxen, or long whippletree or evener for horses, and loosen up the dirt with a

FIG. 130½.

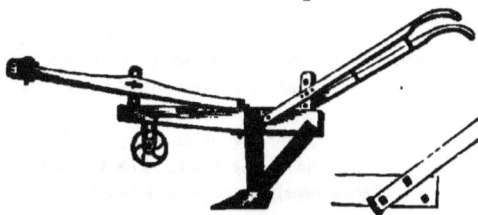

MILTON ALDEN'S DITCHING PLOW, AUBURN, N. Y.

Sub-Soil Plow, or with a Ditching Plow, shown at Fig. 130½, which is a most efficient and superior tool, and can be obtained of the inventor, Milton Alden, Auburn, N. Y.* When the ditch

* Since this chapter on Draining was written, M. Alden, Auburn, N. Y., has made a great improvement in ditching plows. His improved plow is made with two standards and two points. One standard is bolted to one side of the beam, as in the Fig. of the single standard plow on this page, and the other standard is bolted to a block, which block is

is sufficiently wide for a horse to walk in, let one or two be hitched before it, *ad tandem*, or one before the other.   The bottom of a ditch is a very difficult place for a horse to walk in; consequently a man should steady him, walking by his side, with one hand hold of the back-band to keep him balanced,—or in a narrow ditch a horse will lose his balance so often, by hitting his legs and feet against the sides of the ditch, that he will fall over sideways so frequently, he will become *afraid to move*.   A horse cannot walk in a channel which is barely wide enough for a man to walk in.

GRADING THE BOTTOM OF A DITCH.

403.   Any one can work at ditching until he comes to the bottom; but not one ditcher in fifty, that I have ever seen, knows how to grade the bottom correctly, or dig it *across* the bottom in the most correct form.   The bottom of a ditch, from the outlet to the head, should be of a *straight uniform grade* all the way.   The bottom should not be level for a few rods, and then ascend a few rods, and then be of a water level for a number of rods farther, and then ascend, and so on to the head of it, as they are usually dug.   The idea is, to have the bottom of such an inclination that water will flow at the same velocity through every part of the

bolted to one side of the beam of the plow.   The arrangement is such, that the plow will cut a ditch six, eight, ten, or twelve inches wide.   Instead of being drawn by a chain or clevis attached to the end of the beam, it is drawn by a tongue, the end of which is fastened to the upper side of the beam, near the middle of it, and plays up and down in a tongue guide, which is bolted to the end of the beam.   The handles are adjustable, to enable the man who holds it to walk nearly erect, even when the plow is in a ditch two feet deep.

The advantages of this plow over others are, it will run more steadily with a tongue than without a tongue.   With two standards and two points, a ditch is easily kept of a uniform width, without any difficulty ; and with two points a vast amount of labor in dressing off the sides of a ditch is saved ; and the corners of the bottom are dug out much better than they can be with an ordinary plow ; and by having the team hitched to a tongue, the plowman can prevent the plow from running too deep in soft places ; and he will be able to lift it from a ditch much easier than he can without a tongue.   Every part is made strong and durable ; and the plow is a valuable improvement.   It will work well where any other ditching plow will work, and will *always* do better work than one having but one standard.

drain. In order to do this correctly, a ditcher must have a *mechanical eye*—an eye that can, at a glance, detect a depression or an elevation at any point in the bottom of a ditch. If a ditch is cut where there is but little descent or fall, and the bottom is not as straight as a mathematical line, but is sunk an inch too deep here, and a little farther on two inches deeper than the line of a true grade, water will not run out freely; but the current will be so slow in these level places that in a few years the calibre of small tile will be completely filled up with sediment. But if there is a little inclination all the way, and the inclination is of a true grade, there will be no chance for sediment to lodge and to collect. Whether a ditch is to be filled with tile, stone, or wood, the bottom should be of a true grade. Some men may dig ditches all their lives, and they cannot grade the bottom of a ditch just as it should be, in a difficult place. It is *more* important to have the bottom of a ditch very true, where very small tile is to be laid, than it is where *large* tile is to be used.

404. The accompanying Fig., 131, will give the young farmer

FIG. 131.

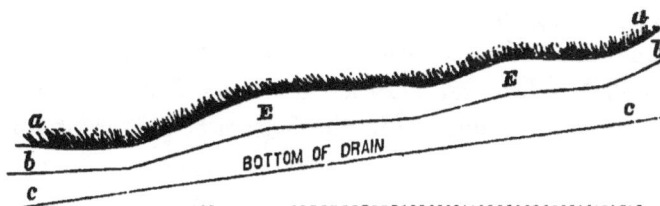

CORRECT MANNER OF GRADING THE BOTTOM OF A DITCH.

a more correct idea of the proper manner of grading the bottom of a ditch. *a a* represents the surface of the ground. The line *b b*, nearly parallel with the surface, shows the common mode of grading the bottom of a ditch, up a slope. The straight line *c c* represents the *most approved* manner of grading the *bottom* of a ditch. A ditcher who possesses little or no mechanical skill, will be puzzled some to grade the bottom just as it should be; but if he cannot make calculations about at what point to commence digging a *little deeper*, and about how deep he must sink the bottom at the highest point on the surface, and about how far he must dig before he runs out, he had better resort to stakes. Stick a stake at the outlet and one at the head of the ditch after it has been dug, like the line *b b*, allowing them to be say four feet high.   Now at the highest places, *E E*, set up stakes four feet high, and then look over the tops of them ; and dig a hole in the bottom of the ditch at *E E*, until the tops of the stakes at *E E* will be in a line with those at the outlet and head of the ditch.   The ditcher should bring his head down in the ditch as near the bottom as is convenient, when he will be able to discover any depression or elevation in the bottom, as far as the eye can distinguish.

405. When a ditch is to be filled with stone, if there is to be a throat made in the bottom, the young farmer should make calculations about how large a throat will be necessary, and about how large will be the *average* size of the *side* stones.   In this case the *corners* of the ditch should be well dressed out, and the middle dug about an inch the lowest, as shown by Fig. 133.   (See Par. 416.)   The object of having the *middle* of the ditch the lowest is, to keep the water from forming a channel between the side-stones and the bank; which would be liable to displace the stone, and thus form an obstruction in the drain.   When the corners are not well dug out in the bottom of a ditch, it is much more difficult to stone it in a complete manner.   There is no necessity for digging out the corners of the *bottom* of a ditch for tile, unless tile of the largest size is to be used, or two rows of tile, as shown by Fig. 132, in which case the bottom should be hollowed out, as shown in the figure.

DEPTH AND SIZE OF DRAINS.

406. It is totally impracticable for any individual to tell *where* a drain should be cut, or *how deep* or *how wide* drains should be made, without going on the ground during a wet, and sometimes a dry part of the season, and examining the sources of the surplus

water and the inclination of the ground where a drain is thought to be needed. The young farmer should never be satisfied with a drain that is not thirty inches deep; and the instances are very rare where it would not be better to cut it thirty inches than *less* than that depth. In some places it *may* be allowable, and drain the soil well, to put *small tile* in a ditch only two feet deep. But for large tile, and particularly for stone, a ditch should never be *less* than thirty inches deep. Drains that are thirty inches deep will be just as effectual in drying some fields as if they were three or four feet deep. On the contrary, drains only thirty inches deep in some fields would not be half as effectual in draining the land as they would if they were forty or fifty inches in depth. In some places it will be necessary to sink the ditches four feet deep in order to "get the water," or to reach the veins. But when the water veins are reached at the depth of thirty inches, it will be incurring a bill of useless expense to sink the ditches deeper than that depth. It is no detriment nor disadvantage to land to have the drains four feet deep; because water will percolate into a deep drain about as soon as it will into a *shallow* drain twenty-five or thirty inches in depth. When land is drained to cut off the water arising from springs, as a general rule the drains need to be deeper than they do where the surplus water does not arise from springs.

407. When a drain is to receive a single row of tile, if the ditch is cut barely wide enough to admit them it will be just as well as if it were a foot wide. When the ditches are to be cut three or four feet deep, they must necessarily be wide enough for a man to work in without being cramped for want of space. The narrower a ditch is, of course the less earth there will be to dig up and shovel out. When a ditch is to receive tile not more than five inches wide, and is to be dug not more than three feet deep, it may be about ten inches wide at the top and five inches wide at the bottom. A man cannot work conveniently in a ditch smaller than this size. When a ditch is to be filled with stone, calculations should first be made how large will be the stream of water, and how much space the stone will occupy. A stoned

13

drain with a large throat should never be *less* than three feet
deep.   The larger the throat is, the deeper a drain ought always
to be made; because the wider the space of the throat the more
liable a drain is to become obstructed by the dirt caving in.
Throats that are much deeper than their width are less liable to
become obstructed than those are which are *wider* than their depth.
Tile, the calibre of which is twice as deep as it is wide, will discharge water with greater rapidity than those will having round,
or half round calibre.   (See MANUFACTURING TILE, 436.)

HOW TO DETERMINE THE PROPER DEPTH FOR DRAINS.

408.   A man who has had a good share of experience in underdraining will be able to *conjecture*, in most instances, about how
deep ditches should be cut in order to operate most effectually.
But the correct and *sure* way is, to "cut and try."   Let the
ditches be cut about thirty or thirty-six inches in depth, not in a
very wet time, nor in a very dry time.   Now, if by digging
thirty inches deep most of the veins of water seem to be cut off,
and but little bubbles up from the bottom of the ditch, it is useless to dig deeper.   When it is very evident that a field needs
draining, and ditches have been cut thirty inches deep, and no
veins of water are reached, it is very conclusive evidence that the
ditches should be sunk deeper.   Again : when ditches have been
cut thirty inches deep, and most of the water issues from the *sides*,
and but little or none bubbles up in the bottom, there will·be no
necessity of sinking them deeper for the sole purpose of cutting
off the veins of water.   It is no uncommon occurrence to see
about all the water that has been the cause of rendering the soil
wet, flow into a ditch at twenty or twenty-five inches from the
surface of the ground, at the sides of the ditch.   When such is
the case, the expense of sinking a ditch more than thirty inches
deep—except for the purpose of securing a bottom with a true
grade, or for large tile (see Fig. 132)—would be entirely useless.
When a ditch has been sunk thirty inches deep, and the subsoil
appears to be full of water, and but little water flows into the

ditch, and most of that bubbles up in the bottom, there is certain evidence that it should be sunk from six to twelve, or perhaps twenty inches deeper. When the soil is *too wet* to plow, a ditch thirty inches deep will often send out a stream of water sufficiently large to fill tile having an inch and a half calibre. But when that soil is dry enough to plow, and such a stream of water can be obtained in a ditch of twenty rods in length, it will drain the ground for a rod or more on each side of it. But when there is an abundance of springs, in some localities there will be four times as much water collected in a given distance as there would be in some others. But it is utterly impossible to give perfect directions for draining every place or field, without having a man of some experience on the ground to examine the ditches, either after they are dug or while the digging is going on. An engineer may give directions for draining a field, with the assurance that if the ditches are sunk three and a half or four feet deep it will be thoroughly drained; when, at the same time, if he were on the ground when the digging of the ditches was in progress, he would decide, without hesitancy, that it would be useless to dig the ditches over thirty or thirty-five inches deep, to collect about all the water that would be collected were they sunk twelve or twenty inches deeper. I would by no means advocate the practice of attempting to drain land with drains *less* than thirty inches deep, even where a drain two feet deep would collect just as much water as a deeper one. But when drains thirty inches deep will subserve as good purpose as *deeper* ones, there can be no plausible reason assigned why they should be sunk deeper. At the depth of thirty inches frost will never affect them, nor the subsoil plow derange any portion of them so as to obstruct the water passages. I refer more particularly to small drains, where there is but little water.

MANNER OF FILLING DRAINS.

409. The sooner drains are filled after they have been finished, the better; and, in some instances, it will be very necessary to make the passage for the water as soon as practicable after the

ditches have been dug, on account of the liability of the sides to cave in. Ditches ought not to be left unfilled during the summer, so that cattle and sheep will be jumping across them, for they will be very liable to fall into them; and if they do not *slip in*, and carry a portion of the bank with them, they will often tread up the bottom so that it will require more labor to prepare it again for the tile than most men are aware of.

410. Before a ditch is filled, if the young farmer does not know positively that water will flow freely from the head to the foot of a ditch, the fact should be ascertained without delay. When there is but little fall, it is the easiest thing in the whole science of underdraining, to be *greatly deceived* with reference to the amount of *fall*. I have seen many instances in which men, who affirmed positively that they had not the shadow of a doubt that water would flow from the head to the outlet of a ditch, were *most wofully disappointed* when they saw water standing a foot deep *above* the outlet. No man can determine, simply by the eye, whether water will run towards the head or the foot of a ditch, when the surface is about level. I have seen men so confident that water would run out, that they have stoned their ditches and filled them with earth, and afterwards had the very unpleasant satisfaction of learning that the outlet of their drain was about a foot *higher* than the middle or the head of it.

411. As levelling instruments are not always at hand on a farm, the most expeditious and most accurate manner for common laborers to ascertain whether or not there is sufficient fall in a ditch is, to pour a barrel or two of water into it at the head. If it will flow onward until it reaches the outlet, we may rest assured that water will not stand in it after it has been filled. When a ditch is thirty or forty rods in length, it may be necessary to pour in three or four barrels of water, as the earth will often absorb one or two in a short distance. It is a good practice to grade the bottom of a ditch while there is a small stream of water in it, as it can be done much more accurately than it usually is performed when there is no water in it.

412. This is a part of draining which requires the exercise of more good judgment than anything else in making a drain. When tile are all very straight and true, and the ends square, if the bottom of the ditch is as true as it should be there will be little difficulty in laying them in the best manner ; but when some of them are crooked, and the ends of many by no means as square as they should be, it is often difficult to lay them as well as they should be laid. I must condemn the practice, which is too frequently recommended, of placing the tile in the ditch with a *tile-hook* and *staff,* while the workman is standing on the surface of the ground. In order to lay tile as they *should be laid, the workman must stand in the ditch.* Of course, he will understand that, in tiling or stoning a ditch, he should always commence at the *head* of it, so that nothing can flow down and enter the water passage. Now, the idea is, to have the calibre of each tile placed so that a smooth passage will be formed throughout the entire length of the drain. Place the first tile at the upper end of the ditch, and stop the upper end with a stone, and stamp the tile down firmly with one foot. Now place another to the end of it, and stamp it down, so that the ends will exactly correspond. If a tile is crooked, and is of such a form that it will not answer to turn it over in order to make it fit better on the ground, or if the middle or one end of it is kept too high by a small stone in the bottom of the ditch, I always use a rammer of some description, and sink the earth until the tile will lie in the most desirable position. Sometimes the ends of one tile will *pitch down* more than the tiles at each end of it. In such a case, I use *hard dirt,* well rammed down, and lay the tile on it and stamp it down, or place a thin piece of flat stone under one or both ends, to raise it to the desired position. The ends of tile are very seldom so square that a *dime* could not be dropped into the calibre after they have been placed in the ditch, and frequently the ends are so untrue, that the upper side of the joints will be open from half to three-fourths of an inch. In such a case I usually try another tile, or change ends with it, or turn it on the side, or upside down. If then I fail to make the ends fit as closely as they should, I place a lot of small flat stones over and on the sides of the open joint, and then cover the stones with hard dirt *with my hands*, so that nothing will be displaced when the dirt is plowed or shovelled in. A tile that will not endure hard stamping, for the purpose of sinking it into the dirt, is not fit to be laid in a ditch. The aim of the workman should always be, in laying tile, to place them in such a manner that they will never sink, so that the ends of them will not be uneven with each other. If the bottom of a ditch is neatly graded, and the tile are very true, an experienced workman will be able to lay three thousand, or even more than that number in a day. But if tile are crooked, and the ends not true, and the bottom of the ditch is full of little stones which must be rammed down to a level, a laborer may sometimes labor most faithfully and not lay more than one thousand in a day. It is always desirable to have the joints between tile so close that there will be barely room to receive a knife-blade of ordinary thickness; but if there is, in some places, a space of three-eighths of an inch at the joints of tile which have a calibre of over three inches, any substance that would find its way into a joint or space of that size would be swept out by the force of the stream of water. When the calibre of tile is *less* than three inches, and there is but little fall in the ditch, the workman should be unusually particular in securing "*a good fit*" at each joint, as the current of water in small tile would be so slow, where there is not more than six or eight inches fall in one hundred feet, that it would not be very apt to carry dirt or very small gravel out of the tile. Some men seem to prefer a little channel in the bottom of a ditch, to lay small tile in; but I have always found that with such crooked, untrue tile as we are obliged to use, I could secure a better fit at the joints, when the bottom of a ditch was about five or six inches wide, with *no* channel in the middle. When very large tile are used, or when two rows of tile are laid in one ditch, with a water-passage between them, as shown by Fig. 132, it is best to sink a channel, not more than an inch deep, between the tile, for the purpose of preventing the water from *undermining* any of the tile. The preceding remarks refer solely to *pipe tile.* But, as many knowing ones will persist in having half-round or horse-shoe tile—although I do not approve of that form of tile (see paragraph 438)—I will give directions for

Fig. 132.

LAYING HALF-ROUND OR HORSESHOE TILE.

413. If the young farmer *will have* horseshoe tile, they should always be placed on *soles*, which are flat pieces of burnt clay, of the same length and width as the tile, and not less than half an inch thick. These soles are placed firmly in the bottom of a ditch, and the tile placed on them so as to break joint near the middle of the soles. But both soles and tile are so frequently warped and twisted, that there is sufficient room, in some places, between the soles and the tile, for meadow mice or moles to enter the water-passage and haul in dirt, and thus obstruct the flow of the water. Some farmers lay a narrow board or plank in the bottom of a ditch, and place a row of horseshoe tile on the boards; but such a practice cannot be denounced too strongly. Boards are so liable to decay in places, and thus allow some of the tiles to sink below others, that we cannot calculate with certainty that a drain will not be obstructed within a few years, when the tile are laid on boards. Perhaps most of the boards might last, in the bottom of the drain, thirty or forty years; but if there should be only *one* or *two poor places* in the boards, an obstruction would be formed in a few years. When the bottom of a ditch is very hard, large half-round tile may be laid in the bottom, and subserve a good purpose; but they should never be placed on boards. When the ground is hard they will never sink one-eighth of an inch; but, where they would be liable to sink without a board under them, soles or sole-tile should be used, but boards never. When small horseshoe tiles are laid in a ditch with boards, it would be far better to sink a narrow channel in

the bottom of the ditch, and place the tile in it, *upside down,* and cut up the boards into short pieces, and lay them *crosswise* on the row of tile. I should have far more confidence in the durability of a drain made in this manner, than if the boards were beneath the tile.

MANNER OF LAYING STONE IN A DITCH.

414. Any one can *pitch* stones into a ditch, and cover them with dirt; but, in order to have a stoned drain carry off the water as well as it should, and not become obstructed in the water-passage, it is very important to have every stone placed *just right.* The most common cause of obstructions in a stoned drain is, the side stones, which, in consequence of not being placed most correctly, *fall over* into the middle of the water-passage, or the stream forms a channel *between* the side stones and the sides of the drain, and thus displaces the stones. As stones of almost every form and size must be worked in when the throat is laid, a laborer needs much judgment and skill to place every one in such a manner that it will not be displaced.

415. Writers on draining with stone, in years past, recommended *breaking the stone* as small as the size of a hen's egg for filling ditches, and, also, to have ditches filled with stone to a point within about one foot of the surface of the ground. But the observation and experience of our most successful farmers, who have used stone for filling their ditches, have induced them to come to the deliberate conclusion that drains are but little, if any, more effectual in draining the land, when they are filled with small stone one foot above the throat, than they are when nothing but a *throat* is made of stone, well chinked with small stone. The expense of digging ditches three feet deep, and of laying a good throat in them for the water, is quite as large as most farmers are willing to incur, without incurring the additional and useless expense of breaking a large lot of stone into small pieces. Any one who knows anything about breaking stone in very small pieces, knows, that it is a very laborious and expensive job. As a good throat is all that is necessary in a ditch,

and as drains are less liable to become obstructed in the water passage when there is only a throat than they are when small stones a foot or more deep are placed above it, let us attend par-ticularly to the manner of placing the stones in the bottom of a ditch, so that they will not be displaced by the water.

416. If most of the stones are cobble or bowlders, both the side stones and covering stones, place them as shown in Fig. 133

MANNER OF STONING WITH COBBLE STONES.   IMPROPERLY STONED.

It will be discovered by the figure, that if the covering stone is removed, the side stones will fall into the water channel. But the covering stone being convex or circular on the under side, it keeps them from falling inwards. When side stones will not stand alone until the covering stone is placed on them, I hold them up with one foot. This is the most approved manner of stoning a ditch with small bowlders.

417. When the side stones are flat on one side and convex on the opposite side, as shown at Fig. 134, which represents a stone drain improperly stoned, they should be placed, not as shown in the figure, but with the *flat side* against the *side* of the ditch, and the convex side *inwards*. It will be seen by the figure, that there is a passage for water *between* the side stones and the sides of the ditch,—which is very objectionable. And, besides, when the flat sides of the side stones are placed against the side of a ditch, and not as shown in the figure, the superincumbent pres-sure will all be near the *corners* of the bottom of a ditch; and not near the *middle* of it, as here represented. When stone are placed as represented by this figure, they are very liable to *slide*

13*

inwards, as they appear to be sliding in the figure, and obstruct the free passage of the water. If two such stones were turned *around,* with the covering stone remaining as it is represented in the figure, the throat would carry a larger stream of water, and little or no water would run *between* the side stones and the sides of the ditch ; and the superincumbent pressure would tend to keep the side stones in their proper places.

418. Fig. 135 represents the *side* stones placed very improperly. Great care should be exercised in placing the *side* stones,

FIG. 135.   FIG. 136.

VIEW OF SIDE STONES
IMPROPERLY PLACED.

MANNER OF STONING
WITH THIN SIDE STONES.

so as to have them of a *uniform height,* or of such a height that *the covering stones will rest on every side stone.* If large and small side stones are placed together, as shown in the figure, those that the covering stones do not *rest* on, will be very liable to fall or roll over into the water passage. When covering stones are broad, the beginner should see that every side stone sustains some superincumbent pressure. It is necessary, sometimes, to make a little depression with a pick, for a side stone of peculiar form, in order to have it lie well.

419. Fig. 136 represents the most approved manner of stoning a ditch, where most of the side stones are nearly or quite flat. The sharpest edge of the side stones should be placed in the *corner* of the ditch, in order to make the throat as spacious as possible, and to prevent the water from forming a channel *outside* of them.

420. Fig. 137 represents a very good mode of laying the

throat of a drain, when the covering stones are flat, and a little wider than the bottom of the ditch. This man-

FIG. 137.

ner of forming a throat with flat stones is far preferable to the one in which the stones are placed like the rafters of a building.

421. *Chinking with small stones* is a very important part of laying the stones in a ditch. Great pains should be taken to chink the entire surface so thoroughly, that there will not be an open space as large as a mouse-hole. When

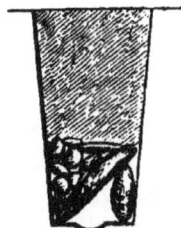

STONING WITH ONE ROW OF SIDE STONES.

flat stones are used for covering stones, small flat stones should be used to cover the cracks and for chinking; and, when bowlders are used for covering the side stones, small round stones will be the best for chinking. After the chinking has been thoroughly performed, it would be a good practice to spread coarse gravel on the stones, for the purpose of keeping out the moles and meadow mice. It would hardly pay, however, to haul gravel for such a purpose any considerable distance, as the surplus water would find its way into the throat of the drain quite as well *without* the gravel. Let those who doubt this, try the experiment for a few years; and I am confident they will coincide with me in every respect.

SIDE-HILL DRAINS.

422. When drains that are filled with stone, have a fall or inclination of more than one foot per lineal rod, if the bottom of the ditch is not very hard, should there be a stream of water sufficiently large to fill a four-inch tile, the water would be very liable to form gullies, where it runs swiftly, and to undermine the side stones, thus causing derangement and obstructing the free passage of the water. When a stream of water as large as a man's arm is confined and pressed a very little, and its passage is down a slope, which may not be very steep, it will carry in it large gravel and stones, as large as hens' eggs; which, rolling and rumbling and tumbling along, will cut a gully in a few weeks even in very compact earth. It is often very desirable to make

a stone drain beneath a stone wall, which runs up and down a steep slope, or beneath a hedge row. (See Par. 195 and 261.) In such localities, a farmer does not feel willing to purchase tile for that purpose when suitable stones are very abundant. Now, in order to form a throat with stone in such a drain, which will be as permanent as the hills, let the bottom of the ditch be finished in a *triangular form*, as represented by Fig. 138, which represents the manner of forming a throat with thin flat stones. In order to perform the job in a workmanlike manner, the workman should have a light stone-hammer for dressing off the edges,

FIG. 138.

in order to make them fit well. Should the stream be a small one, and the stones small, the *throat* may be made small. But should the stone average in size about one foot wide, the channel should be dug about one foot deep, and two inches wide in the bottom, and eight or nine inches at the top. When flat stones are scarce and rather small, it would be best to place a row of them lying flat in the bottom of the ditch; and then form a throat with bowlders for the side stones, and for covering stones. This manner of forming a throat with the bottom *flagged* with flat stones, would be worthy of adoption where the subsoil is so soft that a drain is liable to sink in it.

MANNER OF STONING A DITCH WITH THIN FLAT STONES ON A SIDE HILL OR THROUGH QUICK-SAND.

FILLING IN THE EARTH.

423. Every writer on underdraining, whose writings have come under my observation, has recommended placing *sods directly on tile* or *stone* when filling in the dirt. My experience in underdraining teaches me that this practice is by no means a good one; and I am confident that every intelligent farmer, who will or who has given the subject a proper investigation, will coincide with me. When sods are placed over stone or over the joints of tile in an inverted position, they will exclude most effectually the loose dirt from the joints of the tile and from the interstices between the stones. But it must be remembered, that sods in such

places will very soon decay, forming a complete bed of *mellow, fine earth,* which will be very easily washed into the calibre, or worked in by moles or mice. When straw or shavings are used, they soon decay, and furnish an abundance of the right kind of substance to obstruct the water passage. When mellow earth is placed on the stone, moles and mice will haul it down and fill the throat full in one season. But if *hard earth* is placed directly on the stones, they find it impossible to work holes through it; and, therefore, they will not be able to obstruct the water passage with earth. I was once accustomed to put straw on the stones in my drains, and to place sods, inverted, next to the stones; but I found that the moles and meadow mice made holes so readily from the throat to the surface of the ground, and hauled in so much dirt, that I abandoned the use of straw entirely; and instead of putting the sods on the stones, the hard subsoil is *always* placed directly on them.

424. My practice now is—and I find that all our best farmers are adopting it—to return not less than six inches in depth of the hardest sub-soil directly on the tile or stone. I always prefer to *shovel* it in when it is *wet,* as it will *set,* and form a more compact covering when it is *wet* than it will when the dirt will crumble. In covering tile, I always fill with a shovel about six inches above the tile, and exercise great care that small stones do not fall on the tile, and crush them. In covering stone, I shovel in about six inches of hard dirt, and then tread it down firmly—not with a horse, as I have read of in some agricultural journals, but with my own feet. After this, plow in the dirt with one horse. One horse is better than two horses, even when they draw by a long whippletree, because they are usually afraid of getting into the ditch. After the ditch has been filled so that one horse can travel on the dirt in it without danger of displacing the stone or tile, it is best to plow with two horses. Great care should be exercised by the workmen not to allow a horse to step in a ditch when there is but little earth over the stone or tile, as he will surely displace some of them.

425. Of the many hundreds of rods of underdrains which are

on my farm, of tile and stone, my own hands have laid every foot; and there is not a rod of it that does not work very effect-ually. I have never dared to trust those men to fill my ditches who were employed by my neighbors; because they do not, in some instances, know how to perform such a job in the most approved manner; and, when they *do* know, they are too apt to slight it. Being unable, once, to use a shovel myself, I em-ployed a man to fill a short ditch after the tile had been laid, and, although he had put straw over the tile, he had allowed small stones to drop on them, which had *broken* them in three different places, and obstructed the water passage. A stone as large as a hen's egg, when allowed to fall on tile in a deep ditch, if it should strike just right, would break it. I pen these observations that the young farmer may see the importance of being very careful in placing the first earth on the tile.

HOW TO FIND WHERE A DRAIN IS OBSTRUCTED.

426. If the locality of a drain is known exactly, when the water passage is obstructed dig down to the tile or stone; and if water does not rise in the hole where you dug, the obstruction is *above* that place. (See Par. 6 and 7.) Now pass on up stream, until it is thought best to dig again, or until the soil appears to be full of water, and dig another hole. Now, if water rises in the hole from the calibre and stands in the hole, the obstruction is *below* that point. If there is not more water than the drain can carry, the soil will be dry a short distance *down stream* from the obstruction. If the exact locality of a drain is not known, it may be found sometimes by running a crowbar down for every six inches; and when it is thrust in over the drain, it will go down much faster and more easily than it will when the subsoil has not been disturbed.

HOW TO FORM THE OUTLET OF DRAINS.

427. Both stone drains and tile drains are very apt to be dis-turbed and displaced by the frost at the *outlets*. In order to pre-

vent the frost from injuring them, lay a few feet of the outlet with scantling and plank; or, with scantling for the sides and flat stones for covering. Timber for such places should be of the most durable kind. The earth should be shovelled away at the outlet as often as it works inward so as to obstruct the water from flowing freely. The practice is too prevalent, even among some good farmers, of leaving the earth some three or four inches *higher*, a few feet below the outlet, than it is at the end of the calibre. When left in such a condition, drains are very liable to fill up in the calibre near the end of the outlet. The young farmer should not neglect to have the earth cleared away in the spring and in autumn, so that the stream of water may wash out all gravel and fine earth which has found its way into the calibre. But if water is forced to "back up" at the outlet, gravel and earth will be carried down almost to the outlet, where it will lodge and soon close the water passage.

HOW TO FORM SMALL POOLS IN A DRAIN FOR WATERING STOCK.

428. On farms where all the water is collected in underdrains, it is often very convenient to have some arrangement so that animals may obtain water. Water is collected in underdrains, on my own farm, which run the whole length of it. At the lower side of each field I cut a gully with plow and scraper, directly across the drain, wide enough for a span of horses and plow to pass back and forth, and not less than six inches *deeper* than the bottom of the drain, after the tile or stone have been removed. Now, place a box *without* a bottom in it, made of good plank, three or four feet long and about two feet wide, and one foot or more high, with the corners *halved* or *rabbeted* together in the channel of the drain. In the upper end of the box cut a hole a little larger than the calibre of the tile or stone; and in the lower end of the box, bore a dozen or more—according to the size of the calibre—inch holes, close together. At the lower end of the box, *on the outside*, make a large calibre with flat stones, for a foot or two from the box, so as to direct the water, as it flows

through the holes in the box, into the calibre of the drain. Chink it well with small stones, so that mice cannot haul in dirt and stop the passage. Now, let the box be well staked to keep it in its place. The box should be the widest at the *bottom* so that the frost will not lift it. In lieu of stakes, if a man has an abundance of plank, it would be better to allow the ends of the *side* plank to extend into each bank, above and below the main box. On each side of the box the earth should be kept shovelled away, so that cattle when drinking may stand as low as the surface of the water is in the box. In times of high water, such watering places will be overflowed; but if there are enough holes in the lower end of the box, the drain will never be injured by the water.

429. The object of having the box sunk *deeper* than the calibre of the drain is, to allow all gravel and dirt that may be washed out to lodge in the sink, so that it can be shovelled out when the water is low. The gully should be so wide across the ditch that cattle can go down and drink, and turn around and come up again, without difficulty. By having the earth excavated on each side of the box so that they can go down and drink, if a small animal should get cornered by a large one, it may jump over the box and escape on the other side. Such watering-places should be examined very often, and cleaned out, if necessary, as cattle are very liable to drop their excrement in and about the pools where they are accustomed to drink.

DITCHES OR OPEN DRAINS.

430. When there is a stream of water so large that it would be too expensive to have it run in an underdrain, it is necessary to have open drains. These can be made with a plow and scraper very much cheaper than they can be excavated with spades and shovels. Open drains should be made so wide that the banks will not be continually caving in; and so deep that where the water from underdrains flows into them it may flow freely. The banks of an open drain should slope not less than at

an angle of forty-five degrees. Accordingly, when a ditch is cut thirty inches deep, and is ten inches wide on the bottom, it should be forty inches wide at the top.

431. In localities where the water flows with such a rapid current as to wash out deep gullies in a short period of time, the bottom and sides of open drains should be paved or flagged with small stones. The sides need not be paved more than one-third or half way to the top of the banks—according to the amount of water that usually flows in it. In places where water flows only a part of the season, in order to prevent it from forming gullies, the bottom and sides of open drains should be scratched over with an iron-toothed rake, and grass seed—red-top seed is best—sown on them in the fore part of summer, in order to form a sod. But where the water seldom or never dries up, the bottom and sides must be paved, or simply covered with flat stones. The gutters along some highways, where flood-water is apt to form gullies, should be smoothed off, and grass seed sown to form a sod; or, they should be paved or flagged with small flat stones.

FILLING DITCHES WITH WOOD.

432. I would never advocate the practice of filling ditches with wood, in any form, where stone of suitable sizes or tile can be readily obtained. But where timber is cheap, and stone and tile scarce, it is infinitely better to fill them with plank than to attempt to drain land with open ditches. I have known many farmers to use split timber about the size of rails for the side pieces, and split slabs for covering them. But with materials in such a form it is always very difficult to perform a job in a proper manner. There will be so many large cracks between the side pieces and the cover, that such drains always become obstructed in a very few years. I have filled several ditches on my farm with plank, because tile and stone were scarce; and I see no good reason why such drains will not work well for thirty or forty years, providing the outlets are kept clear, and the earth is not allowed to enter at the head.

433. Fig. 139 represents the best manner of filling with wood.

FIG. 139.

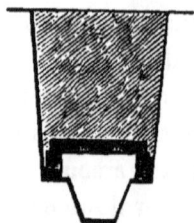

MANNER OF FILLING
DRAINS WITH PLANK.

Where there would be a stream of water as large as a man's leg, the bottom of the ditch is dug about ten inches wide, with the corners dressed out very true, and a channel sunk in the bottom, as shown in the figure, from four to six inches deep. Great care should be exercised in cutting the channel, so that each bank be not broken up. Now, have a log sawed into strips an inch and a half by two inches square, for the side-pieces. I have always had my logs sawed into plank, and then the plank were slit with a circular horse-saw into two-inch strips. (See SLITTING TABLE, Par. 689.) I have sometimes slit up inch boards into strips two inches wide; and I think they are quite as good as if they were an inch and a half thick. The covering should never be *less* than two inches thick; and plank should never be placed *lengthways* of a ditch, but always *crossways*. Because, when a plank is placed lengthways it is very liable to split, in consequence of a heavy superincumbent pressure, and thus obstruct the water course. But when placed *crossways* there is no danger of their splitting. And, more than this, when plank are placed crossways there is no *waste*, as plank of any width can be used; whereas, if laid *lengthways* they must be all of a uniform width. I saw up the covering plank, with a horse saw, as long as the width of the ditch. Now place two side-pieces in the ditch, and lay a plank on them, and nail it. Nail a plank at the end of every side-piece. The plank should be placed about half an inch apart, if they are a foot wide, and *seasoned*, so that when the water expands or swells them, the joints will not be so tight that there will be no space for the water to enter. If there is but little water to flow in a drain, and the subsoil is very hard, I dispense with the side-pieces, and lay the plank over the channel, *on the earth*. *Seasoned* plank in a drain will last twice as long as *green* ones; and they will be much more durable in a *deep* ditch than they will in a *shallow* one; and in a ditch where there is water nearly all the year, they will outlast those that are laid where there is no water during the summer. Necessity compelled me to use hemlock or elm plank. But the better the timber is, the more durable a drain will be. As plank is costly, I have in some instances sawed up *slabs* for covering.

434. The young farmer should be very careful not to lay any *poor pieces* of plank in a drain. Plank sawed out of logs near the tops of trees, in most kinds of timber, will not be as durable as plank cut from the *butt* logs. Let the best plank be laid at the *lower end* of a drain; and if poor pieces *must be* used,—although they had better be thrown among the firewood,—let them all be placed together at the *upper end* of the drain. Now return about a foot in depth of the *hardest* dirt, and tread it down well; and should the plank decay in less than twenty years, in which time they probably will not, the earth will be so compact that a water-passage would remain in the earth for ages to come. In filling in the earth on plank, I am always careful to see that no stones lie *directly on the plank.* My plank drains seem to drain the land as soon and as effectually as tile or stone.

ON THE COMPARATIVE VALUE OF STONE, TILE AND PLANK
FOR FILLING DITCHES.

435. In making small drains, where two-inch tile will carry the water, providing tile do not have to be hauled more than four or five miles, the expense in dollars and cents of purchasing two-inch tile and laying them, would be *less* than the expense of picking up and laying the stone for a given number of rods. But a tile drain is always *better* than stone or wood drains. The expense of purchasing, hauling, and laying four-inch tile will *greatly exceed* the expense of a stone or plank drain, which will carry a stream of equal size. I always consider it the best policy to use up my stone in making drains, as far as they will go, and then, if there is but little water, use tile; and if there is a stream large enough to fill a four-inch tile, use plank. Four-inch tile cost at our works, eighteen miles from me, forty dollars per thousand; and a thousand tile fourteen inches long will lay about seventy rods. Now if stone are not too scarce and scattering,

a man can pick up and haul stone sufficient for ten rods of drain, and lay them, in a day.   Where there is an abundance of good stone, he will accomplish *more* than that.   Almost any intelligent school-boy will be able to determine how many feet of plank it will require to fill a rod in length of a drain having a water-passage of a given size.   When there is a large stream of water, the side-pieces might be *three or four* inches wide, and the covering plank *twelve* or *fourteen* inches long. (See Fig. 139.) Suppose, for example, that it costs fifty dollars to fill seventy rods of drain with tile having five-inch calibre, making no account of the expense of hauling them.   If they are thoroughly burnt, a drain made with them would remain good during all time.   Now, then, if a channel is cut in the bottom of the ditch three inches deep, two inches wide on the bottom and four inches wide at the top, with side-pieces two inches high and an inch and a half thick, covered with plank eight inches long, a calibre or throat would be formed which would be equal in size to the calibre of a tile, the superficial measure of which is equal to twenty-two square inches.   A throat of the size just mentioned would carry a larger stream of water than tile having five-inch calibre; and it would require for seventy rods about two thousand one hundred feet of lumber, which would cost in many localities fifteen dollars per one thousand feet; but in many other places, lumber of equal value would not cost over five dollars per one thousand feet.   Now, allowing that a plank drain would last only fifteen years before it would need to be newly planked; and allowing that it would cost twenty cents per rod to *re-dig* the ditch every fifteen years, which would use up $14.00; and reckoning the interest on the money, being the difference between the first cost of tile and the first cost of plank, we find that it will not cost half as much, in dollars and cents, where large tile is used, to keep drains in order one hundred years, *filling with plank* every fifteen years, as it will to use large tile.   But who would like an arrangement in which all the leading drains of a farm must be *re-dug* and *re-planked* every twelve, or fifteen, or even *twenty* years?   It is better to use plank than not to have drains, where tile nor stone are not at hand.

ON THE MANUFACTURE OF DRAIN TILE.

436. After the clay has been worked by machinery so that it is of the right consistence, it is forced through *dies* in the side of a strong box, which is usually made of iron, with the inside planed smooth and true; and as several of them are forced out side by side, they are received on a table of small rollers, until they are several feet in length, in one piece. A small frame is then lifted, by which small wires cut the tile of the desired length. An instrument like a wooden fork, with round tines or fingers, is run in the calibres of the tile, and by this they are lifted from the table and placed carefully on shelves to dry, in a building which is open on the sides. After they have become so dry that they will sustain the superincumbent pressure of each other, they are placed in a kiln and burned for several successive days and nights, until they are so hard that they will not disintegrate or fall to pieces when they are placed in a ditch. In handling tile when they are in a plastic state, careless workmen often handle them roughly, and thus deprive them of their true form, by bunting the ends against the shelves, or by allowing them to be bent with the fingers of the fork. If farmers would insist on *rejecting* every ill-shaped tile, manufacturers would soon learn to handle them *with care*. Some of them will *spring* a little when they are being burned, but that will not injure them if the calibre and ends are true. Sometimes a kilnful of tile is about *half burned*. But honest tile-makers will not allow those that are *not thoroughly burned* to be sold until they have been *re-burned*.

437. Good tile, when they are handled, will *ring* like stoneware, if they are not saturated with water. But those that are not thoroughly burned will emit a *dull sound*, and should be rejected. When good tile are saturated with water they are nearly one-third heavier to haul, and will not emit a clear sound when struck.

THE BEST FORM OF CALIBRE FOR TILE.

438. Tile having the calibre of the shape of a turkey's egg, placed with the small end down, are preferable to those of any other form, because the *narrower* the channel is on the bottom, the more rapidly the stream will flow; and the swifter the stream flows, the more gravel and dirt which may find way into the calibre will be carried out with the stream. Therefore sole tile, with egg-shaped calibre, when they are made true, are preferable to tile of any other form. But when we must take up with those that have been *jammed* and *pinched* and *heedlessly knocked* into the shape of a cocked-hat, when in a plastic state, *round* tile are preferable to those of any other form, because one can make *better joints* in laying them. Half-round or horseshoe tile will become obstructed with sedimentary matter *much sooner* than sole tile with egg-shaped calibre. Pieces of tile, for the *junction* of drains, are manufactured with one or two *branches* on the sides, or with *two* calibres at one end like a fork, and one at the other end.

COST OF DIGGING DITCHES.

439. It will cost twice as much to dig a ditch of a given depth and breadth in some localities as it will in others; and even on the same farm, and sometimes in the same field, a man will be able to dig twice as much as in others. If the subsoil is so hard and stony that it must be all picked up with a sharp pick, if a laborer cuts six or eight rods in length, of thirty inches deep, in a day, he performs a faithful day's work. It is acknowledged by every experienced ditcher that it is *proportionally* more expensive cutting *deep* ditches than *shallow* ones. After a ditch is dug thirty inches deep, it is worth, in some ground, from eight to ten cents more per rod for the next foot in depth. In ordinary digging, all good ditchers will be able to dig a rod in length of tile ditch, thirty inches deep, in an hour. Very many ditchers will perform more than this, while many who have had but little experience, and handle their tools awkwardly, will not be able to do more than one rod in length in *two* hours. Where ditching is performed as recommended in paragraph 402, ditches for a single row of tile, three feet deep, ought not to cost over ten or fifteen cents per rod, according to the compactness of the subsoil; and the cost *will not exceed* that sum, if laborers are willing to do a faithful day's

work. Where the subsoil is so free from stone that a ditching machine can be used advantageously, the cost, per rod, is still less. When a man can spade most of the earth, if he is a good ditcher, and willing to do a faithful day's work, he can make good wages by digging ditches thirty inches deep, and eight or ten inches wide on the bottom, for fifteen cents per rod. If a laborer is not able to do this, he may safely conclude that he is an inferior laborer, and should be willing to work for wages in proportion to the amount of work performed. I have had several hundred rods of ditch dug, not less than thirty inches deep in the lowest place, and eight inches wide on the bottom, for fifteen cents per rod, the ditchers boarding themselves. And they earned, in some instances, at that price, from $1 to $1 75 per day. A faithful laborer will shovel out a long piece in a day; and when a man can procure laborers who are willing to do an ordinary day's work for one dollar, or one dollar twenty-five cents, it is the most economical way to use the plow, as recommended in paragraph 402. The habits of most ditchers are so detrimental to their health and strength, that their powers of endurance fail when they attempt to perform a day's work; and therefore they increase the price per rod in order to make fair wages by performing less labor. For this reason ditches of a given depth, which a few years ago cost fifteen cents per rod, will now cost twenty and twenty-five cents per rod. But even at those prices, drains will often pay for themselves in the first crop.

RECAPITULATION.—CONCLUDING REMARKS.

440. Underdraining will pay, and pay well, too, and no intelligent farmer will attempt to deny it. If the young farmer feels incompetent to lay out his drains most economically, it may save him hundreds of dollars eventually to confer with some experienced, successful farmer, who has had much experience in draining. This confiding in the directions of some *would-be* engineer, who knows so much that his wisdom is a decided disadvantage to him; or laying out ditches, according to the notions of some ditchers, who know more than experience ever taught

about ditching, will sometimes drain land and sometimes not. Don't be a *three-cent* farmer, especially in underdraining. If drains thirty inches deep will drain the land effectually, it is unnecessary to sink them deeper. If a three, or four, or five, or even six feet drain is needed, never stop to compute the cost. Insist on having everything performed *just right*. Never yield to the suggestions of any one to make a drain according to the *good-enough-for-the-present* system. If one or two day's work in a drain seems to be necessary, drop every other job and have it done in time. When a laborer has completed a job of ditching *by the job*, and a ditch is not as deep as it should be in some places, if he has dug as deep as he agreed to dig, employ him a day or so to complete it. Never commence filling a ditch until you have seen water flow from the upper end to the lower end, except one knows positively that it will flow as directed. Water, in such places, never deceives us. Levelling instruments may be incorrect, or may vary, or an inexperienced hand may not adjust them correctly. Water is the cheapest and the best, and always at hand, even if it is not found in a ditch. Never spoil a drain for the sake of using up every tile, both good and poor. If you are a little suspicious that a tile is not hard enough, if it must be used, lay all of that kind *at the upper end* of the ditch, and lay them all together. Thousands of rods of drain have been stopped, simply from this cause,—laying, occasionally, a tile among good ones, which was *so soft* that it disintegrated in one season. Never make a drain with two-inch tile to carry a stream of water which will be large enough to fill a *four*-inch tile. Let every tile and stone and plank be laid by some one who is a little interested in having it done well. Do not trust a man to work at filling a ditch who insists that he can stand on the surface of the ground and do it just as well as to get into the ditch. If it is likely to ruin a man's reputation should he be found with India-rubber boots on, and other ditching duds, filling a ditch, then let it go. In filling a ditch with stone, endeavor to make the throat or calibre of a uniform size. If the side stones are so large that they will extend nearly across the bottom of a ditch, place a bowlder on one side, and a flat one on the other side. Allow nothing to be done in a *superficial, perfunctory* manner. Keep sods, and mellow earth, and straw, and all such substances out of a drain until *after* several inches in depth of *hard earth* have been placed on the stone or tile. Never allow a stream of water to flow on the surface of the ground directly *over* a drain, because if it is a stone drain, the water will most certainly find a hole downwards into the calibre, and wash in dirt, and thus obstruct the water passage. In places where water is apt to flow on the surface in times of high water, have a furrow on one side of the drain for the flood water to flow in, and have the earth *raised over* the drain a few inches *above* the common level. If a drain is filled with tile that are not open on the bottom, if a stream flows along the surface directly over the drain, there is' no danger that it will injure a drain. Always keep a vigilant eye on drains; and, above all, keep the outlets clear. If a main drain prove to be too small to carry all the water, let another one be made a short distance from it. Never allow the water flowing from a *stoned* drain to flow into small tile, lest some obstruction lodge in the tile. Where a part of a drain is filled with tile, and a part with stone, if the calibre of the tile is *less* than four inches in diameter, always put the *tile* at the *upper* end of the drain. I have seen drains filled with tile, and then a row of flat stones laid on each side of the tile, from the top of the tile to the bottom of the drain, form-ing a water passage on both sides of the tile. This practice is very objectionable, because the water is very liable to undermine and displace the tile. We usually reap our best and most abun-dant crops directly over good drains. In wet seasons, vegetation suffers far less from too much moisture directly over good drains; and in dry seasons, when crops are suffering extremely for want of moisture, vegetation will suffer much less directly over a good drain, than it will for a rod on either side of it. Let very dry knolls be well drained with drains five or six feet apart, and they will retain more moisture than they did before they were drained. Truly, the entire surface of the earth which is devoted to agricul-tural purposes, needs to be underdrained.

14

441. Drains should never intersect at right angles. If they are made at right angles to each other, the one that intersects with a larger one should be dug in a circle for a few feet from the main drain.   Tile should be manufactured expressly for receiving side drains.   They are commonly made with a hole in one side of a tile.   But the correct way is, to have a large tile made like a *tree*, with a large limb on one side of it, which should stand at about an angle of forty-five degrees with the main tile; or a *crotched* tile placed at the junction would subserve a good purpose.   (See Par. 438.)

DITCHING WITH MACHINES.

442.. There have been several kinds of ditching machines invented and put into successful operation in some localities.   But where there is much *hard-pan*, or many stones or bowlders, large and small, firmly imbedded in the subsoil, it is almost impossible to accomplish much with any that have as yet been invented. When the subsoil can be nearly all spaded, some ditching machines operate very satisfactorily.   The best ditching machine with which I am acquainted is drawn by two horses, one walking on each side of the ditch, having a small plow to loosen the earth, with a system of revolving spades to bring up the earth; and when each spade stands in a perpendicular position, the earth drops down, and slides or rolls off on each side of the ditch.   After such a machine has accomplished all it can perform, in most places it is necessary to have a good practical ditcher to grade the bottom of a true inclination.   For such a machine the ground must be free from stone.

443. In J. J. Thomas' Farm Implements, page 139, is a cut of a draining plow which is said to operate very successfully, cutting the ditch and laying the tile at one operation.   But the cost for ordinary farmers is too great; and besides, it would not operate where there are many stone in the subsoil.   And, more than all else, the tile when strung on a rope would be liable to be left many times in such a position that when the ground came to settle down some of the ends would settle *by* each other.

CHAPTER VI.

PLOWS AND PLOWING.

"Speed the plow ! Speed the plow !
O'er the fields away ;
And turn the furrows up and down
All the summer's day."—N. Stone.

444. Our country is full of ill-shapen, clumsy, awkward, and almost worthless implements, which pass for plows, in the manufacture of which nearly every correct principle in mechanics has been set at naught. But while there are so many plows of an exceptionable form and character, it is very gratifying to know that there are scores of them which have been manufactured according to the most philosophical and correct mechanical principles; and many of them have been brought to so good a degree of perfection that it is impossible to point out a single imperfection in any part of them. The common plow, because of its great efficiency, and almost universal application in the thorough pulverization of the soil, is *the* implement on which common farmers must almost entirely rely; therefore, to aid the young farmer in the proper selection of plows, I will endeavor to point out some of the defects and imperfections which are too commonly met with in the manufacture of plows.

DEFECTIVE PLOWS.

445. A very heavy plow is objectionable for a single team, because it increases the draught of the team ; and a light or indolent plowman will not perform as good work with it as if it were lighter; because in one instance they are not *able* to handle it, and in the other they *will not*. Another very great defect in our

common country plows is, there is not a sufficient *dip* of the point *below* the sole of the plow, or the bottom of the landside. (See Par. 449.)   Another defect is, a little short stub of a mole-board. Another is, the wing of the share is too narrow, and rises very abruptly from the entering edge.   Another very great fault or imperfection is, a very short, low standard, having an acute edge, and connected with the beam at an acute angle, by which every sod and straw is sure to ciug it.   Another defect is, the point of the share is not half as far *forward* of the *throat* of the plow as it should be.   The throat of a plow is the space beneath the beam, just forward of the junction of the standard and the beam. Another defect in the manufacture of common plows is, the handles do not extend far enough behind the plow, but stand so straight up and down that the plowman too often stubs his toes against the plow; and he cannot handle it, because it is too near his feet.   Another defect is, the handles are too high; and the *left* handle stands too much behind the plow.

WHICH IS THE BEST PLOW?

446. Many farmers are often puzzled, and are in great doubt to know which is the best plow for them to purchase.   A joiner might with the same propriety ask, What *plane* shall I purchase, as the best for every kind of planing.   For plowing some kinds of soils a certain kind of plows will operate in the most satisfactory manner, while on a *different* soil those very plows will not operate with any degree of satisfaction.   Many plows will work well in plowing stubble ground, and in cross-plowing, which would be almost worthless for plowing sod ground.   One farmer will laud a certain kind of plows, and pronounce them the very best for plowing sod; while his neighbor, just on the other side of the fence, and in the same kind of soil, with the same kind of plows, does his work intolerably bad.   The first one mentioned plows just deep enough for the plow to operate as well as possible; while his neighbor, having adjusted his plow to run a little too deep for the shape of the mold-board to turn the furrow-slice well, is entirely unable to plow in a workmanlike manner.   Hun-

dreds and thousands of plows are now manufactured, which will operate as well as any man can desire, while they cut a furrow only four or five inches deep. But when they are put into the soil seven, eight, or nine inches in depth, the draught is unaccountably hard, and all the strength of a strong plowman is necessary to hold them; and even then they will not operate well. Some plows have such a peculiar shape that an increased depth of the furrow only one inch will so affect their operation as to make them work decidedly bad.

447. At a plowing match of the New York State Agricultural Society in 1856, there were two steel plows entered, which were made as nearly alike as two plows could be made. The plowing done by one of them was done most neatly, while the other performed intolerably bad. The teams and plowmen were good, and the soil where both plowed exactly alike. One plow cut just six inches deep and eleven inches wide; while the other cut from eight to nine inches deep and from ten to eleven wide, and left the furrow-slices all standing on the edge, to the great chagrin and mortification of both the manufacturer and the plowman.

448. This showed very conclusively, that plows for deep and for shallow plowing must be of a little different form to operate well. A plow that works well for plowing deep, may cut a shallow furrow well; but a plow may cut a shallow furrow well and will not a deep one, and turn it well.

HOW TO SELECT A GOOD PLOW

449. In selecting a plow for every kind of plowing, the surest and best way is, to purchase it *on trial*, and not take it because A or B pronounces it "*the plow that beats the world.*" Perhaps your manner of adjusting a plow and of plowing, and your soil, are all so very different from his who pronounces that kind of plow a most complete implement in every respect, that you cannot possibly make it operate at all satisfactorily. Such a plow no man desires to purchase; and, as different plows are calculated

for plowing different kinds of soil, and for cutting a furrow of a given depth, it is always best after selecting a plow, the various parts of which are as nearly perfect as possible, to purchase it *on trial.* When the first cast-iron plows were manufactured, the stand was made very low, and the mold-board also was very low. For plowing three or four inches deep they operated very well,— as most plows will which have a low standard ·and low mold-board, when turning only a very shallow furrow. But most farmers have learned that mines of untold wealth lie just beneath this thin stratum of super soil, which our ancestors merely scratched over with these imperfectly constructed plows; and that when they attempt to bring it up with such plows, they need more team to draw such imperfectly-shaped implements, when they are driven an inch or two deeper than they were calculated to run; and that they do not turn the furrow-slice well, but *shove* it off, and turn a portion of it over, while the greater part is merely set on one edge, ready to fall back into the furrow. With the foregoing considerations, we will attend to

THE POINTS OR CHARACTERISTICS OF A GOOD PLOW.

450. A good plow is one the shape of which is such, that the *draft* will be *as light as possible;* and will *turn* a furrow-slice well, whether the furrow is four or eight inches deep; and will maintain easily a *uniform depth* of furrow; and will hold easy, without much exertion of the plowman; and which will glide along as smoothly as a goose glides over the gentle-rolling waves of a lake. The mold-board should be rather long, and so high that the furrow-slice will not be constantly falling over it into the plow and furrow; and the plow should be several inches narrower at the sole than it is at the hind end of the mold-board at the top of it; and the mold-board should have a *good twist* at the hind end; and the standard should be of a good height; and the throat open and circular, so that every little sod or bunch of manure will not clog the plow; and the plow should be of a good length from the end of the point to the middle of the throat or standard; and should not rise too much in a short distance; and

the *point* and *wing* of the share should be in such a position— "lying down flat," as common plowmen express it—that they will enter the earth several inches, straight in, before it raises the furrow-slice any. When the furrow-slice must begin to rise as soon as the wing of the share begins to enter the earth, and must rise more and more, until it reaches the mold-board, the draft of that plow will be full one-third greater than it would be if the wing of the share were very wide, and the *surface* of it for two or more inches almost horizontal. When the share of a plow can enter two or three inches, so as *to cut the furrow-slice loose* before it begins to rise, it requires but little force to raise the furrow-slice and turn it over. The wing of the share should extend beyond the sole of the plow never *less* than three inches; and farther than this, as the size of the plow increases, in order to *cut loose* the furrow-slice so that it will turn over more readily. When the wing of the share extends but little beyond the sole of the plow, the furrow-slice is not cut loose; and it is far more inclined to fall back into the furrow than if it were cut loose on the bottom. The wing should always be " cold chilled "—hardened—on the *under* side, and should be so thin that it will wear off as fast on the *upper* side as it does on the under side. When the wing of the share is half an inch thick, and chilled or not, it will wear off the fastest on the *under* side; and will affect very greatly the running of the plow.*

451. The *point* of the share should always be cold chilled on the *under* side; and if the soil is free from stone it should be much longer, and more slender, and thinner than it should be for plowing ground that is full of fast stone. When there are no fast stone against which a plow may be broken, the point of the share may be so thin that the upper side will wear away as fast as the under side wears off. When plow points are very thick—

---

* Plow points and any other iron is " cold chilled " by running the liquid iron on a smooth piece of cold iron, which is placed in the sand when the pattern is molded. Iron being so much better to conduct heat than wet sand, the liquid iron is cooled so rapidly that it is rendered as hard as it can be made. It costs no more to cold chill plow points than it does to cast them without cold chilling. And one plow point cold chilled will outlast two, and sometimes four—if they are made of soft iron—which are not cold chilled.

up and down—the under side wears off much faster than the upper side ; consequently, after the under side of a point has become worn off but little, there is a tendency of the plow to run up out of the ground. For plowing ground that is full of fast stone, a thicker plow point is necessary, as thin, slender ones will break too frequently. But as every plowshare should be made with a *fin-cutter* to separate the furrow-slice from the unplowed land, the lower part of the fin may extend almost to the end of the point, which will strengthen the point very much. Plowshares should always be made with *fin-cutters*, because they lessen the draft of a plow ; and a plow works much better with them than without them.

452. Plow points as well as plows, should always be ground so smooth before using, that the earth will not adhere to them. Grind any kind of cast-iron *without* water, as a grindstone will grind it much faster than it will when wet.

453. When the young farmer has found a style of plow to suit him, when he is about to purchase a new one, order one made, and charge the manufacturers to make the mold-board of old iron, such as old stoves and old plow-points ; as such iron will form new iron which will wear far better and longer than if it were run out of pig-iron. Tell them to endeavor to make the mold-board as smooth as possible, as a rough mold-board is a very disagreeable thing to plow with. Charge him to use the best of timber in wooding it ; and give him directions, in feet and inches, just how high to make the handles. Have the *left* handle bent to the left not less than seven inches from a right line, so that the plowman can walk in the furrow without the *left* handle close to his side. A plowman cannot exert as much strength in hold-ing a plow, when the handles are as high, or even higher than his hips, and when the left handle is constantly against his side. The best and most proper height for plow handles is, just high enough for the plowman, when he stands erect, to grasp them with his hands without bending his body forward, and having his arms straight. When the handles are so low that the plowman can just grasp them without bending his arms, he can hold a

plow very much easier and better than he possibly can when the handles are so high that he is obliged to bend his arms when his hands are hold of the handles. It is better to have the handles too low than too high. Plow handles are almost always too high for boys ;—and this is one good reason why they are not able to plow as well as they might plow, if the handles were of a proper height. When the handles are low, a plowman can throw his whole weight and strength on one handle ; but it will be very difficult and inconvenient for him to do so when the handles are as high as his ribs.

454. *Steel plows.*—In some of the Western States, and in some parts of the Empire State, plows are manufactured with *steel mold-boards*. Steel plows cost several dollars more per plow ; but for plowing some kinds of soil, and especially very light soils, they are far superior to the best cast-iron plows, because the surface of the mold-board is smoother, and admits of a finer polish ; and in some kinds of very light soil, where the dirt will not slip well when a cast-iron plow is used, a steel plow will perform most complete work. For heavy, stiff soils steel plows are little, if any, better than cast-iron plows, providing they are made of old iron, and have a very smooth surface.

ADJUSTING THE DRAFT OF THE PLOW.

455. There are so many collateral and conditional considerations which influence and affect the proper adjustment of the draft of the plow, that it seems almost an impossibility to lay down any infallible rules to enable the tyro to adjust his plow correctly. When a plow is correctly adjusted it will glide along with a steady motion, requiring very little effort of the plowman to hold it, in smooth ground; and it will not seem inclined to run too much on the point, nor on the heel. When the draught is improperly adjusted, the plowman is often obliged to exert all his strength in order to make his plow work at all satisfactorily. Sometimes it will run too much on the point; and the most skillful plowmen are unable to adjust it so that it will glide along

14*

smoothly, resting equally on the point and heel. The draft may be correctly adjusted for plowing one kind of soil, but for plowing a different soil—perhaps not eight rods distant—that adjustment of the draft would be very incorrect. Let a plow be adjusted correctly for plowing stubble ground of any kind, where the soil is very compact and hard, and it will be found that for plowing sod of the same kind of soil the plow will run too deep. The soil often varies very much in the same field; so that a plow in one part of the field runs well, and in another part, with the same adjustment, runs very badly.

456. The idea which the expert plowman keeps in mind is, to have the plow cut a furrow-slice just so thick and just so wide, with the least draft to the team, and the least exertion for himself. To secure this end, the team is hitched as close to the plow as it can be and not have the whippletrees hit their heels in turning at the corners. As the length of traces is increased, in plowing, the draft increases. Now put the connecting ring, or link, or dial clevis, at the end of the beam, in the lowest notch; and if it will not run deep enough, raise it another notch at a time, until it will run just deep enough. Now alter the clevis from right to left, or from left to right, as may be necessary, until the plow will cut a furrow-slice just wide enough to turn it over well. If the plow crowds the furrow-slice into the furrow, without turning it over, it shows that the furrow-slice is too narrow for its depth; and the plow must be adjusted to cut a wider slice. On the contrary, if the plowman is obliged to push the furrow-slice over with his foot constantly, if the ground he is plowing be very smooth and even, it shows that there is an imperfection or fault somewhere. Sometimes by adjusting a plow to run an inch deeper it will do very bad work. (See Par. 447.) And sometimes it is necessary to adjust it to cut a little wider, or a little narrower, before it will turn the furrow-slice as well as it ought to be done. When a good plow is correctly adjusted, it will glide along where there are no obstructions, without being held, for many rods. When a plow is constantly inclined *to fall over* either way, and the plowman must hold it up all the while to keep

it erect, there is either an imperfection in the *construction* of the plow, or it is not adjusted correctly. When a plow "*tips up behind*," and does not keep down flat on its sole, or when it seems to run all on the point, either the point is *too blunt*, or is worn off too much on the *under* side, or there is not "*dip enough*" —pitching of the point downwards—to the point. Sometimes I have found that a plow could not be adjusted by the clevis so correctly as all the parts were arranged; and that by shortening the traces or draft chain, or giving them a little more length, it would run like another plow. When a plow is adjusted to run just right, as the point wears off it is necessary many times to give a little more length to the draft chains, or to adjust it with the clevis to run a little deeper. It is sometimes impossible to adjust a plow to run just right with the style of clevis which is on the end of the beam. The arrangement ought always to be such that the draft can be adjusted half an inch at a time, either up or down, or to the right or left. Then if the beam of the plow stands as it should, so that the most correct line of draft *will cut the end of the beam*, it can be most correctly adjusted in a few seconds.

457. To make a plow run deeper, *raise* the connecting point at the end of the beam one or more notches higher in the clevis; or lengthen the draft chains. To make it run more shallow, *lower* the draft a notch or more in the clevis; or shorten the draft chains; or, which should never be done, shorten the *back-bands* or *hip-straps* of the harness. To make a plow take a *wider* furrow-slice, carry the connecting point one or more notches in the clevis *to the right hand*. A notch or two to the *left hand* will make a plow cut a *narrower* furrow slice. Or, which is seldom allowable, a plow may be made to run *more shallow* by putting the gauge-wheel *lower*, (see Par. 459) so as to raise the end of the beam. And a plow may be made to cut a *narrower* furrow-slice by carrying the handles *to the left hand;* or wider by carry-ing and holding them to the *right*, beyond an erect position; neither of which is allowable, except for a temporary purpose. (See HOLDING PLOW, 466.)

458. I always go with my plowmen to the field and show them how to adjust the plow until it will run just right; and at least once every day I take hold of the plow with my own hands, to see if it runs correctly. It would be no difficult thing to tell, if I were blindfolded, when a plow runs correctly or incorrectly, and how to adjust it properly in case it seemed to run wrong. Any good plowman can tell by the touch when a plow runs right.

THE GAUGE-WHEEL.

459. Were the soil which is to be plowed always very smooth on the surface, and of a uniform depth, and of equal solidity, and could the share always be kept as sharp as when first put on the plow, a gauge-wheel under the beam to regulate the depth of the furrow would be not only a useless but a cumbersome appendage. A plow should always be adjusted to run as nearly as may be the desired depth *without* the wheel; and if the plow is inclined to run a little too deep in some places, while most of the time it runs just deep enough, the wheel may be lowered not more than half an inch at a time, until it appears to be exactly right. When the share is very dull and the soil variable—being very hard in some places and mellow and light in others—it is almost impossible to plow a furrow of a uniform depth without a wheel. In such a case a plow must be adjusted to run deep, and then the gauge-wheel lowered under the beam, until it will make the plow cut a furrow of a uniform depth. But such an adjustment of a plow increases the draft more than we are wont to suppose; and makes it hold harder; and it does not, as a general thing, run as well. Take off that dull point and put on one that is fit to plow with, and then the plow will operate enough better to repay the expense of a new share.

460. A gauge-wheel for general purposes should never be less than one foot in diameter. Very small gauge-wheels never operate as well as wheels of a larger diameter, unless the ground is very smooth. When the ground is rather rough, small wheels are apt to strike obstructions in such a manner as to require a

much greater force to draw the plow than if the wheel were. much larger.

461. In plowing deep with a double team, where the soil was variable and very uneven, we have found *two* gauge-wheels to operate very advantageously; one under the beam, and one over the heel of the plow, fastened to the *side* of the beam. The plow is adjusted to run about the desired depth, and then the hindermost gauge-wheel is attached to the *side* of the plow in such a manner as to allow the plow to enter only a given depth. In plowing over knolls, it is many times very difficult to turn the furrow-slice well without this wheel, because the plow will run so very deep. The plow should not be adjusted to run deep, and then the wheel lowered under the beam, to make it run more shallow; because that would increase the draft of the plow and make it hold harder; and if the wheel is nearer the standard of the plow than it is the end of the beam, the plow will be very much inclined to fall over to the right. In plowing a field where the soil is so light and mellow in some places, that a plow would run in up to the beam if it were adjusted to run of the desired depth through the hard portions of the field, *two* gauge-wheels are very necessary. Although very many farmers denounce a gauge-wheel as a useless appendage, I must be allowed to say that *I know* a plowman can plow better, as a general rule, with one, and sometimes two gauge-wheels, than he can without them. Every good plowman will coincide with me in this assertion.

THE CORRECT ADJUSTMENT OF THE COULTER

462. Of a plow is something which not one plowman in fifty understands. My manner of adjusting the coulter is, to have the lower end of it from two to three inches *above* and *forward of* the plow point, and standing as far to the left as the *left side of the end of the plow point.* The coulter works best when it cuts just as wide as the plow will cut. When it is adjusted to cut a half-inch *wider* or *narrower* than the plow would cut, the plow will not run well, and will hold hard. Most plowmen adjust the coulter as shown at Fig. 140, Par. 464, with the end of

the coulter directly over the left corner of the point. But in plow-ing where there are some stone in the soil, it will be found that stones will throw out the plow much oftener when the coulter is adjusted as in the figure, than they will if it is adjusted *forward* of the point so far that most of the stone will pass *between* the end of the coulter and the point of the plow, when they will not throw the plow out. And I am fully persuaded—and my expe-rience coincides with all the good plowmen with whom I have ever conversed on this subject—that when the blade of a coulter is of a good length, and sharp, and of the form shown by the next figure, and stands about as slanting as shown in the figure, with the point from two to three or four inches *forward* of the plow point, it will work better than it will in any other position. It requires but little force to draw a sharp coulter through the sod, and when the blade of it is made of the form shown in the figure, common sense teaches us, that if it stands slanting—as a knife for ripping—it will *clog less*, and lessen the draft of the plow. Always keep the coulter *sharp-pointed*, and the edge sharp.

464. Fig. 140 represents a very useful instrument for prevent-ing weeds, manure, grass, &c., from clogging a plow. It was invented by Mr. E. C. Bills, Perry, Wyoming co., N. Y. It consists of a corrugated conical cylinder, attached to the coulter, as represented in the figure, which turns freely either way. The bearing of the lower end of the cylinder plays in a hole in the front side of the coulter, and the upper end plays in a hole in a clasp, which is fastened to the coulter by means of a set-screw. When straw, or clover, or manure, comes in contact with the coulter, it slides up against the cylinder ; and as it is free to turn, as one side of such materials will usually draw more than the other, the cylinder revolves and carries it all on one side of the plow, and thus keeps the coulter clear. With such a contrivance a plow will seldom clog.

FIG. 140.

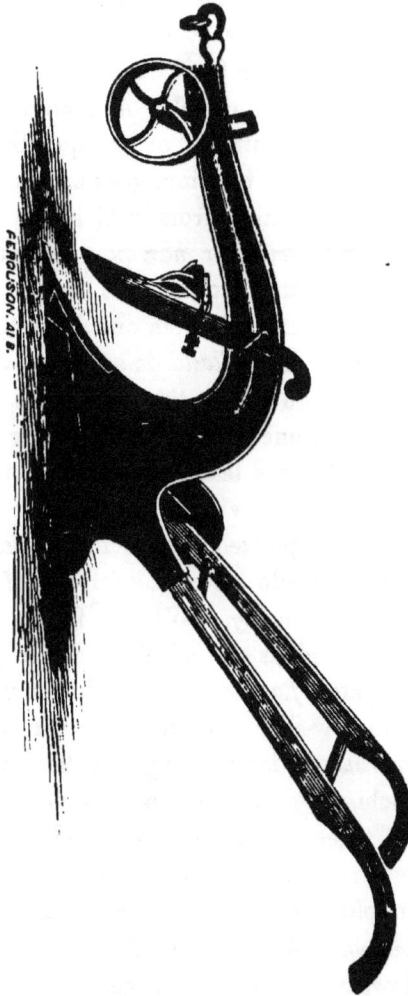

BILLS' PATENT COULTER-CLEARER.

PLOWING TECHNICALITIES.

465. A *furrow* is the trench or channel made by the plow when it is drawn through the soil; and it is said to be *wide*, or *narrow—deep*, or *shallow*. The *furrow-slice* is the strip of soil which the plow separates and turns away from the unplowed soil when making a furrow; and it may be wide, or narrow—thick, or

thin. A *back-furrow* is two furrow-slices turned towards each other so that their edges will meet; or, one may overlay or lap on the other. A *dead furrow, middle furrow,* or *open furrow,* which are only different names for the same thing, is the channel that is left when a land is finished. A *land* is the unplowed ground between two back furrows, or the quantity of unplowed ground which a plowman, in plowing, goes around, when he turns about in the opposite direction from which the furrow-slice is turned. A land may be *wide,* or *narrow.* A *ridge* embraces a part of two lands, or all the ground from one middle furrow to the other; while a *land* extends from one back furrow or centre of a ridge to another. A *headland* is a narrow strip of ground at the ends of the lands on which the team turns when plowing. When a team goes from one end of the plowing to the other, it is called a *through.* When a team goes to the other end of the land or ridge, and returns plowing a furrow, it is called a *bout* or a *round.* When land is plowed two or more times before seeding, if the furrows are made *across* the furrows of the last plowing, it is termed *cross-plowing.* When a furrow-slice is turned into a furrow, and the edges of each furrow-slice just touch each other, it is denominated *flat-plowing,* or plowed with a *flat furrow.* When the furrow-slices lap on each other, it is called plowing *with a lap-furrow,* or lap-plowing. When plowing is performed with a Michigan Sod Plow, with which a narrow furrow of the sod two or three inches deep is rolled up, and the whole covered with well pulverized soil, it is called *round-plowing.* When a common plow is run twice in a place, it is called *trenching,* or *trench-plowing.* When a subsoil plow is run in the furrow of a common plow, it is called *subsoiling.*

HOLDING PLOW.

" The plow with ill-holding goes quickly aside."—Tusser.

466. After the plow has been correctly adjusted, the young farmer, if he would make a skillful and complete plowman, must be careful to observe and to practise the following rules : Always keep the plow as nearly level as is practicable. Stand up straight

between the handles, and never fall into the unworkmanlike practice of walking two or three feet *behind* the handles. Take a firm hold of the handles, and make the arms so stiff, if it is necessary, that the handles will take the plowman off his feet before it can deviate from a right line. If a stone or anything else should *cant* the. plow from its erect position, with a quick jerk with one hand set it instantaneously erect. Keep the eye a good portion of the time on the furrow-slice, to see if it is not cut too wide, and to see if it all seems to be broken up, and whether there is not a narrow strip which remains unbroken. Some plowmen, too indolent to step up to their work, will support themselves, in part, by the handles, and will roll to the right and left as a huge ship does in a storm, carrying the handles of the plow with them, until the plow almost loses the furrow-slice, or cuts one so wide that it cannot turn it, when they will begin to "*right up.*" Such plowmen always make crooked furrows; and no plowman can perform a job neatly who does not cast his eye forward of the team and plow, and endeavor to cut *straight furrows.* By *riding* on the handles of the plow from an indolent habit, or for the purpose of keeping the plow from running too deep, *increases the draft* of the plow always; because, when the handles of a plow are long and the plowman rests heavily on them, the fulcrum being at the *heel* of the landside, and the weight at the end of the beam where the draft is downwards, the draft is increased as much, many times, as it would be if a number of hundred pounds of stone were carried on the plow. On the contrary, when a plowman walks up square with his handles, and instead of *riding* on them, *lifts* a little, and at the same time *leans a little forward,* he will *diminish* the draft of his plow from twenty to fifty pounds, and at the same time plow a furrow just as deep and wide as he who indolently rides on his handles.

467. Many a good plowman, understanding this principle, when the committee at our agricultural fairs and plowing matches have been testing the draft of his plow with the *dynamometer*, has secured the first prize by *lifting* and *shoving* a little on the handles, instead of *riding* on them. The movements of a good

plowman must be as quick and agile as a weasel; and if his plow deviates to the right or left, he must set it up as quickly as it turned from its course. A slow-bellied, indolent Jonathan, who always desires to *ride* through the world, never can make a complete plowman.

468. In breaking up the prairies of our Western country, which are as level and free from stone and other obstructions as a barn floor, the plow being drawn by three or four yoke of oxen and sustained by four wheels, with a seat on it—like the devout and submissive Paddy, who "let the *world* slide along ' *azy,*' and jump on and ride"—the plowman holds his plow when *riding* on it. But let a plowman adopt any such arrangement on our compact, stubborn, and stony soils, where our good plowmen do not know half of the time whether they are on their feet or in a passive state between the heavens and the earth, and he would find his quiet seat disturbed very abruptly so frequently, that he would choose "to foot it" until he became somewhat tired.

BEGINNING TO PLOW.

"Clear the brown path to meet the coulter's gleam !
The plowman comes, behind his smoking team !
Line after line, along the verdant sod,
Marks the broad acres where his feet have trod.
At every round the loosening chains resound,
And glittering mold-boards sleek the furrowed ground."—GRAHAM.

469. The principles of adjusting and of holding the plow being well understood, and the team being correctly hitched to the plow (see Par. 456), and the mold-board being well polished, so that the dirt will slip, we are ready to start the plow. Now, then, it is not desirable to have huge ridges thrown up along the fence, nor to have deep furrows there; but the surface should be kept as smooth there as in any other part of the field. Where fields are about level, it is best to plow them one way at one time, and across the middle furrows at the next plowing. This will keep the surface of the ground about level and smooth. In plowing with a double team or with a single team, the plowman must

first determine how wide his *headland* (see Par. 465) must be in order to give the team sufficient room to turn at the ends of the lands. If a field is to be plowed by going directly around the outside, there will be nothing to do but to go ahead and keep plowing until the field is all plowed. But when a field is to be plowed by *lands,*—having determined which way to plow it, run the plow along say ten, or any number of feet distant from the edges of the field, which will be at the ends of the furrows, making a shallow *mark*—not plowing a furrow—with the *point* of the plow. Now always turn out the plow and set it in *exactly at these marks.* Now measure off a strip with the rod-pole (see Par. 695) on both sides of the field, just as wide as the headland strips. This strip entirely around the field must be left to be plowed last. Now plow a back furrow on the *farther side* of the field, leaving a strip as wide as the headland. Commence on the farther side first, so that the team will not trample the plowed soil in going to and from work. Now if grain is to be sowed by hand, (see SOWING GRAIN BY HAND, 493,) it is best to have the *middle furrows* of exactly equal distances apart, and the *ridges* exactly as far apart as the middle furrows are. I always calculate to sow about forty-two feet at two rounds. Therefore, measure off forty-two feet from the *first ridge,* and turn another ridge, as straight as a line, and back-furrow just as many furrows on every succeeding ridge as there were furrows on the *first* ridge ; and commence to turn a ridge every time at the same end that you commenced at when the first ridge was turned. If a plowman commences at one end in striking out one ridge, and at the other end of the field for the next ridge, and plows one or two furrows *more* on one ridge than he does on another, the ridges may be equidistant apart ; but the middle furrows will be of very *unequal* distances apart. This will be a bad arrangement when grain is sowed by hand, with ridges and furrows for guides.

470. When striking out a land or a ridge, the *first* furrow always requires much more strength of team to turn it than is required after one furrow has been turned. And the draft of a plow needs a different adjustment with the clevis, usually, to run

at the same depth in striking out a ridge, and in plowing after two or three furrows have been plowed. Therefore, if a team is very spirited or fractious, and disinclined to press steadily into the yoke or collar,—which is no uncommon occurrence with many good teams,—adjust the plow to cut *a very shallow furrow*, and go twice in one place until the team will work steadily. Many a valuable horse has been balked, and "fooled," and well-nigh spoiled for service, simply because this precaution was not observed. When a team has lain idle for a long, and sometimes for only a short period of time, and they are hitched to a plow, and it is put in the soil at the ordinary depth, their necks and shoulders are very often *tender*, and they will *flinch* at a heavy draft. Therefore they must be hitched to something, and made to haul it about until they will not flinch when drawing a plow when it runs at the ordinary depth.

471. In order to strike out a ridge straight, plant not less than three stakes in a row; and if the distance is over twenty-five rods there ought to be four stakes. Let the plowman put the lines *around his body*, and keep an eye on the stakes, between the horses, and have the lines just tight enough to enable him to guide his team by turning his body to the right or to the left. This is a far better way than to have the lines on the neck and shoulders. I have always found, that with the lines *around my body* I could strike a ridge fifty or sixty rods long as straight as a line, without touching my lines; whereas, if they were about my neck I could not do it.

472. The beauty and excellence of plowing are, to keep the furrows as straight as a line, and of a uniform depth. He who cannot take a team alone and strike out his lands and finish them, and adjust and *re*-adjust his plow to suit all circumstances, and perform a job in a neat manner, cannot expect to receive the appellation of *a complete plowman*.

473. In order to finish a land neatly when plowing sod ground, the plowman must make calculations to leave a strip of sod just as wide as two ordinary furrow-slices. Now elevate the end of the plow-beam by lowering the gauge-wheel so that the plow will

run about *half* as deep as usual; and turn *half* of this strip with the team going *up the slope*, if the ground is not about level. In turning the *last* furrow let the team go *down the slope*, because the last furrow is much more difficult to turn than any other ; and it is less difficult to turn it when going *down* hill. Remove entirely, or raise the gauge-wheel higher than usual, while plowing the last furrow, and then let the plow run along once or twice to break up the soil where the next to the last furrow was cut shallow. This leaves the middle furrow full of *mellow earth*, instead of leaving a space about two feet wide with little or no super-soil on it. Having finished the field in this manner, the last thing will be,

PLOWING THE HEADLANDS.

474. If the soil is about level and smooth, plow the headlands by passing round and round the field, turning the furrows *inwards*. If the soil was turned *away* from the fence when plowed last, turn it *towards* the fence. This manner of plowing headlands is infinitely better, and more plowman-like, than it is to plow the headlands in a *land*, or back-furrow, which is the common practice. If a strip twenty feet wide is left entirely around the field, there is no disadvantage in it. It is as important to keep the surface of the soil smooth along the *margin* of a field as it is near the middle of it.

475. Many plowmen will insist on plowing very wide back-furrows and lands, and will plow across the *ends* of the lands. But the practice is by no means so good a one as it is to leave a wide headland. The headlands should always be plowed last; because, if plowed *first* the soil in many places will be trodden down so firmly that it would need to be plowed again when the field is finished.

476. *Plowing side-hills* and throwing the furrows down hill year after year is not a good practice, because every plowing removes the soil of the entire field down the slope about one foot farther; and on the lower side of the field the soil would be piled up in a huge ridge, while there would be in a few years a wide

strip at the *upper side* of the field, from which all the super-soil had been removed.   When it is not impracticable, side-hills should always be plowed up and down the slope.   The soil will work down hill sufficiently fast without plowing it downwards.

PLOWING A FIELD BY BEGINNING IN THE MIDDLE AND TURN-ING THE FURROWS INWARDS.

477. Every plowman knows that when a field is plowed by going around it and turning the furrows outwards, all the soil is thrown at each plowing nearly a foot towards the outsides of the field; and if a field is plowed in this way many times, a high ridge is formed at the outside, and in the *middle* of the field the soil is all thrown outwards so far that a large excavation is made where the plowing was finished.   And, furthermore, when a field is plowed by going around it and finishing in the middle, there is always a dead-furrow from every corner of the field to the middle, where the plowing is finished; and, beside these dead-furrows, there is a strip of plowed ground on which the team turns, which often becomes so much trodden as to injure it very much, especially if the soil be of a clayey nature, and is a little too moist when the plowing is performed.   But by commencing to plow in the *middle* of a field, and by turning the furrows *inwards*, there will be no dead-furrows, no plowed ground trampled down by the team in turning, and no ridges at the outsides of the field; and the team will turn on unplowed ground until the field is finished.   Plowing a field by beginning in the middle is the neatest way in which a field can be plowed.   The only difficulty in plowing a field by beginning in the middle is, *to get started correctly ;* and if the plowman has a little geometrical skill he will find no difficulty in plowing a field of almost any shape, unless it is some-what hilly, and have every side finish up with the greatest accuracy.   The main idea to be kept in mind is, after a field has been plowed by commencing on the outside and finishing in the middle, to commence in the middle and turn each furrow *inwards*, with the same precision that they were turned outwards.

478. The first step, then, will be, to find the middle.   This

process will be readily understood by Fig. 141. *A B C D* represents the outside of a plot of ground, to be plowed in the form of a parallelogram. At *E E*, at equal distances from *E F*, *E G*,

FIG. 141.

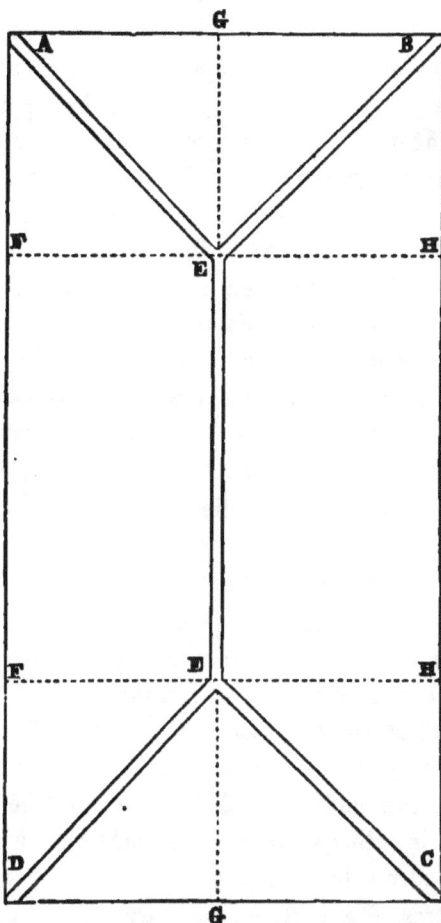

MODE OF PLOWING A SQUARE FIELD BY COMMENCING IN THE MIDDLE.

and *E H*, which is found by measuring in the direction of the dotted lines, stick a stake at both centres, *E E*. Now, as it is not very practicable to turn a plow at a right angle when it is in the ground, let a back-furrow be turned from each corner of the field to *A E B*, and *C E D*, and from *F* to *E*. Now, the land is laid out, and the plowman has only to keep his furrow-slices of a uniform width on every side, in order to have the field finish alike on every side. If he is careless in setting in his plow, and is not particular at each corner to have the team go straight out, and takes a furrow-slice in one place a little too wide and in another place too narrow, he will have a very undesirable job to finish the plowing up ; because, at one place it may be finished, and at another it may lack many feet of being finished to the margin of the field. The plow should be set in and come out at each corner with the greatest precision. It will not hurt a plow-man to exercise his geometrical faculties a little at every corner, by measuring the width of each furrow slice with a mechanical eye ; and, after a field has been plowed in this way, every one will acknowledge that it is enough better to "pay" for any *apparent* extra trouble or care in laying out the work and in finishing it. By plowing in this manner there will be neither ridges nor dead-furrows, which is very desirable, especially where hoed crops are to be planted; and also, when a field is to be pre-pared for a meadow, the entire field is left as level as can be desired.

479. Fig. 142 shows the manner of plowing a field of an *irreg-ular* form by commencing in the middle. The same letters in this figure refer to the same points as in Fig. 141. It will be seen that the point *E* is found by measuring from the outside of the field *G H F*, at *right angles* to each side. The centre *K* is found by measuring at the dotted lines *N L M*, at a right angle to the centre of the field. It will be seen that the point to set a stake at, *K*, is in a line with *E M*, *M* being equidistant from *D* and C. Now, turn a back-furrow from each corner of the field to the two centres, *E* and *K*, and also from *E* to *K*. Now, com-mence plowing by going around the centre, *E*, and be very par-ticular, in commencing, *to have the furrows run parallel with the outsides of the field*. After plowing a few hours, measure from the outsides of the field to the furrows on every side, and if the distances from the last furrow, represented by the dotted lines *O O O O O*, are all equal, the field will be finished alike on

every side. If the distances are *unequal*, let stakes be stuck on every side, at equal distances from the outsides of the field, and plow up to those stakes on every side, until the last furrow is exactly parallel to the outsides of the field, like the dotted line at *O O*, &c. When the plowman has arrived at *K* in plowing,

FIG. 142.

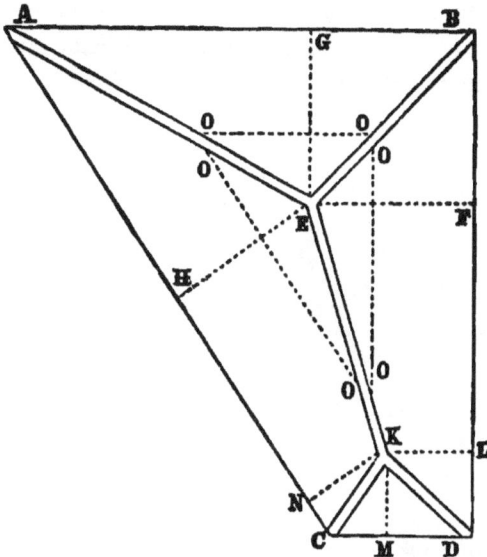

MODE OF PLOWING A FIELD OF IRREGULAR FORM BY COMMENCING IN THE CENTRE.

cut off just the point of the unplowed ground across the end at *K*. After plowing a few furrows across the end, measure from *K* to the last furrow on each side, and if the distances are equal, " speed the plow," and you will come out square on every side.

480. The first field that I ever undertook to plow in this way was a field of irregular form. But by following the directions here laid down, the field finished up on every side very exactly. If the young farmer is not able to carry these directions in his mind, let him take them to the field with him, and refer to the figure as he measures.

481. In order to determine at what point to start in measur-

15

ing, in order to measure on a line at a right angle to the outsides or margin of the plot to be plowed, nail two narrow strips of thin boards together at a right angle, and place them on a carpenter's steel square on a high stool or box, or on three stakes driven in the ground, and place one arm of the square *parallel with the margin of the field,* and if the other points to the centre, *E* or *K,* as the station may be, commence measuring from that point. In about half an hour a field of ordinary size can be laid out and all the stakes stuck, ready for the plow.

CHAPTER VII.

" A harrow to dig up and mellow the path,
And roller to smooth it, good husbandry hath."—ANON.

482. THE *styles* and *forms* of common harrows are so numerous, and all good, that I shall here give illustrations of but three of them. A farmer in moderate circumstances does not feel willing nor able to pay fifteen or twenty-five dollars for a common harrow, which could be afforded for less than half that sum. It is with harrows as with many other farm implements: there are many times several dollars expended in fitting them up, which is of no *practical* utility whatever. Common farmers, who obtain every dollar and dime by the most rigid economy and hard-fisted industry, expend their cash somewhat grudgingly when it goes to pay for redundant, unnecessary work in the manufacture of implements. A manufacturer will soon use up $5.00 in *unnecessary* hammering and filing and polishing portions of implements which would be just as good, in every respect, if they were merely coated with paint or coal tar; and the same implement, while costing much less, would be equally good and durable.

483. Fig. 143 represents a triangular hinged harrow,—which I have used for fifteen years, and it is good still,—which cost me $7.25 ; and it is a very substantial one. Timber, 30 cts.; making, 75 cts.; 26 teeth, $4.00; hinges, $1.00; draft chains, 50 cts.; 4 carriage-bolts, 15 cts.; painting, 30 cts. ;—total, $7.00. The timber is 3x3, of the best of white-oak. The two centre-sticks are six feet long, and the forward wings are six feet. The hindermost wings are a few inches shorter. The wing-pieces are thirteen

inches apart. The slats are an inch thick, four inches wide, of the toughest timber, and driven in firmly, with the joints painted. The forward ends of the wings are let into a mortise, with a good fit, as shown by the dotted lines, and *bolted* with carriage-bolts, which may be obtained at the hardware stores. The teeth are

FIG. 143.

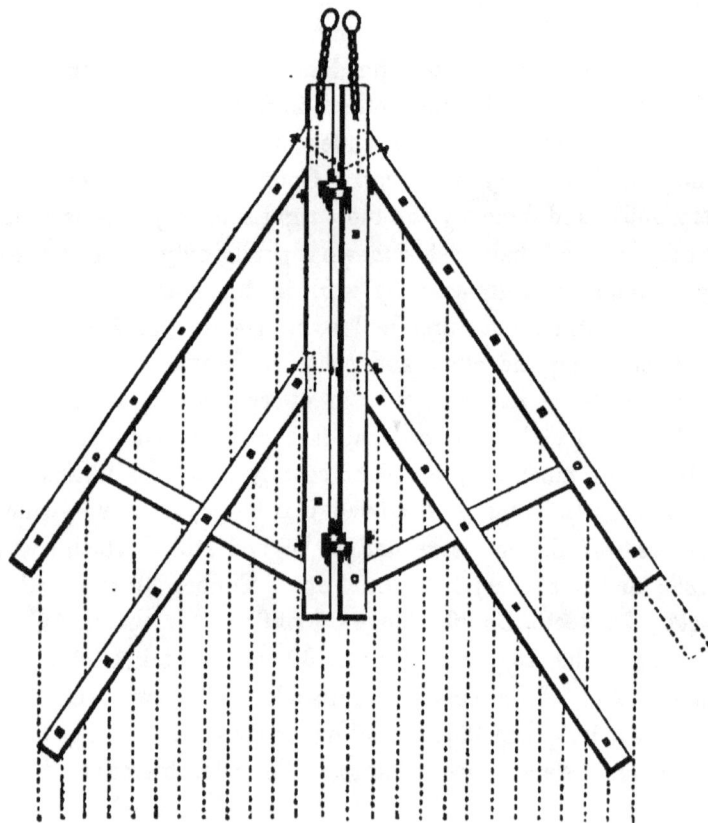

A TRIANGULAR HARROW.

less than an inch square, and three inches apart, from centre to centre. If it is desirable to have a wider harrow, make the wings longer. The hinges are put through the centre-pieces, which are placed close together to prevent the middle of the harrow rising. One of the hinge-hooks has a spring-key in it, and the harrow is readily taken apart. The draft-chains need not be heavy chains; and one end of them is attached to an *eye-bolt*, which is put through the centre-pieces.

484. Harrows similar to this are manufactured all over the country, with iron bars bolted across all the sticks where the slats are placed, with hinges at one end of them. But that mode of hinges increases the expense, and they are not as strong as they would be if made in this manner, because in this style the draft is on the centre-pieces, while the hinges are put through them; whereas, in the common style the draft is at the *hinges*, which are bolted with small bolts to the wood. A carriage-bolt should be put through the pieces at every tooth, to keep them from splitting.

485. In order to get the wings at the proper angle, strike two chalk-lines on the floor at a right angle, and measure three feet one way from the corner, and two feet and one inch on the other line, and strike a diagonal line, which will give the desired angle.

486. Always have the teeth extend below the wood not less than eight inches, and have them even on the points. The longer they are the less liable they are to clog. A harrow should be supported on the points of the teeth, and not by the frame.

487. Fig. 144 represents one of the very best styles of harrows for pulverizing any kind of soil,

FIG. 144.

and especially sod ground. It will pulverize sod ground more with one harrowing than two harrowings with a common harrow. It will not clog, nor tear up manure that has been plowed

COULTER HARROW.

under, nor turn over sods, even when it is drawn *across* them. It draws easier than a common harrow, and I know it to be a most useful implement. It is manufactured by Pease and Egglestone, Albany, N. Y.

488. The frame of it is made similar to a common harrow, of timber two by six inches square. The coulter teeth *c* are thin

plates of iron inclining forward, or turned up like sleigh runners, so as to prevent their clogging. The mold-board, *M*, and standard between *c* and *M*, are all cast in one piece, and the edge of *c* is cold chilled to make it wear well; and they are bolted to the wood with carriage-bolts. For preparing stiff soils for hoed crops, or for any other crop, such a harrow is worth two ordinary harrows. J. J. Thomas says of this harrow: "Every farmer who cultivates a farm of any considerable size, especially if the soil be strong and adhesive, would certainly pay for this harrow in one year, by the work it would enable him to perform. Nothing can exceed it in preparing inverted sod for corn, or for any other crop. It is one of the best inventions of late years for the farmer."

HERALD AND TOMPKINS' PATENT IRON HARROW.

489. Fig. 145 represents an iron harrow, which promises eventually to supersede and supplant every other form of tooth harrows. Messrs. Herald & Tompkins, Trumansburg, Tompkins Co., N. Y., are the manufacturers and patentees. It has recently been patented, and is a genuine implement. They manufacture of various sizes, and the prices vary from $5.00 to $22.00, according to the number and size of teeth, and weight of harrow. The teeth are *bolt* teeth, with a nut and screw on the upper end. The frame is made of round rods of iron, which cross each other at the angle shown in the figure, and are held in their proper places by two small collars of cast-iron, which have grooves in them to fit the round rods, and a hole through the centre of each collar for the tooth. Three-quarter-inch round rods are used for the largest size. The frames are made in two parts, hinged together as shown by the figure. The above cut is a perspective view of one tooth, and the collars, or flanges, as they clasp the rods. One flange is placed *beneath* the rods and one *above* them, when the tooth is put in its place, and screwed up firmly.

The chief advantages of this harrow are,—it is as durable as

FIG. 145.

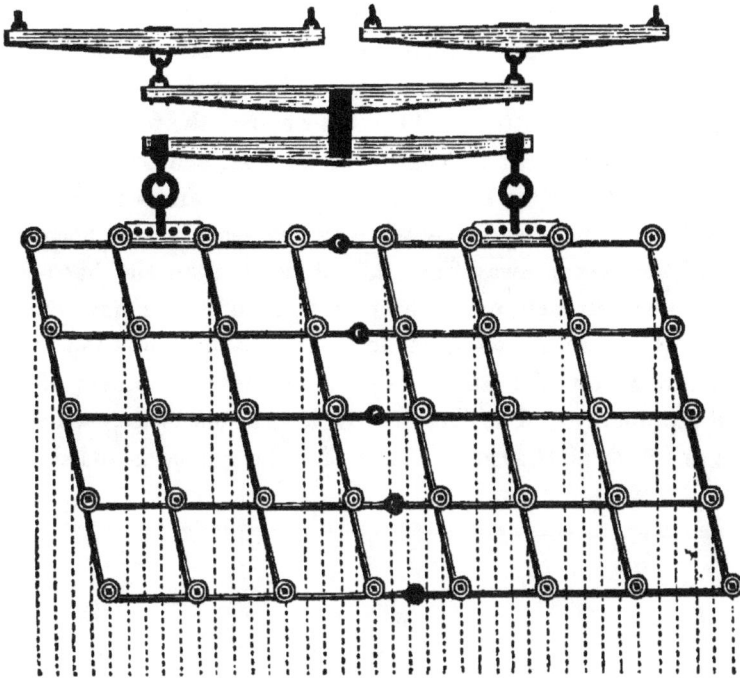

HERALD AND TOMPKINS' PATENT IRON HARROW.

iron; it is less liable to clog than harrows having wooden frames; it is more substantial than wooden-frame harrows; the teeth can be taken out, and sharpened, and replaced, much more readily; and it is a neat, farmer-like implement.

HARROWING.

490. Sod ground should always be harrowed the same way that it was plowed, so as not to tear up any sods, unless the *coulter* harrow is used, when the harrow may be run directly across the furrows, or diagonally. In harrowing stubble that has just been plowed, harrow across the middle furrows the first time, in order to level the ridges, and fill up the middle furrows before the grain is sowed or drilled in. Some farmers never harrow their land before sowing, be it ever so uneven and rough. But I never feel that grain is well put in if the soil is not harrowed

previous to its receiving the seed. If the teeth clog, they should be unclogged at once. Harrow teeth will clog much sooner in harrowing damp or wet soil than they will when it is rather dry.

491. When beginners are learning to harrow, I always walk with them, and tell them to keep their eye on the fore feet of the animal that is nearest the harrowed ground, and keep him just so far from it. If he keeps his eye on the harrow most of the time, he will be very liable to have his team on the harrowed ground, or too far away from it. Always allow the harrow to run one or two teeth on the harrowed ground, so as not to make balks. One can harrow faster to go directly back and forth than he can to go round a land. Always harrow the borders of the field thoroughly. I seldom harrow a field but twice,—once before and once after sowing, after which the ground is rolled.

CHAPTER VIII.

" Scatter ye seeds, and flowers will spring !
Strew them at broadcast o'er hill and glen :
Sow in your garden, and time will bring
Bright flowers with seeds to scatter again."—Anon.

492. Not every one is *fit* to sow grain broadcast, and not one man in a score is able to scatter seed with his hands as evenly as it should be, and *no* man can sow grain as evenly as a good drill, or a good seed-sower. But in some instances a drill cannot be used ; and sometimes a seed drill is not at hand ; and sometimes scores of very good farmers have imbibed the erroneous notion that, all things considered, it is better to sow broadcast and harrow in the seed, than it is to put it in with a drill. Some men may sow grain as long as they live, and they will throw it in ridges or streaks. It is very important to know how to sow, even if a drill is used for putting in most of the grain on a farm.

493. There are two modes of sowing by hand broadcast ; one is by *ridges* and *furrows* (see Par. 469), and the other is *by stakes.* A person can sow much more correctly by furrows and ridges, than he can by stakes, and can sow much faster, also, as it consumes much time in moving the stakes.

494. A good-sized bag, with one corner of the bottom tied to the mouth of it, hung over the shoulder, is about the most convenient thing to sow out of. Have grain at each end of the field, or if the field is not more than forty rods long, have the grain in the middle of it. Now, measure off half an acre, and calculate about how much you desire to sow on an acre. Sow handfuls of a given size while sowing the half acre, and if the proportion

15*   (351)

seems to be about right per acre, endeavor to take about so much at every handful.

495. Always throw grain as the opposite foot rises. If the foot on the same side with the hand that sows, rises as the hand throws the grain, a man will find it much more difficult to go forward. But if the *opposite* foot rises with the forward motion of the hand, the sower will move much easier than if he raises the foot on the same side of the hand that sows.

496. In sowing, either by furrows or stakes, always throw the grain *from* the margin of the field, because one can sow much more evenly up to the margin by throwing *away* from it, than he can to throw *towards* it. Let the grain slip off the ends of the fingers, and not *between* the thumb and fingers, nor *between* the fingers. Make calculations how wide to sow at *one through* or once across, and endeavor to give the grain such a cast that it will come down as evenly as possible.

497. In sowing by middle furrows and ridges, which, if the plowing has been done correctly, will be just twenty-two feet apart, I always sow just eleven feet to a *cast*. I can usually sow more evenly by walking about midway from each edge of the strip that I am sowing. It matters little where a sower walks, if he only distributes his grain evenly.

498. *Casting the grain all one way* is the most approved manner of sowing, with many farmers. When sowing is performed in this manner, some farmers *mark out* the ground with marks just eleven feet apart, and the sower travels in the marks ; and if he commences sowing east and west on the north margin of the field, he starts at the east end, travelling on the margin, and casts the grain to the south with his *right* hand, sowing up to the first mark. Now, when travelling to the east, he walks in the mark and casts his grain to the south with his *left* hand, and so on, until the entire field is finished.

499. Some farmers walk in the middle furrow, and cast the grain half way from the furrow to the ridge, and in returning *travel on the ridge*, and with the same hand cast the grain from the ridge, half way to the middle furrow, and then return on the

ridge, sowing with the same hand half way to the next middle furrow.

500. Some farmers sow from a basket suspended from their neck, walking in the middle of the strip to be sowed, and casting at every step, alternately, *with both hands.* I never could discover any advantage in this manner of sowing. Indeed, I do not approve of it, because it requires a long practice before a man can become an *ambidexter*—able to use both hands in sowing with equal facility. There are those who can sow very evenly with both hands, alternately, but if the sower is not exceedingly careful he will sow more unevenly in this manner than when he sows with only one hand.

SOWING BY STAKES.

501. When the ground is not prepared by furrows and ridges, nor by marks, (see Par. 498,) the idea is to sow by one or two rows of stakes, placed at a given distance. In sowing with *one* row of stakes, which should be not more than eight or ten rods apart, set a stake where you commence, twenty-two feet—or seven paces is my rule—from the margin of the plot to be sowed. Sow along the margin eight or ten rods, and plant another stake seven paces from the margin, and so on clear across the field. Now, in returning, sow from the row of stakes half-way to the margin of the field, or up to where it has been sowed. Now, set the *first stake* seven paces farther on, at the end where you first commenced, and sow up to the row of stakes. According to this mode the sower casts with only one hand in sowing both ways.

502. When *two* rows of stakes are used in sowing, they are placed eleven feet apart, or as far apart as the width of the strip, which is sowed at one through, and one row of stakes is carried by the other row, at every through or time across the field. Sowing with *two* rows of stakes consumes too much time in removing them. When a sower uses *two* rows of stakes, he usually walks between them; although some sowers choose to walk in the *line* of one row, and sow with the *right* hand when going one way, and with the *left* hand when going in the opposite direction.

503. Whatever the manner of sowing may be, the sower should endeavor to travel with an *even* step, and in a straight course, and not step sometimes three feet or more, and sometimes one foot or two feet, because any variation in the steps will tend to sow the grain unevenly. A sower who has long legs and takes long steps, is too apt to get over the ground so fast that he will not distribute a sufficient amount of seed, unless he has a very large hand. On the contrary, he whose legs are very short, and who takes short steps, if he has a large hand, is very liable to sow too thick. Most sowers are quite apt to scatter much grain in bunches and streaks, when they bring their hands back from the grain preparatory to casting it. The hand should grasp as much as is thought proper, and be brought back even with his side, as high as the hips, and extended the entire length, when the hand, in the act of casting the grain, should always move *horizontally*, and not rise nor fall, when in the act of sowing. (See Par. 496.) Beginners are very apt to cast their grain in streaks three or four times as thick along their tracks as it is a few feet distant. Some sowers give their grain an upward heave as they cast it, throwing so far that the courses will *overlap* each other several feet. This practice is not as good as it is to have the courses overlap a very little. When they overlap too much, the grain will be too uneven. A sower should not cast *too high* nor *too low*. If he casts *too high*, the grain will be too thin in the *middle* of the courses; and if he casts too *low*, the grain will be too thin at the *junction* of the courses. A sower who casts his grain low, if he casts it the most proper distance, will always sow more evenly than he who casts his grain very high; and this is more particularly true in

SOWING GRAIN WHEN THE WIND BLOWS.

504. No sower, however skillful, can sow grain evenly when the wind is blowing furiously, or hard enough to change the course of the grain as it is cast from his hands. If the wind

always blew steadily, a sower could make calculations how far the grain would be drifted, and could thus sow it tolerably even. But as the wind blows in sudden *gusts*, a sower may calculate how far to cast his handfuls, and may cast a number of them with all desirable precision, and in an instant a gust of wind would drift two or three handfuls in one place, leaving a space without a dozen kernels of grain on it. A sower can sow any kind of grain *with* the wind, far better than he can when he casts *towards* the wind, whether he travels with the wind blowing *in his face* or *against one side*. If grain *must* be sowed when the wind blows, I always endeavor to manage so as to sow *with the wind*, and never *against* it. One way is, to have all the grain on the *windward* side of the field and sow towards the *leeward* side, returning with empty vessel. Another way is, if the wind blows from the south, commence on the south side, and if the wind is north commence on the north side, and *cast the grain all to the south*. In travelling to the east on the north side, cast the grain with the *left* hand, and when going to the west, cast it with the *right* hand. (See Par. 498.) Let a sower do the best he can, if the wind blows very hard the grain will be very uneven.

MANNER OF GAUGING THE HANDFULS.

505. If it is at all difficult for the tyro to gauge his handfuls when he grasps a large or small quantity with all his fingers, he must try several expedients. Sometimes he must close the little finger only when taking a handful, and sometimes close both the second and third fingers also. Sometimes, in sowing buckwheat, or flax-seed, or any kind of seed, where but a small quantity to the acre is needed, some sowers hold a round stone with their third and fourth fingers. Some sowers grasp a large handful, and cast a small portion of it at every step, casting *both ways*, as the arm moves back and forth. But I could never recommend this mode of gauging the handfuls, because twice or thrice as much is apt to be cast at once as there should be; and sometimes as the sower empties his hand there will not be in it enough for half a cast. In gauging the handfuls when

506. The tyro would sow more evenly to hold a *round* ball of wood, as large as a hen's egg of ordinary size—not an ill-shapen polygon—in his hand, grasping the desired amount of seed with the thumb and fore finger. In sowing grass seed—not in the chaff—it is best to sow the field *both ways*, sowing half the desired amount each way. This is far better than to sow it all at one sowing, because it distributes it more evenly.

507. If the ridges and middle furrows are about forty-two feet, equidistant,—twenty-two feet from ridge to furrow,—it is better to sow such a strip at *five* throughs instead of four, as in sowing grain. In sowing grass seed by stakes, and especially very light grass seed, it is best to sow at one through only about eight and a half feet. Some farmers sow at one through twelve feet in width. But it is difficult to sow so wide a strip at one through without making balks.

THICK AND THIN SEEDING.

508. It seems hardly necessary to state, that if grain is sowed very thick on the ground, but little or no seed will be produced; and if it is sowed *too thin*, not so much grain will be produced as there would be if it were sowed thicker. There is little danger of getting grass seed of any kind too thick. Not half of our best farmers sow as much per acre, by one half or more, as would be most profitable. But there *is* danger of sowing grain too thick, and too thin also. Now if grain can be too thick and too thin, in order to produce the largest amount per acre there must be a *medium* quantity, which, if sowed, will produce more grain per acre than any other amount, either smaller or greater. The idea, then, is, to determine with any degree of certainty how much grain per acre, when evenly sowed, will produce the greatest amount of grain. There are very many collateral considerations which must not be disregarded in deciding how much grain to sow per acre. Different kinds of grain, in order to obtain the largest amount, require a different amount of seed per acre. Dif-

ferent soils, also, require a different amount of seed; and a different amount of the same kind of seed is very necessary in order to produce the greatest amount of grain per acre. Sometimes 60 lbs. of a given kind of winter wheat will produce only half as much as 60 lbs. of the same kind of wheat,—both kinds being of first quality,—if the kernels were large in the first, and half as large in the second mentioned. We have no *standard size* for the kernels of any kind of grain. If we had it would be an easy task to determine, with the greatest accuracy, how much grain of any kind we must sow in order to obtain the greatest amount per acre. Some grain tillers to a certain extent, if it is not sowed too thick. Therefore, if one hundred kernels of grain are sowed at such a distance apart that by *tillering* they will produce just six heads each, or six hundred heads; and if six hundred kernels are sowed in the same space of ground and do not tiller at all, the evidence cannot be gainsayed, that, although the first amount mentioned *may* be too small, six times that amount will be less profitable than the *first*, or an amount a *little* larger. One kernel of buckwheat or of flax-seed, when sowed alone, will usually produce more seed than half a dozen kernels, when sowed within the compass which is occupied by the one plant. Now the question arises, how may the tyro know, or be able to determine with tolerable certainty, how much to sow per acre in order to get the largest amount of grain. A will tell him so much, and B will say double that amount; while C will affirm that in both cases the amount is too small. They may all be correct, and under different circumstances all be very wrong.

509. In order to settle the point most satisfactorily, let a farmer measure off a number of plots of good soil, as nearly equal in every respect as practicable, and sow them all with the same kind of grain. Now in one acre of ground there are 43,560 square feet. One bushel of wheat weighs sixty lbs. Now we will have the plots for sowing wheat contain just one sixtieth of an acre; so that by sowing one pound on a plot it will be at the rate of one bushel per acre. One sixtieth of 43,560 is 726. Now a plot of ground twenty-seven feet square—*not twenty-seven*

square feet—is as nearly one sixtieth of an acre as we care to measure. Measure off five such plots. On the first sow one lb. of good wheat, and label it as sown at the rate of one bushel per acre. On the second sow two lbs., or one lb. and a half. On the third sow two, or two and a half lbs. On the fourth sow three, or three and a half lbs. On the fifth sow four lbs. Sow them all very evenly, having a space of a foot wide between each plot, and cover the seed with a hand-rake. At harvest, cut and weigh each plot separately, and note the result. Notice particularly the size of the kernels, and then make an estimate of how many kernels in a pound, &c., and the young farmer will have in his possession some valuable, tangible data, which will aid him in determining this point with more correctness than the *opinion* of all the best farmers in his vicinity.

510. In determining how many lbs. of oats to sow per acre, when the kernels are of a given size, and the soil of a given quality, as thirty-two lbs. constitute a statute bushel in the Empire State, measure off four or five plots, each plot containing one thirty-second part of an acre, which is $1,361\frac{1}{4}$ *square feet*,—not feet square,—equal to a plot forty-five feet and three inches long and thirty feet wide. One pound of oats evenly sowed on such a plot will be at the rate of one bushel per acre. Two lbs., at the rate of two bushels per acre. Two and a half lbs., at the rate of two and a half bushels per acre. Sow five plots in this manner, and note the result, as in Par. 509.

511. Forty-eight lbs. make a statute bushel of barley; and the size of the kernels varies as much as almost any other cereal grain. If the kernels are very large, it will be necessary to sow more pounds per acre than it would if they were only half as large. But in order to test the matter as directed in 509 and 510, 43,560 square feet in an acre divided by 48, the number of lbs. in a bushel, gives $907\frac{1}{4}$ square feet, which is equal to a plot of ground about $30\frac{1}{4}$ feet long and 30 feet wide. One lb. of barley sowed on this plot will be at the rate of one bushel per acre; two lbs., two bushels, &c.

512. On my soil I have been accustomed to sow not more than

three bushels of oats, two and a half to three of barley, and one and a half of wheat. When more than that amount of wheat is sowed it tillers but little, and the heads are very short, and the grain small. I have sowed at the rate of four or more bushels of oats per acre, and the straw was slender, the kernels small, and but a small number on each straw.

513. I am well satisfied, beyond a doubt, that it requires at least half a bushel of seed per acre *less* when it is drilled in than when it is sowed broadcast; and that I always obtain several bushels more per acre when the seed is put in with a drill than when it is sowed broadcast. When grain is drilled in, it is all covered of a uniform depth, and consequently it vegetates alike, and grows more uniformly and evenly, and stands more evenly on the ground. When grain is sowed broadcast, even with some machines, the grain in some places is scattered at the rate of four or five bushels per acre; while in other places, when the wind blows, the proportion is less than one bushel per acre. And more than this, some of the kernels are not covered at all, and some of them are covered two, three, and four inches deep; and a vast deal of it is covered so deep in mellow soil by the feet of the team that it never comes up at all; and much of it that does come up after a long time never amounts to anything at all but straw. The question now arises,

WHAT IS THE MOST PROPER DEPTH TO COVER SEEDS?

514. We all know that if seeds are covered so deep that all the substance of the kernel is exhausted in forming the roots and stems before it reaches the surface of the ground, the sprout must die. And we acknowledge also that if a kernel is not covered deep enough it does not flourish luxuriantly. That the depth at which seeds are covered materially influences the germination of them no one will deny. The shallower grain is covered, providing it is covered sufficiently deep to insure a healthy and good germination, the better it will be for the plant. Small seeds need only a light sprinkling of earth. If they are covered deep, if

they germinate at all there is not substance enough in them to push a stem to the surface of the soil, and of course they die. Oft-repeated experiments and extensive observation prove very conclusively that if our cereals are covered about two inches deep every good seed will germinate readily, and be as productive, and perhaps more so, than if covered at any other depth. As they are covered deeper than two inches, they are longer in coming to the surface of the ground. Grass seed vegetates better, and more of the seeds grow, if they are sowed after the last harrowing, or after the roller. When it is harrowed or rolled in, a good portion of it is covered so deep that it is forever lost. A good shower will cover grass-seed as deep as it ever needs to be covered.

> " Soon as the soil receives the fruitful seed,
> Make no delay, but cover it with speed."—VIRGIL.

ROLLING THE SOIL.

515. There are several objects in rolling the soil after it has been harrowed. One is, the pulverization of the lumps. The roots of grain seldom or never enter hard lumps of earth. Another is, to cover the grain that the harrow has failed to cover. This it does by mashing the lumps. Another object is, to form a smooth surface to work on, with mowers or reapers, cradles, scythes, or rakes, when cutting and securing a crop. Another is, to leave the *surface* of the soil as smooth as practicable, so that the next plowing may be neatly performed. Never roll up and down a slope, if a field can be rolled by going along the slope, because a heavy roller draws hard up a slope. I would as soon dispense with my harrow as with my land roller. I always entertained a poor opinion of small rollers, because they draw heavily, and are not as effective as a larger one in levelling the surface of the soil. Rollers usually cost too much. A common farmer in moderate circumstances, does not feel willing to expend thirty or forty dollars for a roller. Therefore, I will give directions to the young farmer, who is unwilling to pay four times as much as a good roller will cost,

516. That will do good service for an age, and be worth two small cast-iron rollers which will cost fifty dollars each. I have a roller which has run sixteen years, and rolled thousands of acres, and has not cost twenty-five cents for repairs, and which will be good for thirty years to come. It cost less than ten dollars for materials and labor, at cash prices. A roller should always be double, so as to turn more easily for a team. It should be not less than four feet in diameter—so as to be heavy and run easy—and about eight feet long. If a young farmer has sufficient ingenuity to make a neat "cider peg," he will be able to make a good roller. If he will keep it under shelter it may be made of elm, maple, beech, or any other hard wood. The axle of mine is sugar maple.

517. *Specifications.*—Fig. 146 represents the principal parts of a wooden roller; *a a* are the two end pieces of the frame, seven feet four inches long, and three by four inches square, framed to the front and rear girts, three by three, nine inches apart, with inch and a half tenons. The tongue is bolted to the forward girts, with whipple-trees on the *under* side. The girts are eight feet three inches between joints. *E* is the shaft, six inches square, of hard timber, seasoned, with four gains turned in it, *h*, four inches in diameter and three inches wide, and a bearing at each end three inches in diameter, to fit a hole in the wooden box *F* which is bolted to the under side of *a a*. From one bearing to the other, eight feet three inches. From bearing to first gain, three inches. Middle gains, six inches apart. Get it turned at the turning-shop, or machine shop. A turner will turn it in less than an hour; and it will cost not over thirty cents. *b* is one of the roller *heads*, in two parts, with a four-inch hole in the centre. They are made of plank three inches thick, forty-four inches in diameter, and united in the middle with four $1\frac{1}{2}$-inch dowel pins in each head. The pins must be of the best of timber, and well-seasoned, and must be *pinned* or nailed, to keep the heads from separating in case the dowel pins should shrink. After the frame is made and the shaft *E* fastened in its place,

place the ends of the frame *a a* on two benches, and put the
heads *b* in their places, and nail four small braces, *d d*, from the
shaft to the head, to hold it true as it revolves. Now, saw off

Fig. 146.

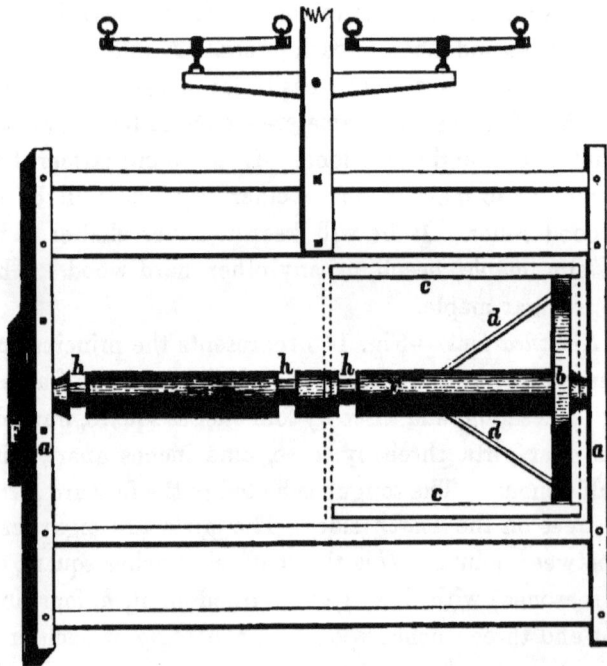

A LAND ROLLER FRAME.

the staves, *c c*, which are two inches thick, four inches wide, and
three feet eleven and a quarter inches long, and with a carpenter's
adz, dress the *inside* of each stave hollowing so as to fit the heads,
and nail them with forty-penny nails. If the staves are very
hard, bore holes for the nails. It is not important to have the
edges of staves bevelled very neatly. Some men never bevel
them at all. The shaft will wear three times as long if the
holes in the heads are *bushed* with thin band or hoop-iron, as
iron and wood will wear much longer than wood running in
wood. It is not necessary to have hoops to hold the staves.
Nail a piece of leather over the end bearings to keep the dirt

out of the boxes. Use soft grease instead of oil on the bearings. The two parts of the roller should be one inch and a half apart, as at the dotted lines, and should run as close to the *hind* girt as practicable, in order to scrape off any dirt that may adhere to it. But soil should never be rolled when it is wet enough to stick to the roller. It will require 192 feet for the heads, about 192 feet for the staves, about 50 feet for the frame, 27 feet for the shaft; tongue ten cents, turning thirty cents, eight pounds of nails thirty-six cents, eight carriage-bolts fifty cents, for bolting-tongue and bearing-boxes, and two and a half days' work, $3 13. Reconing the timber at one cent per foot, the cost of a good roller will not exceed 192+192+50+27+10+30+36+50+$3 13 =$9 00. Mechanics will scout at these figures, but I *know* that I can get up a roller according to these figures, and not lift a finger toward it. But those who would like a very neat and more expensive roller, should procure

GILES AND TOMPKINS' IMPROVED FIELD ROLLER.

Fig. 146½ represents a perspective view of a most superior

FIG. 146½.

GILES & TOMPKINS' IMPROVED FIELD ROLLER, WITH SEED AND PLASTER SOWER ATTACHED.

field roller with cover, and with grass seed and plaster-sower attached. They are manufactured by Herald & Tompkins, Trumansburg, Tompkins co., N. Y. The prices vary from $40 to $70. With cover to the roller, and box for holding stone when hauling them off the field, and with Seymour's grain-sowing attachment, for sowing all kinds of grass seed, and plaster, lime, ashes, and other kinds of fertilizers, the price is $70. They are made in a very neat and substantial manner, in two parts; and the manner of *hanging* them, and of attaching the staves to the heads, has been secured to them by letters patent. The heads are made of cast-iron, with a flange at the circumference of each head, which fits a gain in the ends of each stave, so that no bolts or nails are used in fastening the staves to the heads. There are cast-iron gudgeons bolted to the ends of the frame, which work in the hub of the cast-iron heads. An iron cross-bar passes between the two parts of the roller, and is bolted to the frame behind and before, and in the middle of the cross-bar are two gudgeons, which play in the centre of the middle heads. Those who desire a superior roller, will do well to confer with the manufacturers already alluded to. It weighs about eight hundred pounds, and can be loaded with stone to make it heavier if desired.

CHAPTER IX.

" The farmer's workshop now our notice claims ;
The work-bench, screw, the yawning jaws and planes,
Augers to bore, chisels to mortise, grinning saws
To cut and rip, hammers with potent claws ;
The shaving-knife, and set of bits and brace,
All well arranged, each in its proper place."

518. EVERY farmer needs a good workshop, where he can appropriate to some useful purpose his leisure days in winter, and stormy days at any season of the year; and every energetic and thoughtful farmer will have a shop, and will avail himself of the advantages and conveniences which a shop and a few tools afford. There are scores of farmers (and be it said to their shame) who squander away time enough in one season in loafing about places of public resort, to make all the harrows, gates, etc., that are needed on a small farm, and to do all repairing of implements, if they only had a bench and a few tools. Furthermore, it is a good *discipline* for any farmer to exercise his skill in the use of tools, and if a skillful and ingenious farmer will only become accustomed to repair his implements, if he prepares his timber for such purposes beforehand, he will have the satisfaction of knowing that, all things considered, his repairing is done better than he is accustomed to have it done by regular mechanics. The idea that farmers should have a set of tools, may appear somewhat ridiculous to many people, and mechanics will sometimes deride such a thought. But it is not to be expected that a farmer, unskilled in the mechanic arts, will be able to handle tools with all the facility and exactness of an expe-

(365)

rienced mechanic. Still, with a little practice, and with the instructions we shall impart, any one whose apprehensions are not too blunt, may do his own repairing of the common implements of the farm, and make many new tools in a neat and workmanlike manner. It is impossible to do a piece of work well without tools, and if the tyro has tools, and they are in good order, he will often do a piece of work infinitely better than he had ever thought it were possible for him to do it.

519. The Fig. 147, on the opposite page, represents in part one side of a farmer's workshop. It ought not to be smaller than sixteen by twenty-four feet. A larger shop than this is always convenient. There should be a window at each end of the bench on the same side of the shop, and the more windows there are on the other sides the better.

520. The bench should be not less than twelve feet long, and the front plank not less than three inches thick, of some hard wood. Two feet and six inches is wide enough for a bench for ordinary purposes. The height should be in proportion to the height of the man who works at it. The correct height is, just so a man can sit on it by standing on tip-toe. If it be too high, he cannot shove a plane easily, and if too low, he will be obliged to stoop too much.

521. The *jaws*, of which *a* is the movable one, and *b* the stationary one, should be made of hard timber, four by five inches square, and should extend *above* the bench six or seven inches, so that the shaving-knife can be used in dressing out timber. The bench-screw should work in a nut cut *in the jaw, b,* and should be above the bench rather than under it. There are several patent devices for keeping the jaws parallel with each other, when holding a stick of timber, but the one shown in the figure is the cheapest, and good enough for any one. The ends of the jaws should be mounted with cast-iron flanges, as shown in the engraving, fitted neatly to the jaws.

522. *c* is a rest, which may be placed in any of the holes in the bench, for the purpose of supporting one end of anything that may be held in the vise when dressing it out.

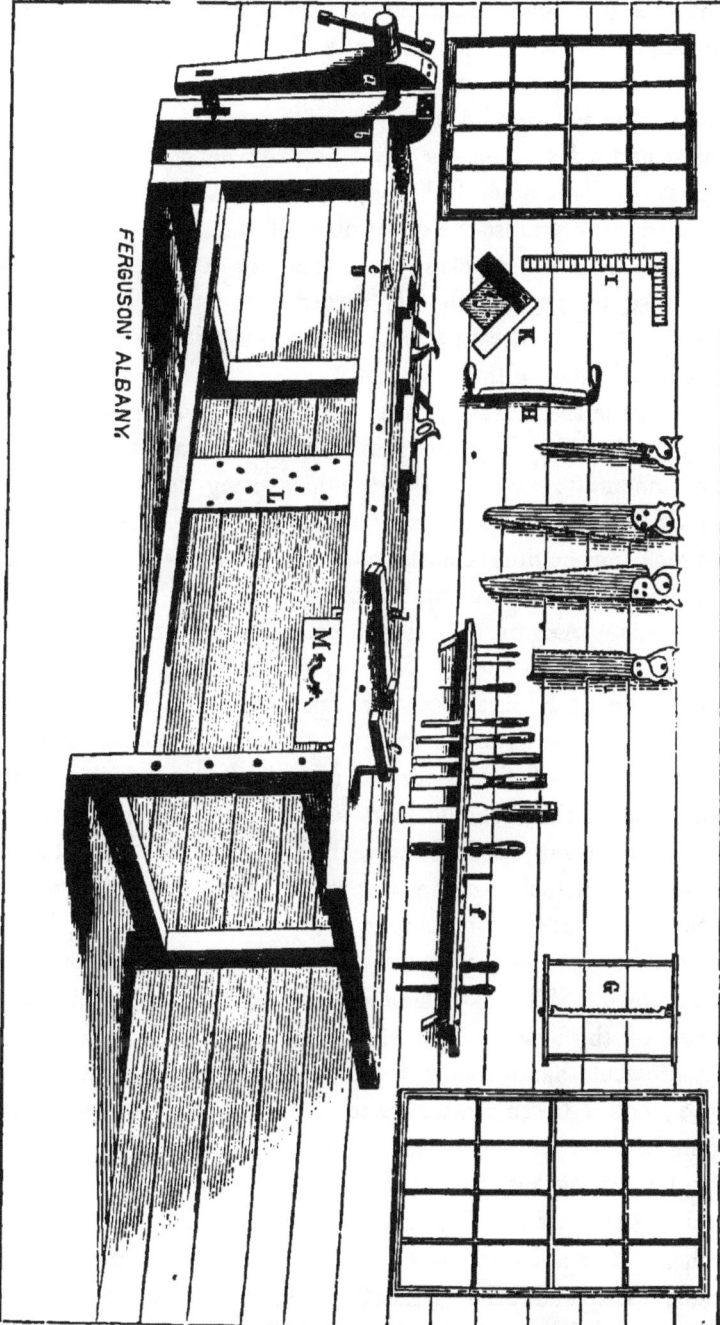

FERGUSON' ALBANY

FIG. 147.—A FARMER'S WORK-BENCH.

16

523. *L* is a board made to slide in a groove in the frame of
the bench, and a pin is put in any of the holes in it, to support
one end of a board when jointing the edges.

524. *d* is a "grab-hook," made of a piece of wood two inches
square and a foot long, for laying on the bench, with one notch
against the front side of the bench, and whatever is to be sawed
is placed on it against the other hook of it.

525. *c* is a dog or plane-hook, made of an old steel file, and
teeth filed in the end that is turned over for holding anything
that is to be planed. It should fit so tightly in the bench that it
must be adjusted with a hammer.

526. *H* is the shaving-knife, which should hang on a wooden
pin, opposite the jaws, so that standing on either side of the
jaws one may reach it. *I* is the measuring carpenter's square,
and *K* is the *try-square*, hanging on a square block. *f* is the
tool-rack, for holding chisels, bits, &c., which is a kind of shelf
with holes in it for holding them. The brace should hang close
to the bits. Augers should hang at the front end of the bench,
on the side of the shop. They should not hang all together, so
as to touch each other, lest the lips become injured and dulled
by knocking one against another. The framing chisels should all
be at one end of the tool-rack, and the firming chisels next to
them. Each chisel should have its place, and so should each bit
and screw-driver ; and the tyro should adopt the plan *at once* of
putting every tool back in its proper place when he is working
at the bench, even if he uses it every two minutes. It is a bad
habit to lay bits on the bench because they are to be used again
in a moment. The saws should hang on wooden pins about the
middle of the bench. The slitting-saw, the back or tenon saw,
the crosscut hand-saw, and compass-saw, should each have its
place ; and if taken down only to cut off a stick, let it be hung up
again at once, and never laid down on the bench. *c* is a felloe-
saw, for sawing out circular work, and at one end is a stirrup for
straining the saw, having a nut and screw on the outside of the
frame. *M* is a drawer with apartments in it for screws, cotters,
brads, nails, and other trinkets. Let the mallet be hung up

under the saws, near the chisels. Other tools which it is not necessary to enumerate, should have a place on a shelf or in a closet. If one has an *iron* vise, it should be attached to a bench on the other side of the shop, because it would be very much in the way on one end of the work-bench when planing a long board. A large, heavy piece of cast-iron will answer for an anvil. The planes should be placed opposite the plane-dog, *e*, and the ends should rest on a couple of strips nailed across the bench, so that when they are set on the bench the edges of the plane irons will not be dulled against any grit which may be on the bench. Iron chips, and iron filings, and all such substances, should be brushed from the bench so that edge tools will not get dulled on them. Remember, that it is the most skillful part of a trade to put tools in order, and to *keep* them in order. It is bad policy to work with dull tools.

EDGE TOOLS.

And now we speak of edge-tools long and slim,
With edges straight, or curved, or thick, or thin ;
Of furbished knives to cut, and rip, and shave ;
Of piercing forms to separate and cleave ;
Of tiny needles, awls with double edge,
And other forms that sunder like the wedge.

527. Every instrument that has a cutting edge, whether it is formed for *piercing* substances, for shaving off the surface piece-meal, or for cutting them in *two*, operates like a wedge. Pocket-knives, cambric needles, grass scythes, and shears of all kinds, are *wedges;* and their efficiency usually depends on the *completeness of the cutting edge*, and on the *acuteness or obtuseness of the angle with which they are formed*, and on the *trueness* and *smoothness of their surfaces*. (See WEDGES, Par. 344.)

528. Mathematically speaking, a perfect edge in any tool is an absolute impossibility. The finest and keenest edge that can be produced on the very best razor, when viewed through a micro-

scope appears full of *serrature*—more like the edge of a huge saw
than a razor. So with the finest cambric needle, whose point is
as delicate as it can be made, when viewed through a microscope
the point appears like a blunt, dull crowbar. When we attempt
to cut a very fine hair with a very sharp razor, by holding the
hair between the thumb and finger, with one end of the hair hanging free, we can perceive the serrature by the slipping or jerking
of the hair from one to another.. In the sickle the serrature may
be seen with the naked eye. In a scythe, and in many other
tools, we can *feel* them by drawing a finger along the edge, when
the tool has a good edge. When a grass scythe is in good order
the serrations are not as fine as they can be made, because if they
were the scythe would not be most effective. (See PUTTING
SCYTHES IN ORDER, 551.)

529. Why may we not make a razor, or a knife blade, or any
other cutting instrument, out of a piece of cast or wrought iron?
Why can we not make a needle or an awl out of a piece of wire?
Because there is not sufficient *firmness* and solidity between the
particles of such materials to retain their shape and position when
brought in contact with other substances. We have seen (see
WEDGES, Par. 344) that a piece of very tough and hard wood
always makes the best wedges. This holds good in respect to
edge tools : the cutting edge must be made of such material as is
capable of being made not only *hard*, but *tough and hard*. If
iron that is capable of being made very hard would make the
best edge tools, there would be nothing better than good cast-
iron ; because that can be made as hard as we can desire. But
such iron possesses no more tenacity than glass, and of course is
unfit for edge tools. If an edge tool were made of the very
toughest iron, it might appear to the naked eye to possess all the
qualities of a very effective tool. But when brought into use,
the edge would readily yield by bending and turning every way,
because the cutting edge lacks *firmness* and *hardness* in addition
to its *toughness*. And, more than these qualities already mentioned, the serrations of the cutting edge of a tool made of either
wrought or cast-iron would be very coarse; and if they possessed

tenacity and hardness they would lack a very important quality —*fineness of particle.*

530. Now good steel possesses every desirable quality for making the best of edge tools. It possesses *refinement* of particles, and is capable of being made very hard and brittle, as glass, or tough and soft, as wrought iron; or any degree of hardness and tenacity combined, from its softest to its hardest condition, may easily be secured. Many kinds of tools are made wholly of steel; and some are made of a part iron, and faced with steel; and some are made of entire steel, excepting the shank or the eye.

531. Framing chisels, for example, are made with the whole face steel and the back iron; but *firming* chisels are usually all steel. Large, heavy tools, the edges of which are bevelled only on one side, are made with a steel face, for the sake of economy in the cost of tools, and are just as good, and sometimes better, than if they were all steel. The cutting edge of an axe, or a pick, or crowbar, or any other tool the edge of which is bevelled on *both sides*, must be all steel for a few inches back of the cutting edge. Large knives for some kinds of straw-cutters, shingle-machines, and such like, the edges of which are bevelled only on *one* side, are just as good, and much cheaper, by having their faces laid with a thin plate of steel. When it is desirable to have tools of a given size, they should always be forged a very little larger, wider, and thicker than it is necessary to have them, so that there will be room or space for finishing them up well. The forging should be done as true and smooth as practicable, and the tools partly ground or filed off a little, and then tempered.

TEMPERING EDGE-TOOLS.

" The tempered metals clash, and yield a silver sound."—DRYDEN.

532. Tempering edge tools is the art of giving them a certain degree of hardness. If a tool be made of the *very best* of steel, and has not the correct temper, it is in one respect no better than if it were made of steel of a very inferior quality. It requires the exercise of much skill and wisdom to temper tools right. A man

may be able to forge and finish up edge tools in the neatest manner, and be incompetent to temper them well. This is an art which is acquired by the exercise of mechanical skill, and long experience. A workman may "*hit*" upon the right temper in one tool, and then, if he is not a natural mechanic, and if his observation be not very close, and perception very quick and keen, he may fail to get the correct temper in tempering a score of tools exactly like the one he had tempered so well. The idea to be kept in mind in tempering edge tools is, to have the *whole steel* tempered so as to make a good cutting edge as the edge wears away. Tools are tempered many times so that the cutting edge is first-rate until one-fourth of an inch or so is worn off, and then they become poorer and poorer as the edge is worn away, when they are worthless until they are re-tempered. And many times the *first edge* of a tool is very poor; but after it has been ground two or three times the edge will continue to grow better until it is worn out. But if a tool is tempered as it should be, it will hold as good an edge when it is half worn out as it did when it was new.

533. When a piece of steel is heated to redness, and immediately plunged into cold water, it is rendered as hard as it can be made, and as brittle as a file, which possesses no tenacity. When steel is heated to certain different degrees it emits different colors, each color corresponding to the different degrees of heat. For example: if we heat the end of a steel bar, or chisel which has good steel on the end, to redness, and thrust the end into cold water and cool it for an inch or two from the end, if the steel is not rusty, by looking attentively at the steel between the hot and the cold steel we shall discover several colors. As the cold steel is being heated up, a kind of *greyish* color will be perceived, and a little farther towards the hot part of the tool the steel will assume a kind of *straw* color; and between this color and the hot portion the steel will assume a *sky-blue* color. Now when all these colors are discovered in ordinary steel, if the whole were plunged into cold water and cooled, those parts of the tool which presented different colors would possess different degrees

of *hardness.* If the cutting edge of the tool were formed in that part which presented a *greyish-white* color, it would be so hard that it would not retain a cutting edge, either for cutting iron or wood. Now if this hard or grey portion of the tool were ground off until the cutting edge is formed in that part which was of a *straw* color, the cutting edge would usually be *hard and tough,* suitable for cutting iron. Now grind off all the straw-colored portion, so that the cutting edge will be in the *sky-blue* part, and in good steel we would have an edge most suitable for cutting wood. Now the idea always is, if we know about how hard it is desired to have the steel of which tools are made, we have only to heat the whole tool to such a degree of heat and plunge it into cold water, when the entire steel will possess a given degree of hardness. Sometimes one kind of steel must necessarily be made a little harder than another kind, for the same purpose; and sometimes the steel of which a tool is made is of such an inferior quality that it is *impossible* to give it such a temper as will retain a good cutting edge. Tools are sometimes heated to redness, and plunged into cold water and partially cooled, and then heated in the fire until they exhibit the desired color, when they are plunged into the water and cooled. Large tools, such as saws, scythes, &c., are heated in large ovens to a given degree of heat, when they are slipped instantaneously into a large tank of oil or water to cool them.

534. Different steel requires different degrees of heat. Now, when the young farmer has an axe *jumped,* or a pick repaired, he should tell the workman to remember and *note the color* or degree of heat at which the edge was tempered, and if the edge upon trial proves to be *too hard* or *too soft,* if he is a skillful workman he will be able the *second time* to temper the edge of the desired *hardness* and *toughness.* I find that almost all kinds of edge tools as the cutting edge is worn off become *softer,* and will not retain an edge well. I heat such tools in a *charcoal*—not mineral coal—fire to redness; and cool about two inches of the cutting edge, and then if it is desired to have a *cold-chisel* edge, cool it just as the straw-color begins to appear at the edge. If for cut-

ting wood, cool it just as the *sky-blue* begins to cover the end. Should it be too hard or too soft, try again. Great care should be exercised in heating the steel, not to get it *too hot*. Steel is often injured very materially by being heated to a *white heat;* and sometimes if steel is heated a little too hot, it is spoiled completely for good edge tools.

535. If a farmer has many tools to be tempered, whoever tempers them should use *charcoal* instead of mineral coal for heating the steel, because with *charcoal*, steel is heated more gradually and uniformly *entirely through it;* whereas, the heat of mineral coal fire being so *intense*, the steel is heated too hot at the *surface before* it is sufficiently heated in the middle. Consequently, it is quite liable to be injured or "burned" by too intense heat. No good manufacturer of edge tools will work in mineral coal fire: he will use *charcoal*.

536. Our common blacksmiths usually work in mineral coal fire, and they seldom get half as good temper in drills, picks, and such like, because it is impossible to do it without charcoal. I can always obtain a better temper in small tools by heating them in a common stove, than our ordinary blacksmiths can in a fire of mineral coal.—Although *grinding* tools is the next operation after tempering them, it is necessary to have the grindstone in good order first. Therefore, although rather out of place, I shall notice here

THE GRINDSTONE.

" Noiselessly the grindstone's standing
In the willow's cooling shade ;
O'er it now no workman 's bending,
Grinding up his tempered blade.
Faithful grindstone ! useful grindstone !
Who does not thy service prize."—EDWARDS.

537. Allow me to see a farmer's grindstone, and I will not ask to see *him*, nor his *tools*, nor his *farm*, nor his *gates*, nor his *fences;* and I will "*grind out*" for you his traits of character with infallible certainty. If it is "as hard as a nether mill-stone," and hung upon a wooden crank, and supported by a couple of old

rails set against the fence, or on two stakes driven into the
ground, and bobs up and down, and wabbles sideways when
revolving, like an old rickety, "drunken" carriage-wheel, and
utters a mournful squeak, which sounds like the last requiem of
an old dilapidated New England ox-cart, he may be set down as
a slack, unskillful, unsuccessful, thriftless, penny-wise-and-pound-
foolish sort of a nonentity, who does not take an agricultural
journal; and who always performs every job just as if he felt
that his time was consumed to no good purpose, and his money
thrown away.   On the contrary, if the grindstone is a good one,
and neatly hung, we may rest assured that its proprietor will
eventually distinguish himself in the world—if he has not already
done so—as a thorough, successful and worthy citizen.   The
grindstone is the most useful implement among all the tools of
the farm.   How shall we put all our tools in order without a
good grindstone?   Therefore, because of its great utility and
efficiency, it must of necessity be *itself* a good one, and be in
good order.

HOW TO SELECT A GOOD GRINDSTONE.

538. A good grindstone should not be *too hard* nor *too soft*.
If it is *too hard*, it will require a long time to grind a tool; and if
it is *too soft*, itself will wear out much more rapidly than it will
grind a tool.   For ordinary tools, the grit should not be too
coarse nor too fine.   Very coarse stones are used for grinding
heavy tools with coarse edges.   (See GRINDING TOOLS, Par.
548.)   Grindstones often are full of *hard spots* and *hard streaks*.
Therefore, the young farmer should always purchase a grindstone
on trial, and if it should be found to have no hard streaks or
spots in it, if the grit is about right, it will doubtless prove to be
a good stone.   Select one for ordinary use, which weighs about
two hundred pounds.   It is impracticable to grind tools well on
a stone that is full of hard spots or streaks.   Small ones may be
cut out with a cold-chisel, but as a general rule it is best to reject
every stone that has hard spots in it.

16*

HANGING THE GRINDSTONE.

539. In order to be able to grind tools well, the stone must run as true, both on the *sides* and *edge*, as a circular saw. It is as impracticable to grind tools properly on a stone that *wabbles*, and *bobs up and down*, as it would be for a miller to grind grain well with the mill-stones in bad order, or not balanced correctly. Many a good grass scythe or cradle scythe has been condemned and returned to the manufacturer as not having a good temper, simply because it could not be properly ground on that miserable apology for a grindstone.

540. There are various modes of hanging a grindstone true, but I shall notice in this place only one of them. Grindstones will often wear away on one side much faster than on the other side. In such a case, if the stone is *wedged* on with wooden wedges, it must be *un*hung, and *re*hung in order to make it run true. But

FIG. 148.

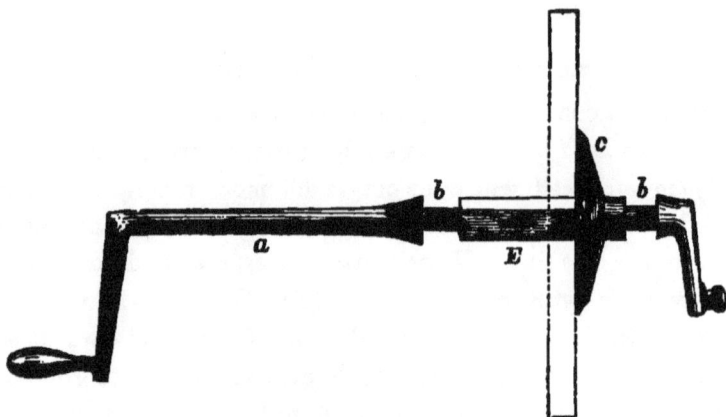

AN IMPROVED GRINDSTONE SHAFT.

if it is hung on a shaft with *collars*, as a circular saw is hung, it will require but a few moments to *un*hang it, and *re*hang it. There are grindstone shafts for sale, fitted up like the journals of circular saws, with collars and a nut to fasten the stone. But they cost several dollars, and are no better than the style of shafts represented by Fig. 148. *a* is the shaft, not less than three feet long, with a crank at each end of it, and the bearings, *b b*, 1½ inches in diameter and three inches long, turned smooth, with a collar, *c*, six or eight inches in diameter, *cast* with the shaft having a square key-hole through it at *E*. Put the shaft in the eye of the stone, as shown by the dotted lines, against the stationary collar, *c*, and put a *loose* collar like *c* on the opposite side of the stone, and drive in the key a little. Place the shaft on the frame, and if it does not revolve true on the side, adjust it with a few thicknesses of paper, or with a piece of thin leather. The shaft should be smaller than the eye in the stone, so that it can be made to run true on the *edge*. If the stone is too thin for the space between the collars, put in a thin piece of board. Drive with a hammer, on the stationary collar to the right or left, and not on the surface of the stone, when adjusting it to run true on the circumference. With such a shaft a grindstone can be well hung in fifteen minutes. Do not drive in the key too hard, because it requires but little to hold a stone. If the shaft of a grindstone is short, the crank is always in the way when grinding the knives on cutter-bars, grass scythes, axes, &c.

541. Fig. 149 represents a grindstone complete, running on friction rollers; although if the bearings of the shaft are neatly polished it is a matter of indifference whether there are any friction rollers or not, because there will be so *little* friction at the bearings that there will be no perceptible difference in the running of the stone. The bearings of my grindstone run in *lead* boxes, (see FITTING UP MACHINERY, in next vol.,) and I would not exchange them for friction rollers. *a* is the frame, made of 3x3 scantling. *b* is the water-trough, which should be well smeared on the inside with coal tar. *c* is the treadle, by which the grindstone is turned by the foot. *d* is the dash, to protect the workman from water. I sometimes place a board on each side of the stone, to turn the water into the trough when grinding. When a stone revolves so rapidly that it will throw all the water from the trough, a vessel containing water may be suspended above it, and a small hole

FIG. 149.

A GRINDSTONE WITH CLAMP FOR HOLDING TOOLS WHILE GRINDING THEM.

made near the bottom of it with an *awl*, so that the water will drop just fast enough to keep the stone wet.

542. Grindstones should always be *protected* from the influences of the weather, and especially from the rays of the summer's sun. Sometimes the sun will affect them so as to render them *very hard ;* and sometimes the rain, frost and sunshine will *check* them, or cause them to crumble. In order to grind edge tools correctly, the workman should understand very well the difference between a

CRUSHING STROKE, AND A DRAWING OR SLIDING STROKE.

543. Edge tools of every description operate most effectively by being *drawn diagonally* as they enter the materials to be cut ; and any substance can be cut with far less force when the cutting instrument is made to operate in a *diagonal* direction than if it were forced square through it. When a cutting instrument is forced straight into or through any substance, it is said to have a *crushing stroke ;* and when the cutting edge is made to enter, and

to slide along as it enters, the stroke is called a *sliding*, or a *drawing* stroke. The stroke of an axe is a *crushing* stroke. A chisel in mortising, an auger in boring, and a plane in planing, have a *crushing* stroke. A sickle, a grass scythe and cradle scythe, have a *drawing* stroke. (See SHARPENING GRASS SCYTHES, 551.) A shaving knife, a pocket knife, a razor, and many other instruments, are used with either a *crushing* stroke or a *drawing* stroke. When an edge tool is used with a *crushing* stroke, no matter what the substance to be cut may be, the cutting edge should be whetted on a whetstone that will produce as fine an edge as possible. An edge tool that has a coarse edge re-quires the exercise of much more force in working it than if it had a very fine edge. A first-rate chisel will not work at all well in mortising dry, soft timber, when the edge is coarse. But give the same chisel a fine edge and it will shave like a razor. It is impossible to make a good plane-iron work well in planing when it has a *coarse* edge; but give it a *fine* edge and one can shove it in very hard wood with ease. For cutting wood with any instrument, having either a drawing or crushing stroke, and for cutting any kind of metal, either with a drill, or turning it with any kind of chisel, or for planing it, the cutting edge should be whet on an oil-stone having very fine grit. The cutters of mowers and reapers usually operate with a *crushing* stroke; and they require a very fine edge in order to have them work with the least amount of force. Edge tools that are used with a *draw-ing* stroke for cutting such substances as cornstalks, operate much more effectively with a *coarse* edge than if it were *very fine*. A very fine edge on a sickle would require the exercise of *double* the strength that a *coarse* edge requires. But any edge tool for cutting wood having the serrature of the edge as coarse as the edge of a sickle, would require more than twice the amount of power to work it that would be necessary if the edge were very fine.

544. Straw-cutters, and some kinds of shingle machines, the knives of which are attached to a gate, are made to cut with a *sliding* stroke by having the gate work *diagonally* instead of

playing straight up and down. A very little slide or draw when an instrument is cutting, often gives it more efficiency than we are wont to suppose.

545. When a young lad begins to whittle, he very soon learns, without any instruction, to give the knife blade a *diagonal* motion across the stick. In using a drawing knife a workman soon learns, when shaving a hard stick, to draw the knife *across* the stick, as he draws it towards him. A man may clasp the edge of a sharp tool or razor very firmly and it will not cut his hand, but *draw* the instrument or hand a very little, and with one-fourth the pressure the edge will enter readily. When a young man first begins to pass the razor over his face, he often finds that even with a good razor he is not able to cut his down-like beard unless he *draws* his razor; and even then some of it is so very slim and limsy—like the down on a young gosling—that it will *slip between* the serrature of the edge. (See PUTTING RAZORS IN ORDER, 550.)

546. In trimming fruit-trees, or shrubs, or hedges, if the cutting instrument makes a *crushing* cut, more than *twice* the force is required in cutting off a small branch than is necessary when it is cut with a *sliding* stroke. And more than this, the work is much better, and more neatly performed, if the cut is *sliding*.

547. *Pruning shears*, represented at Fig. 150, by having a slot

FIG. 150.

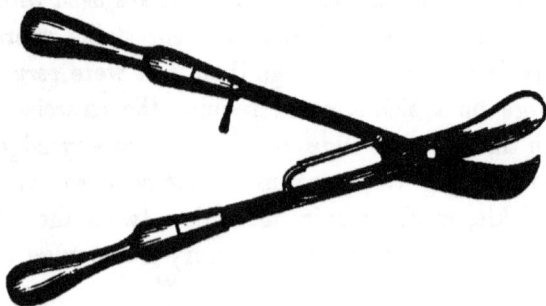

SLIDING-CUT PRUNING SHEARS.

in one of the blades, so that the centre-pin will move easily back and forth in it, make a *sliding* cut when cutting off branches, or the long hoofs of sheep. Common shears make a *crushing* cut; but when this kind of shears is opened, the connecting rod, in closing them, slides one blade along, so that the centre is at the other end of the slot. They can be obtained at Allen's Agricultural Warehouse, 89 Water street, N. Y. city.

GRINDING EDGE TOOLS.

" The flashing knives upon the grinding disk
Are held, with grating and discordant sound."—T. B. READ.

548. The young farmer doubtless understands that the process of grinding and whetting tools is performed very similar to reducing the thickness of a board, by planing it with a gouge-shaped plane. The grit of the stone enters the steel, and scratches numerous little furrows in it, removing the metal as soon as it is cut loose. If the grit is *coarse*, the scratches will be much *deeper* and *wider*, and farther apart than if the grit is fine. If the scratches extend to the cutting edge of the tool, the edge will be full of serrature, coarse or fine, corresponding with the grit of the stone. If the scratches are made at a *right angle* with the cutting edge, the serrature will stand at a right angle also. But if the tool when grinding is held in such a position that the scratches are made at *different angles*, the serrature will be *hooked*, or stand at the same angle with the scratches on the sides of the tool. Now, when a tool is designed for cutting wood or iron, or any other kind of hard substances, it is best to grind it and whet it while it is held in such a position, that the scratches and serrature will stand at a right angle with the cutting edge, whether the tool makes a *crushing* cut or *drawing* cut. But when a tool is designed for cutting soft, spongy substances, and is used with a *draw* cut, it should be ground and whet so that the serrature will stand at an *acute* angle, or be "*hooked.*"

549. Let a *case-knife* be ground so that the scratches will be at an angle of forty-five degrees towards the handle, and let it be whet by drawing it on a fine-gritted stone, from heel to point *across* the stone, and attempt to cut a loaf of soft bread with it by drawing the knife *towards* you, and if the knife is a good one

soft bread can be cut *neatly*, which could *not* be cut with a *crushing* cut.

550. *Sharpening razors* is a job which every man ought to understand. If a man's beard is very fine, and the serrature of his razor almost as coarse as his beard, the serrature will *jerk* from beard to beard, and "*pull hair*" intolerably hard. If a razor is very dull, draw it fifty times or so on a very fine-gritted oil-stone, from heel to point *across* the stone, with sweet oil on it, (see Par. 565,) and then *strap* it on a razor-strap which has three or four sides, each being a little finer gritted. There is grit in wood and in leather. The idea is to make the serrature as fine as possible. Then, as the beard is composed of the same substance as our finger nails, by *wetting* it *thoroughly*, and by having a thick lather to hold the ends of the beard from vibrating, and by shaving with a *drawing* cut, any bachelor whose face is tolerably plump, will be able to shave his beard so closely and smoothly, that the fair, soft cheek of the belle of the town, when cheek to jole, would not recoil on account of the "prickers." It will not dull a razor half as much to cut *wet* beard as it does to cut *dry* beard.

GRINDING GRASS SCYTHES AND CRADLE SCYTHES.

"They sharp their blades with many a shrill che-whet."—READ.

551. When scythes are handled most correctly, they make a *sliding* cut; therefore, in order to have them "take hold" of the grass or straw, the serrature of the edge should stand *towards* the point, or in an opposite direction from the serrature of a grain sickle, which stand *towards the handle.* Now, in order to have the serrature all standing at the proper angle, and hooked *towards the point,* both sides of the blade must be *ground* and *whet,* so that all the scratches will be *diagonally* across the basil of the blade, from heel to point, as represented by Fig. 151, which exhibits a microscopic view of a well-ground scythe.

552. Now, with one hand holding the *heel* of the scythe *firmly,* so that it cannot *rock* either way, and with the other

hand towards the point, hold the scythe on the grindstone, with the edge *towards* you, so that the scratches of the grindstone will be at about an angle of forty-five degrees with the cutting edge, as shown in the figure. Move the scythe gradually from heel to point when grinding, and grind clear to the point *at just*

FIG. 151.

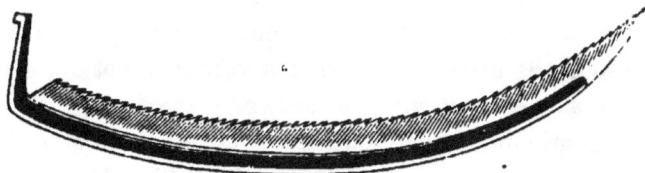

A MICROSCOPIC VIEW OF THE EDGE OF A SCYTHE IN GOOD ORDER.

such an angle. After grinding one side in part, remain in the same position, and turn the scythe over, taking the heel of it in the other hand, and grind that side at the same angle *clear to the point.* Grind no more on one side of a *scythe* than on the other.

553. Always hold a scythe so that the stone will revolve *towards* the edge, and never *from* it; because, when a stone revolves *towards* the edge, it cuts the steel smooth and clean entirely to the edge, and a workman can see distinctly when a tool is *ground up to a good edge.* But when a stone revolves *from* the edge, if a tool is not *very hard,* the steel will not be swept clean from the edge, but a very thin stratum of it will hang to the edge, sometimes more than a sixteenth of an inch wide, which will all come off when the tool is whet. And besides, when grinding a very wide cradle-scythe, it is almost impossible to grind it in a proper manner, if the grindstone revolves in the direction from the *back* to the *cutting edge.* Let a workman of but little experience grind up a new cradle-scythe by grinding *from* the edge, and if he does not grind it so thin as to spoil it, he will be an exception to the general rule.

554. I once had a young man in my employ who knew far more than I about grinding up new scythes, who ground *from* the edge, and reduced the basil of the scythe so thin for half an inch *back* of the cutting edge, that it would not retain an edge

to cut grain one rod, but would *crumble* like a thin plate of cast-iron.   No *good* scythe will retain a good edge for any reasonable length of time if it is ground *too thin*.

555. If a scythe is ground *square across* the basil, the serrature will stand at a *right angle* with the cutting edge ; and a workman will be obliged to exert more force when using it to make it cut well.   If the scythe is ground so that the scratches on the basil and the serrature are made in the *opposite* direction from those in the preceding figure, a scythe will not cut grass or grain near as well as if made as shown in the figure.   A workman, when grinding a scythe, should avoid *rolling* and *rocking* a scythe on the stone, because such a motion will make the surface of the basil *circular* or *convex*, and the cutting edge will be very blunt.   Avoid also letting the grindstone *catch* the edge, as it will round it off so much that a rifle or rubstone will not touch the edge.

556. *Whetting scythes* requires more judgment and skill than to whet a razor.   To whet a scythe correctly, set it up before you on the small end of the snath, and move the rifle from heel to point *slowly* and alternately on each side of the scythe, drawing the hand *downwards* as it is thrust forward, so as to make *very fine* scratches on the basil, in the same direction of those which are made by the grindstone.   Stop the rifle suddenly and see if you do not whet *too rounding* on one or both sides.   No scythe will cut well if it is whet too rounding or blunt.   The idea is, to hold the rifle in such a position that it will sharpen the cutting edge, and *lie flat on the basil* when it is on either side of the scythe. If a rifle is not held in a correct position, the more a laborer whets his scythe the worse he makes it.   Boys, and some men, too, when whetting their scythes, will *thwack away* with all their might, sometimes hitting the *back* of the scythe, and sometimes making a very rounding stroke on the *edge*, and sometimes the rifle will not touch the edge on *either* side, and sometimes a careless stroke *backwards* will remove more good edge than can be restored by whetting half an hour.

557. More good scythes are *spoiled* and *worn out*, and rendered

useless by improper grinding and careless whetting, than by all the grass and grain which they cut. Let a man who understands well how to grind and to whet scythes, have a good scythe, and he will wear it out by cutting grain or grass, and not *by whetting* it. Good scythes, when properly ground, do not need to be whet every ten rods. When I see laborers whetting their scythes at every ten rods, the conclusion is a *correct* one, that they have *poor scythes*, or that they do not know how *to whet* them correctly, or that they prefer "to stop and whet" to *using* them. I have often cut around a ten-acre field without whetting my scythe; and I always observed, even when I was in my teens, when mowing or cradling with a lot of hands, that they could not cut as far as I did without whetting, and cut it well.

558. Different scythes require rifles and rubstones of different grit. Sometimes a *new* rifle will produce *too coarse a serrature* on the edge, and sometimes a new rifle will produce an edge which a rubstone or *old* rifle will not. And sometimes an old rifle which is about worn out, will give a scythe a keener edge than anything else. If a scythe is rather soft, keep rubstones and coarse rifles off it, and use some old rifle nearly worn out. The grit of both rifles and rubstones should be very fine, in order to form a keen edge.

CLAMPS FOR HOLDING EDGE TOOLS WHILE GRINDING THEM.

559. At edge-tool manufactories, different styles of clamps are used for holding edge tools on the grindstone, so that a workman can grind the basil of any tool very true at any desired angle, by the application of a little strength. But common farmers do not always feel willing to expend several dollars for a clamp which they will not use but a few times in a year. Every one who has ever ground many tools, knows that it is a very difficult and laborious job to grind up some kinds of tools while holding them with the hands alone.

560. To facilitate the grinding of small edge tools, like knives of straw-cutters, or any knives which are difficult to hold in the hand, I have been accustomed to use a very cheap but efficient

clamp, shown at Fig. 149. *E* is a board ten inches wide, bolted to the frame *a*, with the bolts put through slots or mortises in *E*, so that it may be raised or slid along to the right or left. *F* is a square stick fitted to a mortise in *E*, and extending from *E* across the grindstone. With wood-screws or small iron bolts, fasten a straw-cutter knife to the under side of the handle *F*, and place it on the grindstone with the handle in the mortise *E*, and adjust the board *E* so that the knife will rest on the stone at the desired angle, and fasten *E* with the bolts. As the grindstone revolves, slide the knife across the stone back and forth by taking hold of *F*. The handle may be four or five feet long, and if it fits the mortise well, a knife can be ground as true as is practicable with any other clamp. With only one hand a man can set a span of horses with ease.

THE MOST PROPER ANGLE FOR THE BASIL OF TOOLS

561. Is a subject in relation to which the opinions of all good mechanics coincide very well. The more acute the angle of the basil is, the less will be the force required to make it cut. But when tools are used for *prying* as well as for cutting, the angle of the basil must be more *obtuse* than if the tool is designed simply for cutting. The angle of the basil of a scythe is usually about five degrees—very acute.

562. Fig. 152 represents a side view of a cold-chisel, which every farmer needs. If no old file is at hand, purchase a piece of octagonal steel, and have one end forged like the figure, and tempered, and then grind the edge on both sides, as shown in the figure, at an angle of about twenty-five degrees.

563. Framing chisels, and plane-irons, and drawing-knives, and knives for straw-cutters, &c., I usually grind at an angle of about *twenty degrees*. And even when plane-irons and chisels are ground at an angle of twenty degrees, the edge will not stand when cutting hemlock knots, and such like, unless they are made of superior steel. All such tools should be held on the grindstone, so that the scratches and serrature will be at a right angle to the cutting edge.

FIG. 152.

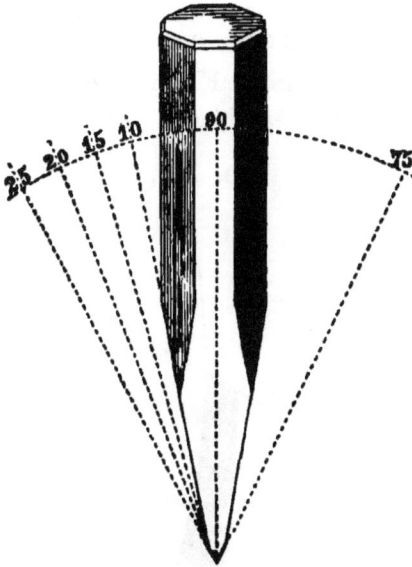

SHOWING THE PROPER ANGLE FOR GRINDING COLD-CHISELS.

564. The knives of mowers and reapers usually cut with a crushing stroke. Therefore, the more acute the angle of the basil the more easily they cut. But if they are ground too thin they are more liable to be dulled by breaking out at the edge, than if they were ground at a more obtuse angle. All things considered, if such knives are ground at an angle of twenty degrees, the basil will be acute enough for all kinds of work.

OIL-STONES

565. Are almost as indispensable as a grindstone. Indeed, it is very impracticable to produce a fine, keen edge without one. They may be obtained at the hardware stores for about fifteen cents. Set it in a wooden block, and use *sweet oil* on it when whetting a tool instead of water, because oil will aid in giving a tool a keener edge. Nail a strap of old leather on one side of the oil-stone case, and after a chisel or plane-iron has been whet,

strap it a little on the leather, and if the steel is good and properly tempered, it will clip a hair.

566. Is a very short job. Fig. 153 represents a transverse section of one of the shear blades ground at a proper angle.

FIG. 153.

A TRANSVERSE SECTION OF A SHEAR BLADE PROPERLY GROUND.

Never grind any shears on the flat side of the blade. The grindstone should run very true, and the blade should be held *square across it* as it revolves *towards* the edge. If the edges of the blades have become worn off on the. *flat* side where they cut, they must be ground off on the edge—not on the *flat side*—until the flat side is most prominent at the cutting edge. Whet sheep-shears and *wife's* shears on an oil-stone, and if they will cut wet newspaper they are in good order. If shears are ground at an angle as acute as chisels, in cutting thick hard substances the edge would yield bv bending or breaking.

BENCH PLANES.

567. A farmer needs a good set of planes, consisting of a *jack-plane* for rough work, a *fore-plane* or *short-jointer*, larger

than the jack-plane, for dressing stuff truer than can be done with the jack; a *jointer*, for making straight work, and a *smoothing-plane*, for smoothing boards when it is not necessary to joint them.

568. Select planes that are made of good white beech, in preference to any other wood. Apple-wood and cast-iron planes shove much harder than beech planes, because they set so close to the stuff which is being planed. See that the grain of the wood runs *up and down*, and not *parallel* with the face of them. Before they are used they should be thoroughly soaked in linseed oil, to render them more durable and heavy, as a workman will usually be able to plane more easily with a *heavy* plane than with a *light* one.

569. The face of a good plane must always be very true, not *hollowing*, nor *rounding*, nor *winding*. They are very liable to wear *untrue*,—when they must be "*faced off*" with a jointer, similar to the manner of dressing out a gate stile. (See Par. 240.) New planes are very apt to be *winding* on the face. When they are so they must be *faced* true.

570. Planes with *double irons* are best, because with them we can plane smoothly cross-grained or eaty timber. But it is not practicable to do so with a plane having a *single* iron. The adjustable iron or *cap* is designed to break the shaving when planing, by turning it at so short an angle that slivers cannot be torn up as they often are with a single iron. In planing straight-grained timber, a single iron is preferable.

PUTTING PLANES IN GOOD ORDER

571. Is a job that every wood-mangler is not able to perform. If the irons or bits are not ground correctly and whet on a fine stone, no man can plane well. Fig. 154 represents a view of the *face side* of a jack-plane iron. Hold it in grinding so that the grindstone will revolve *towards* the edge, and grind the *basil* at an angle of about twenty degrees, if the stuff to be planed is hard and knotty. (See Fig. 152.) Set the bevel square at the desired angle, and try the angle when grinding. Grind it about

FIG. 154.

SHAPE OF THE EDGE OF A JACK-PLANE IRON.

as circular on the edge, from corner to corner, as the figure. Place the *try-square* against one of the edges of the iron, to see if one corner is not being ground off too much, as shown by the dotted line. If a jack-plane iron is ground *straight* on the edge, as shown by the dotted line, it will cut a shaving so wide that the plane will *choke* or clog. The edge should be ground on as true a circle as is practicable, from corner to corner, and if the basil should be found upon trial to be too thin for planing hard and knotty stuff, let it be ground a little more blunt.

572. Fig. 155 shows the correct form for the jointer and smoothing-plane irons. The edge, from corner to corner, should be ground convex but little. If it is ground very true, and the middle is about one-thirtieth of an inch more prominent than the

FIG. 155.

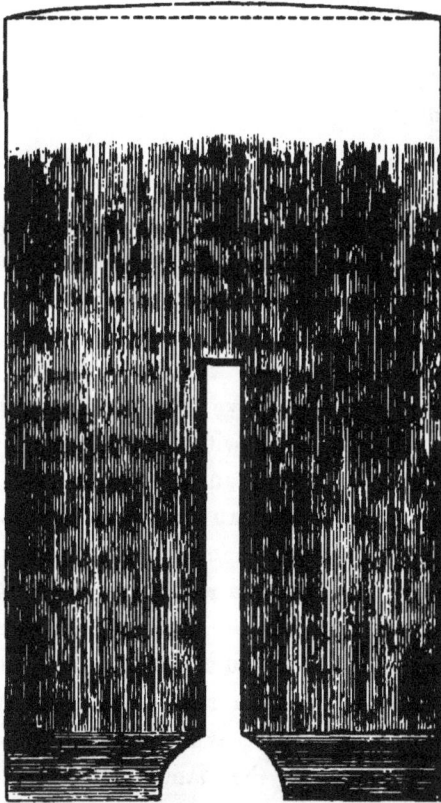

SHAPE OF THE EDGE OF THE JOINTER IRON.

corners, it will work well, and the plane ridges will be hardly perceptible. In order to plane smooth, the irons must be as straight on the edge as they can be, and not make a *square cut* at their corners, for if they do they are very liable to choke or clog. In order to plane well, the edge must cut like a razor. (See OIL-STONE, Par. 565.)

ADJUSTING THE PLANE BITS

573. Requires considerable skill in order to do it just right when it is done with a wedge. There are in limited use several patent arrangements for adjusting plane bits, but they increase

17

the cost to such an extent that ordinary mechanics are not willing to purchase them. The old way of adjusting and keying them with a wedge is good enough for any mechanic, and will without any doubt supplant and triumph over every other mode of adjustment.

574. Set the plane on the hind end, holding it erect with the left hand, with the *left thumb* in the throat, placed on the face of the bit. Rest the fore end against your chin and look *lengthways* of the face of the plane, and put the plane iron through the throat until the eye can just see *a little* of the edge. Hold it then with the left thumb while the wedge is crowded in with the right hand. A *light* tap with the hammer will fasten it. Never drive in the wedges as if they were never to be again withdrawn. Try the plane; and with *light* taps with the hammer start it in until it cuts deep enough. For planing cross-grained, eaty timber, sharpen the bit, and set the cap or shaving breaker (see Par. 570) as close to the cutting edge of the bit as practicable. To *withdraw* the bit, hold the plane with one hand, with the thumb in *the throat* at the lower edge of the wedge. Press upward with the *thumb* on the wedge as you strike on the fore part of the plane, on a rivet head which is put in the plane to hammer on. Or turn the plane upside down, and withdraw the wedge and bit *with one hand*, by thumping the plane downwards on the bench.

575. Mechanics many times dispose of their old planes because the *mouth* is too wide. Such a defect may be obviated by setting a piece of band iron in the *face* of the plane so that the mouth will admit only a thin shaving. When planing straight-grained stuff, *raise* the cap, or shaving breaker; because more force is required to shove a plane when the shaving breaker is set near the edge of the bit. If a wedge is driven in very hard in keying the bit, there is danger of springing the plane.

THE WAY TO PLANE A BOARD TRUE AND SMOOTH.

576. If a board is pretty true, not warped nor winding, it is a short job to plane it. Lay it on the work-bench, with one edge about even with the front side of the bench. With the jack-

plane, well sharpened, commence at the end of the board, and shove the plane at the first stroke along the edge of the board nearest to you about two or three feet. Cut another shaving now a little farther on the board, and then another, until you have planed entirely across the end of the board. Now step along and plane about three feet in length more of the board, and so on until the whole board is planed. Now go over it with the smoothing-plane in the same manner as was done with the jack-plane. Make as long strokes as you can conveniently without stepping forward. Endeavor to avoid this planing at *random*, as many workmen often do; and be very careful not to plane off the *sides* of the board more than the middle. A few random, careless strokes with a plane near the edge of a board, will in some instances make the side of it so uneven that the entire board must be dressed down even with the deep cuts; which might consume nearly half an hour of time. Let the sides at the edges of the board be left a shaving or so the highest, if anything, until the finishing strokes are applied, when it will be found much easier to plane the sides down even with the middle than it is to plane the middle down even with the sides. If the face of a board is required to be straight, after it has been jacked off with the jack-plane the *fore-plane* or short-jointer should follow the jack-plane, and after the short-jointer use the long-jointer. When the board is cross-grained, and cannot be planed smooth by shoving the plane one way, the tyro should learn to plane in an opposite direction. After the face of a board has been dressed with the short-jointer as smooth and true as seems to be practicable by shoving the planes forward, or lengthways of the board, if there are numerous ridges made by the plane it shows that the edge of the plane iron is *too circular,* or *convex, from one corner to the other.* Sometimes, after a board has been dressed pretty true, it is best to plane *crossways* of it, cutting a thin shaving, after which it must be planed lengthways, cutting a very thin shaving. It is just as well, in planing timber which is not "eaty" or cross-grained, to cut a thick shaving at first as it is to take a very thin one. But in finishing it, in order to leave it true, and destitute of plane ridges, it must be done by taking a very thin shaving. When a board is very rough, and covered with a mat of fine slivers, resembling wool more than wood, which is often the case with baswood and other soft woods when the boards have been sawed with a dull saw, the jack-plane iron must be *very sharp* or it will not cut these fine slivers when planing lengthways of the timber. When such is the case, it will be well to try planing crossways of the grain until the board is jacked off. Sometimes one can cut a very thick shaving with a jack-plane, and thus take off all the fine slivers at one planing much better than to cut only a thin shaving. In planing hard wood, if the boards are not pretty true it is best to plane crossways with the jack-plane until the short-jointer or smoothing-plane can be used to plane lengthways.

If a board is warped, or is winding, it can usually be made true more easily by planing it crossways first, and then planing lengthways. In planing *crossways* of a board, the tyro must be careful to turn up his plane or make the shaving *run out* just before the cutting edge of the iron arrives at the opposite side of the board; otherwise, instead of cutting a smooth shaving entirely across the board, it will split a sliver from the opposite corner, and mar the face of the board at the corner. In planing off long boards, if they are a very little winding they may -be dressed out winding; but when a workman intends making a bee-hive, or chest, or nice box, the side boards and end boards must not be winding. If they are dressed out winding, the whole box is liable to be winding, unless the boards of two opposite sides wind equally towards each other, or from each other, when they are placed side by side. The tyro will perhaps find it much more difficult to plane a board true and smooth that is but one foot long than to plane one that is two or three feet in length; because beginners at planing usually cut a thicker shaving at each end of the board, in consequence of not keeping their plane level on the board. When the iron begins to cut at the end of the board, the forward end of the plane must be held down firmly until it arrives at the other end of the board, when the hindmost end of the plane must be kept down until the plane iron is beyond the end of the board. This last direction is very important in jointing or planing the edges of boards, in order to have them straight.

577. When one side of a board is planed true, which may be determined by holding the straight edge of a steel square across it, if the board is to be planed on both sides, and brought to an *even thickness*, run a gauge-mark along the edges and across the ends, and then plane it down with the jack-plane almost to the mark near the edges of the board first; and then plane down the middle, and be very careful and not plane the middle *lower* than the sides are. Plane crossways or lengthways as already directed; but do not try to plane with an iron that has not a sharp edge, because with a *dull* plane iron the tyro will do poor work. *Sharpen the plane irons very often* in order to plane true and smooth. Sometimes the grain of about half of the board runs in a contrary direction from the other half. In such a case the board must be turned the other end forward, or the workman may shove his plane with the other hand in an opposite direction. Good workmen accustom themselves to shoving the plane both ways, as it is often much more convenient to plane the other way than it is to change ends with a board.

578. In planing some kinds of hard timber that is eaty, tough, and with the grain doubled and twisted, it is necessary to take a very thin shaving. And even then, should the throat of the plane be rather large, one cannot plane smooth. If the plane iron be a double one, the *cap* or shaving-breaker must be set as close down to the edge of the cutting iron as it can be, and not prevent its cutting a shaving. In such a case the iron must be very sharp or the workman cannot plane at all. The nearer the shaving-breaker is to the edge of the plane iron, the greater will be the force required to shove the plane. If the grain of a stick be very straight and not eaty, the shaving-breaker may be raised one-fourth of an inch from the cutting edge of the plane iron, as it will plane just as smooth, and much easier.

JOINTING BOARDS AND PLANK.

579. Let the board be put in the vise on the edge, vertically,

not leaning to or from you, and have it as low, if possible, as the top of the bench; because one cannot plane well when he is obliged to hold his plane on a board as high as his arm-pits. Jack off the edge the entire length, and then look over it to see where it is a little the highest or lowest, and jack the high places until the edge looks about straight, and then apply the jointer. Be careful to keep the edge of the board at a right angle with the side by using the try-square. In jointing a board or plank, beginners —and many old workmen, too—plane off the edges near the ends, in starting their plane and in running out, so that the edges are *convex* from end to end. When a workman is apt to fall into this error in jointing, he should not allow his plane to cut within a foot of the end, until it seems highest at the end. Some workmen think if they cut a shaving the entire length of a board it must be straight. But one may plane a shaving the entire length of a short or long board, and it may not be straight by half an inch. When the workman cannot tell by a glance of the eye over the edge of a board whether it is straight or not, he had better, if the edge of a board is a little rounding or hollowing, strike a line on the side of it with a very small chalk line, and then, with the drawing-knife and planes, it can be made straight very easily and quickly. Some pretty good joiners cannot tell always, simply by the eye, whether the edges of two boards will make a close joint when placed together. The beginner may find it to his advantage to place the edges of two boards together when he is jointing them, and then he will be able to discover without any difficulty, how much must be planed off in order to make a close joint.

580. Some mechanics, when they look over the edge of a board, cannot tell with accuracy whether it is convex, concave, undulating, or entirely straight. And when it is undulating they cannot go and put their finger on the highest point of the edge of the board. The chief reason of this failure is, they close one eye, when looking at the edge of a board, and then endeavor to keep the eye on the highest place, until they can get to it with the plane. This is all well enough. But when they

come to open the eye that was closed the vision is so affected that the exact point is lost sight of for a moment, and it is impossible to determine where it is.   The best and most correct way is, to look with both eyes open, as they always are, and then the exact point can be kept in view until the workman can reach it with the plane.   It will require a little practice and ingenuity to look over the edge of a board with both eyes open and determine whether it is straight or not.   But in order to do it, the head must be placed in such a position that the edge can be seen with one eye *only*.   Then it will not be difficult to keep the eye on any point on the edge of a board, until the workman can step to it with his plane.   In looking at anything, which is often expressed by different mechanics as " *ranging*," " *squinting*," "*sighting*," or " *shooting*," in order to discover whether it is straight or not, it is always best to keep both eyes open ; because the vision is less perfect when one eye is closed.   And if a person becomes accustomed to " take sight " with both eyes open, it will be found a better way than to close one eye.

581. In jointing the *end* of a board or plank with the square and sharp point of a knife, cut a deep mark on each side of it, and then with the drawing-knife shave the end almost to the marks, and afterwards use the jointer or smoothing-plane.   Never shove the plane entirely across the end, lest it stave off slivers from the opposite corner.   Place the board in the vise, if it is a short one, and if a long one, lay one end of it on a low bench on the edge, and joint the end while standing astride of it.   Have the plane iron very sharp for this purpose.   If these directions be strictly followed, there will be no more difficulty in making the joints of a box *water-tight* at the ends, than there is on the sides of it.

CHISELS.

" Chisels here, with faces bright,
Framers, firmers, heavy, light,
Corner-chisels, duck-bill, too,
True and crooked, now we view.

582. Fig. 156 represents a *face* view of a good framing-chisel.

Figs. 156,   157,   158,   159.

FRAMER.   FIRMER.   CORNER CHISEL.   DUCK-BILL CHISEL.

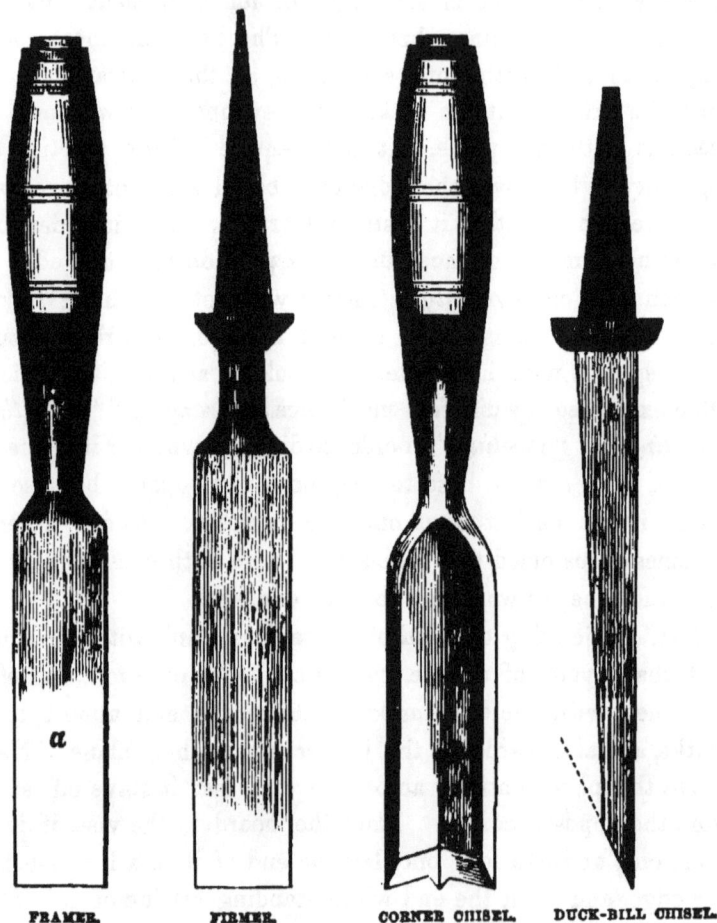

a is the *face* of the blade, *b* is the socket-shank, which receives
the handle, which has an iron ring on the top of it to keep it
from splitting.

Fig. 157 exhibits a face view of a *firmer* chisel, which is
usually made of the *best* of steel,—blade, shank, and all. Such
chisels are designed for light work, such as hanging doors, and
for shaving and fitting by hand without a mallet.

583. Fig. 158 is a perspective view of a *corner* chisel, which
is worth a score of common chisels for mortising. As such

chisels are seldom kept on hand at hardware stores, get one forged, with the wings at a right angle, which will cost about seventy-five cents. Take it, before it is tempered, to a machine-shop, and have the *blade planed* true, at a right angle, both on the *face* and *back*. Have the *edges* planed down so that each wing will be about seven-eighths of an inch wide, so that it can be used in making inch mortises. After tempering it, grind it on a stone that runs very true, and whet it like any other chisel. *File* the basil in the corner to the desired depth with a triangular file. Do not file off the *projecting point* at the middle of the basil, as that will aid very much in mortising. Planing it and tempering it will cost not over forty cents.

584. The superiority of such a chisel, when compared with *straight* chisels, is this; in heading down a mortise, it makes a *clean*, true cut in the corner, and a workman can mortise very much faster with it than with another chisel, and a *beginner* can make a very good mortise with it when he would not have sufficient skill to make a mortise " half-way decent " with a *straight* chisel. (See MAKING MORTISES, in next vol.)

585. Fig. 159 represents a *side* or *edge* view of a *duck-bill* chisel, which is designed for making deep mortises, and is ground about as every kind of chisels should be ground.

FORMS OF CHISELS, AND GRINDING THEM.

586. No mechanic can mortise well and easily if his chisels are not of a good shape and well sharpened. In order to have a chisel enter a mortise easily and not *stick*, so that it is difficult to withdraw it, it must be a trifle *wider* at the cutting edge than it is at the upper end of the blade. When a chisel is *narrower* at the cutting edge, like Fig. 163, it will *bind* so tightly in a mortise that it will be difficult to withdraw it. If the two side edges are *exactly parallel* with each other, like the blades of 156 and 157, they will *stick* in mortising but little. In order to have a chisel enter straight inwards, the face should be as straight as shown at Fig. 162, which is an edge view of a framer. Never

17*

grind the edge of a chisel like Fig. 161 ; because, when of such
a form it is very difficult to mortise true with them.   Chisels are
sometimes *made* and sometimes *bent* like Fig. 160.   But they
are very awkward, inconvenient tools to mortise with, because
the edge will always run *inwards* from the mark, making a mor-

FIGS. 160,   161,   162,   163.

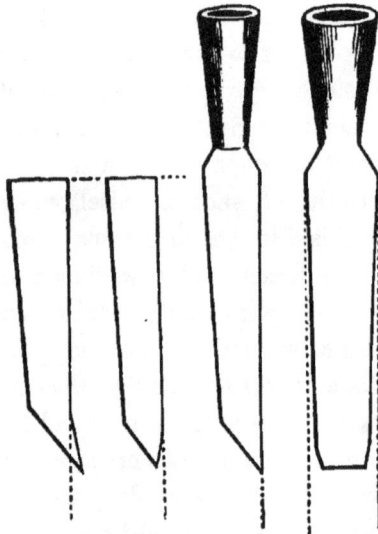

MANNER OF GRINDING CHISELS.

tise larger in the middle of it.   The *side edges* of every chisel
should be ground *at a right angle* with the face.   If they are
bevelled but little either way from the face, they will *stick* when
mortising.   If the face and *side edges* are polished as they *should*
be, so that you can see the color of your eyes in them, and kept
oiled when mortising, they will never stick.   Rough, untrue
chisels make hard work in mortising.

TURNING-GOUGES AND TURNING-CHISELS

587. Of all sizes, and *firmer*-gouges also, may be obtained at
hardware stores, and are often of great service in the farmer's
workshop.

AUGERS AND BITS.

" An auger once to boring went,
And bored until the shank was bent ;
The screw encountered a tough knot,
And stopped the boring on the spot.
The pod untwisted, and the lips
Refused to cut and heave out chips."—PUNCH.

588. The principal parts of an auger or bit are, *a* the *screw*, *b* the cutters, or *lips*, *c* the *pod*, or twist, and *d* the *shank*. Pointed projections on the under side of the lips of some kinds of augers and bits are called *spurs*.

589. It will be seen by these figures that the lips are *circular*, and not square, as most augers are. This is a patentable feature in the manufacture of augers and bits, and Mr. Ransom Cooke, Saratoga Springs, N. Y., the patentee, informed me that he "*re-ceives four hundred dollars per month for his claim, during the life of the patent,* from Messrs. Lamson, Goodnow & Co., Shelburne Falls, Mass., who are the sole proprietors for manufacturing this kind of augers and bits. I *know* them to be far superior to any other auger that was ever made. They bore with the greatest possible ease at any angle of the grain of the wood, without *crush-ing* or breaking and tearing out the wood which adjoins the hole bored. These augers now stand without a successful rival in the world, and can be obtained of any size of the manufacturers, at ·79 Beekman street, N. Y. city.

590. Fig. 166 represents a small bit, with a single lip and a single twist; and for boring any kind of wood it is infinitely su-perior to a centre-bit. (See PATENT EXTENSION BIT, Fig. 123.)

SHARPENING AUGERS AND BITS

591. Is usually done with a *file*, while the pod is held in the visc. The lips should be filed at as acute an angle as will be consistent with strength on the *upper* side, and on the *under* side they should be filed as flat as possible and have the cutting edge a little *more prominent* than it is *back* of the edge. This style of augers and bits should be filed with a very fine *round* file. When augers have *spurs*, the spurs should never be filed on the *outside*,

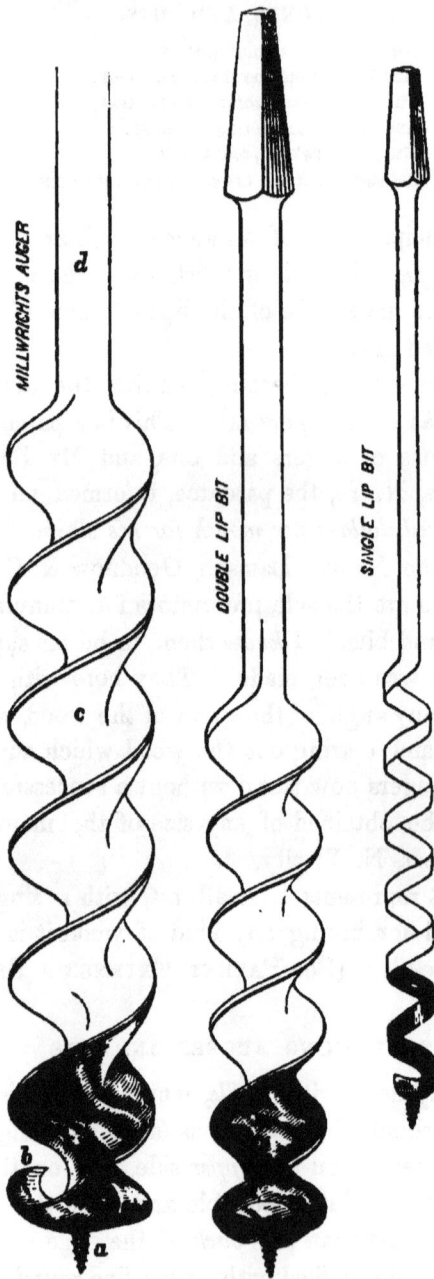

FIGS. 164,   165,   166.

MILLWRIGHTS AUGER

DOUBLE LIP BIT

SINGLE LIP BIT

d

c

b

a

DOUBLE-LIP AUGER.   DOUBLE-LIP BIT.   SINGLE-LIP BIT.

(402)

but always on the *inside*, so that they will mark out the size of the hole, and cut so large that the pod will not *bind*, or be "pinched" in the hole. As augers and bits cut with a *crushing* stroke, (see Par. 543) after filing the lips whet them a little with a small piece of oil-stone, to give them a keen edge.

DEFECTIVE AUGERS AND BITS.

592. Good augers and bits are sometimes rendered almost worthless by improper filing. If the under side of the lips is more prominent *back* of the cutting edge than at the edge, the screw will not draw it in, and a workman must necessarily *bear on* in boring. (See the remedy, Par. 591.) Sometimes the screw has become very dull, and needs a little filing in order to make it *draw in* when boring. Sometimes the pod is larger than the hole which the lips cut; and sometimes it has been bent a little, so that it *binds* on one side of the hole. In either case the pod must be dressed off true, so that it will not bind in the hole. Sometimes one lip cuts a chip twice as thick as the other. Bore a hole close to the end of a stick, so that you can see which lip cuts the thickest, and file it off a little on the *under side*. Should the screw of a large auger get broken off, if there is substance enough in the auger another screw may be put in for a few dimes by a gunsmith or watchmaker.

BORING HOLES.

593. In order to bore holes straight and true, the stick to be bored should lay about level, both endways and sideways; for an auger can be kept in a vertical position much easier than it can be inclined a little to correspond with the inclination of a stick that does not lie level. Carpenters, when framing a building, always want their timber to lie as nearly level as practicable, so that they will be able to bore the pin-holes more exact. In boring a hole *diagonally*, the tyro will be able to bore it truer if the stick be held level one way and inclined the other way, so as to bring the auger in a vertical position. In boring a hole *lengthways* through a stick, put it in the vise and plumb it, and then

start in the auger and plumb that also, and keep it in an erect
position until the auger has entered the length of the pod, when
if the pod be true the auger will run very straight through. In
this way I have often bored a hole through a piece of scantling
twice the length of the auger, by boring at both ends. After an
auger has entered the length of the pod, the chips should be cleared
out often, especially in green timber, by turning the auger backwards just enough to loosen the screw, and then drawing it
straight out, turning it forward as it is drawn out. If it be turned
backward it works the chips towards the bottom of the hole. Sometimes an auger refuses to bore, in consequence of a shaving getting on the cutting edge; and sometimes the screw will fill with
wood, and will not draw the auger in. This may be prevented
by *filing* the screw a little, and by sharpening the cutting edge.
If this does not remove the defect entirely, oil the screw, and bear
on the auger a little when boring.

594. In boring pump logs, or wooden tubes which may be
eight or twelve feet long, or anything else of that description, a
long lathe is necessary, or something equivalent to it, by which
means the centre of each end of the stick and the screw of the
auger and the end of the shank will all range exactly in a
straight line. But the auger must be drawn out often, lest the chips
clog so firmly that there will be difficulty in withdrawing it at all.

595. The neatest auger for this business consists of a pod some
eight or ten feet long, made very true, fitted neatly to turn in an
iron tube of the same length as the pod. The tube may be two
or more inches in diameter, and the lips of the auger cut a hole
just large enough for the tube to enter easily; and the chips are
all brought out through the tube. Such an auger will bore
very true, and will not clog. The lips of such an auger cut a
hole just as large as the tube. This arrangement was patented,
and is now in use by a man in Elmira, N. Y.

596. The tyro should be very careful, in boring hard wood,
not to thrust the shank of the auger or bit *sideways*, from right to
left, when first starting it in, because there is danger of bending
or breaking the screw.

597. There are many patent devices for attaching augers to the handles; but I shall notice none of them, because they increase the cost of an auger too much. A thin plate of iron screwed on the under side of the handle, with a square hole in it just large enough to receive the end of the auger shank, which is passed through the handle and secured on the upper side by a small nut and screw, is about as good a device, all things considered, as any one can desire. Keep augers sharp and bright, and it is good fun for boys to bore.

598. When bits cannot be used with the brace, make a small handle for them, and use them as a gimlet.

FIGS. 167, 168.

AWLS.

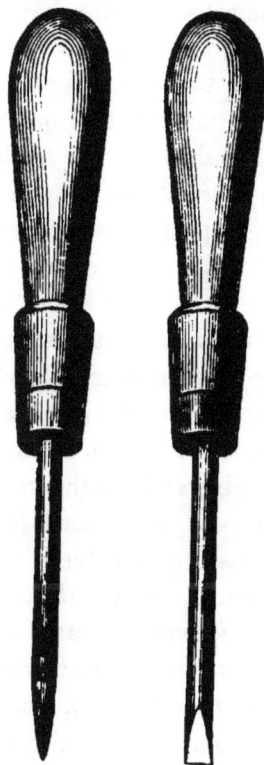

599. Fig. 167 is a harness-awl, for making holes in leather. From the point to the part where it begins to taper it is ground rather flat, so that the edges will cut when entering the leather. A *round* awl does not enter leather easily.

600. Fig. 168 is a *brad-awl*, for making holes in wood. The edge is made square across the awl, in order to *cut off* the grain of the wood as it enters. A pointed round awl will *split* a stick when such an awl would not.

601. *Scratch-awls* should always have a round point. Harness-awls and brad-awls should be whet on an oil-stone, else they will not enter easily. All such awls can be obtained at the hardware stores for two or three cents each.

HARNESS-AWL.   BRAD-AWL.

SAWS.

" The saw hangs glittering in the quiet shade,
  With sharp and grinning teeth, and burnished blade.
  The well-set teeth laugh at the stubborn oaks,
  And knots and gnarls yield to its potent strokes.
    Now starting, and stopping, and darting,
    And ripping, and slitting, and splitting,
    Dividing, and cleaving, and riving,
    And shivering, and quivering, and slivering,
  Inspiring with terror, amazement and awe :
  Such are the manœuvres cut up by a saw."—EDWARDS.

TECHNICALITIES IN RELATION TO SAWS.

602. *Hanging a saw* means, putting it in the frame or gate previous to using it, or fitting a buzz saw to a journal or mandrel. The two irons on the mandrel which hold the saw in its position are called the *flanges*, or *collars*. The collar which is keyed fast to the mandrel is called the *fixed* collar, and the other one the *loose* collar. The distance from one tooth to another is called the *space*. *Gumming* a saw is the act of making the spaces deeper, or wider and deeper, according to the shape of the teeth. The *face* of the teeth is the edge which is *forward* when the saw is in use. The *back* of the teeth is the edge opposite to the face. The *hook* or *pitch* of the teeth is the inclination of the face of the teeth forward from a line drawn at a right angle with the cutting edge, or points of the teeth. *Setting a saw* is the act of spreading the points of the teeth, either by hammering or bending them sideways, so as to make the saw cut a kerf wider than the thickness of the saw. *Jointing* a saw is the act of making the *points* of the teeth *true*, both on the edge and on the *sides* of the points, so that in a buzz saw every tooth will extend just so far from the centre of motion. The *roots* of the teeth are the bases of them at the bottom of the spaces. The *rake* of a saw is the inclination of the cutting edge forward towards the timber to be sawed. This is only applied to saws which work up and down, or horizontally. *Fleam-pointed*, or *fleaming*, means having the teeth filed on the face and back diagonally. A circular saw is said to be *fast* when the rim is largest, which is caused by stretching the edge when gumming it. When a saw deviates

from a straight course in sawing off a stick, it is said *to run*. The young farmer should make himself familiar with each of these terms, as they will often be used in the succeeding paragraphs.

NAMES OF DIFFERENT KINDS OF SAWS.

603. Saws that are *circular* on the cutting-edge are denominated sometimes *buzz* saws, or *crosscut-circular*, or *slitting-circular*, according to the form of the teeth. Hand-saws are denominated *hand-crosscut*, or *hand-slitting*, or *panel saws*, according to the form of their teeth. Saws that have their backs inserted in a bar of brass or iron are called *back*, or *tenon saws*. A *compass* saw has a narrow, tapering blade, with a handle on one end for sawing round holes in anything. Saws that are used by two men when sawing logs are called *crosscut*, or *crosscut log* saws. (Any saw that is filed to cut *across* the grain of wood is called a *crosscut*, and when filed *square across* the teeth, *slitting*, or *rip* saws.) Saws that are used for sawing logs into short cuts for staves, or shingles, or firewood, when attached to a pitman are called *crosscut-butting* saws, or *drag* saws. *Felly*, or *felloe* saws are put in a frame and filed to cut both *crossways* and *lengthways* of the grain of wood. *Pit* saws are long, two-men saws, for slitting long timber, while one man stands on the timber, and the other beneath the stick that they are sawing. *Billet*, or *wood-sawyer's* saws, are put in a frame for sawing fire-wood. *Bow*, or *billet-web* saws, are put in a small frame and strained, and used for sawing circular work. Cast-steel webs are used for sawing iron and brass. *Mulay*, or "mooly" saws, are used in sawmills where the pitman is attached to one end of the saw, and the saw is not hung in a gate. There are many other kinds of saws which we will not notice here.

SELECTING SAWS, AND THE EXTERNAL SIGNS OF GOOD SAWS AND POOR ONES, AND NUMBER OF TEETH IN SAWS.

604. In selecting a saw of any kind, it is always the wisest policy to get a *good one*, even if it be a little more costly. A *poor* saw is always a source of vexation and loss to any one who

has much sawing to do; and a man never regrets having paid a few dimes more for a good saw.

605. A good saw is usually distinguished by a *bright polish— a clear and lively ring—freedom from flaws in the blade and in the teeth—its great elasticity, and a good degree of hardness.* A coarse-looking, leaden-colored, dull-sounding, non-elastic, pewter-plate, coarsely-polished saw should be avoided. A *hard* saw is worth a score of soft ones. A saw that is so soft when it is filed that a thin sheet of steel hangs to the edge of the teeth, is a poor thing. The two ends of a good hand-saw, or a crosscut saw, if the blade is not too thick, may be brought together without any danger of kinking or breaking it. A saw that will *kink* very easily is not as good as it would be if it were harder. Such a saw will never retain its set of the teeth like a harder one.

606. Another thing of great importance in selecting a saw is, to select one that has teeth, many or few, adapted to the kind of sawing to be done. The materials which a farmer has to saw are so variable, that it is best for him to select a hand-saw for ordinary purposes having a pretty stiff plate, and about *seven teeth* to the inch. A saw with fine teeth will cut much smoother than a saw with coarse teeth. Indeed, for some kinds of sawing a saw with *coarse* teeth would do the work intolerably bad; while if the same saw had four times as many teeth it would saw *neatly*, and just as fast, and sometimes much faster, with the same power. If the materials to be sawed be of good thickness, the teeth should be farther apart; and if the materials be small, or thin, the teeth must be fine, else they will take too rank a hold, making a very rough, jagged cut. For sawing hard wood, both across and lengthways of the grain of the wood, a saw with fine teeth is best. A hand-saw, whose teeth are half an inch or three-eighths of an inch apart is an ugly thing to saw a thin, hard board with, or even hard plank. The teeth of a saw, for any purpose, ought to be so fine that not less than *four*, in sawing soft wood, and *six* or eight in hard wood, shall be cutting at once. In slitting hard plank, the teeth must be *fine* or the work will be very rough. The *reason* of this is, when the teeth are far apart each

tooth is made to cut *deeper* than it is capable of cutting without *staggering* or *springing aside;* and when the cut of a saw is all notched and jagged, it is very evident that each tooth is made to cut *too deep.* If the plate of a saw is very thin, the teeth must be fine, else it will spring, and work badly. If the plate is a *thick* one, the teeth may be farther apart without danger of springing, but the cut will not be as smooth as if there were more teeth. A saw having fine teeth will require more filing and setting, but it will do the work enough better to compensate for any extra expense in putting it in order.

607. The teeth in circular saws from twenty to thirty inches in diameter, for cutting firewood, ought not to be more than an inch or an inch and a fourth apart to work the best, taking hard wood and soft, large and small, together. Each tooth can cut only a certain distance to good advantage, and this distance is in proportion to the *hardness* or *softness* of the timber. In sawing *soft* wood, if there are a great many teeth the saw-dust is cut very fine; and each tooth does not cut as deep as it should, especially if the power is limited. Consequently there is a loss of power.

608. A buzz saw, for slitting boards and plank, for both hard and soft timber, should have rather fine teeth, where smooth work is any object, unless the velocity with which such a saw revolves is *unusually* great. (See VELOCITY OF SAWS, 680.) A tenon saw for ordinary purposes should have about eight teeth in an inch. Such a saw will cut about right for sawing the limbs of trees preparatory to grafting.

609. Circular slitting saws, as a general thing, have *too few* teeth to do smooth work, unless the materials to be slit are pretty thick. In a saw forty-eight inches in diameter, for sawing soft wood good sawyers say there should be about twenty-four to thirty teeth, and for hard wood about forty teeth. A small circular saw ten or twelve inches in diameter, for slitting hard wood plank and boards, should have the points of the teeth about half an inch apart. The thinner the blade the finer the teeth must be.

610. I am now using a circular saw about one foot in diameter, the teeth of which were about three inches apart at the cut-

ting edge. It was impossible to slit hard timber smooth with it until I cut the teeth all away and made new ones in it about half an inch apart. Now it saws as true and smooth, with the same power and velocity, as it is possible for a saw to cut. I used for several years a 22-inch circular wood-saw, whose teeth were three inches apart at the points, and it always worked very unsatisfactorily. Another one was put in its place, having teeth an inch and a fourth apart, and with the same power it would saw nearly twice as fast, and do it very smoothly.

PUTTING SAWS IN ORDER

611. Is an operation that requires the exercise of much dexterity and mechanical precision. If the teeth are all filed to a sharp point, unless they are perfectly *even* and *true* on the points, a saw will not cut as fast as it ought, nor as fast as it *would*, if it were well filed. When a saw is well filed and the teeth set properly, by casting the eye over the teeth, lengthways of the saw, not the least variation in the length of the teeth can be discovered. Where some of the teeth are longer than the rest, the *long ones only* will cut; and so far as cutting is concerned, the short ones might as well not be there. When a few teeth only have been dulled, the saw will cut no faster by filing these dulled ones to a point, unless the rest of the teeth are jointed off and made of a corresponding length. In such instances it would be as well to let them remain as they are until the remainder of the teeth need filing. In filing, the aim should be to keep the teeth of a uniform *shape*,—*i. e.*, the *angle* of what is called the *hook* of the teeth, should be retained as much as possible. Many farmers, not understanding the importance of this, continue to file with a file that is nearly worn out on its corners, and thus the hook of the teeth becomes not only very *obtuse*, but the teeth are not kept as long as they should be. It is poor policy to file a saw with a file the corners of which are worn out. It is very important that the corners of file should be sharp, in order to keep all the teeth as long as possible. If a tooth has been shortened on the point by dulling or filing, it should be filed to its

original length as it is filed to a point. Much care should be exercised lest the teeth on one side become *smaller* and *shorter* than those on the opposite side. Whenever this is the case with a saw, the file, in filing, should be pressed *harder* against the larger teeth than against the smaller ones.

612. It is very important when filing a saw, to have it held *firmly* in a proper position. For this purpose a saw-clamp is

Fig. 169.   Fig. 170.

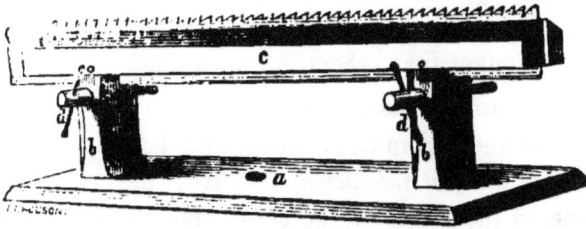 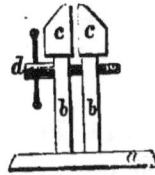

SAW-CLAMP.   END VIEW.

necessary, a perspective and end view of which is represented by Fig. 169, with a saw in it. *a* is a heavy plank, two inches thick or thicker, a foot wide and three feet long. Fig. 170 is an end view of the same. *b b* are four standards, one and a half by four inches square, of hard wood, driven into mortises in *a*, and are about eight inches long. *c c* are the jaws, about four feet long, and fastened to the upper ends of *b b*, by mortise and tenon. *d d* are screws, which pass through *b b*. They may be nothing but iron bolts. The standards *b b* should be about one-eighth of an inch apart, to give room for a saw. Put the saw in the clamp and screw up the jaws, and if the clamp is not heavy enough to remain still when filing, bolt it to the bench. If the jaws are straight and true, they will press against the saw from one end to the other. If the saw rattles or works between the jaws, they are not true, and must be straightened.

PUTTING HAND-SAWS IN ORDER.

613. Put the saw in the clamp with the teeth extending a little above the jaws. Always have the clamp set *as level* as practicable, and never attempt to file a saw in a place where it is not as light as is desirable. It is very important to have

enough *light*, that the points of all the teeth may be seen dis-tinctly. No man can expect to file a saw well when the light is dim. Sometimes one can file by candle-light, if he has good sight, quite as well as by daylight. In dark, cloudy days, the clamp can be carried out of doors when filing; but it should always be placed in a level position.

614. Now, the idea is, to file *just so deep* between every two teeth, and to file the *face* and *back* (see TECHNICALITIES, Par. 602) *at a given angle*, and to have the teeth on both sides of the saw of *equal length and size*. Cast the eye over the teeth, and if some of them are longer than others the teeth must be jointed.

HOW TO JOINT SAWS.

615. Put a saw in the clamp as for filing, and, holding a large file in the hands *with the flat side down*, and *level*, run it along as you would a plane on the points of the teeth, until the long ones are all filed off on the points even with the short ones. Great care should be exercised in jointing a saw, and not joint off the teeth on *one side* of the saw more than they are jointed off on the other side. Run the file from end to end of the saw, and exam-ine it at every stroke to see if the teeth are not jointed off enough. One careless stroke in jointing, or one stroke too much, will cause much unnecessary filing.

616. *To joint a circular saw*, set it to running moderately by hand *backwards*, and hold a large file on a plank placed close to the edge of the saw, so that the longest teeth as they revolve will touch the file. Place the edge of the plank at a right angle with the saw, in order to have some guide for holding the file at a right angle. If this particular is not strictly observed, the saw will not be *round*. I have seen workmen, when jointing circular saws, hold their file so unskillfully that all the *short* teeth as well as the *long* ones, were jointed off, and the saw was no more round than it was when they commenced jointing it. Hold the file *firmly*, and move it towards the teeth only a *hair's-breadth* at a time.

FILING SAWS.

617. After having put the saw in the clamp, as in the figure,

and placed it on a bench that will bring the teeth about as high as "the *pit* of your stomach," put the shank of the file in a handle not less than one foot long, and put it in as *true* as practicable. The beginner will be able to hold his file more correctly with a long handle than with a short one. Now, hold the file firmly, so that it will not turn to the right nor to the left, and file every tooth to a point; and as soon as a tooth *is filed* to a point, do not give it another stroke. Great care and skill are necessary when filing with a triangular file, lest while one tooth is being filed, the tooth on the opposite side of the file should get filed off *too much*. Always make the strokes *from you;* and when a tooth is almost to a point, make each stroke with precision and care, and rather slowly.

THE PROPER ANGLE FOR FILING THE FACE OF THE TEETH

618. For cutting across the grain, varies very much among different filers. The work to be done with a saw must determine, in a measure, the proper angle for filing the face of the teeth. If the wood be hard, and knotty, and gnarly, the teeth must be filed for *chipping* or removing the sawdust. And the best kind of tooth for removing sawdust is one that is filed *square across on the face*. But a tooth filed square across on the face of it will not *cut off* the fibres of the wood well; therefore, the face of the teeth must be filed more or less diagonally. If filed very diagonally on the face, the teeth will be very *fleaming*, or *fleam-pointed*. (See TECHNICALITIES.) When filed of this shape, they *cut* very fast, but they remove the core very slowly. Some men prefer to file four teeth or six teeth very fleam-pointed, at an angle of about forty or forty-five degrees on the face, and then file one tooth *square* on the face for taking out the core, leaving the point a little *shorter* than the others. For all kinds of work, for hard and for soft wood, when a man keeps but one saw, if the teeth be filed at an angle of about ten or fifteen degrees on the face, it will be found to subserve the best purpose for hand-saws. If a man keeps a *slitting*-saw, his *crosscut hand*-saw may be filed a little more fleaming on the face of the teeth. When the wood

to be sawed is all soft wood, a saw will cut the fastest if four teeth—two on each side—are filed quite fleaming on the *face,* and every *fifth* tooth filed *square across it* on the face and back, without setting them. When teeth are *all* filed very fleaming, and none filed square to clean out the chip or core, it will be necessary to bear on in sawing.

619. Slitting-saws are always filed *square across* on the *face* of the teeth, and *usually* square on the *back* of them; although some filers contend that it is better to file a little *fleaming* on the backs at the points. As it is very difficult for beginners to retain the proper angle in-all the teeth, and to file every tooth of exactly such a size and form, with nothing but the eye for a guide,

A SAW-FILER,

620. A perspective view of which is shown at Fig. 171, is found to be a very useful implement. With such a filer, any

FIG. 171.

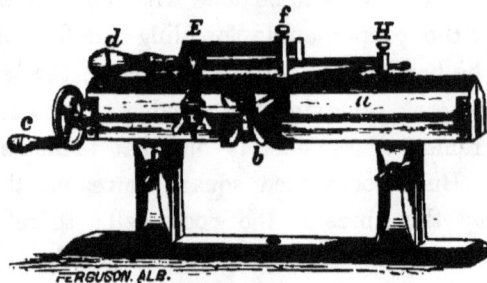

SAW-FILER.

farmer can file his saws in a most complete manner, giving every tooth *exactly* a certain angle, both on the face and back, and of a given hook, and just so long and no longer, nor shorter; and besides, if every tooth is filed to a point, the saw will be neatly jointed. It consists of a clamp like Fig. 169, with an iron plate, *a,* screwed firmly to the jaw of the clamp. *b* is an iron slide, which is neatly fitted by notches or gains to the true edges of *a,* which is slid along the jaw, back and forth, from end to end, by the endless set-screw and wheel *c,* fastened in front of the iron plate *a.* *d* is the handle of the iron plate which holds the file which plays back and forth in the iron post *E,* which is fastened to an adjustable iron plate, which is bolted to the slide b. f is a thumb set-screw, to regulate the proper depth to file the teeth. H is another set-screw, for holding the file at any desired angle.

621. When a saw is filed with such a filer, put it in the clamp very true, with one end just as high above the jaws as the other. Adjust the file to file hooked or not, and, with the set-screw and wheel, run the slide b to one end of the clamp. Now, adjust the post E by the thumb-screw on the lower end, to hold the file at the desired angle. File the teeth on one side of the saw, and carry the post E around, so as to bring the file at the same angle in the opposite direction. After having filed one tooth, turn the set wheel around once or twice, more or less, according to the size of the teeth, which will draw the slide b along *just so far*. If the slide is drawn along only a trifle *too far* at one time, and not quite so far the next time, the teeth will not all be of a uniform length. The file is so hung that in thrusting *from* you it will cut, and can be raised a little when drawing it back. There are several styles of patent filers. The proprietor of this one is Mr. H. Miller, Ithaca, N. Y., who will furnish both filers and rights to manufacture.

622. Fig. 172 exhibits a section of a *slitting hand-saw* well filed. It will be seen by the figure that the *faces* of the teeth

FIG. 172.

SLITTING-SAW WELL FILED.

are at right angles to the cutting edges, or points, and are all filed square across. It is not practicable to saw *across* the grain with a saw filed in this manner.

613. Fig. 173 is a *crosscut* section of a hand-saw well filed. The faces of the teeth are at right angles with the dotted lines along the points. Many filers contend, that if the faces of the

18

teeth are filed at right angles they will be *too hooked.*   But if filed in this style a saw will cut much faster and easier, and it

FIG. 173.

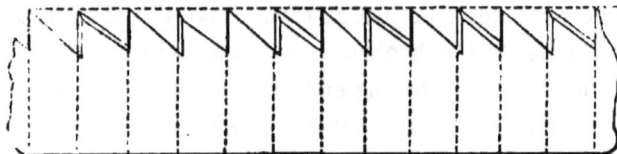

CROSSCUT WELL FILED.

coincides with the manner of filing adopted by our best mechanics.

624. Fig. 174 shows a saw *badly filed;* but it is an exact rep-

FIG. 174.

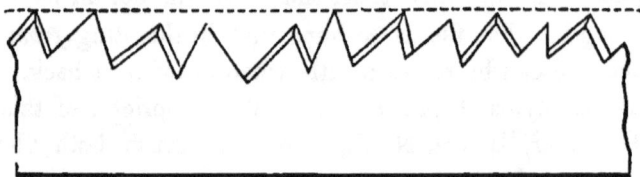

BADLY FILED.

resentation of many saws that have been filed by those who do not understand the *principle* on which saws are sharpened.   By a glance at the dotted line along the edge it will be seen that *a few* teeth only must do all the sawing.   (See Par. 611.)   I have taken this figure from a saw that was brought to me to be filed; and some parts of it had been filed worse than this.   It had been filed with old worn-out files until its proprietor found it impossible to cut off a narrow board with it.

625. Now in order to put it in *sawable* order it was put in the clamp and jointed, and all of the teeth started in filing of the proper form, and then the teeth were set.   It is not always most advisable to restore such teeth to the most proper form at *one* filing unless one has much sawing to perform.   If a saw-filer is used it will be much easier to restore the correct form of the teeth than it will be when filing by hand.   When filing such a saw by

hand, after it has been jointed place a try-square against the edge, and with the sharp point of a file make a scratch across the blade 'or the face of each tooth, as shown by the dotted lines Figs. 172 and 173, and then file the teeth only in part to a point the first time across from end to end.   Some filers always *change ends* with a saw after filing one side.   But it is of little consequence how a man files, if he only does it in a workmanlike manner. After a saw has been filed, in order to have it cut a kerf a little *wider* than the blade the *points* of the teeth must be *set*.

SETTING SAWS.

FIGS. 175, 176, 177.

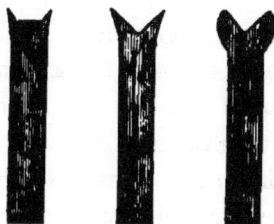

CROSS SECTIONS OF SAWS.

626. Fig. 175 represents a cross section of a saw with the points of the fleam-pointed teeth set, showing the *cleaners*, or teeth that are filed square across.   (See Par. 653.)

627. Fig. 176 is a section of saw in which all the teeth have been set.   When a saw is well filed it will appear like these figures when viewed endways, and a cambric needle may be slid along between the points of the teeth, from one end of a saw to the other.

628. Fig. 177 is a section of a saw, the teeth of which are set *more* than they ought to be for the thickness of the plate ; and the *whole teeth* having been set too much, the *points* have been *worn off*, so that it will work very hard, and perhaps not at all without great power.   This shows the importance of setting *as little of the points as practicable*.

629. There are two kinds of *set* for saw teeth,—*bent* set and

swedged set. *Bent* set is used for both crosscut and slitting-saws; but *swedged* set is used only for saws that cut lengthways of the grain. There are two kinds of *bent* set, but we shall notice but one in this work.

630. The least possible amount of set, in either a crosscut or ripping-saw, and have the saw work easily, is the best. The greater the amount of set the wider will be the kerf; and the wider the kerf the greater must be the power to drive a saw. Soft wood requires more set than hard wood. A good saw often does bad work in consequence of *too much* set. If there is too much set, a saw will sometimes *run* in consequence of it; and sometimes, especially if the feed is heavy, if there is too much set, a saw will often make a *rough* and *jagged* cut, which makes a saw run hard.

631. The rudest and simplest mode of setting a saw is, to lay the blade of it on a smooth end of a block of hard wood, and with a punch and hammer bend the point of every other tooth by a single blow, and then turn the saw over and set the other side, being careful to place the punch on each tooth in the same place, and to gauge the force of each blow as nearly as may be. If the

FIGS. 178, 179. punch is placed near the *points* of some teeth and near the *roots* of others, the teeth will be set very unevenly. Two or three teeth on each side should be set near the end of the saw *first;* and then, if there appears to be too little or too much set in these teeth, let the blows be lighter or heavier, as may be necessary.

632. Fig. 178 represents an *edge*-view of a slitting-saw having the teeth set by bending the points.

633. Fig. 179 is an edge-view of a slitting-saw having the teeth *set*, or *spread*, by *swedging*. It is not practicable to set *small* saws by swedging the points.

EDGE VIEW OF SLIT-TING-SAWS.

634. Of many different styles, may be obtained at hardware stores. It matters little what the set is, if it will only set all the teeth *true*. *Bow*-saws, *billet*-saws, and all other saws having a very narrow blade, must sometimes be set with a punch, or nail sct. (See Par. 631.)

635. Fig. 180 represents a punch for setting a rip-saw, which

FIG. 180.

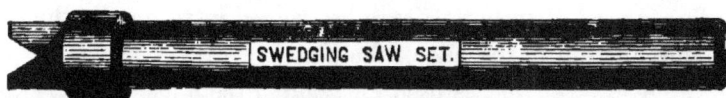

SWEDGING SAW SET.

is made of steel, and well hardened, with an iron band around it, near the crotched end, to prevent its splitting. The fork is made with a triangular file, while the steel is yet soft, of an angle more obtuse than the saw teeth, and left a little crowning at the bottom of the fork, from side to side. Before the set is hardened, make the crotch a little deeper with a sharp cold-chisel, to prevent dulling the points of the teeth.

636. To set with a crotched punch after the saw has been jointed and filed, let the punch be held steadily and firmly against the point of the tooth, parallel with the side of the saw, and with light blows with a hammer weighing about a pound, (with a still lighter hammer if the teeth be small,) spread the points of the teeth like the tail of a dove (Fig. 179), both ways from the centre. *Heavy* blows will be liable to *bend* the teeth. As the crotch of the punch is a little *convex* lengthways of it, by varying the position of the punch the point of the tooth may be spread to the required extent. After the points are spread enough, the cutting edge of each tooth may be drawn out with the hammer by holding a heavy piece of iron firmly against the face or bottom of the tooth. This operation saves a vast amount of filing. In spreading the teeth of a circular saw, the set may be gauged by allowing the saw to revolve slowly, when every tooth must be spread sufficiently to just touch the end of a stick of hard wood. In

case a tooth should get set a little *too much*, the side of the point may be dressed off a little with a file, being careful to have the *side edge of the face* of the teeth more prominent than they are *back* of the face edges.   If there should be any play of the man-drel *endways*, it must be held against one shoulder of the bearing while it is being set.   This mode of setting will make a circular saw of uneven thickness, or that has little *kinks* in it, cut much truer, and work easier, than if the set of the teeth were gauged by the *side* of the saw plate.   The teeth of circular saws for cut-ting *across* the grain of wood, the points of which are spread by bending instead of swedging, may be gauged in setting by the end of a stick instead of the side of the plate.

637.   A saw set that is used for *bending* teeth should have not only a set-screw to gauge the amount of set, but should have a brass or copper plate for the points of the teeth to rest against when the saw is being set, which plate may be adjusted to allow the teeth to enter the set just so far and no farther.   A saw set that has no adjustable plate, but receives some teeth half their length, and only the points of others, is an improper instrument to set teeth with.   If a saw set, for instance, takes hold of one tooth near its point, and bends it as much as the gauge-screw will admit of, and if the set is then put on the next tooth *farther* than it was on the first tooth, the teeth on which the set was placed the *farthest*, will receive the most set, even if the set-screw is made to touch the plate alike in setting each individual tooth.

638.   There is great danger, in setting the teeth of saws which have a high temper, or which are very hard, of breaking them, especially in cold weather.   Whenever a hard saw or a thick one is to be set, it should be well warmed before any teeth are set. The teeth of some good saws when they are very cold will snap almost like glass when we attempt to set them.   The best way to warm the teeth is, to pour hot water on them before setting, unless the saw can be taken into a warm room.   This applies not only to circular saws, but to all kinds of long saws; and the tyro will ever regret that he did not warm his saw previous to setting

the teeth, after having broken several teeth of a good saw in consequence of not warming it.

639. The teeth of a very *soft* saw will require more set than a hard saw of the same thickness; because, in the hard saw the edge is more perfect, and the cut of such a saw of course will be *cleaner* and *smoother*. On the contrary, a very coarse edge, instead of cutting the fibres of wood smoothly, *tears* them in two, leaving the sides of the kerf very rough, which makes a saw work hard. Avoid setting the teeth too wide in *any* saw.

640. To take the set *out of* a saw which has *too much* set in the teeth, lay it on a smooth stick of timber, and lay a hard, smooth plank on the sides of the teeth, and strike on it with a heavy hammer; or, use a set.

TWO-HAND CROSSCUT SAWS.

641. Fig. 181 represents a two-hand crosscut saw, with teeth of a proper form at one end, while at the other end they are represented as they are too often filed in old saws which have been filed with old files. The dotted lines show how much should be filed out in order to make them of the proper form. Although there is the same number of teeth per foot when filed at such an obtuse angle as is shown at the left hand, the teeth will not cut half as fast as they will when filed like those at the *right*

FIG. 181.

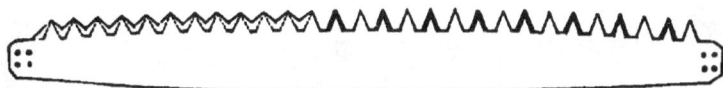

A CROSS-CUT SAW.

hand. When teeth are filed *short* and *blunt*, they require more force to make a saw cut, on the same principle that a man with a *thin* axe will be able to chop faster than he will with one having a *very thick* blade.

642. The teeth in crosscut saws are almost always *too far apart* to work well. Many a good saw has been spoiled by some *knowing know-nothing*, who has cut away every alternate tooth

with a view to make a saw cut *faster*. Suppose, for instance, that we cut away *four-fifths* of the teeth, how fast will a saw cut? For sawing timber of ordinary size, the teeth should not be more than one inch apart. When a saw *jumps* and *jerks* along, it is very certain evidence that the teeth are too far apart. The smaller in diameter the timber is, the closer together the teeth should be, in order to work best and smoothest. As the teeth of *two-hand crosscut* saws are filed without any *hook*, they should be filed rather slim and narrow at the base or roots, in order to cut the fastest.

643. *Improved* two-hand crosscut saws are now manufactured with every third tooth formed like a *cat's claw*, and filed square across, and about a sixteenth of an inch *shorter* than the others, which are filed very fleaming. They are much superior to the common kind of saws.

PUTTING TWO-HAND CROSSCUT SAWS IN ORDER.

644. Dress out two strips of board, with one edge of each one of the same circle as the cutting edge of the saw, and screw them together with the saw between them, like Fig. 182, which shows a combined clamp and jointer, with the longest teeth of a saw extending above the edges of the clamp. The screws are

FIG. 182.

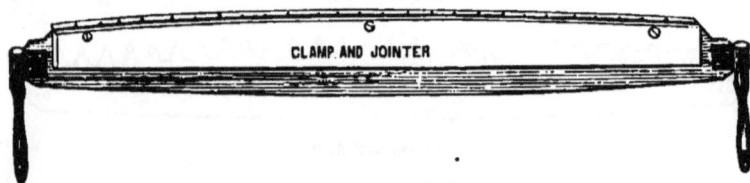

CLAMP AND JOINTER

A CROSSCUT SAW WITH HANDLES.

put between the teeth. Adjust the clamp so that the long teeth will extend a little above the edge, and with a file dress them off even with the edge of the clamp. After it is jointed take out the screws, and place the saw in the bench-vise, and file it.

645. In filing, always endeavor to file the spaces as deep or

deeper than they were originally made. This will keep the teeth of a good length, and a saw will never need to be gummed. Never file with an *old worn-out file ;* because, although the teeth may be filed to a *point,* the spaces will not be deepened ; and in a short time it will cost far more to *gum* a saw than it would to keep the teeth of a suitable length by filing them. If the teeth are filed very fleaming, or diagonally, it will be necessary to file about every seventh tooth *square across,* and a little shorter than the others. When all the teeth are filed fleaming, if they are filed at an angle of about ten or fifteen degrees with the face of the teeth, they will remove the core or dust as fast as they cut.

646. After filing, set the *points* of the teeth a very little. The least possible set, and have a saw work easily, will cause it to run the truest and the best. If a saw is kept as sharp as it ought to be, it will seldom need any more set when cutting *soft* wood, than it will when cutting hard wood. When a saw cuts a jagged, rough, uneven cut, it is a sign that the saw is not set *true,* or that the set has been taken out of some of the teeth.

647. When the *whole tooth* is set, the set is very liable to be taken out by allowing the saw to be pinched between the ends of a log when it is nearly sawed in two. This may be the cause of its *running.* Perhaps a few teeth are a trifle *shorter* on one side than on the other, made so either by filing or dulling. In this case the teeth should be jointed and filed of an equal length. If the set is out and the saw runs towards the *top end* of the log, give the teeth on the *opposite* side a little more set. In sawing logs for staves, spokes, and shingles, it is important that the saw run true, else there is danger of sawing one side of the log *too short.*

HANDLING A CROSSCUT SAW

648. Requires the exercise of a little activity and agility, else the work will be rendered laborious. The hands of the sawer should merely *hang loosely* on the handles, allowing the handle freedom to play up and down, as the saw adjusts itself in its passage through the log. After a saw has entered a log sufficiently

18*

to keep itself erect, if a sawyer is inclined "to ride," as it is called, it would be well to pass a rope or strap of leather around the handle for him to pull by. A good sawyer must make long, elastic motions with the arms, and let the saw play lively, lightly, and freely through the log, and if the saw is in good order, the ends of the log will be as true as if they had been turned off. Let the saw be kept well-jointed and properly set, and not allowed to become rusty, and it will work easy and cut fast.

THE MANNER OF FILING COMPASS SAWS.

649. Compass saws, and billet-web saws, and such as are used in a frame, for sawing felloes, and other circular work, cut as much *lengthways* of the grain as they do *crossways;* and if filed for crosscutting, they do not work well in sawing lengthways of the grain; and if filed exclusively for ripping, they will not work *at all* when they come to that portion of the circle which crosses the grain of the wood. Most mechanics file such saws but a *little* fleaming, but I think they will cut smoother and faster by filing every third tooth for *ripping,* making it a little shorter than the teeth filed fleaming. The object of this is, when the saw comes to that part of a circle which runs lengthways of the grain, teeth filed fleaming will not *chip* well; therefore, every third tooth being filed for ripping, and not set, will cut away the *centre* of the kerf as fast as the fleaming teeth cut the *sides* of it. Compass and billet-saws being so narrow, they cannot advantageously be set with an ordinary set, but must be set with a nail set, or punch and hammer, by laying them on the square end of a block of hard wood, and by giving each tooth an equal blow with the hammer.

650. The blades of compass and all other saws for cutting circular work, should be thinner on the *back* than they are at the cutting edge. When of this form they will turn in sawing a small circle with less set than they possibly can when the blade is all of a uniform thickness.

CIRCULAR SAWS.

651. Fig. 183 represents a circular saw with four different kinds of teeth. Three kinds, *C B*, *B A*, and *A D*, are for *ripping*, and the portion between *D C* is for cutting *across* the grain. To find the angle for filing the *face* of the teeth, strike a circle, the dotted line *a*, half the diameter of the saw, and a line from the points of the teeth to one side of this circle, will give

FIG. 183.

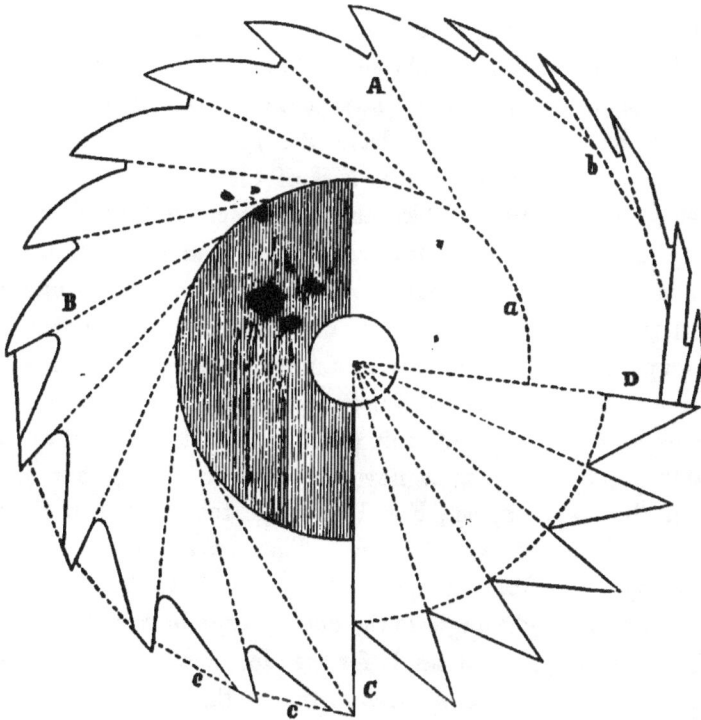

A CIRCULAR SAW HAVING FOUR KINDS OF TEETH.

the *hook* of the teeth. The marks may be made with the sharp point of a steel file. The angle for the *hook* of the teeth may be more obtuse or *acute*, as at *b*, from *A* to *D*. The teeth between *B* and *C* are kept in order with less filing than those with circular backs between *A* and *B*. Those teeth between *A* and *B* are the strongest, and if the spaces at the roots of them be filed with a half-round file, the teeth will be still stronger. The *backs* of the teeth for one-fourth or half an inch back from the points, according to the size of the teeth, should be on a line drawn from the point of one tooth to a point as much *below* the point of the tooth *behind* it, as each tooth is required to cut *in depth*, as at *c c*. If, for example, a saw cuts one inch in one revolution, and has forty teeth, the teeth *back* of the points must be filed *below* the points, so as to be on a line drawn from one-fortieth of an inch *below* one point, *c c*, to the point of the tooth *forward* of it. Such a shape will allow the teeth to cut just as easily as if the backs of them were like those between *C* and *D*. The filer should be very careful to have the *points* of the teeth more *prominent* than they are just *back* of the cutting points. These teeth, that are formed like those between *A* and *D*, will cut very much faster, and with less power than either of the other kinds. They seem to *cut* a kerf through a stick, while teeth with less hook *scrape* or *file* out the kerf. But teeth of such a shape must be made only in a saw of the very best materials, and for sawing hard and knotty wood there is great danger of breaking them. For all soft wood such teeth work most admirably. Such teeth must never be bent in setting, but *swedged* with the swedging set, Fig. 180. The teeth between *C* and *D* are for cutting across the grain. The correct hook is found by drawing a line from the points of the teeth to the centre of the saw ; or, at a right angle to the cutting edge of the saw. This is allowed to be the best angle for the face of all crosscutting saws, except such as have *no hook* to the teeth, like Fig. 181. It is of very little consequence so far as cutting is concerned, what the shape of the *back* of a tooth is, if the part *back of the point* is far enough back of, or *below* the line of motion, in which the points move, for all the teeth to enter the wood freely. If the *back* of a tooth be *higher* than the point, a tooth must *wear* its way through a stick instead of *cutting* through.

JOINTING A CIRCULAR SAW.

652. If a circular saw is not as round as may be, the teeth on one side will cut too deep at each revolution, and on the other side will not cut as deep as they ought to cut; and, therefore, at every revolution one side will sometimes take such a rank hold as to produce a *jar*, or spring the teeth, thus making a rough cut. Some mechanics use for jointing circular saws, a kind of *templet* or template, one end of which is rested on the collar of the mandrel. But that is not as correct and easy for *beginners* as the manner recommended at Par. 616. When a large circular saw is jointed by being made to revolve backwards while a file is held against the points, the impact or friction is so intense, that the teeth will *wear out* a file wherever it touches the saw. When large teeth need much jointing, hold a bar of lead near the points for every one to touch as they pass it; lead will not dull them: and then *file off* the points of the long teeth until the facet made by the jointing-file on the *ends* of them, will be even with the points of the shortest teeth. Now, set it and file it.

FILING CIRCULAR SAWS.

653. The best and most convenient place for filing a circular saw is on its mandrel, providing there is sufficient light to enable one to see the points of the teeth. Some mechanics always take the saw off the mandrel and put it in a vise when filing. But any contrivance which will hold a saw firmly on the side which is being filed is all that is necessary. I always have used for this purpose two sticks, one on each side of the saw, extending from the saw to some part of the frame. Every tooth should be brought to the top of the saw when it is filed; because any one can file better on the *top* of a saw than on the *sides* of it. And, if, every tooth is brought to just such a position before it is filed, they are more likely to be filed *alike*. If the teeth are to be filed *square across*, every tooth may be filed while standing on one side of the saw; but if the teeth are to be filed *fleaming* or bevelling, it is better to file the teeth on *one* side while standing on

one side of the saw, and to file the other side when standing on the *opposite* side. The same rules hold good for filing circular saws that are observed for filing long saws. A circular saw for cutting across the grain should have not less than four teeth— one on each side of the saw—filed square across, and a little shorter than the others, to cut out the chip. These teeth should have a good hook. All the teeth should be kept as nearly of a size and length as possible; and for this purpose the templet (see Fig. 184) should be placed on every tooth before it is filed, in order to show whether or not a tooth has the desired shape. It is sometimes a very good practice in filing any kind of saw, and especially if it is a very *soft* saw, to go over all the teeth with a very fine file, or with one that is nearly worn out, after they have been brought to an edge with a *sharp* file. This process gives the teeth a *more perfect edge.* A good fine edge can never be obtained with a coarse file, if the strokes be made ever so light. The finishing strokes with the file should always be made *from you,* and if the teeth be fleam-pointed, the strokes of the file should be made in the same direction that the teeth are bent in setting. My twenty-four-inch circular saw, for cutting fire-wood, with teeth an inch and one-fourth apart, is filed *fleaming,* at an angle of about forty-five degrees; and every *fifth* tooth is filed *square,* and a sixteenth of an inch *shorter* than the others; and I have never met with a saw before which will run through large knots and gnarls so *noiselessly,* and with so little power, and cut so neatly.

654. There are several styles of saw-filers for filing circular saws. But a man should have more saws to file than a common farmer usually owns, in order "to make it pay" to purchase a filer, which costs from $10 to $15. A little practice and skill are more important than a *saw-filer,* unless some cheaper article shall be invented than any with which I have ever met.

WHERE TO OBTAIN THE BEST PATENT GROUND SAWS.

655. The best saws of every kind with which I have ever met, were manufactured by R. Hoe & Co., 29 Gold st., New

York city, and by Andrews & Burbage, Elmira, N. Y. Their patent ground circulars sustain an *unrivalled* reputation through-out the States, not only for sawing lumber, but for farmers' wood-saws. The patent ground circulars are *thicker* in the centre than they are at the *cutting edge*, and are ground of a uniform taper from the centre to the edge, which shape renders them *stronger* than those which are ground in the usual manner; and they require *less set*, and, as a consequence, less power is required to drive them; and they are less liable to become heated; and they do not wear out so many *files*, because the teeth are *thinner;* and, more than all, they possess a *superior temper;* and are made of the best of steel. I have two of them in use, and although I am a stranger to the manufacturers of these saws, I would not exchange one of these saws for a *gross* of common saws. If a farmer desires a *good saw* of any kind, and made of any thick-ness, or of any style of teeth, or if he has an *old* saw which needs to be *re-toothed*, or *re-tempered*, or straightened, he need not fear to confide in either of these companies.

HANGING CIRCULAR SAWS.

656. It is a pretty nice piece of work to hang a circular saw just right. It is an impossibility to make a saw *mathematically* true, or to hang it to run with mathematical precision; but it is easy for a good mechanic to approximate as near perfection in this respect as is of practical use. A good saw is often con-demned when the whole fault is in the mandrel on which it turns; and a badly fitted mandrel is liable to spoil a good saw.

657. The idea to be kept in mind is, to have the collars or flanges turned as true as possible; and any deviation in the col-lars from trueness, will *multiply* this deviation in the saw just as many times as the saw is larger than the collars. The bearings of the mandrel should be turned first, and then the face of the collar should be turned off very true, without changing ends of the mandrel in the lathe. Sometimes the centres or points in a lathe *deviate* a trifle, and by changing ends with the mandrel, and finishing a part of it with the ends in *opposite directions*, the

bearings will not be true with the collars. If the lathe be rather light, and it springs when the collars are being turn-----he man-drel should be put in the lathe, and the face of th-----collar turned while the mandrel revolves *on its own bearing*-----not merely on the *centres* of the lathe. Sometimes the collars must be turned a little *concave*, to fit the saw well, and sometimes one must be a little concave and the other one correspondingly con-vex or straight, as the shape of the saw requires. The mandrel should fit snugly the eye of the saw without any play. When the saw is placed on the mandrel, if it deviates any in revolving, it may be adjusted by a piece or two of paper, between the col-lar and the saw, and be made to run with the greatest precision. The bearings should be so neatly fitted to the boxes, that there will be no working of it up and down, nor any play endways. (See FITTING UP MACHINERY, in the next volume.) In sawing anything where exactness is not necessary, if there should be a little play of the mandrel endways, it matters not; but in sawing to a gauge, if there be much play of the mandrel endways, some pieces will be thicker or longer than others, according to the amount of play.

BALANCING SAWS.

658. When saws are hung on a mandrel having a fly-wheel on it, if it is not well balanced the saw will vibrate or flutter at the edge, and the frame will shake like a person who has been attacked with the quotidian ague. When a saw is well balanced the frame will not tremble, even when the motion is very high. (See HOW TO BALANCE A SAW, in next vol.)

GUMMING SAWS

659. Is the act of making the teeth longer by making the spaces between them deeper. This is performed in several ways. The best mode, but most expensive, is, to gum with a file; be-cause by gumming with a file there is no danger of breaking or bending a saw, nor of *stretching* the edge. And if the spaces

were filed deeper, as the points wear off there would be no necessity for ⬛⬛ gumming saws at all.

660. ⬛⬛ming is often done with a cold-chisel and hammer while ⬛⬛ saw lies on the smooth face of an anvil, or an equivalent to an anvil. If gummed in this way, it must be done with a thin, sharp chisel and a rather light hammer ; and the operator cannot be too particular in having the part of the saw opposite the chisel rest level on the anvil. One careless blow has often broken a good saw, or damaged it by kinking it or cracking a tooth. Both ends of the saw should be supported as high as the surface of the anvil, and then, with a narrow cold-chisel, about one-fourth of an inch wide, *work crossways* of the saw, with the edge of the chisel *parallel* with the edge of the saw. Never cleave at one cut more than one-eighth of an inch, unless the chip be cut loose *first* on the ends. If the chisel *stands crossways* of the saw, in working the spaces deeper there is great danger of *stretching* the edge of the saw, or of starting the teeth near the roots.

661. Gumming saws with a machine is done with a kind of punch playing in a die of the shape of the spaces, which is attached to a strong lever, and the saw is placed between the die and punch, and the spaces are worked deeper by *nipping* a little at each descent of the lever. In gumming with a machine every alternate tooth should be gummed with the saw the *other side up*. If the gumming be all done on one side it is apt to *bend* the saw; and straightening it back *stretches* the edge ; and, in stretching the middle, by striking the saw a few smart blows on opposite sides with a hammer having a roundish face, when the saw lies on a true anvil so as to make the edges straight, there is great danger of *breaking* a saw. The cutting edge of the punch should have about three-sixteenths of an inch *bevel*, so as to make a cleaner and easier cut when gumming it.

662. There is always more or less danger of damaging a good saw while gumming it; therefore it is far better to expend a dollar in gumming with a *file* than to pay a dollar for gumming with a chisel or gummer.

663. In order to have all the spaces and the teeth of a uniform

FIG. 184.

MANNER OF MARKING OUT THE CORRECT
SHAPE OF SAW TEETH.

size, they should be marked out with a templet, shown at Fig. 184, which is made of a piece of sheet-iron, or a thin piece of board wood, and is placed with one end on the collar against the side of the saw; and as each tooth is filed the templet may be placed against the saw, in order to determine whether the *face* or *back* of a tooth requires *more* filing or not.

664. Fig. 185 shows the form of a templet for marking out

FIG. 185.

new teeth on a saw like the shape of the teeth at *b*, Fig. 183. The templet may be formed to mark out any style of teeth.

MILL SAWS.

665. Why is lumber often sawed of all shapes and of variable thicknesses at the great majority of saw-mills? In most instances it is in consequence of the saw being in improper order. Should the set get out of any of the teeth on either side, by passing a hard knot a saw will most assuredly *run*, and make the lumber thicker or thinner in the middle than it should be. From what has been said of filing and setting other saws, the tyro will be able to file and set a mill saw in a proper manner. Where both hard and soft logs are to be sawed, it would be good policy to have a saw for each kind of wood. For sawing hard wood logs the plate should be rather thick and stiff, with the teeth nearer together, and rather *short*, to retain the set longer, than in a saw designed solely for soft wood. In order to saw lumber or timber of an exact size, and very true and smooth, the saw or saws must

be in perfect order. A few practical directions may not be amiss on the ▮▮▮▮ct of

▮▮▮F TEETH IN SAWS WHICH WORK UP AND DOWN.

666. Fig. 186 represents a mill saw having five different forms of teeth. At *a* the teeth are filed on the face, at a right angle with the cutting edge of the saw, and the backs, or upper sides, at an angle of forty-five degrees. This is the oldest and most common form of teeth, and whether filed square or bevelling, more power is required to drive a saw having this kind of teeth, unless they are hammered as at *e*. Teeth of this form remove the sawdust by *scraping* instead of *cutting*. It requires less skill to keep such teeth in good order than either of the other kinds.

667. At *b* much the same kind of teeth is shown, with the faces filed at an acute angle, giving them a greater *hook*, while the *backs* are of the same angle. If the motion were high, such teeth will cut much faster, with the same power, than the kind at *a*. But if the motion be very slow, teeth with much hook are liable to draw into the log farther than they are able to cut without *staggering* or *trembling*, as if having too much feed.

668. At *c* and *d* are two different kinds of teeth, which operate with far less power than those at *a* and *b*, but they require much more skill to keep them in order. But by using a templet (see Fig. 185), any one who is able to put the teeth of any saw in order will find little difficulty with these. The

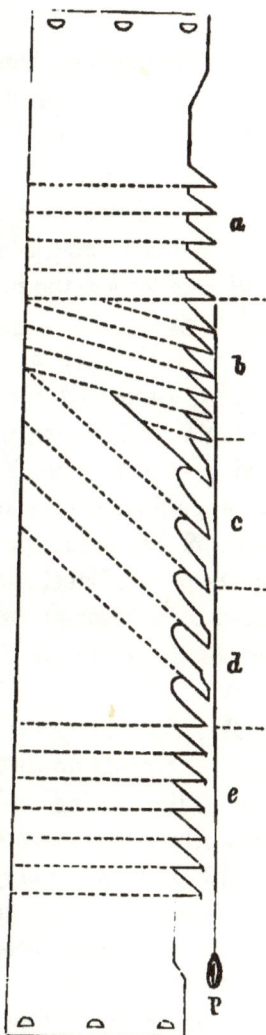

FIG. 186.

teeth at *c* should be filed so that the cutting points shall be one-sixteenth or one-twentieth of an inch more *prominent* than they are back of the points. (See Fig. 183, *c*.) If the material to be sawed be such that each tooth is required to cut one part of an inch, by filing the ends of the teeth so that a line drawn from the point of one tooth would strike one-sixteenth of an inch *below* the point of the first tooth *back* of it, the saw cannot draw into the log any farther than it will cut without *trembling*, even if the teeth be filed very hooked.

669. At *d* is a form for teeth having a *heel* or guide to prevent the saw from drawing into the log when sawing. The guides or heels are dressed in a line with each other, at a given distance back of the cutting edge. If, in sawing, the saw is inclined to *haul into the log*, the heels prevent its entering any farther than is desirable.

670. At *e* teeth are represented with the points *hammered;* i. e., with repeated blows on the *back* of a tooth, near the point, with a light hammer, the edge is turned *downward*. There is a saving of nearly one-half the power by hammering the teeth, if it be performed very skillfully. If this spur should not all be worn off before filing again, it is necessary to hold a smooth and square piece of steel against the *face* of the tooth, and with a few blows of a hammer *upwards*, bring this spur on a line with the face of the tooth, so that it will not be filed off in dressing the tooth.

671. As *hammering* teeth, either for the purpose of setting them or turning down the points, *refines* the steel and renders it harder, the cutting quality of an inferior saw is often improved by working the points with a hammer when cold.

672. It is of primary importance that a saw which works up and down, should be jointed *straight* on the edge. If a saw is allowed to become *hollowing* on the cutting edge more than one-fourth of an inch, if everything is not made doubly strong, we may surely expect that the saw or something else will break. If the cutting edge is *crowning* from end to end, a saw cannot be made to work up to its greatest capacity. A jointer for a mill

saw may be made with its edges straight and square, like the
jointe████ crosscut saw. (See Fig. 182.) In order to have a
saw ████ well, it should be jointed every alternate time it is
█████████llful filer will take a square block a foot long, and
one by three inches square, and place the flat side of it against
the side of the saw, and, holding the jointing-file on the edge of
the block, joint the teeth very true.

LENGTH OF THE CUTTING EDGE OF A SAW.

672½. When a saw is worked by a crank and pitman, all the
teeth beyond a given point had better be cut away; because, it
is only a waste of time and tools, to keep them in order with the
teeth that do all the sawing. The teeth *below the rabbet* on the
head-block, when the crank is *up* never cut any, unless in sawing
a log with a *bow downwards*. If the stroke of the crank be
twenty-four inches, and the logs one foot in diameter, three feet
of the cutting edge is all that is brought in contact with the log;
and a cutting edge of *greater* length would be useless. If the
logs be two feet in diameter, and twenty-four-inch stroke of the
crank, the cutting edge should be four feet long. If the logs be
three feet in diameter, the cutting edge of the saw should be not
less than four and a half feet long. When the crank is down,
all the teeth above the log are useless.

673. This rule holds good in regard to saws that are worked
horizontally. In sawing off logs two feet in diameter with a
crank having a twenty-eight-inch stroke, the cutting edge should
be four feet and four inches long. With the same crank, for sawing off logs only *one* foot, three feet four inches of the cutting
edge is all that saws.

674. There is, many times, two or three inches in length of
the cutting edge of hand-saws near the handle, which never saws
any, and is worse than useless; because, the teeth must all be
filed off in order to keep them of the same length as those in the
middle of the saw. These suggestions will enable the young
filer to understand how large a number of teeth near the ends of
his saw are useless.

RAKE OF SAWS.

674½. Saws are hung in a gate working up a̲n̲d̲ ̲d̲o̲w̲n̲, not only for sawing logs, but for sawing out boat-knees, r̲u̲n̲-ners, felloes for wheels, wagon thills, scrolls, and o̲t̲h̲e̲r̲ work, and they are always dressed to cut *only when they descend.* If the material be forced on to the saw when it is ascending, unless it should be very heavy, the material with the carriage will be jerked up and down in a most frightful manner. To avoid this difficulty the saw is hung with a *rake*, (see TECHNI-CALITIES, Par. 602,) in order to allow the material to be brought up to the saw with facility when it is *ascending.*

675. I knew a mechanic once who got up a little saw for saw-ing out felloes and sleigh-runners, and not understanding this principle, he hung his saw without any rake. He could not make it operate with any degree of satisfaction until he hung the saw with a *rake.*

676. The *amount* of rake which should be given to a saw, *should be equal*, usually, *to the greatest amount of feed*, measuring from the tooth which is found at the upper side of the timber when the crank is down. Many sawyers hang their saws with-out any rake.

677. To ascertain the amount of rake, set the crank up, and suspend a plumb, *P*, Fig. 186, with a small line from the upper tooth, and lean the saw *forward* as far as is desirable, as shown in the figure, and fasten it there.

678. *Rake*, in saws which work horizontally, is something which is seldom recognized or even thought of. But when a *drag* or a *butting* saw is attached to a pitman, and it is filed to saw only one way, if the cutting edge is not exactly parallel with a line cutting the centre of the pitman, it *may* or may not be hung with a *rake.* If the farthest end falls *below* a parallel line cutting the centre of the pitman, it will have a *rake* just in proportion to the distance it falls below a parallel line.

RANGING SAWS

679. Is a very important consideration where a carriage or

table is used. The carriage or table should always move *parallel* with the sides of the saw. An ingenious sawyer will be able to determine by simply glancing his eye along the sides of the saw on the carriage, whether the saw and carriage are in range or not. When the carriage or table is fitted up, the saw must be hung to correspond with it; but, when the saw is already in the desired position, the table or carriage must be fitted to the *saw*. To determine whether the carriage or table of a circular saw for cutting wood is in range with the saw, push the carriage back as far as it will go, and then place a board having a straight edge on the carriage, with the straight edge as close to one side of the saw as it can be and not hit it. Move the carriage back and forth, with the straight-edged board on both sides of the saw, and if the board remains just so far from the saw, it is all correct. When there is a long carriage, run one end of the carriage to the saw, and stick a nail where the edge of the saw hits. Now, move the carriage so that the other end will be at the saw, and stick another nail. Now, hold a long straight edge against the *side* of the saw-plate; and *if in range*, the straight edge will point directly to these nails. If the feeding-table of a circular wood-saw does not range with the saw, it will be almost impossible to saw off a large stick, because it will *bind* against the sides of the saw, and almost stop the motion of it if the power is limited.

THE VELOCITY OF THE CUTTING EDGE OF SAWS.

680. There is little danger of having the teeth of any saw move too fast. The faster the cutting edge moves, the more work a saw is capable of performing. When there is an abundance of available power, it is well to have a buzz-saw run with a frightful velocity; for it will saw much smoother and faster than if it moves with less rapidity. But when the power is limited, and it is desirable to *lose* none of that power, it is very important to have the cutting edge move at the *most effective* velocity for the power which drives it. Some engineers say that the cutting edge of a crosscut circular saw should move about seventy-five

feet per second, while others, of equally good authority, say one hundred feet and more per second. The dia██████ of the saw has much to do in this respect. A circular sa██████y-two inches in diameter, has a cutting edge of sixty-nine ██████ if it revolves twelve hundred times in one minute, th███████ edge will move one hundred and fifteen feet per second, or six thousand nine hundred feet per minute; and if the wood to be sawed be as large as that saw will cut in two without turning it over, by putting another saw of the same thickness, having teeth the same distance apart, which is twenty-six inches in diameter *on the same mandrel*, the same amount of power will saw *more* than it will with the saw *twenty-two* inches in diameter. It will require a little more power to drive the twenty-six-inch saw, because it is a little heavier; but the difference is so small that it cannot be perceived. And the diameter of the saw being *greater*, there will be a greater leverage to absorb the driving power. But the velocity of the *cutting edge* of the twenty-six-inch saw being (at 1200 revolutions per minute) one hundred and thirty-six feet per second, together with the greater diameter of the saw, by reason of which, in sawing materials of the size already mentioned, fewer teeth cut at the same time, both operate in favor of the large saw. Consequently, a twenty-six-inch saw will do *more* with the same power than a twenty-two-inch saw, in sawing wood that is nearly all as large as a twenty-two-inch saw will reach through; the teeth and thickness of the plate being the same. If, now, the speed pulley on the saw mandrel be made so large as to give the cutting edge of the twenty-six-inch saw a velocity of one hundred and fifteen feet per second, the same amount of power will saw more than when the velocity of the teeth was one hundred and thirty-six feet per second. If the tyro should have much sawing to do, and his power limited, it would be well worth while to have two or three different speed pulleys to put on the saw mandrel. The size of the pulleys would very soon decide whether too much of the power was absorbed in producing a higher velocity than will be most effective for the amount of power employed. The driving wheel may be so large and speed-pulley so small, (in a one or two-horse power) to absorb *all the available power* in getting up a good velocity. These should be just large enough to allow the horses with their ordinary gait. Intimately connected with this subject, as elucidating and rendering it more intelligible, is

THE INFLUENCE OF THE THICKNESS OF THE MATERIALS TO BE SAWED.

681. Every one who has ever sawed a board in two with a hand-saw knows that it will require three times more time and power to saw off a board one foot wide, if the saw be made to cut *entirely across the width* of the board, than it does to saw it having the saw cut only across the *thickness* of the board at once. A man will saw in two with a hand-saw twelve boards one foot wide and an inch thick, twice as quick as he can saw in two a stick of timber one foot square. A man will saw with a slitting-saw, eight feet in length of a board one inch thick, quicker and easier than he can saw one foot in length of a four-inch plank with the same saw, unless the teeth were very coarse.

682. In sawing fire-wood with a two-horse-power, if the wood be nearly all from six to eight inches thick, by splitting it in two before sawing it can be sawed with the same power in about half the time that it would require, without being made smaller. With an abundance of power a cord of *large* wood could be sawed sooner than a cord of small wood. A span of horses on a two-horse railway power will do a good business at slitting boards and plank from one and a half to three inches thick. As the thickness of materials to be sawed increases, in order to do a fair business an increase of power is necessary. With a circular saw about one foot in diameter, driven by two horses, a man can saw seventy feet in length of hard lumber one inch thick—if he is able to handle the lumber as fast as the saw will cut it—sooner than he can saw through a plank twelve feet long and three inches thick.

683. A circular saw ten or twelve inches in diameter, for slitting boards and two-inch plank, will do much neater and smoother work than a saw twice as large in diameter. This is particularly

19

so with hard-wood lumber, for slitting which a saw that is just large enough to reach through a board or plank to be ▉▉▉ will saw smoother than a larger saw, that will cut more s▉▉ ▉▉ across the lumber.

684. In sawing logs into boards, either with an up-and-down saw or with a circular saw, the larger the logs are the greater must be the power in order to do a profitable business. A power that will do a good business at sawing logs from one to two feet in diameter into lumber, if the power be all absorbed in sawing such logs, will be insufficient to drive a saw at a good velocity through logs from three to four feet in diameter. It is all folly to attempt to do a fair business in sawing anything thick and heavy, with a weak or limited power. If, in erecting a steam saw-mill, the logs are of an average large size, it would be infinitely more profitable to the proprietor to have an engine say of not less than thirty-horse-power, that would drive a saw with a good speed through any log, however large and hard it might be, than it would to use an engine of ten or fifteen-horse-power.

685. In slitting lumber with my two-horse-power, with a circular saw one foot in diameter, I found by experiment that with a pulley six inches in diameter on the mandrel I could saw only about half as fast with the horses travelling at a given gait as I could when the pulley was about eleven inches in diameter. With the small pulley too much of the power was absorbed in producing a given velocity. The difference was not so perceptible when sawing thin stuff as it was when sawing plank two or three inches thick.

A WORD ABOUT FILES.

686. My rule in selecting files is, to choose those that have a clear, bright, and lively appearance, and that are well cut, having *sharp corners.* If the *corners* are full—*which is of the greatest importance*—the sides will be correspondingly sharp. If the corners are *not* full, it is a pretty certain evidence that the temper is not right,—generally too hard,—and they will not do good ser-

FIG. 187.

SLITTING TABLE.

SETOFF

ROLLER

TABLE

vice. Always examine the corners of files, and select those that have the sharpest corners.

THE SIZE OF THE FILES

687. Should be in. proportion to the teeth. Files about the size of the teeth to be filed are generally the most economical, because there are *more corners* in proportion to the sides. I always use very small triangular files for filing small teeth. The *double-cut single* files, although they cost a trifle more, are preferable to the *single*-cut ones, because they make a cleaner and neater cut when filing.

688. Save all the old files and have them *cut over*, in nearly any of our cities, at less than half their original cost.

THE SLITTING-TABLE.

689. Fig. 187 is a representation of a bench and slitting-table for slitting boards, plank, and anything else of that character. When a man has a wood-saw, he may bolt two extension benches to the frame, as shown in the Fig., and put a small slitting-saw on the mandrel, and he will find it a most convenient arrangement for slitting all kinds of lumber. I have such a table, the frame of which is twenty-four feet long, and the movable carriage or table is sixteen feet in length. This table is moved back and forth close to the saw, on *rollers* in the frame, and boards or plank, when being sawed, are placed on the *table* and pushed towards the saw. With two horses I can saw lath, door-casings, stiles for doors, and such like, *faster*, and very much *truer*, than ten active men would be able to saw with hand-saws. (See Par. 38.) The rollers—one of which is shown at the left hand in the Fig.—which support the table, are about five inches in diameter, sixteen inches long, with a gain in each one for the *guide* to run in, which is fastened to the under side of the table. A gauge is shown behind the sawyer, which is adjusted by two set-screws, *a a*, which screws pass through a long mortise in the stick *under* the gauge. The *nut* is beneath the long mortise. At

the left hand is shown a portion of the table, with an iron dog, d, screwed to the top of the table for holding the plank.

SQUARES AND MEASURING RULES.

690. A carpenters' steel square is an indispensable tool in laying out any heavy work. Steel squares are usually graduated correctly, and are as "square" as they can conveniently be made. The common iron squares are almost always a nuisance ; because they are not square, are not graduated correctly, are always bending and twisting, and the edges are not straight. No one who is possessed of much mechanical talent, will be satisfied to use an iron square. *Steel* squares are usually graduated and figured on both sides, with a rule for measuring lumber on one side, which is many times very convenient.

691. In addition to the carpenters' square, a *try-square* and *bevel* are very useful, and it is not very practicable to perform many little jobs without them. These can always be obtained at hardware stores, of almost any desirable size.

692. A *pocket rule* is another very convenient instrument, both for laying out any piece of small work in the shop, and for taking the dimensions of anything that comes in our way that we wish to measure. Pocket-rules and carpenters' steel squares are usually graduated as small as sixteenths of inches, and the tyro should be careful to see that in purchasing a square he does not get turned off with an *iron* square. A good steel square will ring when struck while it hangs on one's finger, but an *iron* one will give a very dull sound.

693. Mechanics who make many patterns for moulding for cast-iron, when they wish to have their casting of a given size, use a graduated rule twelve inches and one-eighth in length, or one-eighth of an inch to a foot *longer* than the sealed or statute measure. The object of using such a rule is, to make the necessary allowance for the contraction or shrinkage of the iron in cooling. When such a rule is not at hand, it is necessary to make calculations for the contraction of the iron, by making the pattern twelve inches and one-eighth long, if the iron is to be just twelve inches

in length when cold. But when such a rule is used there is no allowance to be made and no liability to make mistakes.

694. Squares are not always "*square*" or true. They may be readily tested when purchasing them, by holding them against the straight edge of a board, and making a mark *across* it, and then reverse it; and if the arm of the square is exactly parallel with the mark, the square is true. Let squares and rules be kept bright by rubbing them with a piece of white chalk.

695. *Measuring poles* are very convenient many times. I have three of different lengths. One is six feet in length, three-eighths of an inch thick at the ends and an inch wide at the ends, and half an inch thick at the middle and two inches wide, graduated to three inch spaces at the ends. Another is ten feet long, one inch wide and half an inch thick at the ends, and in the middle two inches wide, graduated in feet. Another, of the same size as the ten feet pole, is sixteen and a half feet long, correctly graduated to half feet. These are all made of baswood, very straight and true, and varnished with three coats of shellac, (see next vol.,) and a piece of sheet copper, just the size of the ends, is neatly fitted and screwed on the ends, to keep them true and square. All these poles have their appropriate place in the shop, where they will lie in a straight position; and when they are not in use they are returned promptly to their places. It will injure them very much to get very wet, by springing and warping them.

696. Instead of poles, many men have a graduated tape, two or four rods in length, which is wound up in a circular case of stiff leather, and can be carried in the pocket. In measuring, the tape is drawn out of one side of the case, a part or the entire length. The tape is usually graduated on one side into feet and inches, and on the opposite side is a graduation into *links* for measuring land. But for ordinary purposes, and especially for correct measuring, and for cheapness, *poles* are far the best, and the most convenient. One man can measure alone with a rod pole very expeditiously, while with a tape it would be very difficult for him to measure alone.

697. There have been of late several patent improvements in squares and measuring rules. But I shall notice none of them except the one in which the blade of a common hand-saw is graduated on both sides, at its back edge. There can be no particular objection to this manner of having a measuring rule. But they who use this kind only, will find it, many times, very inconvenient; and, besides, the teeth of the saw would be very liable to get a dulling oftener than we like to file them, and it makes an awkward, clumsy rule at best. A saw and a good carpenters' square cannot very well be judiciously and conveniently combined.

698. For measuring the circumference of anything, or the outside or inside of the rim of a wheel, or drum, it is not very practicable to do it with a straight rule. For such purposes a measuring wheel is made use of, which is represented by Fig. 188.

FIG. 188.

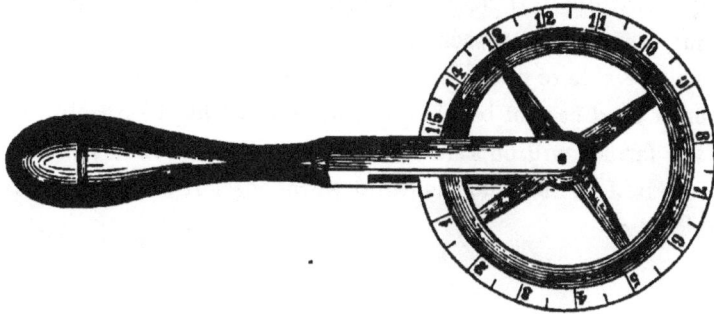

A MEASURING WHEEL.

The wheel should be about six or eight inches in diameter, and instead of being flat on the surface of the circumference, the wheel at the circumference should be formed to a sharp edge entirely around it. If it is three or four eighths wide at the circumference, it is much more liable to vary from the correct measurement of anything which is measured with it. In measuring with the wheel, the operator must be careful to have it roll in a straight direction, and not from right to left, as that would indicate a greater distance than it really is.

799. Mr. Louis Young has invented an improvement in the measuring wheel, in which there is a neatly graduated circular disk in the end of the handle, which is moved by a *pawl*, working in a ratchet wheel at the disk, which pawl is worked by a *cam* on the shaft of the measuring-wheel. When the wheel is rolled forward, the distance traversed over is accurately indicated in feet, inches, and fractions of inches on the disk. But it is too expensive for farmers, otherwise I would have given an illustration of it in this place.

700. For measuring the circumference of small bodies, in the absence of a measuring-wheel, use a piece of small wire, and then take the length of it with the rule afterwards. There is a no more correct way to measure a round body than this.

701. This chapter on edge tools has been revised and very much abbreviated, and a goodly number of tools which every farmer ought to have, have been excluded in order to bring the chapter within a proper limit for such a work as this. But if the young farmer is possessed of sufficient skill to put these in order, he will be able to put all others in order. When tools of a desired form or kind cannot be obtained at country hardware stores, the young farmer will be able to procure anything which he may desire at R. L. Allen's agricultural warehouse, 189 Water st., New York city.

INDEX.

A.

B.

19*

E.

F.

K.

L.

M.

N.

O.

P.